LITERACY

Exmouth

7 Day

University of Plymouth Library

Subject to status this item may be renewed
via your Voyager account

http://voyager.plymouth.ac.uk

Exeter tel: (01392) 475049
Exmouth tel: (01395) 255331
Plymouth tel: (01752) 232323

LITERACY

Major Themes in Education

Edited by David Wray

Volume III

Writing: Processes and Teaching

RoutledgeFalmer
Taylor & Francis Group

LONDON AND NEW YORK

First published 2004
by RoutledgeFalmer
2 Park Square, Milton Park, Abingdon, Oxfordshire OX14 4RN

Simultaneously published in the USA and Canada
by RoutledgeFalmer
270 Madison Avenue, New York, NY 10016

RoutledgeFalmer is an imprint of the Taylor & Francis Group

Editorial Matter and Selection © 2004 David Wray; individual
owners retain copyright in their own material

Typeset in Times by Wearset Ltd, Boldon, Tyne and Wear
Printed and bound in Great Britain by MPG Books Ltd, Bodmin

British Library Cataloguing in Publication Data
A catalogue record for this book is available from the British Library

Library of Congress Cataloging in Publication Data
A catalog record for this book has been requested

ISBN 0-415-27708-6 (Set)
ISBN 0-415-27711-6 (Volume III)

Publisher's note
References within each chapter are as they appear in the original
complete work.

CONTENTS

CONTENTS

CONTENTS

ACKNOWLEDGEMENTS

The publishers would like to thank the following for permission to reprint their material:

National Council of Teachers of English for permission to reprint Donald H. Graves, 'An examination of the writing processes of seven year old children', in *Research in the Teaching of English* 9, 1975, pp. 227–241. Copyright © 1975 by the National Council of Teachers of English.

National Council of Teachers of English for permission to reprint James Britton, 'The composing process and the functions of writing', in Cooper, C. R. and Odell, L. (eds.), *Research on Composing*, Urbana, IL: NCTE, 1978, pp. 13–28. Copyright © 1978 by the National Council of Teachers of English.

National Council of Teachers of English for permission to reprint Linda Flower and John R. Hayes, 'A cognitive process theory of writing', in *College Composition and Communication* 32, December, 1981, pp. 365–387. Copyright © 1981 by the National Council of Teachers of English.

National Council of Teachers of English for permission to reprint George Hillocks, Jr., 'The interaction of instruction, teacher comment, and revision in teaching the composing process', in *Research in the Teaching of English* 16(3), 1982, pp. 261–278. Copyright © 1982 by the National Council of Teachers of English.

National Council of Teachers of English for permission to reprint Sheridan Blau, 'Invisible writing: investigating cognitive processes in composition', in *College Composition and Communication* 34(3), 1983, pp. 297–312. Copyright © 1983 by the National Council of Teachers of English.

Boynton/Cook, a subsidury of Reed Elsevier, Inc., Portsmouth, NH for permission to reprint J. Emig, 'Non-magical thinking: presenting writing developmentally in schools' in Goswami, D. and Butler, M. (eds) *The Web of Meaning: Essays on Writing, Teaching, Learning and Thinking*, Upper Montclair, NJ, 1983, pp. 135–144. Copyright © 1983 by Janet Emig.

Cambridge University Press for permission to reprint Daniel Chandler, 'Writing strategies and writers' tools', in *English Today* 9(2), 1993, pp. 32–38. Copyright © Cambridge University Press, reprinted with permission of the author and publisher.

Taylor & Francis for permission to reprint David Wray, 'What do children think about writing?', in *Educational Review* 45(1), 1993, pp. 67–77, http://www.tandf.co.uk/journals/carfax/00131911.html.

American Educational Research Association for permission to reprint Ann Hume, 'Research on the composing process', *Review of Educational Research* 53(2), 1983, pp. 201–216.

American Educational Research Association for permission to reprint Jill Fitzgerald, 'Research on revision in writing', *Review of Educational Research* 57(4), 1987, pp. 481–506.

The Helen Dwight Reid Educational Foundation for permission to reprint Vicki L. Brakel Olson, 'The revising processes of sixth-grade writers with and without peer feedback', in *Journal of Educational Research*, 84(1), 1990, pp. 23–29. Published by Heldref Publications, 1319 Eighteenth St., NW, Washington, DC 20036–1802. http://www.heldref.org. Copyright © 1990.

National Council of Teachers of English for permission to reprint Taffy E. Raphael, Carol Sue Englert, and Becky W. Kirschner, 'Students' metacognitive knowledge about writing', in *Research in the Teaching of English* 23(4), 1989, pp. 343–379. Copyright © 1989 by the National Council of Teachers of English.

The International Reading Association for permission to reprint J. Richard Gentry, 'An analysis of developmental spelling in *GNYS AT WRK*', in *The Reading Teacher*, 36(2), 1982, pp. 192–200.

Sage Publications Inc. for permission to reprint Peter Smagorinsky, 'Graves revisited: a look at the methods and conclusions of the New Hampshire study', in *Written Communication* 4(4), 1987, pp. 331–342. Copyright © 1987 by Sage Publications Inc. Reprinted with permission.

Australian Council for Educational Research and Bill Green for permission to reprint Bill Green, 'Subject-specific literacy and school learning: a focus on writing', in *Australian Journal of Education*, 32(2), 1988, pp. 156–179.

University of South Africa and Myra Barrs for permission to reprint Myra Barrs, 'Genre theory: what's it all about?', in *Language Matters* 1, 1991, pp. 9–16. Copyright © Centre for Language in Primary Education (http://www.clpe.co.uk).

Cambridge University Press for permission to reprint James R. Martin, 'Genre and literacy: modeling context in educational linguistics', in *Annual Review of Applied Linguistics* 13, 1993, pp. 141–172. Copyright © 1993 by Cambridge University Press.

Sage Publications Inc., for permission to reprint Marilyn L. Chapman, 'The emergence of genres: some findings from an examination of first-grade writing', in *Written Communication* 11(3), 1994, pp. 348–380. Copyright © 1994 by Sage Publications Ltd. Reprinted with permission.

National Association for the Teaching of English for permission to reprint Gunther Kress and Peter Knapp, 'Genre in a social theory of language', in *English in Education* 26(2), 1994, pp. 4–15.

National Association for the Teaching of English for permission to reprint Leslie Stratta and John Dixon, 'The National Curriculum in English: does Genre Theory have anything to offer?', in *English in Education* 26(2), 1994, pp. 16–27.

Lawrence Erlbaum Associates, Inc. for permission to reprint Steve Graham and Karen Harris, 'The effects of whole language on children's writing: a review of the literature', in *Educational Psychologist* 29(4), 1994, pp. 187–192.

Routledge for permission to reprint Jane Medwell, 'Contexts for writing: the social construction of classroom writing', in Wray, D. and Medwell, J. (eds), *Teaching Primary English: The State of the Art*, London, 1994, pp. 112–121.

National Association for the Teaching of English for permission to reprint David Tomlinson, 'Errors in the research into the effectiveness of grammar teaching', in *English in Education*, 28(1), 1994, pp. 20–26.

Australian Literacy Educators' Association for permission to reprint David Wray and Maureen Lewis, 'Teaching factual writing: purpose and structure', in *The Australian Journal of Language and Literacy*, 20(2), 1997, pp. 43–52.

Disclaimer

INTRODUCTION TO VOLUME III

Writing: processes and teaching

Introduction

Rather surprisingly, writing and its teaching has received much less research attention than the parallel process of reading. There have been many fewer studies of the process of writing, and, in comparison with the field of reading, a mere handful of studies exploring teaching procedures. Writing has still had its share of controversies, however, some of these of long standing. Of particular importance has been developing an agreed definition of writing. Evidence suggests that, although most teachers would agree that writing has to involve the creation of meaningful symbols on paper, screen, and so on, many of them, in their teaching of writing, prioritise the technical aspects such as handwriting, spelling and grammar. This is possibly because the actual teaching of writing, that is, the composition of meaning, has always been perceived as quite difficult and demanding. Until fairly recently there was a lack of well-grounded pedagogies for the 'second R'. Teaching the technical aspects is undoubtedly easier.

This volume is structured around three central themes in thinking about writing and its teaching.

Theme 1: the writing process

Writing often seems a very mysterious process. When we write, somehow or other, ideas which are in our heads, perhaps only in the very vaguest of forms, have to be shaped into coherent representations in language and transferred onto paper, screen or other media so they can be inspected by some other person. Although we vary greatly in the amount of writing that we do, we all have a tendency to take the process for granted. Even those who write a great deal will, when asked to describe the difficulties of writing, tend to focus upon the original development of ideas rather than on the process of shaping these into language. The term we use to describe having difficulties in writing, 'writer's block', is understood by most people to mean having difficulty in getting ideas for writing rather than difficulty in transferring these to the page.

Yet the process of writing is not so simple. How exactly do we shape our ideas into writable forms, and does the process then simply involve the transferring of these ideas to a page? Do we all follow the same process in writing, or does the process vary according to how skilful we are at writing, how experienced we are, our individual styles or personalities, or any other dimension? These questions have all been explored by research.

There are clearly several stages to the process of writing. In order to produce a piece of writing, the writer needs to:

- have something worth saying;
- decide that writing is the most appropriate medium for saying this;
- have an audience in mind for what will be written;
- think about how ideas will be expressed;
- put these expressions down on paper;
- reconsider what has been written, and perhaps make alterations;
- pass on the writing to where it was intended to go.

These stages do not include the pencil sharpening, false starts, coffee making and various other activities that some writers find essential! Very few adults are able to produce a neat, accurate piece of writing that says all that they want to say in the appropriate style and form at one short sitting. Interruptions and disruptions are normal in experiences of writing rather than exceptions.

Research has revealed the multiple dimensions involved in the writing process. There are two fundamental dimensions and one which might be described as the orchestration of these two.

1   In order to communicate ideas, the writer must compose. This involves:

- getting and evaluating information;
- evolving and synthesising ideas;
- shaping information and ideas into a form that can be expressed in writing.

This is essentially a creative act involving the moulding of ideas and the creation and ordering of knowledge. Composition is, therefore, a learning activity in its own right rather than simply a way of presenting pre-formed ideas. This view of composition, and writing in general, puts emphasis on the role of language as a means of making sense of the world.

2   The writer must also transcribe the composition. This involves choosing an appropriate form and presenting a correct layout. Transcription

also sometimes requires attention to accuracy in spelling, grammar, punctuation and handwriting. It is clear that transcription assumes different levels of importance depending upon the purpose of, and audience for, a piece of writing. A letter to a bank manager or an application for a job requires much more care to be given to features such as spelling and handwriting than does a shopping list or the notes we may take during a lecture. Yet transcription always takes place and always demands some of our attention in writing.

3   Ideally, the writer should be able to co-ordinate these two dimensions of writing, but this is often not the case. Composition and transcription may inhibit one another and orchestrating the two may be very difficult. Many adults find that they make more mistakes and changes when writing something important because their minds are so involved with composing the ideas. For children, who may have less than complete mastery of the processes involved, this co-ordination is doubly difficult.

The result of this problem of co-ordination is sometimes that children come to believe that particular parts of the writing process are more important than others and should take the lion's share of their attention. Some research (see Chapter 49) has explored the important issue of pupil perceptions of writing.

Perhaps the most significant development in our understanding of the writing process has been the shift from seeing it as a linear process to a recognition of its recursive nature (see Chapter 47). Most writers will agree that, in all but the simplest of writing tasks, they do not move forward in a straight line from conception to completion: all planning is not completed before words are put onto paper; all the words are not on paper before writers begin to review and revise what they are writing. Writers move backwards and forwards among each of these components of the process. For example, as writers plan, they may revise these plans even before committing anything to paper; they may formulate new plans in the very act of trying to transcribe their original ones; they may not even fully realise what the precise aims of their writing are before almost completing it (see Chapter 50).

Certainly in research terms a linear model has proved less than useful because, as Flower and Hayes put it, it describes 'the growth of the written product, not ... the inner process of the person producing the product'. If this model of writing as a collection of simultaneously operating and recursive processes is accurate, as suggested by an increasing volume of research, then it seems likely that great emphasis needs to be laid upon the mechanisms whereby these processes are controlled and co-ordinated in the writer. What have been termed 'executive control processes' (Raphael, Englert and Kirschner) have become a focus of interest precisely because they are a means of linking together diverse and complex component processes.

Theme 2: genre theory and writing

There has been an increasing interest in the idea of encouraging students to write for a particular purpose, for a known audience and in an appropriate form. However, what constitutes an appropriate form has often been described in very general terms, such as the listing of different types of texts – for example, 'notes, letters, instructions, stories and poems in order to plan, inform, explain, entertain and express attitudes or emotions' (Department of Education and Science, 1990).

This listing of text types implies that teachers and students know what distinguishes the form of one text type from another. At a certain level, of course, this is true – we all know what a story is like and how it differs from a recipe, etc. Most of us are aware that a narrative usually has a beginning, a series of events and an ending, but it is still relatively rare, however, for teachers to discuss texts in this way with students – drawing on our knowledge of the usual structure of a particular text type to improve our students' writing of that form.

Recently it has been argued (for example, by Martin, see Chapter 58) that our implicit knowledge of text types and their forms is quite extensive and one of the teacher's roles is to make this implicit knowledge explicit. Theorists in this area are often loosely referred to as 'genre theorists' and they base their work on a functional approach to language, arguing that we develop language to satisfy our needs in society. They see all texts, written and spoken, as being 'produced in a response to, and out of, particular social situations and their specific structures' (Kress and Knapp, see Chapter 60) and as a result put stress on the social and cultural factors that form a text as well as on its linguistic features. They see a text as a social object and the making of a text as a social process. They argue that in any society there are certain types of text – both written and spoken – of a particular form because there are similar social encounters, situations and events which recur constantly within that society. As these 'events' are repeated over and over again, certain types of text are created over and over again. These texts become recognised in a society by its members, and once recognised they become conventionalised, i.e. become distinct genres.

Imagine you are the inspector appointed to review the proposed route of a new road and you have invited written evidence. You receive a great many letters from the general public all wishing to put forward arguments in favour of or against the road. Some letters make their case clearly – arguing a point, elaborating on it before moving onto another point and ending with a summary; others, although obviously deeply felt, are rambling, move randomly from point to point, are at times incoherent, and leave you with no clear idea of the arguments being expressed or the evidence to support them. Which letters are you more likely to take account of when making your decision?

This imaginary situation is just one example of how important being competent in the use of some written genres is in our society. Persuasion, explanation, report, explanation and discussion are powerful forms of language that we use to get things done. They have been called the 'language of power' and it can be argued that pupils who leave our classrooms unable to operate successfully within these powerful genres are denied access to becoming fully functioning members of society.

Theme 3: pedagogies of writing

As pointed out earlier, the development of effective pedagogies for writing has taken rather longer than the development of an understanding of the writing process. There have been bitter controversies about the teaching of grammar and its effect on writing. There have also been debates about the teaching of spelling. More recently a pedagogy has begun to develop which focuses on the importance of teacher modelling of writing and subsequent student guided practice. It is rather too early in the game yet, however, to make claims about the universal application of such a pedagogy. Research into effective pedagogies in writing is a current high priority, with the potential to significantly enhance student experience of education generally. It is, after all, through writing that most students interface with the school curriculum, and are assessed on their understanding of it. Teaching effective writing can improve learning and achievement in all areas of education.

42

AN EXAMINATION OF THE WRITING PROCESSES OF SEVEN YEAR OLD CHILDREN[1]

Donald H. Graves

Source: *Research in the Teaching of English* (1975) 9: 227–241

The complexity of the writing process and the interrelationships of its components have been underestimated by researchers, teachers, and other educators, because writing is an organic process that frustrates approaches to explain its operation. Three major "Needs for Research" summaries in the last eleven years reflect specific concern for dealing with the issue of complexity (Braddock, 1963; Parke, 1960; Meckel, 1963). All three recommend extensive investigation of developmental issues, issues that focus much more on individual differences than on the "procedural-methodological" matters which have historically received research emphasis.

A review of research since the summaries indicates that most efforts have focused on correlative studies or the examination of the effects of single or multivariate interventions. The data from these separate studies make it difficult to produce a sound, organic understanding of what is even involved in the writing process. Furthermore, only two studies seem to have involved the actual observation of the behaviors of writers while they are in the process of writing. One of these studies (Emig, 1969) involved the composing processes of twelfth graders and the other (Holstein, 1970) was primarily concerned with the use of metaphor by fifth grade children.

This investigation was undertaken to explore the writing processes and related variables of a group of seven-year-old children. Through the gathering of data in a case study procedure, an analysis of broad samples of writing, and the naturalistic observation of children while writing in two types of classroom environments, formal and informal, the study sought to avoid both a fragmentary approach and teacher intervention. From this study a profile of writing in the early years emerges sufficient in depth and scope to make effective research hypotheses and recommendations.

7

In recent years new focus has come to the case study approach as a means to investigation of the variables involved in new areas of research. Indeed, the case study approach in the field of comparative research is most often recommended when entering virgin territory in which little has been investigated. Because of a lack of studies on the writing process or the actual observation of children while actually writing, the use of the case study to investigate the writing processes of children was considered as one of the appropriate methodologies.

The emphasis in this report of the study of the writing processes of seven year old children will be placed on a detailed description of the procedures used, and the conclusions and hypotheses formulated from the findings. This was done because the complexity and extent of the actual findings from case studies, small and large groups precluded their reporting in short space.

Procedures

The sample

Two formal and two informal second level (second grade) classrooms in a middle class community were chosen for the principal focus of a five month investigation. The classrooms selected met specific criteria that identified them as being either formal or informal. These criteria concerned the degree to which children were able to function without specific directions from the teacher and the amount of choice children had in determining their learning activities.

Figure 1 depicts the makeup of the sample for the different phases of data gathering in the study. The First Phase involved ninety-four children (forty-eight boys and forty-six girls) with a mean age of seven years and six months at the beginning of the study. In Phase II fourteen seven year old children (eight boys and six girls) from each of the four rooms were observed while they were writing. In Phase III, seventeen seven year old children (nine boys and eight girls) from each of the four rooms were interviewed as to their views of their own writing and concepts of the "good writer." Finally, in Phase IV, eight children (six boys and two girls), two from each of the four classrooms, were chosen for case study investigation. The eight children selected were considered by teachers and administrators as representative of "normal" seven year old children; thus pupils of unusually high intellectual capacity and those with learning or emotional problems were excluded.

Data collection procedures

Throughout the data collection period from the first week of December, 1972, to the middle of April, 1973, the primary emphasis was placed on

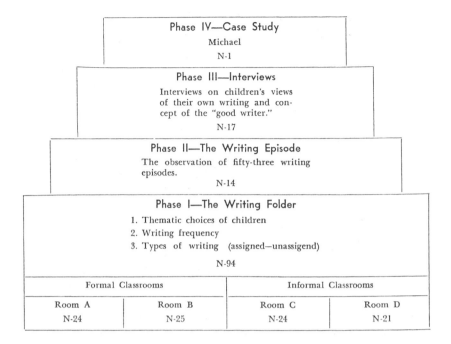

Figure 1 Study phases and procedures

gathering case study data on two children in each of the four environments. Secondary emphasis was placed on gathering data from larger
groups in the same four classrooms. Data were collected from: (1) the
logging of five categories of information secured from the writing of
ninety-four children; 1,635 writings were logged for theme, type of
writing, number of words, use of accompanying art, and teacher comments; (2) the naturalistic observation of fourteen children while they
were writing in their classrooms; (3) the interviewing in four different sessions of the eight case study children as to their views of their own writing
and of seventeen children as to their concepts of "a good writer"; (4) the
gathering of full case study data about eight children through parent
interviews, testing, assembling of educational-developmental history, and
observating the children in several environments. The purpose of this
form of data gathering and reporting was to provide a range of cross-
validation of data to support the findings and, thus, to add power to the
research recommendations and instructional hypotheses posed. This
approach made it possible to follow findings from the several larger settings to an individual case and, conversely, from the case and/or small
group findings to all-class profiles and to the entire group of seven year
old children studied.

Phase one – the writing folder

Writing folders were kept by all children in each of the four classrooms in the study. The purposes of having all children keep a writing folder were the following:

1   to reduce focus on the eight children chosen for case study work;
2   to provide background data of a total classroom nature in order to view the writing of the eight children with greater objectivity;
3   to assess the general writing habits of the children in terms of writing frequency, assigned-unassigned writing, use of illustrations accompanying writing, writing length, and the thematic interests of children.

The definition of writing that was employed to determine paper selection was as follows:

> Any writing intended to be at least a sentence unit that was completely composed by the child.

Teachers distinguished between two types of writing—assigned or unassigned—when they reviewed the writing folders. Assigned was defined as writing that children were required to attempt and for which completion was expected. Unassigned writing was defined as unrequired writing. In this situation the child chose on his own initiative to write. There was no expectation by the teacher that specific work would be completed. Thus the child made choices as to mode, length of writing, and the disposition of the writing product.

Phase two: writing process observation (the writing episode)

In this stage of the investigation, fifty three writing episodes of fourteen seven year old children (mean age – 7:7), made up of eight boys and six girls from all of the four rooms were observed. Writing of the children in the episodes was observed within the classroom in order to gain a more valid view of their writing processes. Writing episodes were not structured by the researcher. Rather, recordings of the children's writing behaviors were made when they chose to initiate writing in assigned or unassigned work. For this reason, approximately 250 hours were spent observing children while waiting for them to enter into a writing episode.

Within each of the four environments two children were chosen as case studies. These eight children were the prime focus of classroom observation. Because these cases were not always engaged in writing, were absent, or were working with the teacher, it was possible to record some of the writings of other children in the rooms. Twelve of the fifty-three writing episodes recorded were from six children who were not case studies.

There is more to a writing episode than the children's act of composing and writing down words. The observation of writing at only one point in time limits an analysis of the writing process and may result in conclusions which overlook important variables. Therefore, a single writing episode was considered to consist of three phases of observation: prewriting, composing and postwriting. Definitions of these phases and the factors in each phase for which data were obtained are given.

> *Prewriting phase.* This phase immediately precedes the writing of the child. Examples of factors related to writing observed in this phase were the contribution of room stimuli to thematic choice, art work behaviors, and discussions with other persons.
>
> *Composing phase.* This phase begins and ends with the actual writing of the message. Examples of phase factors were spelling, resource use, accompanying language, pupil interactions, proof-readings, rereadings, interruptions, erasures, and teacher participation.
>
> *Postwriting phase.* This phase refers to all behaviors recorded following the completion of writing the message.

Examples of these behaviors were product disposition, approval solicitation, material disposition, proofreading, and contemplation of the finished product.

Recording of the episode

Whenever the researcher noted that a child was structuring materials for a writing episode, he moved close to the child and usually seated himself directly in front of his desk or table. Although the researcher was viewing the child's work in the upside-down position, it was the best location to record behaviors accompanying the writing episode. In this way the child's body posture, use of overt language, and rereading could be better observed.

For many children drawing was a major step in the prewriting phase. Michael, the case study chosen for reporting, apparently needed to draw before he was able to write in the composing phase. As he drew he would talk, often making appropriate sound effects to go along with the figure being drawn at the moment. While drawing the dinosaur referred to in Table I, Michael made growling noises to simulate the dinosaur's presence. To aid the recording of such data the observer reproduced the drawing, at the same time numbered each operation to indicate the

11

Table I Example of a writing episode

A whale is eating the
  1   2   3   4   5
	10:12
	R
		9–Gets up to get dictionary. Has the page
		   with pictures of animals.

men. A dinosaur is 6 7 8 ⑨⑩ ⑪ 12		
triing to eat the whale. 13 14 15 16 17 ⑱	IU R	10–Teacher announcement. 11–Copies from dictionary and returns book
A dinosaur is frowning ⑲⑳ ㉑ 22 23 ㉔		to side of room.
a tree at the lion, and		18–Stops, rubs eyes.
㉕ 26 27 28 29 30 31 32	RR	19–Rereads from 13 to 19.
the cavman too the men	OV	20–Voices as he writes.
33 34 35 ㊱ 37 38	OV	21–Still voicing.
are killed. The dinosaur	IS	24–Gets up to sharpen pencil and returns.
39 40 41 42 43		
killed the whale. The	RR	25–Rereads from 20 to 25.
44 45 46 47 49 ㊽	RR	36–Rereads to 36. Lost starting point.
cavmen live is the roks.		48–Puts away paper, takes out again.
50 51 52 53 54 55 ㊻		
	RR 10:20	56–Rereads outloud from 49 to 56.

KEY:
1-2-3-4–Numerals indicate writing sequence. ④–Item explained in comment column on the right. ////–erasure or proofreading. T–Teacher involvement; IS–Interruption Solicited; IU–Interruption Unsolicited; RR–Reread; PR–Proofread; DR–Works on drawing; R–Resource use. Accompanying Language; OV–Overt; WH–Whispering; F–Forms letters and words; M–Murmuring; S–No overt language visible.

sequence in which the picture evolved. Notable behaviors that accompanied each step were also recorded.

As soon as Michael completed his drawing, he started to write about information contained in the picture. At this juncture he began the composing phase. The researcher immediately recorded the time in the center column (Table I). When the child completed his writing the time was also recorded at the bottom of the column. In this way, the length of time the child was engaged in the composing phase could be computed.

The procedure for recording behaviors in the composing phase are contained in Table I. The left column records exactly what Michael wrote. The sequence of the writing and significant acts are indicated by the numerals. Since specific behaviors were noted from time to time by the observer as the writing was done, reference is made to these by circled numerals, with explanations of them given in the right column. For example, the circled eleven in the left column is explained following the eleven in the right column. That is, as Michael wrote dinosaur, he copied the word from the dictionary. Other behaviors were recorded during the composing phase and noted in the right hand column. To assist the summary of these behaviors, lettered symbols were placed in the center column from the key below to indicate the classification of the child's behaviors in the episode. For example, in the center column opposite the numeral twenty in the right column, the symbol "OV" was recorded. This symbol indicates that in step twenty Michael voiced words as he was writing them.

In the key at the bottom of the page in Table I the range of behaviors monitored when a child engaged in a writing episode were listed. Teacher involvement (T) was any form of teacher interaction with a child during his writing episode. Interruptions (IS-IU) were monitored for their effect on the continuance of the child's writing. Two other behaviors, rereadings and proofreadings (RR and PR) were important indices of other writing habits. Re-readings were the child's rescanning of writing composed prior to the current word being written whereas proofreading was defined as an adjustment of a previously composed writing operation. In a number of instances children would adjust a picture to go with a new idea in the text (DR). The use of resources to aid writing (R) such as word banks, phonic charts etc. were recorded during the observations. Finally, the range and type of language used to accompany the actual writing was recorded. This language behavior ranged from full voicing (overt—OV) to the absence of any visible or aural indication of accompanying language (covert—S).

From time to time the researcher would intervene and elicit information from the child he was engaged in a writing episode. The purpose of this procedure was to gain understanding of the child's rationale for a previous operation or insight into his strategies for future operations. The type of intervention varied with the phase of the episode. Examples of interventions and their settings and objectives are shown in Table II. Although there were many types of interventions they were infrequently employed to minimize the observer's effect on the child's writing.

Phase three – interviews

Two types of interviews were used to record children's views of their own writing and writing in general. The first included individual conversations with the eight case study children about the writing in their folders. The purpose in employing the writing folder interview was to gain a profile of the child's view of his own writing. This profile was constructed from the child's rating of papers from his folder, the rationales for such ratings, and his responses to other statements and questions about the papers. In the interview the child was asked to rate writings in his folder from best to poorest

Table II Examples of interventions made by observer during writing episodes

Phase in episode	Setting at time of intervention	Observer's objective	Observer's questions or statements
Prewriting Phase	1. The child was about to start drawing his picture.	1. To determine how much the drawing contributes to the writing.	1. "Tell me what you are going to write about when you finish your drawing."
	2. The child has finished his drawing.	2. To determine how much the drawing contributes to the writing.	2. "Tell me what you are going to write about now that you have finished your drawing."
	3. The child has finished his drawing.	3. To determine in less direct fashion how the drawing contributes to the writing.	3. "Tell me about your drawing."
Composing Phase	1. The child is about to start writing.	1. To determine the range of writing ideas possessed before child writes.	1. "Tell me what you are going to write about."
	2. The child attempts to spell a word.	2. To determine the child's understanding of the resources available for spelling help.	"That seems to be a hard one. How can you figure out how to spell it? Tell me all the different ways you can figure out how to spell it."
	3. The child has written three to four sentences.	3. To determine the range of ideas possessed after the child has started writing.	3. "Tell me what you are going to write about next. Tell me how your story is going to end."
Postwriting Phase	1. The child is starting to put his paper away.	1. To check the child's oral reading in relation to the actual words written by the child.	1. "Would you please read outloud what you have just written."
	2. The child is starting to put his paper away.	2. To check the child's feelings or value judgments about work that has been completed.	2. Question series: "Which sentence do you like best? Tell me about it." "Is there anything you would change to make it better?" "Pick out two words that you felt were the most difficult to write."

and to state a rationale for his choice of the best paper. The second interview consisted of asking questions as to the child's conception of what good writers needed to be able to do in order to write well. The questions were asked of seventeen children, seven of whom were the case study children.

Phase four – case study (Michael)

At the conclusion of the data gathering, a decision was made to report only one case study, Michael, but to use all of the writing observations and interviews of the other cases, as well as the additional information gathered on other children in the four classrooms. The procedures used for gathering case study data involved all of those used in the first three phases, plus additional procedures unique to case study research. The additional procedures were the interviewing of parents throughout the study, the individual administration of test batteries in reading, intelligence, and language; the gathering of the child's educational-developmental history, and the extended observation of the child in areas other than writing at home and in school.

Conclusions

The findings in this study led to conclusions in five areas: learning environments, sex differences in writing, developmental factors and the writing process, the case study, Michael, and the procedures used in the study. These conclusions are reported below.

Learning environments

Since the study distinguished two types of environments, conclusions relative to writing in each are possible. These are the following:

1   Informal environments give greater choice to children. When children are given choice as to whether they write or not as to what to write, they write more and in greater length than when specific writing assignments are given.
2   Results of writing done in the informal environments demonstrate that children do not need motivation or supervision in order to write.
3   The formal environments seem to be more favorable to girls in that they write more, and to greater length, than do boys whether the writing is assigned or unassigned.
4   The informal environments seem to favor boys in that they write more than girls in assigned or unassigned work.
5   In either environment, formal or informal, unassigned writing is longer than assigned writing.

6   An environment that requires large amounts of assigned writing inhibits the range, content, and amount of writing done by children.
7   The writing developmental level of the child is the best predictor of writing process behaviors and therefore transcends the importance of environment, materials and methodologies in influence on children's writing.

Sex differences in writing

Differences in boys and girls were examined in three areas: writing frequency, thematic choice, and their concept of the "good writer." Warranted conclusions relative to these appear to be the following:

1   Girls write longer products than do boys in either formal or informal environments.
2   Boys from either learning environment write more unassigned writing than do girls. Unassigned writing seems to provide an incentive for boys to write about subjects not normally provided in teacher-assigned work. Teachers do not normally assign work that includes themes from secondary and extended territory, the areas most used by boys in unassigned writing. (Secondary territory is defined as the metropolitan area beyond the child's home and school. Expanded territory is defined as the area beyond the secondary which would include current events, history and geography on a national and world scale.)
3   Boys seldom use the first person form in unassigned writing, especially the *I* form, unless they are developmentally advanced.
4   Boys write more about themes identified as in secondary and extended geographical territories than do girls. The only girls who write in these areas are those who are more developmentally advanced than others.
5   Girls write more about primary territory, which is related to the home and school, than do boys.
6   Boys are more concerned than are girls with the importance of spacing, formation of letters, and neatness in expressing their concept of "the good writer."
7   Girls stress more prethinking and organizational qualities, feelings in characterizations, and give more illustrations to support their judgments than do boys in expressing their concept of "the good writer."

Developmental factors and the writing process

Such factors as a child's sex, the use of language, and problem solving behaviors, all of which have developmental roots, are involved as a child writes and interacts in various ways to produce two distinctive types of writers, identified by this study as *reactive* and *reflective*. These characteristics and behaviors are summarized in the following statements:

1   *Reactive:* Children who were identified as reactive showed erratic problem solving strategies, the use of overt language to accompany prewriting and composing phases, isolation that evolved in action-reaction couplets, proofreading at the word unit level, a need for immediate rehearsal in order to write, rare contemplation or reviewing of products, characterizations that exhibited general behaviors similar to their own, a lack of a sense of audience when writing, and an inability to use reasons beyond the affective domain in evaluating their writing.

2   *Reflective:* Children who were identified as reflective showed little rehearsal before writing, little overt language to accompany writing, periodic rereadings to adjust small units of writing at the word or phrase level, growing sense of audience connect with their writing, characterizations that exibit general behaviors similar to their own in the expression of feelings, and the ability to give examples to support their reasons for evaluating writing.

The reactive writer was most often a boy and the reflective writer was most often a girl. The reactive and reflective writers, however, were each composite profiles of a general type of child. Identification of either the reactive or the reflective writer was not dependent on the observation of a single behavioral trait. Rather, the characteristics exist in varying degrees in all children, and can emerge under different types of writing conditions, but they gain greater visibility when viewed at the extremes of the high and low ends of a developmental continuum. The identification of a cluster of traits over a period of time from any one behavioral type (reactive or reflective) can be useful in predicting other writing behaviors of children and thereby be of assistance to teachers in adjusting instruction to their needs.

The case study, Michael

The chief conclusion drawn from the case study of Michael was that many variables contribute in unique ways at any given point in the process of writing. Although the contributions of these variables were specific to each child, the identification of them appears to be transferable to the study of the writing of other children. Table III reports several factors identified as

17

Table III General contribution of specific variables To Michael's writing and writing processes

	Family and home	Teacher room D	Michael developmental	Peers (Kevin)
Writing Clause	Family is generally supportive of his work. Gives Michael encouragement with his drawing. Provides Michael with extra materials for drawing and writing at home.	Provides mostly positive feedback. Provides help with self-direction. Provides freedom of choice, time, and activity.	Writes in order to draw. Writes in order to play.	Boys write up a joint project. Kevin makes suggestion to write.
Thematic Origin	King Arthur, sports ghosts and witches, camping and hunting, fires and explosions	Apollo 17, groundhogs, whales	Secondary and extended territorial use. Use of third person male, no females. Little use of first person Need to express aggression	Mutual interests: Kevin: "Let's write about fires." Request for Michael to draw and write on a subject to help Kevin with ideas and drawing models.

Writing Process— Prewriting Phase	Rehearses for ideas in family discussions. Provided materials and encouragement for drawing. Draws at home.	Provides materials that permit art work before writing. Provides freedom to discuss materials and content.	Needs to draw to rehearse ideas for writing. Interested primarily in drawing. Exhibits action-reaction style of drawing ideas. Demonstrates playing behaviors with sound effects.	Two boys discuss what they will draw.
Writing Process— Composing Phase	Vocabulary backgrounds. Speech interference problems.	Teaching of: spelling reading punctuation proofreading. Provision of resources: Phonic charts Pictionaries Word blanks	Generally reactive behaviors Letter reversal problems. Speech interference problems. Speech interference with spelling. Speech interference with writing syntax.	Minimal contribution to ideation. Some spelling assistance. Affects pace and structure by saying to Michael, "Hurry up, let's paint."
Writing Process— Post-Writing Phase	Unknown	Attempts to teach proofreading.	Quickly disposes of writing product by placing in folder or desk.	Kevin sometimes is in a hurry for Michael to do another activity and may subvert proofreading.

contributing to various components of Michael's writing and writing processes. Findings from the case study data made it possible to chart the influence of four main variables on factors identified as important in the process of writing. In Table III the influence of four main variables, family and home, teacher—room D, Michael's developmental characteristics, and a peer, Kevin, can be viewed in relation to their effect on such writing process factors as writing cause, thematic origin of writing, prewriting, composing, and postwriting. Each of these variables should be viewed in relation to its influence on the writing process. For example, in investigating what causes Michael to write, one can view specific contributions of a positive nature from the family and home, the teacher, the satisfaction of personal need, and the support of Kevin. Any one of these factors alone, or in combination with others could be the cause of Michael's choosing to draw and then write.

The influence of these variables on the thematic origin factor can be both direct and indirect. Examples of a direct factor in Table III is seen in the home's influence on Michael's writing about King Arthur, sports, ghosts and witches. An example of a multiple, and less direct origin, is seen in Michael's drawing in the prewriting phase. Michael may draw because of Kevin's suggestion, extra time given by the teacher, a desire to express a favorite theme, or the need to prepare ideas for writing. Thus, the following conclusions appear to be significant concerning the case study.

1   At any given point in a writing episode, many variables, most of them unknown at the time of composing, contribute to the writing process.
2   Children write for unique reasons, employ highly individual coping strategies, and view writing in ways peculiar to their own person. In short, the writing process is as variable and unique as the individual's personality.

Procedures used in the study

Because the use of the case study combined with data gathering from both large and small groups produced particularly striking findings, a number of conclusions related to the procedure are warranted. First, the case study is an effective means of making visible those variables that contribute to a child's writing. Through the unity of one child's life, the constant focus in observation, interviewing, and testing makes it possible to hypothesize concerning the variables that contribute to the child's writing. In a broad interventive-type inquiry involving many children such speculation would not have been possible. Many of the variables discussed in larger group findings became apparent as a result of the intensive case study. In this sense case studies serve principally as surveying expeditions for identifying the writing territories needing further investigation. Some of the areas identified through case study and reported in larger group findings are the following:

1   The use of first and third person reported in thematic choices.
2   The identification of secondary and extended territoriality reported in thematic choices.
3   The identification of the prewriting, composing, and postwriting phases in the writing episode.
4   The identification of the components making up profiles for assessing developmental levels of children.

Whereas the case study contributed to the identification of variables in the larger group data gathering activities, large-group data provided a means for additional testing of the suitability of certain research hypotheses and directions. For example, large-group data were of assistance to analyzing the case study findings in the following areas:

1   Combining all of the fifty-three writing episodes made it possible to develop and hypothesize about the range and relationship of the developmental variables deemed significant to the writing process.
2   The larger group data confirmed the significance of assigned and unassigned writing and thereby contributed to the recognition of the need to pursue the area with the case study children.
3   The larger group data made it possible to view the differences in boys' and girls' writing shown in the case studies with greater objectivity. Writing frequencies, thematic choices, use of assigned and unassigned writing, and responses to the question on the "good writer" in larger groups are examples of these differences which were observed.

Questions to be researched

The main purpose of this study was to formulate instructional and research hypotheses concerning children's writing. The most significant of these hypotheses grouped into related categories appear to be the following:

Assigned and unassigned writing

1   If given the opportunity in an environment providing the freedom to exercise choice in activities, will children produce more writings on their own than if the teacher gives specific assigned tasks?
2   Will unassigned writing be longer than assigned writing, show greater thematic diversity, and be used more by boys than girls?

3 Will boys in comparison with girls, exhibit distinctive choices with respect to the use of primary, secondary and extended territory as well as first, second, and third person in their writing?

4 Will a survey of teacher-assigned writing in the primary years show that girls are favored through the assigning of topics chiefly concerned with primary territory?

Concepts of the "good writer"

5 Will distinctive responses to the "good writer" question be noted with respect to: boys and girls in general, those rated high and low developmentally, and specific writing strengths and limitations of the respondents?

Developmental factors

6 Will two distinct groups of seven year old children be judged high and low developmentally as a result of the demonstration of consistent behaviors related to writing in the following categories: word writing rate, length of proofreading unit during writing, concept of an audience who may read their papers, spelling errors, rereadings, proofreading after writing, range and complexity of ideas expressed before writing, and in reasons expressed in rating their own writing?

General factors

7 Will general behaviors exhibited by the child in his writing episodes be determined principally by his developmental level and be changed only slightly by the classroom environment?

Needed research directions

To date the need for developmental studies related to children's writing has been virtually ignored. Direct contact and extended observation of the children themselves are necessary to reach conclusions relating to developmental variables involving the behaviors of children. In fields such as psychiatry, child development, or anthropology, the investigation of behaviors would be unthinkable without the direct observation of the persons to be studied.

With the exception of a few studies, researchers have been removed from the direct observation of children at the time of their writing. Furthermore, the scope of even the direct observation at the time of writing needs to expand to include other behaviors in the environment. Such studies, however, cannot be conducted without the successful development of procedures that effectively record the full-range of child behaviors in their natural environment.

In order to improve both procedures and study scope, future research in writing should continue to explore the feasibility of the case study method. Further studies are needed to investigate the developmental histories of different types of children in relation to writing and the writing process. In a profession where there is a basic commitment to the teaching and understanding of the individual child, it is ironic that research devoted to the full study of single individuals is so rare.

Note

1   The report presented here is taken from the author's doctoral dissertation, Children's Writing: Research Hypotheses Based Upon an Examination of the Writing Processes of Seven Year Old Children, completed at the State University of New York at Buffalo in 1973.

References

Braddock, Richard, Lloyd-Jones, Richard, and Schoer, Lowell. *Research in Written Composition*. Champaign, Illinois, NCTE, 1963.

Emig, Janet A., "Component of the Composing Process Among Twelfth Grade Writers." Unpublished doctoral dissertation, Harvard University, 1969.

Holstein, Barbara I. "Use of Metaphor to Induce Innovative Thinking in Fourth Grade Children." Unpublished doctoral dissertation, Boston University, 1970.

Meckel, Henry C. "Research on Teaching Composition," *Handbook of Research on Teaching*, American Education Research Association, Chicago: Rand, McNally and Co., 1963.

Parke, Margaret B. "Composition in Primary Grades," *Children's Writing: Research in Composition and Related Skills*, Champaign, Illinois, National Council of Teachers of English, 1961.

43

THE COMPOSING PROCESS AND THE FUNCTIONS OF WRITING

James Britton

Source: Cooper, C. R. and Odell, L. (eds) *Research on Composing* (1978) Urbana, IL: NCTE, 13–28

Research practices, like those of schools and testing agencies, have some-times mistakenly treated writing as a single kind of ability, regardless of dif-ferences in the reader for whom it is intended and the purpose it attempts to serve. Thus, Kellogg Hunt (1965) bases his index of maturity in writing (the Minimal Terminable Unit) upon any thousand words produced in school by each child in the sample. While it may be held that the intended reader in the children's minds was uniformly the teacher, the nature of the tasks attempted was diverse in a random way. He found significant increases in T-Unit length from grades four to eight to twelve, but then noted that by his measure Faulkner's novels rated a high grade, those of Hemingway a low grade. One might infer that the technique is capable of yielding more information than is to be derived when it is used in a "global" way—that is, when writing functions are ignored. In fact, a member of our research team (Rosen, 1969) applied it to functionally differentiated writings (e.g., a story, a piece of exposition, an argument) and came to a conclusion of a different order, namely that the most able writers tended to produce the greatest vari-ations of T-Unit length from one function to another.

The Writing Research Unit at the University of London Institute of Education was funded by the Schools Council in 1967 for the purpose of studying the development of writing abilities in students throughout their secondary schooling. Our early studies confirmed the suspicion that there were no existing categories adequate to describe differences between one piece of school writing and another. Before attempting to plot develop-ment, therefore, it was necessary to work out a taxonomy, and it is this first stage that will be under consideration in this chapter. In the second stage we made a four-year follow-up study of eleven and fifteen year olds in five schools, but this part of the project is still being completed. Stage one is fully described in a recent publication (Britton, Burgess, Martin,

McLeod, & Rosen, 1975), and I will not attempt to summarize it here. Instead, this chapter will take up one or two points arising from the theory adumbrated in the course of the project and sketch in enough of the research procedures and findings to provide a framework for those points.

We took it for granted that no one set of categories could adequately describe differences among school writings and that a number of variables would have to be identified and categorized. We worked out and applied two such variables and left two others in limbo. Our data comprised 2,000 scripts covering a range of school subjects, produced by 500 boys and girls in their first, third, fifth, and seventh years of secondary schooling in 65 schools scattered over England and Wales. With each script was a brief note by each student's teacher indicating the context in which the work was done and commenting upon the ability of the class.

A study of composing *processes* was focal to the work of the project, and, although we had little more than the products to go by, our taxonomies were developed in the light of our understanding of those processes. We worked on a set of categories that attempted to describe the degree to which a writer appeared to make the teacher-set task his or her own. At one end of the scale were those scripts that reflected perfunctory work, minimal attempts to satisfy demands the writers did not themselves endorse; at the other end, performances in which writers made demands of themselves, so endorsing the teacher's intentions that they became virtually indistinguishable from their own. We noticed that when this happened in the course of the writing (as it frequently did), it was as though a tide had risen and changed the landscape. Starting our analysis with "perfunctory" and "involved" as categories, we found we needed a third, which we called "impelled." Here the work gave the impression that the writer would not have been easily distracted or dissuaded from his or her undertaking, that the writer was in the grip of the topic rather than in control of it. An occasional fantasy story (maybe a retelling of a television drama) came into this category, but it remained a very small set.

We were interested also in the resources a writer appeared to draw upon in a piece of work. We found a few scripts in which a student would attempt to tell a story almost entirely in quoted dialogue. For example:

> "Oh Mummy do you think it would be all right to go and watch daddy? Well I shall want some shopping, it will be closing day tomorrow. All right I will go for you...."

Taking this to be an example of extremely limited linguistic resources on the part of the writer, we thought it might be possible to plot the types of resources reflected in a piece of writing along these lines: spoken dialogue, spoken monologue, the written language of stories, and a particular written model (author or book).

I would not say that "degree of involvement" and "linguistic resources" are blind alleys, but certainly they remain unexplored. By contrast, when we came to tackle two more basic questions about writing—Who is it for? and What is it for?—we found both that we had as much on our hands as we could deal with and perhaps, in terms of the information yielded, as much as we needed for our present purposes.

"Sense of audience" categories

It is inherent in traditional educational procedures that where school writings are concerned, the answer to Who is it for? must usually be the teacher. While we looked also for other audiences such as a peer-group or a public audience, we sought our data mainly by subdividing "teacher" into a number of teaching roles or student-teacher relationships. Thus, the second party named in each of the following categories refers to the teacher who set the writing task:

Child (or adolescent) to trusted adult
Pupil to teacher, general (teacher-learner dialogue)
Pupil to teacher, particular relationship (based on a shared interest in a curriculum subject)
Pupil to examiner

Our trial analysis of 2,000 scripts written by 500 secondary school pupils revealed that 2 categories—pupil to teacher, general, and pupil to examiner—covered between them 88 percent of the scripts (39 percent in the former and 49 percent in the latter). Considering that we had formulated six other categories of audience relationships in addition to the four student-teacher relationships, we were disappointed; but we were somewhat mollified by the fact that some scripts did find their way into each of our ten categories. (For a complete description of the audience categories, see Britton et al., 1975).

"What is it for?": function categories

The purposes that can be served by a piece of writing must surely be manifold. A writer's intentions may be devious or idiosyncratic; the effects upon a reader may be idiosyncratic, unforeseeable, and chainlike, with no clearly defined cutoff point. Yet the function of any piece of writing must be essentially related in some way both to what a writer intends by it and how readers are affected by it. Mercifully, linguists have had to deal with this sort of problem before; their solution is to limit their concern to what is *typical* within the conventions that govern discourse. The context in which an utterance is made must be held to include recognition by writer and reader of these conventions. As Lyons (1964) has put it, "I consider that the idea of context as 'universe of discourse' (in Urban's sense) should be incorporated in any linguistic theory of meaning. Under this head I include the conventions and presuppositions maintained by 'the mutual acknowledgment of communicating subjects' in the particular type of linguistic behaviour (telling a story, philosophizing, buying and selling, praying, writing a novel, etc.)" (pp. 83–84).

Our three principal categories of writing functions—transactional, expressive, and poetic—are intended to mark out two spectra located as follows:

Transactional ⟵——— Expressive ———⟶ Poetic

Behind the two spectra lies a duality that raises most of the issues I want to take up here. The spectrum from expressive to transactional covers what we want to call "language in the role of participant," that from expressive to poetic, "language in the role of spectator." This is a distinction that has origins in Susanne Langer's (1942) "discursive" and "presentational" symbolism and, more specifically, in D. W. Harding's notion (1937, 1962) of "the role of the onlooker."

Harding distinguishes four modes of response to experience: the operative (when we participate in events), the intellectual (when we seek to comprehend without any attempt to modify), the perceptual (when the experiencing and organizing of perceptions is enough), and the "detached evaluative response" of a spectator. While all four modes may contribute to any experience, one is likely to predominate and characterize our response to any situation. In the first mode, as participants we evaluate in order to take part in events, yet our evaluation in this case must subserve our participation; hence, we evaluate under the constraints of self-interest, in the light of our hopes and fears regarding the outcome. In the fourth mode, as spectators we do not stand to gain or lose by the outcome; our evaluation is thus not subject to the constraints of prudence or self-interest. (The femme fatale who watches rival suitors fight a duel is not, in our sense, a spectator!)

Harding's next step is the one that most concerns us here. He goes on to identify as "imaginary spectatorship" all those occasions in which we talk, write, or read about past events, our own or other people's experiences, or about the imagined events of dream or fiction. In gossiping about events, as most of us do every day, speaker and listener are both in the role of spectator: the events recounted are not *taking place*—hence, no one can participate in them—and they are reconstructed solely for contemplation by speaker and listener. Harding points out that in their choice of events to recount, speakers reveal something of the values they place upon events; and in the way they tell their story—their loaded-commentary—

27

they are likely to offer their evaluation even more sharply. What speakers demand from their listeners, whether by nod and grimace or by verbal response, is "feedback" to their evaluation, that is, the sanctioning or modification of the evaluation they offer and hence of the value system by which they manage their existence in the world. If gossip about events constitutes informal language in the role of spectator, then literary fiction—the novel, the story, the play—represents the formal or fully developed end of the scale: "Fiction has to be seen, then, as a convention, a convention for enlarging the scope of the discussions we have with each other about what may befall" (Harding, 1962, p. 139). At the level of social interaction there is, by this view, an exchange of evaluations between authors and their readers, an exchange in which reputations are made and lost, influences wax and wane, values gain and lose currency, and the cultural pattern of a social group is sustained and evolved. Putting the point as broadly as possible, as participants we *apply* our scale of values, as spectators we are concerned to *generate* and *refine* it. While this applies primarily and directly at the level of individuals, it has also its application at the social level. Notice that the agenda of human experience upon which we base our evaluating is not limited to our own firsthand experiences: as participants we have only one life to live; as spectators an infinite number are open to us.

Let me add in parentheses that corroboration of the notion that the tales we exchange about our experiences have an evaluative function has recently come to me from an unexpected quarter. Labov and Waletzky (1967) collected oral narratives of personal experience, mainly from working-class speakers, simply by asking some question as, "Were you ever in a situation where you were in serious danger of being killed?" In carrying out a rigorous linguistic analysis of their recordings, they identified two types of clauses: narrative and evaluative. When occasionally they came across a narrative that had no evaluative clauses and no implied evaluation on other forms, they labeled it an "empty or pointless narrative." In other words, even in the rather artificial circumstances set up for research purposes, the essential evaluative purpose of gossiping about our experiences asserts itself.

For the practical task of classifying written utterances according to function, we reduced Harding's four types of response to two: his first and second modes (operative and intellectual) were conflated into our participant role; his third mode (perceptual) we felt we could safely ignore since there was no obvious way in which language could serve its purposes. His fourth mode is entirely the equivalent of our second, language in the role of spectator. As has been indicated, the two roles are related to three major function categories: transactional language is fully developed to meet the demands of participants; poetic language is fully developed to meet the demands of a spectator role; and expressive language is informal or casual, loosely structured language that may serve, in an undeveloped way, either participant or spectator role purposes. We have said a good deal about the importance of expressive writing elsewhere (Britton et al., 1975)—particularly its educational value as a matrix from which, in favorable circumstances, both transactional and poetic writing are developed. My concern here is with the contrasting spectra: writing in the role of participant (the spectrum from expressive to transactional) and writing in the role of spectator (the spectrum from expressive to poetic).

Writing in the role of participant

As participants we use writing "to get things done," whether it be in an operative mode of informing, instructing, or persuading people or in an intellectual mode of problem solving, speculating, theorizing. An utterance in this category is a means to some end outside itself, and its organization will be on the principle of efficiency in carrying out that end. Of the many types of verbal transactions possible (buying, selling, begging, vowing, etc.), we homed in on two that seemed of importance in school: thus the two principal subcategories of the transactional are the conative and the informative (see Jakobson, 1960, pp. 353 & 357, for a similar distinction). The conative we further divided into regulative (where compliance is assumed) and persuasive (where no such assumption is made). Informative writing we divided in accordance with James Moffett's "abstractive scale," as described in his *Teaching the Universe of Discourse*, but we distinguished seven levels of abstraction where he used four. Our analysis of 2,000 scripts showed that level of abstraction is a highly significant index of development from ages 11 to 18, but that comparatively few students reach the theorizing level and that curriculum subjects vary widely in the rate at which they take students up the scale. The most disappointing finding was the very small percentage of expressive writing at any level—6 percent overall; and this, of course, would cover expressive writing in both the spectator and participant roles.

Writing in the role of spectator

We have suggested that as spectators we take up "a detached evaluative" role with regard to experiences real or imagined; we contemplate narrated experiences, recalled or imagined by ourselves or other people. A word of precaution must be added: we may reconstruct past experiences as a way of *getting something done*, as part of a larger transaction—in other words, for some end outside the utterance. In such cases we are in the participant, not the spectator, role. A witness in a court of law verbally reconstructs past events not in order to contemplate and evaluate them as an instance of what life can be like, but as a contribution towards the court's verdict. If a witness began to savor his or her story and work it up for the enjoyment of the jury, it would soon become clear that the witness was in the wrong mode. Telling a "hard luck story" is a device for securing attention by appearing to invite the listener into the spectator role; but when the demand for a loan comes, the listener knows that he or she was in the wrong role, that the speaker wants cash, not the sanctioning of values!

There is an important implication here: when we move into the spectator role, our utterance itself moves into the focus of attention, becoming an end rather than a means to something outside itself. As such an utterance moves up the scales from expressive to poetic, there is increasing stress upon the forms of the language itself and upon the formal disposition of whatever the language portrays—the pattern of events in a story, the pattern of feelings aroused, the movement of thought in a philosophical narrative such as Wordsworth's *The Prelude*. At the poetic end of the scale, then, a piece of writing is a verbal object, an artifact in words, a work of art: its organization is not on the principle of efficiency as a means, but on the coherence and unity achieved when every part is appropriate to each other and to the whole design. Like any other work of art, a poetic utterance arises from an inner need, and the need is satisfied in the saying. The evaluative function is fulfilled for the writer in the act of presenting *an experience of order* and for the reader in sharing that experience and its ordering effect.

Contextualization

We suggest that there are differences between the way a reader apprehends a transactional utterance and makes it his or her own and the way a reader apprehends a poetic utterance. It is in our view a part of the conventions of transactional writing that a reader contextualizes an utterance in *piecemeal* fashion. Some parts of the discourse readers may ignore because they are too familiar; others they may reject because they judge them, for a variety of reasons, to be unacceptable; others they may reject because they cannot interpret them. Among and around those fragments readers accept, they will build their own connections, articulating the new information with what was already familiar to them. It is within these conventions, for example, that this chapter is intended to be read. But readers of a poetic utterance must resist the process of piecemeal contextualization: their intention is to recreate a verbal object, a piece of discourse that achieves, by internal organization, a single identity marked off from the rest of the world. They can never wholly succeed, of course, since the medium is discourse, discourse is referential, and the responses demanded of readers are deeply embedded in the everyday referential uses of language. The conventions governing poetic discourse are a force operating in a direction contrary to this. Putting it simply, we contextualize facts about social conditions in the nineteenth century as we read *Hard Times*, but we are at the same time aware that such responses are over and above the response we are primarily concerned to make, a response to the work *as a whole* and one which therefore calls for suspended judgement until the shape of the whole has been reconstructed in the reading. Similarly, we know that a novel with a "message" is in danger of being misinterpreted if we locate its message in some detail of plot or characterization: it speaks through the poetic construct as a whole. The conventions of poetic discourse thus call for global contextualization.

When Susanne Langer (1942) first makes her distinction between discursive and presentational symbolism, she contrasts the linear nature of discourse with the simultaneous impact of a visual art form. The idea of a simultaneous communication is suggested in the name she has chosen, *presentational*. Yet the presentational forms of music and the verbal arts have a time dimension, as do discursive forms. Our distinction between piecemeal and global contextualization seems to be one way of resolving this difficulty and is consistent with the advice critics have sometimes offered on how literature—poetry in particular—should be read if we are to preserve its essential unity. Coleridge distinguished a poem from ordinary discourse by calling it "esemplastic" ("molding into one"), and Bateson (1966) stressed the necessity of attention to details of a text *after* a sense of the general meaning of the whole has been established. An interesting field for research offers itself in studying the relationship between "text" and "message" (see, as one starting point, Polanyi, 1958, p. 92) as it varies over types of discourse and, in particular, as between transactional and poetic varieties.

Contextualization and the composing processes

Pursuing the contexualization distinction, we may relate it directly to the processes of composition. The writer of a transactional piece, in having in mind the reader addressed, must try to envisage the initial preoccupations with which that reader will approach the task, since these preoccupations provide the context into which the text is to be fitted. Fitting the text to the preoccupations involves finding a way of beginning that will both open up the topic and enmesh with what the reader has in mind. Shared context builds up between writer and reader as the piece proceeds, so the chances of losing, confusing, misleading, or frustrating a reader are at their greatest in the opening sentences. "Finding a way in" has often been used as a way of talking about the difficulties of writing a transactional piece. It is more, of course, than simply wooing a reader or catching his or her interest: the strategy must be such that the writer-reader interaction sets up a coherent movement towards the heart of the message. How this may vary was something we observed at a simple level in reading the transactional writing produced in school; writers were likely to succeed if they found for their opening a generalization powerful enough to require more than a sentence or two to work out its implications. (Planning in advance is no guarantee of success, for an outline does not necessarily promote the coherence that arises in the texture of the writing—and, indeed, may often militate against it.)

A glance at the opening words of a few poems, stories, or plays is enough to indicate that some quite different principle is at work in poetic discourse. There is no attempt to open by enmeshing with the reader's preoccupations but rather the reverse: an effort to create a dislocation. In Langer's words (1953), "Nothing can be built up unless the very first words of the poem effect the break with the reader's actual environment" (p. 214). The mature writer may make the break in a sophisticated way: *War and Peace* opens with "*Eh bien mon prince*, so Genoa and Lucca are now no more than private estates of the Bonaparte family," and a poem by Kingsley Amis begins, "So, bored with dragons, he lay down to sleep." But even the three year old has a formula for doing it. "Once upon a time." We must not imply that to write the opening words of a story or a poem is a simple matter or one of random selection. What we suggest is that in poetic discourse the writer does not buttonhole readers by attempting to latch on to ideas already preoccupying them, that the writer does not need to "look for a way in." Rather, the writer woos readers by offering them "time out," a holiday from what daily concerns them, with the opening acting as a signal to switch from participant to spectator role. Having said that, it is clear to us that the constraints governing a poetic writer's choice of opening are precisely those that operate at all other points in his or her composition, the rules that produce the internal organization that gives coherence and unity to the artifact.

I should add at this point that while the whole question of piecemeal and global contextualization was most actively under discussion in the research team, we were fortunate enough to have Wayne Booth, author of *The Rhetoric of Fiction*, as a temporary associate, and we owe a great deal to his cooperation. This fact encourages us to believe that there is no fundamental disparity between the views regarding a literary author's relationship to his or her reader as we have set them out here and as Booth describes them in his book. There is, of course, a great deal of speculation in this part of our theory, and the whole area bristles with further problems. There is certainly a need for studies that attempt to connect composing processes with reading processes in systematic ways. A text composed by a writer and "reconstituted" by a reader would provide a useful unit of study; our hypotheses would he in the area of the assumed differences between transactional text and poetic text. Recent approaches to the theory of reading would suggest that one payoff of such studies might be practical help to teachers of beginning reading. (One recent conference on reading produced pretty general agreement with the claim that "the processes of language reception must somehow borrow the machinery of production.")

Preparation, incubation, and articulation

Our study of the processes of writing led us to consider three stages: preparation, incubation, and articulation. While it is clear that incubation plays an important and little-understood role in writing of all kinds, we might speculate that in much poetic writing incubation does duty also for the earlier stage, preparation. Certainly, autobiographical anecdotes that support this idea are in good supply, particularly, it seems, from English poets in the Romantic tradition. This example comes from Siegfried Sassoon (1945):

> One evening in the middle of April I had an experience which seems worth describing for those who are interested in the methods of poetic production. It was a sultry spring night. I was feeling dull minded and depressed, for no assignable reason. After sitting lethargically in the ground floor room for about three hours after dinner, I came to the conclusion that there was nothing for it but to take my useless brain to bed. On my way from the arm-chair to the door I stood by the writing table. A few words had floated into my head as though from nowhere.... I picked up a pencil and wrote the words on a sheet of notepaper. Without sitting down, I added a second line. It was as if I were remembering rather than thinking. In this mindless, recollecting manner I wrote down my poem in a few minutes. When it was finished I read it through, with no sense of elation, merely wondering how I had come to be writing a poem when feeling so stupid. I then went heavily upstairs and fell asleep without thinking about it again.... The poem was *Everyone Sang*, which has since become a stock anthology piece.
>
> (p. 140)

That thinking and utterance may undergo organizing processes at an involuntary level has been demonstrated often enough. This has been shown to be equally true in the production of transactional and poetic utterances. Bernard Kaplan (see also McKeller, 1957), for example, has described the occurrence of hypnogogic images that represent solutions or partial solutions to intellectual problems.[1] It seems surprising that the role of incubation in the writing process has not been experimentally investigated, as far as we know, in recent years. Articulation, the pen-to-paper phase of the writing process, is likewise an area ripe for experimental study. The only attempt to time the process accurately (Van Bruggen, 1946) seems to have been a limited experiment carried out in America many years ago, long before Goldman-Eisler's fruitful studies (1968) of the timing of speech.

The London Writing Research Unit in 1969 developed the design of a transmitting pen which, in conjunction with an electronic recording table, would give a timed record of an individual's performance throughout all the moves of drafting, amending, or redrafting; but shortage of both time and money forced us to abandon the proposal. We continue to cherish our hunch that "shaping at the point of utterance" may be a crucial aspect of the writing process in a great many kinds of writing. We are encouraged in this notion by Polanyi's (1969, pp. 144–146) concept of "focal" and "peripheral" awareness—peripheral awareness of the means, language, being subject to the control of a focal awareness of the end in view, the purposes for which the language is being used. We are encouraged also by our own experiments at writing without being able to read what is written: while in general this proved inhibiting, the degree of interference varied according to function—expressive (a letter to a colleague), transactional (a paragraph in a research paper), or poetic (a poem). The results were consistent with the belief that we focus upon the end in view, shaping the utterance as we write; and when the seam is "played out" or we are interrupted, we get started again by reading what we have written, running along the tracks we have laid down. With the loose structure of expressive writing, a dislocation (due to inability to read what we had written) might barely be noticed; with the transactional paragraph, the frustration lay principally in not being able to read back over the last few phrases. (Had we attempted to write a longer passage other needs would of course have arisen.) With the poetic there was no predicting when the frustration would arise—the need to have the whole in view made itself felt, and the task was virtually impossible.

A more prosaic way of referring to "shaping at the point of utterance" is perhaps to say that a writer develops an inner voice capable of dictating to him or her in the forms of the written language. Yet that is mysterious enough, and there seems to have been no study of how the facility is acquired or how it is related to fluency and other speech factors or to tastes and habits in reading. I have already referred to the fact that we came across cases of children who reach the age of eleven *without* acquiring the ability, whose inner voice is restricted to the dialogue that has assailed their ears.

A final speculation on the articulation process will serve as a link with the general statement that concludes this chapter. We have hinted at the organizing power of a generalization in a piece of transactional writing. A complementary process in poetic writing may lie in the power of a formal feature or features to act as organizing principles. We believe, in fact, that children's writing sometimes demonstrates the "taking over" process in the course of a single utterance. A piece that begins in a loose, unstructured way—perfunctorily, even—may seem to take shape under the influence of the affective power of a rhythm or sound pattern, an image or an idea. It has been remarked that in young children's drawings what has been called physiognomic perception—a dynamic way of perceiving that responds to global expressiveness rather than to detail—may sometimes take over and affect both the objects the child chooses to represent and the mode of representing them. Perhaps there is a parallel here to what we believe we have observed. In this first piece, in many ways typical of the cataloging small children go in for (the writer is a seven-year-old girl), a rhythm seems to take over and exercise a degree of control over what is written:

> Class I had Monday off and Tuesday off and all the other classes had Monday and Tuesday off and we played hide-and-seek and my big sister hid her eyes and counted up to ten and me and my brother had to hide and I went behind the dust-bin and I was thinking about the summer and the buttercups and daisies all those things and fresh grass and violets and roses and lavender and the twinkling sea and the star in the night and the black sky and the moon.

The take-over effect is more powerful in the next example, though it is also more difficult to identify the particular formal feature or features that acted as vehicles for the feeling that drew the piece together. The story was dictated to his teacher by a grade one boy in a Toronto school. We know that, at the time, his father had recently deserted the home.

> Once upon a time there was a little boy, and he didn't have a mother or father. One day he was walking in the forest. He saw a rabbit. It led him to a house.
> There was a book inside of the house. He looked at the book and saw a picture of a pretty animal. It was called a "horse."
> He turned the page and saw a picture of a rabbit, a rabbit just like he had seen in the forest. He turned the page again and saw a cat. He thought of his father and mother, and when he was small, and they had books for him and animals for him to play with. He thought about this and started to cry.
> While he was crying a lady said, "What's the matter, boy?"
> He slowly looked round and saw his mother. He said, "Is it really you?"
> "Yes, my son. I'm your mother."
> "Mother, mother are you alive?"
> "No, child. This is the house that I was killed in."
> "Oh, mother . . . why are you here?"

"Because I came back to look for you."

"Why, mother? Why did you come back to look for me?"

"Because I miss you."

"Where is father?"

"He is in the coffin that he was buried in. But don't talk about that now. How are you son? You're bigger ... and I'm glad to see you."

"It's been a long time, mother."

While the boy and the mother were talking, his father came into the room and said, "Hi, son. How are you?"

"Fine," said the boy, "fine."

Suddenly the mother and father came to life.

The boy was crying, and the mother and father were crying too. God suddenly gave them a miracle ... to come to life. The boy looked at the mother and father and said, "Oh mother, oh, father."

Two sets of rules of use

Susanne Langer's distinction between discursive and presentational symbolism is the foundation stone for her speculations concerning the two modes of organization by which our primary mental operations achieve fullest significance and power. The first is the cognitive order, a superstructure made possible by the invention and use of discursive language. It is the order of objective knowledge; in the course of teaching it, one has to dissociate the cognitive from the affective aspects of one's experience of the world. The uniquely personal responses, the affective aspects, are screened out (as far as they may be) in order to achieve knowledge and control of the environment. Langer claims that we have known and recognized this order and studied its laws so exclusively that we have failed to distinguish the other order from mere chaos. The order associated with presentational symbolism is perfectly represented in a work of art: it is not an organization of *affective* responses, for by the laws of this order the cognitive-affective distinction is irrelevant. A work of art is a projection of our cognitive-cum-affective responses to experience. It is a subjective order, and as such it comes into operation, in a form less intense, less perfect than it achieves in a work of art, in many of our daily activities. Langer's recent volumes (1967, 1973) continue her pioneer work in attempting to describe the principles of her alternative order, the principles by which experience is projected into a work of art. She speculates (1964, p. 61) among other things that "physiognomic perception" may play its part and that the representation of tensions and resolutions may relate the structure of a work of art to the phases characteristic of every "living act," the shape of the elements that make up the continuum of life.

In our proposal to divide discourse into language in the role of participant and language in the role of spectator, we see the two spectra as embodying Langer's two forms of organization. Difficult though it may be for linguists to see the validity of this "first cut" in kinds of discourse, we believe Langer's distinction must in the long run find acceptance. In terms of linguistic competence, then, we see expressive discourse as an area of discourse where the rules of use are at their least demanding. As writers improve in their ability to meet the demands, on the one hand, of participant tasks and, on the other, of tasks in the spectator role, they will internalize two distinct sets of rules of use: from the matrix of expressive writing, they will acquire competence in both transactional and poetic modes of writing. We believe speech-act analysis would improve its explanatory power if it applied its rules differentially and/or applied different rules to the two spectra we have described.

Postscript

Let me say again that the ideas I have explored here have often been highly speculative and may best be regarded as indications of areas where further inquiry is needed. Work on the process we have called *incubation*, for example, is probably still mainly at the case-study level, but I see no reason why experimental situations should not be set up to yield more controlled data. In an intricate and puzzling area of psychological study, one would at least have *texts* to hang on to. Some early experiments on recall (Bartlett, 1932/1964), where time interval was related to stages of modification of the material recalled, might be adapted to serve this somewhat different purpose.

As for the articulation process, I hope people who feel as we do that "snaping at the point of utterance" is an apt description of an actual process may find it worthwhile to investigate the mysteries of the "inner voice" that comes to dictate written forms of discourse, a study that would have to relate to a subject's reading patterns over a period of time, as well as to the subject's drafting procedures. All methods of drafting seem to me to deserve more investigation than they have so far received. Simple interference techniques, such as the one we tried where the writer cannot see what he or she writes and systematically varied interruptions during composing, seem worth further trial. Perhaps the most obvious lack is that of an accurate matching of a fully revised and edited piece of writing with a complete time record of its production. Electronic apparatus would make this matching possible today, and it is high time somebody undertook it. Long-term studies of the development of writing ability are almost as scarce today as they were when I. A. Richards first pointed out their importance some forty years ago. Finally, anyone who has the time and energy to make a full study of Susanne Langer's recent works ought then to fall in behind her in an attempt to define those laws we have glibly referred to as the rules of use governing utterances that are also works of art.

Acknowledgement

In all I have written here, I gratefully acknowledge the work of my colleagues in the Writing Research Unit, Nancy Martin, Dr. Harold Rosen, Tony Burgess, Dennis Griffiths, Alex McLeod, and Bernard Newsome.

Note

1 Lecture presented at a conference on "Symbolization and the Young Child," Wheelock College, Boston, October 1975.

References

Bartlett, F. C. *Remembering: A study in experimental and social psychology.* Cambridge: The University Press, 1964. (Originally published, 1932.)

Bateson, F. W. *English poetry: A critical introduction* (2nd ed.). London: Longman, 1966.

Booth, W. C. *The rhetoric of fiction.* Chicago: University of Chicago Press, 1961.

Britton, J., Burgess, T., Martin, N., McLeod, A., & Rosen, H. *The development of writing abilities (11–18).* London: Macmillan Education, 1975.

Goldman-Eisler, F. *Psycholinguistics.* London: Academic Press, 1968.

Harding, D. W. The role of the onlooker. *Scrutiny,* 1937, *6,* 247–258.

Harding, D. W. Psychological processes in the reading of fiction. *British Journal of Aesthetics,* 1962, *2,* 133–147.

Hunt, K. W. *Grammatical structures written at three grade levels* (NCTE Research Report No. 3). Champaign, Ill.: National Council of Teachers of English, 1965.

Jakobson, R. Linguistics and poetics. In T. A. Sebeok (Ed.), *Style in language.* New York: John Wiley, 1960.

Labov, W., & Waletzky, J. Narrative analysis: Oral versions of personal experience. In J. Helm (Ed.), *Essays on the verbal and visual arts: Proceedings of the 1966 annual meeting of the American Ethnological Society.* Seattle: University of Washington Press, 1967.

Langer, S. K. *Philosophy in a new key.* Cambridge: Harvard University Press, 1942.

Langer, S. K. *Feeling and form.* London: Routledge and Kegan Paul, 1953.

Langer, S. K. *Philosophical sketches.* Baltimore: Johns Hopkins University Press, 1964.

Langer, S. K. *Mind: An essay on human feeling* (Vols. 1 & 2). Baltimore: Johns Hopkins University Press, 1967, 1973.

Lyons, J. *Structural semantics.* Oxford: Blackwell, 1964.

McKeller, P. *Imagination and thinking.* London: Cohen and West, 1957.

Moffett, J. *Teaching the universe of discourse.* Boston: Houghton Mifflin, 1968.

Polanyi, M. *Personal knowledge.* London: Routledge and Kegan Paul, 1958.

Polanyi, M. *Knowing and being.* London: Routledge and Kegan Paul, 1969.

Rosen, H. *An investigation of the effects of differentiated writing assignments on the performance in English composition of a selected group of 15/16 year old pupils.* Unpublished doctoral dissertation, University of London, 1969.

Sassoon, S. *Siegfried's journey.* London: Faber, 1945.

Van Bruggen, J. A. Factors affecting regularity of the flow of words during written composition. *Journal of Experimental Education,* 1946, *15* (2), 133–155.

44

A COGNITIVE PROCESS THEORY OF WRITING

Linda Flower and John R. Hayes

Source: *College Composition and Communication* (December, 1981) 32: 365–387

There is a venerable tradition in rhetoric and composition which sees the composing process as a series of decisions and choices.[1] However, it is no longer easy simply to assert this position, unless you are prepared to answer a number of questions, the most pressing of which probably is: "What then are the criteria which govern that choice?" Or we could put it another way: "What guides the decisions writers make as they write?" In a recent survey of composition research, Odell, Cooper, and Courts noticed that some of the most thoughtful people in the field are giving us two reasonable but somewhat different answers:

> How do writers actually go about choosing diction, syntactic and organizational patterns, and content? Kinneavy claims that one's purpose—informing, persuading, expressing, or manipulating language for its own sake—guides these choices. Moffett and Gibson contend that these choices are determined by one's sense of the relation of speaker, subject, and audience. Is either of these two claims borne out by the actual practice of writers engaged in drafting or revising? Does either premise account adequately for the choices writers make?[2]

Rhetoricians such as Lloyd Bitzer and Richard Vatz have energetically debated this question in still other terms. Lloyd Bitzer argues that speech always occurs as a response to a rhetorical situation, which he succinctly defines as containing an exigency (which demands a response), an audience, and a set of constraints.[3] In response to this "situation-driven" view, Vatz claims that the speaker's response, and even the rhetorical situation itself, are determined by the imagination and art of the speaker.[4]

Finally, James Britton has asked the same question and offered a linguist's answer, namely, that syntactic and lexical choices guide the process.

It is tempting to think of writing as a process of making linguistic choices from one's repertoire of syntactic structures and lexical items. This would suggest that there is a meaning, or something to be expressed, in the writer's mind, and that he proceeds to choose, from the words and structures he has at his disposal, the ones that best match his meaning. But is that really how it happens?[5]

To most of us it may seem reasonable to suppose that all of these forces—"purposes," "relationship," "exigencies," "language"—have a hand in guiding the writer's process, but it is not at all clear how they do so or how they interact. Do they, for example, work in elegant and graceful coordination, or as competitive forces constantly vying for control? We think that the best way to answer these questions—to really understand the nature of rhetorical choices in good and poor writers—is to follow James Britton's lead and turn our attention to the writing process itself: to ask, "but is that really how it happens?"

This paper will introduce a theory of the cognitive processes involved in composing in an effort to lay groundwork for more detailed study of thinking processes in writing. This theory is based on our work with protocol analysis over the past five years and has, we feel, a good deal of evidence to support it. Nevertheless, it is for us a working hypothesis and springboard for further research, and we hope that insofar as it suggests testable hypotheses it will be the same for others. Our cognitive process theory rests on four key points, which this paper will develop:

1   The process of writing is best understood as a set of distinctive thinking processes which writers orchestrate or organize during the act of composing.
2   These processes have a hierarchical, highly embedded organization in which any given process can be embedded within any other.
3   The act of composing itself is a goal-directed thinking process, guided by the writer's own growing network of goals.
4   Writers create their own goals in two key ways: by generating both high-level goals and supporting sub-goals which embody the writer's developing sense of purpose, and then, at times, by changing major goals or even establishing entirely new ones based on what has been learned in the act of writing.

1. Writing is best understood as a set of distinctive thinking processes which writers orchestrate or organize during the act of composing

To many this point may seem self-evident, and yet it is in marked contrast to our current paradigm for composing—the stage process model. This familiar metaphor or model describes the composing process as a linear series of stages, separated in time, and characterized by the gradual development of the written product. The best examples of stage models are the Pre-Write/ Write/Re-Write model of Gordon Rohman[6] and The Conception/Incubation/Production model of Britton *et al.*[7]

Stage models of writing

Without doubt, the wide acceptance of Pre-Writing has helped improve the teaching of composition by calling attention to planning and discovery as legitimate parts of the writing process. Yet many question whether this linear stage model is really an accurate or useful description of the composing process itself. The problem with stage descriptions of writing is that they model the growth of the written product, not the inner process of the person producing it. "Pre-Writing" is the stage before words emerge on paper; "Writing" is the stage in which a product is being produced; and "Re-Writing" is a final reworking of that product. Yet both common sense and research tell us that writers are constantly planning (pre-writing) and revising (re-writing) as they compose (write), not in clean-cut stages.[8] Furthermore, the sharp distinctions stage models make between the operations of planning, writing, and revising may seriously distort how these activities work. For example, Nancy Sommers has shown that revision, as it is carried out by skilled writers, is not an end-of-the-line repair process, but is a constant process of "re-vision" or re-seeing that goes on while they are composing.[9] A more accurate model of the composing process would need to recognize those basic thinking processes which unite planning and revision. Because stage models take the final product as their reference point, they offer an inadequate account of the more intimate, moment-by-moment intellectual process of composing. How, for example, is the output of one stage, such as pre-writing or incubation, transferred to the next? As every writer knows, having good ideas doesn't automatically produce good prose. Such models are typically silent on the inner processes of decision and choice.

A cognitive process model

A cognitive process theory of writing, such as the one presented here, represents a major departure from the traditional paradigm of stages in this way: in a stage model the major units of analysis are *stages* of completion which reflect the growth of a written product, and these stages are organized in a *linear* sequence or structure. In a process model, the major units of analysis are elementary mental *processes*, such as the process of generating ideas. And these processes have a *hierarchical* structure (see p. 379, below) such that idea generation, for example, is a sub-process of Planning. Furthermore, each of these mental acts may occur at any time in the composing process. One major advantage of identifying these basic cognitive processes or thinking skills writers use is that we can then compare the composing strategies of good and poor writers. And we can look at writing in a much more detailed way.

In psychology and linguistics, one traditional way of looking carefully at a process is to build a model of what you see. A model is a metaphor for a process: a way to describe something, such as the composing process, which refuses to sit still for a portrait. As a hypothesis about a dynamic system, it attempts to describe the parts of the system and how they work together. Modeling a process starts as a problem in design. For example, imagine that you have been asked to start from scratch and design an imaginary, working "Writer." In order to build a "Writer" or a theoretical system that would reflect the process of a real writer, you would want to do at least three things:

1   First, you would need to define the major elements or sub-processes that make up the larger process of writing. Such sub-processes would include planning retrieving information from long-term memory, reviewing, and so on.
2   Second, you would want to show how these various elements of the process interact in the total process of writing. For example, how is "knowledge" about the audience actually integrated into the moment-to-moment act of composing?
3   And finally, since a model is primarily a tool for thinking with, you would want your model to speak to critical questions in the discipline. It should help you see things you didn't see before.

Obviously, the best way to model the writing process is to study a writer in action, and there are many ways to do this. However, people's after-the-fact, *introspective analysis* of what they did while writing is notoriously inaccurate and likely to be influenced by their notions of what they should have done. Therefore we turned to *protocol analysis*, which has been successfully used to study other cognitive processes.[10] Unlike introspective reports, thinking aloud protocols capture a detailed record of what is going on in the writer's mind during the act of composing itself. To collect a protocol, we give writers a problem, such as "Write an article on your job for the readers of *Seventeen* magazine," and then ask them to compose out loud near an unobtrusive tape recorder. We ask them to work on the task as they normally would—thinking, jotting notes, and writing—except that they must think out loud. They are asked to verbalize everything that goes through their minds as they write, including stray notions, false starts, and incomplete or fragmentary thought. The writers are *not* asked to engage in any kind of introspection or self-analysis while writing, but simply to think out loud while working like a person talking to herself.

The transcript of this session, which may amount to 20 pages for an hour session, is called a protocol. As a research tool, a protocol is extraordinarily rich in data and, together with the writer's notes and manuscript, it gives us a very detailed picture of the writer's composing process. It lets us see not only the development of the written product but many of the intellectual processes which produced it. The model of the writing process presented in Figure 1 attempts to account for the major thinking processes and constraints we saw at work in these protocols. But note that it does *not* specify the order in which they are invoked.

The act of writing involves three major elements which are reflected in the three units of the model: **the task environment, the writer's long-term memory, and the writing processes**. The task environment includes all of those things outside the writer's skin, starting with the rhetorical problem or assignment and eventually including the growing text itself. The second element is the writer's long-term memory in which the writer has stored knowledge, not only of the topic, but of the audience and of various writing plans. The third element in our model contains writing processes themselves, specifically the basic processes of **Planning, Translating, and Reviewing**, which are under the control of a Monitor.

This model attempts to account for the processes we saw in the composing protocols. It is also a guide to research, which asks us to explore each of these elements and their interaction more fully. Since this model is described in detail elsewhere,[11] let us focus here on some ways each element contributes to the overall process.

Overview of the model

The rhetorical problem

At the beginning of composing, the most important element is obviously **the rhetorical problem** itself. A school assignment is a simplified version of such a problem, describing the writer's topic, audience, and (implicitly) her role as student to teacher. Insofar as writing is a rhetorical act, not a mere artifact, writers attempt to "solve" or respond to this rhetorical problem by writing something.

In theory this problem is a very complex thing: it includes not only the rhetorical situation and audience which prompts one to write, it also

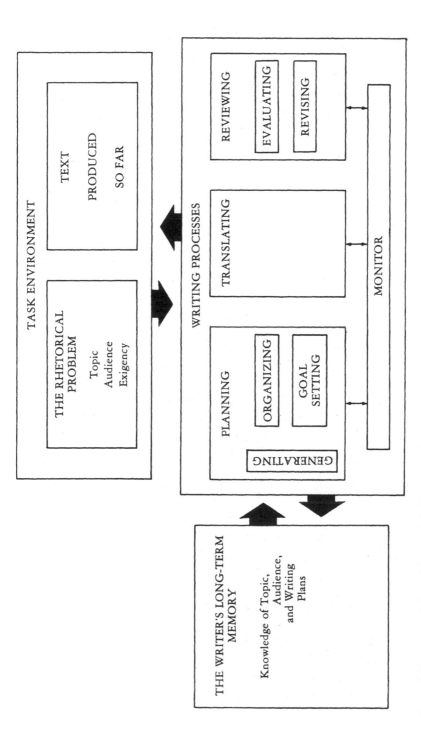

Figure 1 Structure of the writing model. (For an explanation of how to read a process model, please see Footnote 11.)

includes the writer's own goals in writing.[12] A good writer is a person who can juggle all of these demands. But in practice we have observed, as did Britton,[13] that writers frequently reduce this large set of constraints to a radically simplified problem, such as "write another theme for English class." Redefining the problem in this way is obviously an economical strategy as long as the new representation fits reality. But when it doesn't, there is a catch: people only solve the problems they define for themselves. If a writer's representation of her rhetorical problem is inaccurate or simply underdeveloped, then she is unlikely to "solve" or attend to the missing aspects of the problem. To sum up, defining the rhetorical problem is a major, immutable part of the writing process. But the way in which people choose to define a rhetorical problem to themselves can vary greatly from writer to writer. An important goal for research then will be to discover how this process of representing the problem works and how it affects the writer's performance.

The written text

As composing proceeds, a new element enters the task environment which places even more constraints upon what the writer can say. Just as a title constrains the content of a paper and a topic sentence shapes the options of a paragraph, each word in the growing text determines and limits the choices of what can come next. However, the influence that the growing text exerts on the composing process can vary greatly. When writing is incoherent, the text may have exerted too little influence; the writer may have failed to consolidate new ideas with earlier statements. On the other hand, one of the earmarks of a basic writer is a dogged concern with extending the previous sentence[14] and a reluctance to jump from local, text-bound planning to more global decisions, such as "what do I want to cover here?"

As we will see, the growing text makes large demands on the writer's time and attention during composing. But in doing so, it is competing with two other forces which could and also should direct the composing process; namely, the writer's knowledge stored in long-term memory and the writer's plans for dealing with the rhetorical problem. It is easy, for example, to imagine a conflict between what you know about a topic and what you might actually want to say to a given reader, or between a graceful phrase that completes a sentence and the more awkward point you actually wanted to make. Part of the drama of writing is seeing how writers juggle and integrate the multiple constraints of their knowledge, their plans, and their text into the production of each new sentence.[15]

The long-term memory

The writer's long-term memory, which can exist in the mind as well as in outside resources such as books, is a storehouse of knowledge about the topic and audience, as well as knowledge of writing plans and problem representations. Sometimes a single cue in an assignment, such as "write a persuasive ...," can let a writer tap a stored representation of a problem and bring a whole raft of writing plans into play.

Unlike short-term memory, which is our active processing capacity or conscious attention, long-term memory is a relatively stable entity and has its own internal organization of information. The problem with long-term memory is, first of all, getting things out of it—that is, finding the cue that will let you retrieve a network of useful knowledge. The second problem for a writer is usually reorganizing or adapting that information to fit the demands of the rhetorical problem. The phenomena of "writer-based" prose nicely demonstrates the results of a writing strategy based solely on retrieval. The organization of a piece of writer-based prose faithfully reflects the writer's own discovery process and the structure of the remembered information itself, but it often fails to transform or reorganize that knowledge to meet the different needs of a reader.[16]

Planning

People often think of planning as the act of figuring out how to get from here to there, i.e., making a detailed plan. But our model uses the term in its much broader sense. In the **planning** process writers form an internal *representation* of the knowledge that will be used in writing. This internal representation is likely to be more abstract than the writer's prose representation will eventually be. For example, a whole network of ideas might be represented by a single key word. Furthermore, this representation of one's knowledge will not necessarily be made in language, but could be held as a visual or perceptual code, e.g., as a fleeting image the writer must then capture in words.

Planning, or the act of building this internal representation, involves a number of sub-processes. The most obvious is the act of **generating ideas**, which includes retrieving relevant information from long-term memory. Sometimes this information is so well developed and organized *in memory* that the writer is essentially generating standard written English. At other times one may generate only fragmentary, unconnected, even contradictory thoughts, like the pieces of a poem that hasn't yet taken shape.

When the structure of ideas already in the writer's memory is not adequately adapted to the current rhetorical task, the sub-process of **organizing** takes on the job of helping the writer make meaning, that is, give a meaningful structure to his or her ideas. The process of **organizing** appears to play an important part in creative thinking and discovery since it is capable of grouping ideas and forming new concepts. More specifically, the organizing process allows the writer to identify categories, to search for subordinate ideas which develop a current topic, and to search for superordinate ideas which include or subsume the current topic. At another level the process of organizing also attends to more strictly textual decisions about the presentation and ordering of the text. That is, writers identify first or last topics, important ideas, and presentation patterns. However, organizing is much more than merely ordering points. And it seems clear that all rhetorical decisions and plans for reaching the audience affect the process of organizing ideas at all levels, because it is often guided by major goals established during the powerful process of **goal-setting**.

Goal-setting is indeed a third, little-studied but major, aspect of the **planning** process. The goals writers give themselves are both procedural (e.g., "Now let's see—a—I want to start our with "energy"") and substantive, often both at the same time (e.g., "I have to relate this [engineering project] to the economics [of energy] to show why I'm improving it and why the steam turbine needs to be more efficient" or "I want to suggest that—that—um—the reader should sort of—what—what should one say— the reader should look at what she is interested in and look at the things that give her pleasure . . .").

The most important thing about writing goals is the fact that they are *created* by the writer. Although some well-learned plans and goals may be drawn intact from long-term memory, most of the writer's goals are generated, developed, and revised by the same processes that generate and organize new ideas. And this process goes on throughout composing. Just as goals lead a writer to generate ideas, those ideas lead to new, more complex goals which can then integrate content and purpose.

Our own studies on goal setting to date suggest that the act of defining one's own rhetorical problem and setting goals is an important part of "being creative" and can account for some important differences between good and poor writers.[17] As we will argue in the final section of this paper, the act of developing and refining one's own goals is not limited to a "pre-writing stage" in the composing process, but is intimately bound up with the ongoing, moment-to-moment process of composing.

Translating

This is essentially the process of putting ideas into visible language. We have chosen the term **translate** for this process over other terms such as "transcribe" or "write" in order to emphasize the peculiar qualities of the task. The information generated in **planning** may be represented in a variety of symbol systems other than language, such as imagery or kinetic sensations. Trying to capture the movement of a deer on ice in language is clearly a kind of translation. Even when the **planning** process represents one's thought in words, that representation is unlikely to be in the elaborate syntax of written English. So the writer's task is to translate a meaning, which may be embodied in key words (what Vygotsky calls words "saturated with sense") and organized in a complex network of relationships, into a linear piece of written English.

The process of **translating** requires the writer to juggle all the special demands of written English, which Ellen Nold has described as lying on a spectrum from generic and formal demands through syntactic and lexical ones down to the motor tasks of forming letters. For children and inexperienced writers, this extra burden may overwhelm the limited capacity of short-term memory.[18] If the writer must devote conscious attention to demands such as spelling and grammar, the task of translating can interfere with the more global process of planning what one wants to say. Or one can simply ignore some of the constraints of written English. One path produces poor or local planning, the other produces errors, and both, as Mina Shaughnessy showed, lead to frustration for the writer.[19]

In some of the most exciting and extensive research in this area, Marlene Scardamalia and Carl Bereiter have looked at the ways children cope with the cognitive demands of writing. Well-learned skills, such as sentence construction, tend to become automatic and lost to consciousness. Because so little of the writing process is automatic for children, they must devote conscious attention to a variety of individual thinking tasks which adults perform quickly and automatically. Such studies, which trace the development of a given skill over several age groups, can show us the hidden components of an adult process as well as show us how children learn. For example, these studies have been able to distinguish children's ability to handle idea complexity from their ability to handle syntactic complexity; that is, they demonstrate the difference between seeing complex relationships and translating them into appropriate language. In another series of studies Bereiter and Scardamalia showed how children learn to handle the translation process by adapting, then eventually abandoning, the discourse conventions of conversation.[20]

Reviewing

As you can see in Figure 1, **reviewing** depends on two sub-processes: **evaluating** and **revising**. Reviewing, itself, may be a conscious process in which writers choose to read what they have written either as a springboard to further translating or with an eye to systematically evaluating and/or revising the text. These periods of planned reviewing frequently lead to new cycles of planning and translating. However, the reviewing process can also occur as an unplanned action triggered by an evaluation of either the text or one's own planning (that is, people revise written as well as unwritten thoughts or statements). The sub-processes of revising and evaluating, along with generating, share the special distinction of being able to interrupt any other process and occur at any time in the act of writing.

The monitor

As writers compose, they also monitor their current process and progress. The monitor functions as a writing strategist which determines when the writer moves from one process to the next. For example, it determines how long a writer will continue generating ideas before attempting to write prose. Our observations suggest that this choice is determined both by the writer's goals and by individual writing habits or styles. As an example of varied composing styles, writers appear to range from people who try to move to polished prose as quickly as possible to people who choose to plan the entire discourse in detail before writing a word. Bereiter and Scardamalia have shown that much of a child's difficulty and lack of fluency lies in their lack of an "executive routine" which would promote switching between processes or encourage the sustained generation of ideas.[21] Children for example, possess the skills necessary to generate ideas, but lack the kind of monitor which tells them to "keep using" that skill and generate a little more.

Implications of a cognitive process model

A model such as the one presented here is first and foremost a tool for researchers to think with. By giving a testable shape and definition to our observations, we have tried to pose new questions to be answered. For example, the model identifies three major processes (**plan, translate, and review**) and a number of sub-processes available to the writer. And yet the first assertion of this cognitive process theory is that people do not march through these processes in a simple 1, 2, 3 order. Although writers may spend more time in planning at the beginning of a composing session, planning is not a unitary stage, but a distinctive thinking process which writers use over and over during composing. Furthermore, it is used at all levels, whether the writer is making a global plan for the whole text or a local representation of the meaning of the next sentence. This then raises a question: if the process of writing is not a sequence of stages but a set of optional actions, how are these thinking processes in our repertory actually orchestrated or organized as we write? The second point of our cognitive process theory offers one answer to this question.

2. The processes of writing are hierarchically organized, with component processes embedded within other components

A hierarchical system is one in which a large working system such as composing can subsume other less inclusive systems, such as generating ideas, which in turn contain still other systems, and so on. Unlike those in a linear organization, the events in a hierarchical process are not fixed in a rigid order. A given process may be called upon at any time and embedded within another process or even within another instance of itself, in much the same way we embed a subject clause within a larger clause or a picture within a picture.

For instance, a writer trying to construct a sentence (that is, a writer in the act of **translating**) may run into a problem and call in a condensed version of the entire writing process to help her out (e.g., she might generate and organize a new set of ideas, express them in standard writing English, and review this new alternative, all in order to further her current goal of translating. This particular kind of embedding, in which an entire process is embedded within a larger instance of itself, is known technically in linguistics as recursion. However, it is much more common for writers to simply embed individual processes as needed—to call upon them as sub-routines to help carry out the task at hand.

Writing processes may be viewed as the writer's tool kit. In using the tools, the writer is not constrained to use them in a fixed order or in stages. And using any tool may create the need to use another. Generating ideas may require evaluation, as may writing sentences. And evaluation may force the writer to think up new ideas.

Figure 2 demonstrates the embedded processes of a writer trying to compose (translate) the first sentence of a paper. After producing and reviewing two trial versions of the sentence, he invokes a brief sequence of

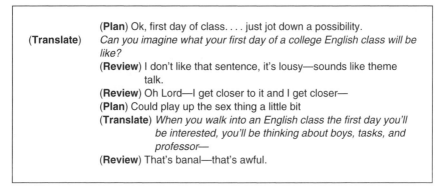

Figure 2 An example of embedding

planning, translating, and reviewing—all in the service of that vexing sentence. In our example the writer is trying to translate some sketchily represented meaning about "the first day of class" into prose, and a hierarchical process allows him to embed a variety of processes as sub-routines within his overall attempt to translate.

A process that is hierarchical and admits many embedded sub-processes is powerful because it is flexible: it lets a writer do a great deal with only a few relatively simple processes—the basic ones being **plan, translate**, and **review**. This means, for instance, that we do not need to define "revision" as a unique stage in composing, but as a thinking process that can occur at any time a writer chooses to evaluate or revise his text or his plans. As an important part of writing, it constantly leads to new planning or a "re-vision" of what one wanted to say.

Embedding is a basic, omni-present feature of the writing process even though we may not be fully conscious of doing it. However, a theory of composing that only recognized embedding wouldn't describe the real complexity of writing. It wouldn't explain *why* writers choose to invoke the processes they do or how they know when they've done enough. To return to Iee Odell's question, what guides the writers' decisions and choices and gives an overall purposeful structure to composing? The third point of the theory is an attempt to answer this question.

3. Writing is a goal-directed process. In the act of composing, writers create a hierarchical network of goals and these in turn guide the writing process

This proposition is the keystone of the cognitive process theory we are proposing—and yet it may also seem somewhat counter-intuitive According to many writers, including our subjects, writing often seems a serendipitous experience, an act of discovery. People start out writing without knowing exactly where they will end up; yet they agree that writing is a purposeful act. For example, our subjects often report that their writing process seemed quite disorganized, even chaotic, as they worked, and yet their protocols reveal a coherent underlying structure. How, then, does the writing process manage to seem so unstructured, open-minded, and exploratory ("I don't know what I mean until I see what I say") and at the same time possess its own underlying coherence, direction, or purpose?

One answer to this question lies in the fact that people rapidly forget many of their own local working goals once those goals have been satisfied. This is why thinking aloud protocols tell us things retrospection doesn't.[22] A second answer lies in the nature of the goals themselves, which fall into two distinctive categories: process goals and content goals. Process goals are essentially the instructions people give themselves about how to carry out the process of writing (e.g., "Let's doodle a little bit." "So

..., write an introduction." "I'll go back to that later."). Good writers often give themselves many such instructions and seem to have greater conscious control over their own process than the poorer writers we have studied. Content goals and plans, on the other hand, specify all things the writer wants to say or to do to an audience. Some goals, usually ones having to do with organization, can specify both content and process, as in, "I want to open with a statement about political views." In this discussion we will focus primarily on the writer's content goals.

The most striking thing about a writer's content goals is that they grow into an increasingly elaborate network of goals and sub-goals as the writer composes. Figure 3 shows the network one writer had created during four minutes of composing. Notice how the writer moves from a very abstract goal of "appealing to a broad range in intellect" to a more operational definition of that goal, i.e., "explain things simply." The eventual plan to "write an introduction" is a reasonable, if conventional, response to all three top-level goals. And it too is developed with a set of alternative sub-goals. Notice also how this network is hierarchical in the sense that new goals operate as a functional part of the more inclusive goals above them.

These networks have three important features:

1. They are created as people compose, throughout the entire process. This means that they do not emerge full-blown as the result of "pre-writing." Rather, as we will show, they are created in close interaction with ongoing exploration and the growing text.

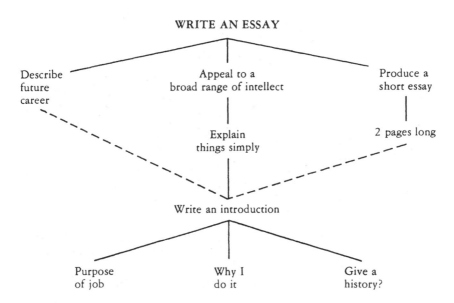

WRITE AN ESSAY

Describe future career

Appeal to a broad range of intellect

Produce a short essay

Explain things simply

2 pages long

Write an introduction

Purpose of job

Why I do it

Give a history?

Figure 3 Beginning of a network of goals

2. The goal-directed thinking that produces these networks takes many forms. That is, goal-setting is not simply the act of stating a well-defined end point such as "I want to write a two-page essay." Goal-directed thinking often involves describing one's starting point ("They're not going to be disposed to hear what I'm saying"), or laying out a plan for reaching a goal ("I'd better explain things simply"), or evaluating one's success ("That's banal—that's awful"). Such statements are often setting implicit goals, e.g., "Don't be banal." In order to understand a writer's goals, then, we must be sensitive to the broad range of plans, goals, and criteria that grow out of goal-directed thinking.

Goal directed thinking is intimately connected with discovery. Consider for example, the discovery process of two famous explorers—Cortez, silent on his peak in Darien, and that bear who went over the mountain. Both, indeed, discovered the unexpected. However, we should note that both chose to climb a long hill to do so. And it is this sort of goal-directed search for the unexpected that we often see in writers as they attempt to explore and consolidate their knowledge. Furthermore, this search for insight leads to new, more adequate goals, which in turn guide further writing.

The beginning of an answer to Odell's question, "What guides composing?" lies here. The writer's own set of self-made goals guide composing, but these goals can be inclusive and exploratory or narrow, sensitive to the audience or chained to the topic, based on rhetorical savvy or focused on producing correct prose. All those forces which might "guide" composing, such as the rhetorical situation, one's knowledge, the genre, etc., are mediated through the goals, plans, and criteria for evaluation of discourse actually set up by the writer.

This does not mean that a writer's goals are necessarily elaborate, logical, or conscious. For example, a simple-minded goal such as "Write down what I can remember" may be perfectly adequate for writing a list. And experienced writers, such as journalists, can often draw on elaborate networks of goals which are so well learned as to be automatic. Or the rules of a genre, such as those of the limerick, may be so specific as to leave little room or necessity for elaborate rhetorical planning. Nevertheless, whether one's goals are abstract or detailed, simple or sophisticated, they provide the "logic" that moves the composing process forward.

3. Finally, writers not only create a hierarchical network of guiding goals, but, as they compose, they continually return or "pop" back up to their higher-level goals. And these higher-level goals give direction and coherence to their next move. Our understanding of this network and how writers use it is still quite limited, but we can make a prediction about an important difference one might find between good and poor writers. Poor writers will frequently depend on very abstract, undeveloped top-level goals, such as "appeal to a broad range of intellect," even though such

goals are much harder to work with than a more operational goal such as "give a brief history of my job." Sondra Perl has seen this phenomenon in the basic writers who kept returning to reread the assignment, searching, it would seem, for ready-made goals, instead of forming their own. Alternatively, poor writers will depend on only very low-level goals, such as finishing a sentence or correctly spelling a word. They will be, as Nancy Sommers' student revisers were, locked in by the myopia in their own goals and criteria.

Therefore, one might predict that an important difference between good and poor writers will be in both the quantity and quality of the middle range of goals they create. These middle-range goals, which lie between intention and actual prose (cf., "give a brief history" in Figure 3), give substance and direction to more abstract goals (such as "appealing to the audience") and they give breadth and coherence to local decisions about what to say next.

Goals, topic, and text

We have been suggesting that the logic which moves composing forward grows out of the goals which writers create as they compose. However, common sense and the folklore of writing offer an alternative explanation which we should consider, namely, that one's own knowledge of the topic (memories, associations, etc.) or the text itself can take control of this process as frequently as one's goals do. One could easily imagine these three forces constituting a sort of eternal triangle in which the writer's goals, knowledge, and current text struggle for influence. For example, the writer's initial planning for a given paragraph might have set up a goal or abstract representation of a paragraph that would discuss three equally important, parallel points on the topic of climate. However, in trying to write, the writer finds that some of his knowledge about climate is really organized around a strong cause-and-effect relationship between points 1 and 2, while he has almost nothing to say about point 3. Or perhaps the text itself attempts to take control, e.g., for the sake of a dramatic opening, the writer's first sentence sets up a vivid example of an effect produced by climate. The syntactic and semantic structure of that sentence now demand that a cause be stated in the next, although this would violate the writer's initial (and still appropriate) plan for a three-point paragraph.

Viewed this way, the writer's abstract plan (representation) of his goals, his knowledge of the topic, and his current text are all actively competing for the writer's attention. Each wants to govern the choices and decisions made next. This competitive model certainly captures that experience of seeing the text run away with you, or the feeling of being led by the nose by an idea. How then do these experiences occur within a "goal-driven process"? First, as our model of the writing process describes, the processes of **generate** and **evaluate** appear to have the power to interrupt the writer's process at any point—and they frequently do. This means that new knowledge and/or some feature of the current text can interrupt the process at any time through the processes of **generate** and **evaluate**. This allows a flexible collaboration among goals, knowledge, and text. Yet this collaboration often culminates in a revision of previous goals. The persistence and functional importance of initally established goals is reflected by a number of signs: the frequency with which writers refer back to their goals; the fact that writers behave consistently with goals they have already stated; and the fact that they evaluate text in response to the criteria specified in their goals.

Second, some kinds of goals steer the writing process in yet another basic way. In the writers we have studied, the overall composing process is clearly under the direction of global and local *process* goals. Behind the most free-wheeling act of "discovery" is a writer who has recognized the heuristic value of free exploration or "just writing it out" and has chosen to do so. Process goals such as these, or "I'll edit it later," are the earmarks of sophisticated writers with a repertory of flexible process goals which let them use writing for discovery. But what about poorer writers who seem simply to free associate on paper or to be obsessed with perfecting the current text? We would argue that often they too are working under a set of implicit process goals which say "write it as it comes," or "make everything perfect and correct as you go." The problem then is not that knowledge or the text have taken over, so much as that the writer's own goals and/or images of the composing process put these strategies in control.[23]

To sum up, the third point of our theory—focused on the role of the writer's own goals—helps us account for purposefulness in writing. But can we account for the dynamics of discovery? Richard Young, Janet Emig, and others argue that writing is uniquely adapted to the task of fostering insight and developing new knowledge.[24] But how does this happen in a goal-directed process?

We think that the remarkable combination of purposefulness and openness which writing offers is based in part on a beautifully simple, but extremely powerful principle, which is this: *In the act of writing, people regenerate or recreate their own goals in the light of what they learn*. This principle then creates the fourth point of our cognitive process theory.

4. Writers create their own goals in two key ways: by generating goals and supporting sub-goals which embody a purpose; and, at times, by changing or regenerating their own top-level goals in light of what they have learned by writing

We are used, of course, to thinking of writing as a process in which our *knowledge* develops as we write. The structure of knowledge for some topic becomes more conscious and assertive as we keep tapping memory for related ideas. That structure, or "schema," may even grow and change as a result of library research or the addition of our own fresh inferences. However, writers must also generate (i.e., create or retrieve) the unique goals which guide their process.

In this paper we focus on the goals writers create for a particular paper, but we should not forget that many writing goals are well-learned, standard ones stored in memory. For example, we would expect many writers to draw automatically on those goals associated with writing in general, such as, "interest the reader," or "start with an introduction," or on goals associated with a given genre, such as making a jingle rhyme. These goals will often be so basic that they won't even be consciously considered or expressed. And the more experienced the writer the greater this repertory of semi-automatic plans and goals will be.

Writers also develop an elaborate network of working "sub-goals" as they compose. As we have seen, these sub-goals give concrete meaning and direction to their more abstract top-level goals, such as "interest the reader," or "describe my job." And then on occasion writers show a remarkable ability to regenerate or change the very goals which had been directing their writing and planning: that is, they replace or revise major goals in light of what they learned through writing. It is these two creative processes we wish to consider now.

We can see these two basic processes—creating sub-goals and regenerating goals—at work in the following protocol, which has been broken down into episodes. As you will see, writers organize these two basic processes in different ways. We will look here at three typical patterns of goals which we have labeled "**Explore and consolidate**," "**State and develop**," "**Write and regenerate**."

Explore and consolidate

This pattern often occurs at the beginning of a composing session, but it could appear anywhere. The writers frequently appear to be working under a high-level goal or plan to explore: that is, to think the topic over, to jot ideas down, or just start writing to see what they have to say. At other times the plan to explore is subordinate to a very specific goal, such as to find out "what on earth can I say that would make a 15-year-old girl interested in my job?" Under such a plan, the writer might explore her own knowledge, following out associations or using more structured discovery procedures such as tagmemics or the classical topics. But however the writer chooses to explore, the next step is the critical one. The writer pops back up to her top-level goal and from that vantage point reviews the information she has generated. She then consolidates it, producing a more complex idea than she began with by drawing inferences and creating new concepts.

Even the poor writers we have studied often seem adept at the exploration part of this process, even to the point of generating long narrative trains of association—sometimes on paper as a final draft. The distinctive thing about good writers is their tendency to return to that higher-level goal and to review and consolidate what has just been learned through exploring. In the act of consolidating, the writer sets up a *new goal* which replaces the goal of explore and directs the subsequent episode in composing. If the writer's topic is unfamiliar or the task demands creative thinking, the writer's ability to explore, to consolidate the results, and to regenerate his or her goals will be a critical skill.

The following protocol excerpt, which is divided into episodes and subepisodes, illustrates this pattern of **explore and consolidate**.

Episode 1 a, b

In the first episode, the writer merely reviews the assignment and plays with some associations as he attempts to define his rhetorical situation. It ends with a simple process goal—"On to the task at hand"—and a reiteration of the assignment.

> (1a) Okay – Um ... Open the envelope – just like a quiz show on TV – My job for a young thirteen to fourteen teenage female audience – Magazine – *Seventeen*. My job for a young teenage female audience – Magazine – *Seventeen*, I never have read *Seventeen*, but I've referred to it in class and other students have. (1b) This is like being thrown the topic in a situation – you know – in an expository writing class and asked to write on it on the board and I've done that and had a lot of fun with it – so on to the task at hand. My job for a young teenage female audience – Magazine – *Seventeen*.

Episode 2 a, b, c, d

The writer starts with a plan to explore his own "job," which he initially defines as being a teacher and not a professor. In the process of exploring he develops a variety of sub-goals which include plans to: make new meaning by exploring a contrast; present himself or his persona as a teacher; and affect his audience by making them reconsider one of their previous notions. The extended audience analysis of teen-age girls (subepisode 2c) is in response to his goal of affecting them.

At the end of episode 2c, the writer reaches tentative closure with the statement, "By God, I can change that notion for them." There are significantly long pauses on both sides of this statement, which appears to consolidate much of the writer's previous exploration. In doing this, he dramatically extends his earlier, rather vague plan to merely "compare teachers and professors"—he has regenerated and elaborated his top-level goals. This consolidation leaves the writer with a new, relatively complex, rhetorically sophisticated working goal, one which encompasses plans for a topic, a persona, and the audience. In essence the writer is learning through planning and his goals are the creative bridge between his exploration and the prose he will write.

Perhaps the writer thought his early closure at this point was too good to be true, so he returns at 2d to his initial top-level or most inclusive goal (write about my job) and explores alternative definitions of his job. The episode ends with the reaffirmation of his topic, his persona, and, by implication, the consolidated goal established in Episode 2c.

> (2a) Okay lets see – lets doodle a little bit – Job – English teacher rather than professor – I'm doodling this on a scratch sheet as I say it, -ah- (2b) In fact that might be a useful thing to focus on – how a professor differs from – how a teacher differs from a professor and I see myself as a teacher – that might help them – my audience to reconsider their notion of what an English teacher does. (2c) -ah- English teacher – young teen-age female audience – they will all have had English – audience – they're in school – they're taking English – for many of them English may be a favorite subject – doodling still – under audience, but for the wrong reasons – some of them will have wrong reasons in that English is good because its tidy – can be a neat tidy little girl – others turned off of it because it seems too prim. By God I can change that notion for them. (2d) My job for a young teenage female audience – Magazine – *Seventeen*. -ah- Job – English teacher – guess that's what I'll have to go – yeah – hell – go with that – that's a challenge – rather than – riding a bicycle across England that's too easy and not on the topic – right, or would work in a garden or something like that – none of those are really my jobs – as a profession – My job for a young teenage female audience – Magazine – *Seventeen*. All right – I'm an English teacher.

State and develop

This second pattern accounts for much of the straightforward work of composing, and is well illustrated in our protocol. In it the writer begins with a relatively general high-level goal which he then proceeds to develop or flesh out with sub-goals. As his goals become more fully specified, they form a bridge from his initial rather fuzzy intentions to actual text. Figure 4 is a schematic representation of the goals and sub-goals which the writer eventually creates.

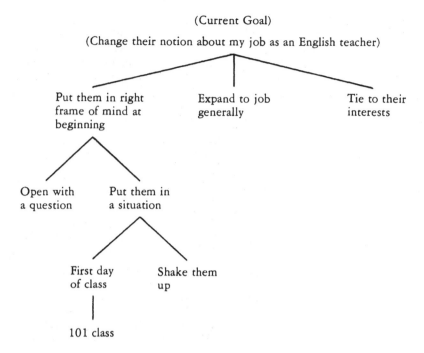

Figure 4 Writer developing a set of sub-goals

Episode 3 a, b, c

The episode starts with a sub-goal directly subordinate to the goal established in Episode 2 (change their notion of English teachers). It takes the pattern of a search in which the writer tries to find ways to carry out his current goal of "get [the audience?] at the beginning." In the process he generates yet another level of sub-goals (i.e., open with a question and draw them into a familiar situation). (A note on our terminology: in order to focus on the overall structure of goals and sub-goals in a writer's thinking, we have treated the writer's plans and strategies all as sub-goals or operational definitions of the larger goal.)

Notice how the content or ideas of the essay are still relatively unspecified. The relationship between creating goals and finding ideas is clearly reciprocal: it was an initial exploration of the writer's ideas which produced these goals. But the writing process was then moved forward by his attempt to flesh out a network of goals and sub-goals, not just by a mere "pre-writing" survey of what he knew about the topic. Episode 3c ends in an effort to test one of his new goals against his own experience with students.

(3a) All right – I'm an English teacher. I want to get at the beginning – I know that they're not going to be disposed – to hear what I'm saying – partly for that reason and partly to put them in the right, the kind of frame of mind I want – I want to open with an implied question or a direct one and put them in the middle of some situation – then expand from there to talk about my job more generally ... and try to tie it in with their interest. (3b) So one question is where to begin – what kind of situation to start in the middle of – probably the first day of class.... They'd be interested – they'd probably clue into that easily because they would identify with first days of school and my first days are raucous affairs – it would immediately shake-em up and get them to thinking a different context. (3c) Okay – so – First day of class – lets see. – Maybe the first 101 class with that crazy skit I put on – that's probably better than 305 because 101 is freshmen and that's nearer their level and that skit really was crazy and it worked beautifully.

Write and regenerate

This pattern is clearly analogous to the explore and consolidate pattern, except that instead of planning, the writer is producing prose. A miniature example of it can be seen in Figure 2, in which the writer, whose planning we have just seen, attempts to compose the first sentence of his article for *Seventeen*. Although he had done a good deal of explicit planning before this point, the prose itself worked as another, more detailed representation of what he wanted to say. In writing the sentence, he not only saw that it was inadequate, but that his goals themselves could be expanded. The reciprocity between writing and planning enabled him to learn even from a failure and to produce a new goal, "play up sex." Yet it is instructive to note that once this new plan was represented in language—subjected to the acid test of prose—it too failed to pass, because it violated some of his tacit goals or criteria for an acceptable prose style.

The examples we cite here are, for the purposes of illustration, small and rather local ones. Yet this process of setting and developing sub-goals, and—at times—regenerating those goals is a powerful creative process. Writers and teachers of writing have long argued that one learns through the act of writing itself, but it has been difficult to support the claim in other ways. However, if one studies the process by which a writer uses a goal to generate ideas, then consolidates those ideas and uses them to revise or regenerate new, more complex goals, one can see this learning process in action. Furthermore, one sees why the process of revising and clarifying goals has such a broad effect, since it is through setting these new goals that the fruits of discovery come back to inform the continuing process of writing. In this instance, some of our most complex and imaginative acts can depend on the elegant simplicity of a few powerful thinking processes. We feel that a cognitive process explanation of discovery, toward which this theory is only a start, will have another special strength. By placing emphasis on the inventive power of the writer, who is able to explore ideas, to develop, act on, test, and regenerate his or her own goals, we are putting an important part of creativity where it belongs—in the hands of the working, thinking writer.

Acknowledgement

The research reported in this paper was partially supported by a grant from the National Institute of Education, U.S. Department of Health, Education, and Welfare, Grant Number IIE G780195.

Notes

1 Aristotle, *The Rhetoric*, trans. Lane Cooper (New York: Appleton-Century-Crofts, 1932), Richard Lloyd-Jones, "A Perspective on Rhetoric," in *Writing: The Nature, Development and Teaching of Written Communication*, ed. C. Frederiksen, M. Whiteman, and J. Dominic (Hillsdale, N.J.: Lawrence Erlbaum Associates, in press.)
2 Lee Odell, Charles R. Cooper, and Cynthia Courts, "Discourse Theory: Implications for Research in Composing," in *Research on Composing: Points of Departure*, ed. Charles Cooper and Lee Odell (Urbana, IL: National Council of Teachers of English, 1978), p. 6.
3 Lloyd Bitzer, "The Rhetorical Situation," *Philosophy and Rhetoric*, 1 (January, 1968), 1–14.
4 Richard E. Vatz, "The Myth of the Rhetorical Situation," in *Philosophy and Rhetoric*, 6 (Summer, 1973), 154–161.
5 James Britton et al., *The Development of Writing Abilities, 11–18* (London: Macmillan, 1975), p. 39.
6 Gordon Rohman, "Pre-Writing: The Stage of Discovery in the Writing Process," *CCC*, 16 (May, 1965), 106–112.
7 See Britton et al., *The Development of Writing Abilities*, pp. 19–49.
8 Nancy Sommers, "Response to Sharon Crowley, 'Components of the Process,' " *CCC*, 29 (May, 1978), 209–211.
9 Nancy Sommers, "Revision Strategies of Student Writers and Experienced Writers," *CCC*. 31 (December, 1980), 378–388.
10 John R. Hayes, *Cognitive Psychology: Thinking and Creating* (Homewood, Illinois: Dorsey Press, 1978); Herbert A. Simon and John R. Hayes, "Understanding Complex Task Instruction," in *Cognition and Instruction*, ed. D. Klahr (Hillsdale, N.J.: Lawrence Erlbaum Associates, 1976), pp. 269–285.
11 John R. Hayes and Linda S. Flower, "Identifying the Organization of Writing Processes," in *Cognitive Processes in Writing: An Interdisciplinary Approach*, ed. Lee Gregg and Erwin Steinberg (Hillsdale, N.J.: Lawrence Erlbaum Associates, 1980), pp. 3–30. Although diagrams of the sort in Figure 1 help distinguish the various processes we wish our model to describe, these schematic representations of processes and elements are often misleading. The arrows

indicate that *information* flows from one box or process to another; that is, knowledge about the writing assignment or knowledge from memory can be transferred or used in the planning process, and information from planning can flow back the other way. What the arrows *do not mean* is that such information flows in a predictable left to right circuit, from one box to another as if the diagram were a one-way flow chart. This distinction is crucial because such a flow chart implies the very kind of stage model against which we wish to argue. One of the central premises of the cognitive process theory presented here is that writers are constantly, instant by instant, orchestrating a battery of cognitive processes as they integrate planning, remembering, writing, and rereading. The multiple arrows, which are conventions in diagramming this sort of model, are unfortunately only weak indications of the complex and active organization of thinking processes which our work attempts to model.

12 Linda S. Flower and John R. Hayes, "The Cognition of Discovery: Defining a Rhetorical Problem," *CCC*, 31 (February, 1980), 21–32.

13 Britton *et. al. The Development of Writing Abilities*, pp. 61–65.

14 Sondra Perl, "Five Writers Writing: Case Studies of the Composing Process of Unskilled College Writers," Diss. New York University, 1978.

15 Linda S. Flower and John R. Hayes, "The Dynamics of Composing: Making Plans and Juggling Constraints," in *Cognitive Processes in Writing: An Interdisciplinary Approach*, ed. Lee Gregg and Erwin Steinberg (Hillsdale, N.J.: Lawrence Erlbaum Associates, 1980), pp. 31–50.

16 Linda S. Flower, "Writer-Based Prose: A Cognitive Basis for Problems in Writing," *College English*, 41 (September, 1979), 19–37.

17 Flower, "The Cognition of Discovery," pp. 21–32.

18 Ellen Nold, "Revising," in *Writing: The Nature, Development, and Teaching of Written Communication*, ed. C. Frederiksen *et al.* (Hillsdale, N.J.: Lawrence Erlbaum Associates, in press).

19 Mina Shaughnessy, *Errors and Expectations* (New York: Oxford University Press, 1977).

20 Marlene Scardamalia, "How Children Cope with the Cognitive Demands of Writing," in *Writing: The Nature, Development and Teaching of Written Communication*, ed. C. Frederiksen *et al.* (Hillsdale, N.J.: Lawrence Erlbaum Associates, in press). Carl Bereiter and Marlene Scardamalia, "From Conversation to Composition: The Role of Instruction in a Developmental Process," in *Advances in Instructional Psychology*, Volume 2, ed. R. Glaser (Hillsdale, N.J.: Lawrence Erlbaum Associates, in press).

21 Bereiter and Scardamalia, "From Conversation to Composition."

22 John R. Hayes and Linda Flower, "Uncovering Cognitive Processes in Writing: An Introduction to Protocol Analysis," in *Methodological Approaches to Writing Research*, ed. P. Mosenthal, L. Tamor, and S. Walmsley (in press).

23 Cf. a recent study by Mike Rose on the power of ineffective process plans, "Rigid Rules, Inflexible Plans, and the Stifling of Language: A Cognitivist's Analysis of Writer's Block," *CCC*, 31 (December, 1980), 389–400.

24 Janet Emig, "Writing as a Model of Learning," *CCC*, 28 (May, 1977), 122–128; Richard E. Young, "Why Write? A Reconsideration," unpublished paper delivered at the convention of the Modern Language Association, San Francisco, California, 28 December 1979.

45

THE INTERACTION OF INSTRUCTION, TEACHER COMMENT, AND REVISION IN TEACHING THE COMPOSING PROCESS

George Hillocks, Jr.

Source: *Research in the Teaching of English* (1982) 16(3): 261–278

This study examines the effects of stressing three phases of the composing process in the teaching of composition. Two of them, feedback (especially in the form of teacher comments and marks) and revision (as implied in the assignment to write first and second drafts) have been assumed for years to be efficacious. The third, observation of data, is related to invention, which has witnessed a revival of interest over the past two decades. These three variables and their control conditions require explanation.

Feedback: the effects of teacher comment

Audience response or feedback is ignored in popular studies of the composing process (e.g., Emig, 1971; Pianko, 1979; Perl, 1979). Conditions and goals of the research, namely the necessity for writers to express thoughts aloud as they write in the presence of an observer or recorder, prohibit explicit feedback. Rhetoricians have long been aware of the importance of both predicting probable audience response and attending to actual response. Teachers and pedagogical theorists (e.g., Moffett, 1968) have attended to the need for feedback, and at least one has incorporated attention to audience response as an explicit element in a model of the composing process (McCabe, 1971).

Audience response may be conveniently divided into three types in school settings: teacher comment, response from peers, and audience response predicted by the writer in the course of writing. Most available studies have been concerned with the effects of teacher comment, and for good reason. An important question about composition teaching is whether or not the time spent in commenting on compositions makes a difference. A number of studies have examined the effect of teacher comment alone. Gee (1972) studied the effects of praise, negative criticism, and "no comment." Four compositions written in four weeks were not preceded by instruction. Nor were the topics linked for instructional purposes. Although he was able to find no differences in the quality of writing, Gee did find that students receiving negative comment and no comment wrote significantly fewer T-units and had significantly more negative attitudes about the four writing experiences than did the praised students. Taylor and Hoedt (1966), Stevens (1973), and Hausner (1975), have all shown that students receiving negative comments display less desirable attitudes toward some facet of writing than do those receiving positive comments. None, however, has shown differences in the quality of writing.

Stiff (1967) and Bata (1972) studied the effects of marginal, terminal, and mixed marginal-terminal comments on the writing of college students over the period of a semester. Both writers report no significant differences among the various groups, and more interestingly, no significant differences from pre-test to post-test.

Other studies have examined the effects of teacher comment in relation to such variables as frequency of writing and revision. Burton and Arnold (1964) examined the effects of frequent writing (one 250 word composition per week) vs. infrequent writing (three 250 word compositions per semester) and the effects of intensive evaluation (marking every error and writing detailed comments) vs. moderate evaluation (grading only an occasional paper or correcting only errors related to skills students were studying at the time). The study found no significant differences among the four groups, concluding that neither frequent practice nor intensive marking will necessarily result in increased writing skill. Sutton and Allen (1964) studied 112 college freshmen divided randomly into six treatment groups. One group did no writing at all. Another wrote a theme a week which was evaluated by peers, while still another wrote one theme per week which was evaluated by professors. All students wrote six pre-test compositions and six post-test compositions. Each composition was evaluated by five raters using the Diederich scale. The mean composition scores for all sections declined significantly ($p < .01$).

Revision

Buxton (1958) studied frequency of writing and teacher comment in conjunction with revision. He used three groups of randomly assigned college students. A control group did no writing. The writing and revision group wrote one 500 word essay per week for sixteen weeks on assigned topics, each with intensive teacher evaluation and teacher supervised revision during a class period. The writing group wrote as many essays but were not required to write on an assigned topic. They received only three to four sentences of comment at the end of the paper and did no revision. Both the writing group and the writing/revision group made significant gains over the control group. All groups made gains from the pre-test to the post-test essays. The revision group's gain was significantly higher than that made by the other groups. However, the design of the study prevents our knowing whether to attribute the difference to revision, intensive marking, the requirement of particular topics, or some combination of these.

Beach (1979) posed a question about the effects of between-drafts evaluation on the revisions made by high school students. Using three groups of randomly assigned students, he asked one group to revise without intervening evaluation. A second group received evaluation from a teacher. The third group used a pre-designed form to evaluate their own writing. Rough and final drafts were mixed together and assigned to three judges for "degree of change" ratings and for quality ratings on various dimensions. The teacher evaluation group received significantly higher "degree of change" ratings than either of the other groups. However, they received higher quality evaluations only on the dimension of support, not on the dimensions of sequence, sentences, language, flavor, or focus. Further, there were no significant differences in quality ratings over the three sets of drafts for any of the groups.

Finally, a carefully designed study by Bridwell (1980) involved 100 high school seniors who were asked to write about a place which they knew well and to write so that another twelfth grader reading the essay would "be able to recognize the thing or place if he or she ever got the chance to see it for real" (p. 202). Students were first encouraged to collect "facts" about the place to bring to class for use while writing. Students had three days for the writing: one for the first drafts, one for revising the first draft, and a third for producing a final draft. In the process students averaged 61 revisions each. Their first and final drafts were submitted to raters trained in the use of the Diederich scale. The results reveal significantly higher scores for the second drafts than for the first (p < .001) on both general merit and mechanics.

Pre-writing activities: invention and observation

A number of rhetoricians and teachers (e.g., Pike, 1964a and b, and Odell, 1974) have argued the necessity of helping students learn to deal with data as a prerequisite for writing. Although studies of the composing process (e.g., Emig, 1971; Pianko, 1979; Perl, 1979) neglect the problem of how writers deal with data before they write, it is intuitively obvious that some processes of screening, differentiating, integrating, and organizing must take place before writing begins. If not, the writing would appear as an undifferentiated mass—somewhat like overcooked rice left out on the table overnight. Though in many ways different from what is generally meant by invention, observational activities have a similar goal—to help students consider more carefully the data they write about (Hillocks, 1975). Odell (1974) strongly suggests that learning and practicing a heuristic results in writing which examines data more thoroughly. Hillocks (1979) indicates that the ninth and eleventh graders in his sample made significantly greater gains in specificity, organization, and support through observing and writing activities than through the traditional study of paragraph structure. Further, such gains are achievable in a relatively short period of time, ten to fifteen hours of classroom instruction.

Design

Instructional variables

Nearly all the studies of teacher comment and revision share one feature in common: they ignore or preclude pre-writing instruction designed to prepare students for particular writing assignments. The studies of Gee, Buxton, and several others view instruction in composition as consisting of an assignment, the writing done by the student, and whatever happens after the fact of the student writing. They assume that the main effects on writing skill derive from an assignment plus the follow-up to the assignment—teacher comment or revision. That English teachers view assignment making as crucial to improving student writing is indicated by the persistence of such publications as *A Thousand Topics for Composition: Second Edition* (Sherer, 1980) and by the continued appearance of such articles as Throckmorton (1980) and its companion piece, "What's a sure-fire topic for non-sure-fire students?" (*English Journal*, 1980, *69*(8), 62–69). Undoubtedly, the more interesting the topic, the better student response is likely to be. But sequences of high interest topics, with or without follow-up, have not yet been shown to bring about change in writing skill. This study examines the assignment assumption against previously tested observational activity.

Writing instruction for half the classes in this study, then, consisted of sets of observing and writing activities with the goal of increasing specificity, focus, and impact in a given piece. Each set of activities led to one of four interim composition assignments. The observing/writing activities, described in detail in Hillocks (1975), included the examination of sets of objects presumably belonging to one person and inferring personal qualities (pp. 7–8), examining various textures tactilely while wearing blindfolds (p. 9), examining and describing sea shells (pp. 9–10), listening to and describing sounds (pp. 10–11), doing physical exercise and describing bodily sensations (pp. 14–16), examining and describing pictures (pp. 16–18), pantomiming and describing brief scenarios (pp. 18–19), developing and acting out dialogues (pp. 19–21), and, finally, examining two model compositions for about one-half of one class period. All of these activities are designed to elicit high levels of student response concerning ideas for describing what has been observed, the listing of more and more precise details, judging the most effective details, and so forth, in small, student directed groups or in whole class teacher-led discussions. The instructional goal is to elicit responses to materials and activities in such a way that students respond to each other's comments with more ideas, questions, and evaluations and, in the process, become more and more aware of what the particular writing task involves and how others are likely to respond to their efforts. (See Hillocks, 1981, for the responses of college freshmen to this "environmental" mode of instruction.)

The control instructional condition consisted of the assignment of interim compositions plus motivational discussions preceding each. That is, prior to the writing, teachers led discussions helping students consider ideas they might use, particular details they might include, how they might focus their ideas, and so forth. Thus, the instructional control classes represent the widespread faith in the efficacy of assignments and follow-up, with the difference in this experiment, however, that all assignments and teacher comments were focused on increasing specificity, focus, and impact.

Teacher comment variables

Previous studies of the effects of teacher comment have examined certain dimensions of teacher comment including negative vs. positive, marginal vs. terminal, and extensive vs. intensive. They have not shown differences in the quality of writing. However, a comparison of the studies suggests an implicit aspect of teacher comment which all have in common: the comments are diffuse, ranging from substance, organization, and style to mechanics and punctuation. If teacher comments over a series of compositions focused on a particular aspect of writing, would they have greater effect? Beach (1979) attributes the higher quality ratings for "support" to the greater emphasis on support in the teacher comments. Experience suggests that concentrating comments on a particular aspect of writing might have a significant effect. Accordingly, this study examines focused comments. That is, all teacher comment, regardless of the instructional condition, focused on increasing the specificity, focus, and impact of the writing. All comments were positive and included suggestions for improvement.

Given the amount of time which teachers spend on writing comments, it seemed worthwhile to determine whether extended comments were more effective than brief comments. Brief comments were arbitrarily limited to ten words or fewer, while extended comments were to average well over ten words. A brief comment was to include a compliment and at least one suggestion for improvement. Extended comments were to include one or more compliments and very specific suggestions for improvement.

Revision variables

Studies of revision have shown that students do make revisions from a first draft to a final draft and that the revisions improve the compositions in quality. However, an important pedagogical question remains unanswered: Does practice in revising increase writing skill? That is, does practice in revising increase the quality of subsequent first drafts? The present study addresses this question in conjunction with its questions about the effects of instruction and teacher comment. Students in half of the classes were asked to make revisions on each of the interim compositions.

Three teachers in two schools were enlisted to participate in this study, two from an upper middle class middle school in Chicago's North Shore area, one from a school in a blue collar community in northwest Indiana. Each of the teachers had four classes which participated in the study. In the Indiana school all four classes were eighth grade. In the North Shore school five classes were eighth grade, and three were seventh. This arrangement was necessitated by the difficulty of finding teachers with four classes at the same grade level. The one year difference in grade level was not considered to be significant.

Instructional sets were assigned randomly to the teachers' classes so that each teacher had one class with each of the following sets: observing and writing activities plus revision: observing and writing activities without revision; assignment plus revision; and assignment without revision. In addition, each class was divided randomly in half with one-half receiving brief comments and the other half receiving extended comments. This results in a $2 \times 2 \times 2$ design to test the following hypotheses:

1   The use of observing and writing activities without revision will result in statistically significant gains comparable to those achieved in earlier experiments (Hillocks, 1979).
2   Revision in conjunction with observational activity will result in greater gains than for observational activities alone or for revision alone.
3   The use of observational activity, revision, or the combination of the two will result in greater gains than instruction through assignment alone.
4   The effects of extended comments will be greater than those of brief comments.

Although interactions among the conditions were expected, no specific hypotheses were developed for interactions. All hypotheses were in the null form for statistical analysis.

Two pre-tests were administered, the first, five days and the second, one day prior to instruction. Two post-tests were also administered, the first on the day following the conclusion of instruction, the second four days later. The pre- and post-tests asked students to write in response to the following two assignments:

1   Write about a person, place, or idea that you feel strongly about. Be as specific as you can so that a person reading what you have written will feel as you do about it, will feel what you feel and see what you see.
2   Write about an experience that you feel strongly about. Be as specific
    . . .

These topics are virtually the same as those used in Hillocks (1979).

The instructional period for each class was approximately four weeks. In the observation classes the time was taken up with observing and writing activities, motivational discussions for the interim compositions, and working on those compositions. Students in non-observational classes used the time for the study of literature or grammar, motivational discussions, and work on the interim assignments. Students in all classes were required to write on the following topics, after a discussion of possibilities which might be pursued:

A   Write about a room at home or some other place. Be as specific as you can so that someone reading your composition will see what you see and understand the character of the room.
B   Write a composition about a place. Give a physical description of the place, but focus on the sounds in that place. Be as specific as you can so that someone reading your composition will hear the sounds you hear or imagine or see the sights you see.
C   Write about one of the following experiences or some other like those that follow. Be as specific as you can to help your reader feel your experience. (All students were presented with a list of possible experiences including those on pp. 15–16 of *Observing and Writing*.)
D   Write a slice of life story about a confrontation between two or more people. Let your reader know what the people look like, how they act, what they say, where they are, and what happens. Be as specific as you can. (All students read and discussed two sample compositions by seventh and eighth graders before proceeding with this assignment.)

Analysis

Teachers saved all the interim compositions along with their comments for later examination. Teacher 1 from School A (northwest Indiana—blue collar) averaged just under 10 words per brief comment and slightly over 41 words per extended comment over the four interim compositions. Typical brief comments by Teacher 1 read as follows:

a   Interesting descriptions. Try to focus on one place next time.
b   Good dialogue. Could detail emotional feelings more.

Typical extended comments by Teacher 1 follow:

a   Good topic. You could include more about how you felt to build suspense. How did your body react to your fear? Did your heart race? How tense were you? Did you panic when you fell? How cold was it?
b   Good use of dialogue. You could also show the increasing nervousness as you waited for the bell. How did you feel inside? What were your friends doing? Focus should be on only one part of the incident.

Teacher 2 in school B wrote an average of nearly 14 words in brief comments and just over 38 words for extended comments. Typical brief comments from Teacher 2 read as follows:

a   Mary Ann—you list many activities here. Describe the sounds with comparisons.
b   Steve—you use some lively language. Watch word choice.

Typical extended comments from Teacher 2 read as follows:

a   Maury—you mention some telling details here. I would like to hear even more. What are the various sounds? What do they sound like? You use verbs well in this paper.
b   Matt—you write a couple of good metaphors here. Use active verbs as often as possible. *To be* verbs just don't accomplish much. With more development of sound, smell, and sight details, this could be excellent.

Teacher 2 preceded nearly every comment with the student's name and often wrote brief marginal comments, most of which were affirmations (good! yes!) of what the student had written. A few of the marginal comments were negative (cliché), and several were hortatory (add comparisons, avoid *there is*).

Teacher 3 also in school B averaged just over nine words for brief comments and about 22 words for extended comments. Both means include

71

marginal comments similar to those written by Teacher 2, but which were primarily of the affirmative type. Typical brief comments for Teacher 3 follow:

a   Quite a good description, but try using more comparisons.
b   Some nice description here—good comparisons. Describe the coughing sound.

The following typify extended comments from Teacher 3:

a   A good start, but you do very little here with descriptive language. What about using some comparisons? Describe voices and facial expressions.
b   You do a pretty sound job of describing the sights, but what other sounds could you work with? What about the sound of skis as they glide over the snow?

The teachers were asked to record the time required to read the papers and write brief or extended comments on the four interim compositions for each of the four instructional sets. Teacher 1 in school A reports spending a total of 17 hours and 35 minutes marking the papers; Teacher 2 in school B reports 30 hours and 5 minutes: Teacher 3 reports 25 hours and 40 minutes. The differences in total time may be accounted for by two factors. Casual inspection reveals that school A students wrote considerably shorter compositions than did school B students. Further, Teachers 2 and 3 both marked mechanical errors in spelling and punctuation. Teacher 1 did not. Despite differences in total marking time, however, the proportion of time required for brief comments and for extended comments is remarkably similar from teacher to teacher. Teacher 1 spent 34.6% of the total on brief comments and 65.4% on extended; Teacher 2 spent 37.3% on brief and 62.7% on extended; Teacher 3 spent 34.7% on brief and 65.3% on extended comments. Providing extended comments required nearly twice as much time as did providing brief comments in each case.

The 1112 pre- and post-tests were coded in such a way that raters could not distinguish pre-tests from post-tests nor students from any given teacher's classes in any way. All identifying information other than the code number was removed from the compositions which were then mixed randomly together.

The five-point specificity scale described in Hillocks (1979) was used to rate the papers. Three raters, not privy to the experimental design, trained for approximately 17 hours, until they reached high levels of inter-rater reliability. Three rater reliability checks were conducted: one at the beginning of the rating process, one when raters had progressed about half way through the compositions, and one near the end. On each occasion, raters

Table 1 Estimates of rater reliability computed by three methods

Pearson product moment correlation				
	Occasion	1	2	3
Rater A and B		.82	.95	.84
Rater A and C		.87	.88	.80
Rater B and C		.90	.93	.89
Ebel's intraclass correlations				
For one rater		.90	.94	.84
For three raters		.96	.98	.95

discussed and resolved their disagreements. Rater's initial judgments on each occasion, were used to compute Pearson product moment correlations for each pair of raters as well as intraclass correlations for one rater and for all three raters using formulas developed by Ebel and reported by Guilford (1954). The resulting estimates of reliability, ranging from .80 to .98, are reported in Table 1.

Total pre-test scores for each student were computed by summing the scores assigned to the two pre-tests. Total post-test scores were derived in the same way. This provides a scale of 2 to 10 for examining changes in student writing. The IQ scores for students in the two schools were converted to standard scores and were used as covariates for analysis of covariance with the teacher and with instructional, revision, and comment conditions as independent variables.

Results

Table 2 summarizes the true means, the mean gains, and the adjusted mean gains (in parentheses) for all instructional sets: pre-writing instruction/revision; pre-writing instruction/no revision; assignment/revision; and assignment/no revision. It also presents mean gains for students receiving long and short comments within each instructional set. Tests of t for correlated groups reveal that all instructional sets made statistically significant gains at p < .005 or p < .0005. As predicted, both of the pre-writing activity groups and the assignment/revision group outperformed the assignment/ no revision group by fairly wide margins. In fact, the gain for the pre-writing activity/no revision group in twice that of the assignment/no revision group. A t-test for groups with pooled variance indicates that the difference between these gains is significant, p < .01 ($t = 2.52$). The differences between the gains of the other two instructional sets and the gain of the assignment/no revision group are not significant at .05.

Table 3 presents the results of an analysis of variance of gain scores using the classical experimental approach in which the covariate effect is estimated first, independent of everything else in the design. This analysis

Table 2 The effects of instruction, revision, and teacher comment on student writing

	Pre-writing activity and revision	Pre-writing activity no revision	Assignment and revision	Assignment no revision
Pre-test Mean	4.453	4.319	4.687	4.938
SD	1.695	1.564	1.616	1.717
Post-test Mean	5.720	6.125	6.254	5.828
SD	1.997	2.245	2.018	2.157
Gain	1.267	1.806	1.567	.89
	(1.246)*	(1.824)*	(1.496)*	(.847)*
SD (Gain)	2.075	2.212	1.925	2.001
N	75	72	67	64
t	5.288	6.927	6.663	3.362
p <	.0005	.0005	.0005	.005
Mean Gains by Comment Type				
Short	1.08	1.69	1.64	1.12
N	39	36	34	33
Long	1.50	1.96	1.43	.55
N	36	36	33	31

Note
* Adjusted mean gains appear in parentheses.

of gain scores by teacher, instructional condition (pre-writing activity or assignment), revision condition (yes or no), and comment condition (long or short) uses IQ as a single covariate. The analysis reveals a highly significant effect by teacher class sets ($F = 18.584$, $p < .0005$) which is difficult to interpret. The difference is between the teacher in the blue collar school and the two teachers in the upper-middle-class school. The mean IQ for blue collar students (96.9) is significantly lower than that for the upper-middle-class students (114.6, $p < .001$). The analysis of covariance controls for differences in IQ and suggests that other differences between the groups of students might well account for the smaller gains by the blue collar students. More importantly for this research, however, there were no significant interactions between teacher and any treatment, indicating that the treatments had similar relative effects for all teachers.

The analysis of covariance (Table 3) indicates two significant interactions, that between instruction and revision ($p < .011$) and that between instruction and comment ($p < .009$). The mean gain for students asked to revise (1.41) differs only minimally for the mean gain of those who did no revising (1.37). The difference, of course, is not significant. However, when revision is combined with assignment only, the mean gain is greater (1.567), though not so high as the mean gain for the pre-writing activity/no

Table 3 Analysis of covariance: mean gain scores by teacher, instruction, revision, and comment

Source of variation	Sum of squares	DF	Mean square	F	Significance of F
Covariate					
IQ	56.226	1	56.226	15.732	.0005
Main Effects					
Teacher	132.836	2	66.418	18.584	.0005
Instruction	9.341	1	9.341	2.614	.107
Revision	0.044	1	0.044	0.012	.912
Comment	2.034	1	2.034	0.569	.451
Two-way Interactions					
Teacher-Instruction	14.728	2	7.364	2.060	.130
Teacher-Revision	11.612	2	5.806	1.625	.199
Teacher-Comment	3.870	2	1.935	0.541	.583
Instruct.-Revision	23.327	1	23.327	6.527	.011
Instruct.-Comment	24.818	1	24.818	6.944	.009
Revision-Comment	0.108	1	0.108	0.030	.862
Three-way Interactions					
Teach.-Inst.-Revis.	2.722	2	1.361	0.381	.684
Teach.-Inst.-Comm.	8.931	2	4.465	1.249	.289
Teach.-Revis.-Comm.	0.049	2	0.024	0.007	.993
Inst.-Revis.-Comm.	0.005	1	0.005	0.001	.969
Four-way Interactions	0.751	2	0.376	0.105	.900
Explained	289.353	24	12.056	3.373	.0005
Residual	822.021	230	3.574		

revision group (1.806). Strong gains for revision alone and for pre-writing activity alone, suggest that taken together, the effects of the two techniques should be even greater. That, however, is not the case. The mean gain for the group incorporating both pre-writing and revision (1.267) is lower than that for either technique alone. Finally, the assignment only condition with no revision has the smallest mean gain (0.89), a gain which is considerably smaller than the others and significantly smaller than the mean gain for pre-writing activity with no revision (p < .01). Clearly then, the type of instruction coupled with the presence or absence of revision makes a difference. One possible explanation for the smaller than expected gain of the group which had both the pre-writing activity and revision will be broached in the discussion section of this paper.

The second significant interaction is that between the teacher comment condition and instruction (p < .009). The mean gain for all students receiving short comments is 1.39; for students receiving long comments the mean gain is also 1.39. By contrast, the mean gains for long and short comments by instructional condition differ sharply. They are presented in Table 4. A *t*-test for groups with pooled variance reveals that the mean gain for long

Table 4 Gains for long and short comments

	Pre-writing activity	*Assignment*
Short		
Mean	1.333	1.463
SD	2.036	2.040
N	75	67
Long		
Mean	1.736	1.000
SD	2.264	1.911
N	72	64

comments with pre-writing activities (1.736) is significantly greater (p < .025) than the mean gain for students who received only the assignments and long comments (t = 2.03). The mean gain for students receiving long comments and pre-writing activities is also greater than the mean gains for both groups receiving short comments, but not significantly. These differences are reflected in the distribution of mean gains for long and short comments by instructional sets as presented in Table 2. The mean gain for the group with long comments but assignment only and no revision (.55) is only half that for any other group and about one quarter that for the students with pre-writing instruction, no revision, and long comments. A Scheffé test indicates the latter difference to be significant at p < .0127.

Discussion

The gain achieved by the observation/no revision group is not surprising in the sense that similar gains have been achieved by similar methods in the past (Hillocks, 1979). But in light of other interventional studies of composition which often show minimal or no gain in a much longer period of time, the magnitude of the gain in this study and in the previous studies is certainly surprising. In this study the gain for the observation/no revision groups is 1.15 times their pre-test standard deviation in only four weeks.

Equally surprising, especially in view of earlier studies, is the gain achieved by the assignment and revision group, a gain which is .96 of the standard deviation of its pre-test score. As far as this researcher knows, this is the first study to indicate that practice in revising has an effect on writing skill—is responsible for better first drafts. But even the assignment/no revision group made a significant gain, though only about .52 times the size of the standard deviation of its pre-test score.

The changes in all these groups may be largely attributable to the fact that all aspects of instruction focused on particular goals. The observation activities, the four interim compositions, the teacher comments, and the student revisions all have the same emphasis: writing more specifically and with a more precise focus in order to convey an experience or set of perceptions to an audience more forcefully.

In contrast, the instruction in other studies of teacher comments, practice in revising, frequency of writing, et cetera, has appeared to be considerably more diffuse in its goals, aiming to improve all aspects of composition. Unfortunately, this study has no control group with diffuse instruction or comment. One is tempted to speculate that a group with assignments, revision, and comments emphasizing a variety of writing skills would have made little or no gain in a comparable period of time.

The results of this research pose a curious problem. If assignment and teacher comment, revision, and pre-writing activities each have beneficial effects on student writing, then why should the use of all not result in the greatest gains? The observation/revision students received all three treatments. They engaged in the pre-writing activities, wrote the four interim papers and received teacher comments encouraging increased specificity, and revised at least part of each of the four papers. Although the gains for this group are not significantly lower than those for the observation/no revision group or those of the assignment/revision group, one might expect them to be higher. Discussion with the teachers has suggested one possible explanation. Students in the observation activity classes worked harder on the first drafts of the four interim papers, many of them producing two drafts unbidden, and in fact, produced better papers which they regarded as final drafts. The teachers involved explained that many of these students complained about having to revise *again*. The requirement of the research design that every student revise *each* of the interim papers may have been regarded as overly burdensome or even as punishment and, thus, have had a depressant effect. One wonders if older students would respond in the same way. It may be that a more selective policy on revision would result in the desired effects. Requesting revision only as necessary or requesting that students rework their choice of two different papers might prove more beneficial.

The results for teacher comment are interesting for a number of reasons. The overall mean gain for brief comment papers is the same as that for extensive comment papers. But when examined by instructional sets, the gain for extensive comment compositions is greater for groups with pre-writing observational activities, somewhat less for the assignment plus revision group, and considerably less for the assignment only group. The difference between the long comment mean in the observation/no revision group and the long comment mean in the assignment/no revision group was shown to be significant by the Scheffé procedure at $p < .0127$. Even though the differences within instructional sets are not statistically significant, the interaction across sets is significant. Longer comments with their increased number of specific suggestions may be more meaningful when they have been preceded by instruction which is related to their content. Indeed, when unaccompanied by related instruction, long comments with a series of suggestions may be interpreted as primarily pejorative or punitive and may discourage seventh and eighth graders. Whether or not extended comments of the same type would have the same effect on more mature students can only be determined by further research.

Most importantly, while the difference between the mean gain of the pre-writing activity/no revision group and that of the assignment/no revision group is .906, the difference between mean gains for the extended comment group and the short comment group is non-existent (less than .001). In fact, short comments appear to be about twice as effective as long comments for students with assignment only. Such contrasts indicate that if a choice must be made between providing extended comments and planning instructional activities, the decision should be for planning. For the three teachers in this study, extended comments required nearly twice as much time as the brief comments. Had teacher #3 in this study written extensive comments for all the interim compositions, we can assume that he would have spent a total of about 37.5 hours commenting on compositions over a four-week period (30 hrs. $\times$ .652 $\times$ 2). Had he written brief comments for all papers, however, he would have spent a total of about 22.38 hours marking papers, thus allowing himself an additional 15 hours for planning instruction.

This research has a number of implications for instruction and research. The following are among the most important. First, in combination with its predecessor (Hillocks, 1979), it indicates, contrary to what has become almost accepted dogma, that significant gains in writing skill are possible over short periods of time. Second, it demonstrates the utility of involving students in dealing with data, as part of the composing process but as a prelude to actual writing. Learning to deal with data in this sense involves far more than the usual pre-writing activity which is simply a warm-up for a particular assignment. Third, it suggests that practice in revising, when focused on particular goals or skills over several pieces of writing, can affect writing skills as displayed in subsequent new pieces of writing, and not simply in subsequent revisions. Fourth, it suggests that teacher comment, when positive and focused on particular aspects of writing over a series of compositions, can be effective. Finally, in view of the number of studies which suggest that teacher comment has little or no effect on writing skill, the present research indicates the usefulness of examining variables in combination rather than individually.

But if this study provides at least tentative answers to some questions, it raises many more. Are gains made in each instructional set retained over a long period of time? Are they retained at equal levels? What particular kinds of comment are most effective in increasing skill? Is there a combination of pre-writing activity, revising, and comment which can increase the effect size? Will pre-writing activities which involve students in data processing strategies other than simply observing have similar effects? For example, will examining data in order to generate and test generalizations increase organizational skill? Do focused teacher comments have greater effect than do diffuse comments, as the comparison of this study with other studies suggests? Experimental studies which pursue such questions may be able to provide important insight into instructional processes.

References

Bata, E. *A study of the relative effectiveness of marking techniques on junior college freshman English composition.* Unpublished doctoral dissertation, University of Maryland, 1972.

Beach, R. The effects of between-draft teacher evaluation versus student self-evaluation on high school students' revising of rough drafts. *Research in the Teaching of English,* 1979, *13,* 111–119.

Bridwell, L. Revising strategies in twelfth grade students' transactional writing. *Research in the Teaching of English,* 1980, *14,* 197–222.

Burton, D. & Arnold, L. *Effects of frequency of writing and intensity of teacher evaluation upon high school students' performance in written composition.* Washington, D.C.: U.S. Office of Education, Cooperative Research Project #1523, 1964 (ED 003 281).

Buxton, E. *An experiment to test the effects of writing frequency and guided practice upon students' skill in written expression.* Unpublished doctoral dissertation, Standord University, 1958.

Emig, J. *The composing processes of twelfth graders.* Urbana. Illinois: National Council of Teachers of English, 1971.

Gee, T. Students' responses to teacher comments. *Research in the Teaching of English,* 1972, *6,* 212–221.

Guilford, J. *Psychometric methods.* New York: McGraw-Hill Book Co., Inc., 1954.

Hausner, R. *Interaction of selected student personality factors and teachers' comments in a sequentially developed composition curriculum.* Unpublished doctoral dissertation, Fordham University, 1975.

Hillocks, G. The responses of college freshmen to three modes of instruction. *American Journal of Education,* 1981, *89,* 373–395.

Hillocks, G. The effects of observational activities on student writing. *Research in the Teaching of English,* 1979, *13,* 23–35.

Hillocks, G. *Observing and writing.* Urbana, Illinois: ERIC/RLS. 1975.

McCabe, B. The composing process: A theory. In G. Hillocks, B. McCabe, and J. McCampbell. *The dynamics of English instruction.* New York: Random House, 1971.

Moffett, J. *Teaching the universe of discourse.* Boston: Houghton-Mifflin. 1968.

Odell, L. Measuring the effect of instruction in pre-writing. *Research in the Teaching of English.* 1974, *8,* 228–240.

Our readers write: What's a sure-fire topic for non-sure-fire students? *English Journal,* 1980, *69(8),* 62–69.

Perl, S. The composing processes of unskilled writers. *Research in the Teaching of English,* 1979, *13,* 317–336.

Pianko, S. A description of the composing processes of college freshman writers. *Research in the Teaching of English*, 1979, *13*, 5–22.

Pike, K. Beyond the sentence. *College Composition and Communication*, 1964, *15*, 129–135. a

Pike, K. A linguistic contribution to composition. *College Composition and Communication*, 1964, *15*, 82–88. b

Sherer, T., Ed. A thousand topics for composition (Fourth edition). *Illinois English Bulletin*, 1980, *67(3)*, 1–32.

Stevens, A. *The effects of positive and negative evaluation on the written composition of low performing high school students*. Unpublished doctoral dissertation, Boston University, 1973.

Stiff, R. The effect upon student composition of particular correction techniques. *Research in the Teaching of English*, 1967, *1*, 54–75.

Sutton, A. & Allen, E. *The effect of practice and evaluation on improvement in written composition*. Washington, D.C.: U.S. Office of Education, Cooperative Research Project #1993, 1964 (ED 001 274).

Taylor, W. & Hoedt, K. The effect of praise upon the quality and quantity of creative writing. *Journal of Educational Research*, 1966, *60*, 80–83.

Throckmorton, H. Do your writing assignments work?—Checklist for a good writing assignment. *English Journal*, 1980, *69(8)*, 56–59.

46

INVISIBLE WRITING

Investigating cognitive processes in composition

Sheridan Blau

Source: *College Composition and Communication* (1983) 34(3): 297–312

I. The background

A recurring feature of the composing process frequently noted is that of rereading or scanning—when the writer pauses in his production of a text to reread parts of what he has already put down on the page. Sondra Perl, who has studied the composing process carefully, observes that few writers write for long periods of time without pausing to reread:

> For some ... rereading occurs after every few phrases; for others it occurs after every sentence; more frequently it occurs after a "chunk" of information has been written. Thus the unit that is reread is not necessarily a syntactic one, but a semantic one as defined by the writer.[1]

James Britton has insisted that this feature of composing, scanning, is an essential dimension of the cognitive processing that takes place when a competent writer is engaged in all but the simplest of writing tasks. Writers need to scan, according to Britton, in order to make alterations in their progressing text and to retain control over their emerging ideas.[2]

To test the importance of scanning, Britton and three of his colleagues in the London Institute Project on Written Language tried writing without scanning, using worn-out ball-point pens:

> We couldn't, therefore, see what we had written, but we used carbon paper so that what we wrote could be read later. We were acutely uncomfortable. When we wrote letters to an absent member of the team about what we were doing, and when we reported recent experiences in a straightforward narrative, we

were able to complete the task with only a few blunders; but when we tried to formulate theoretical principles, even on a topic very familiar to us all, and when we tried to write poems, we were defeated. We just could not hold the thread of an argument or the shape of a poem in our minds, because scanning back was impossible. As we expected, the carbon copies showed many inconsistencies and logical and syntactical discontinuities. They were, in fact, useless.

(p. 35)

II. A preliminary experiment

Britton's experiment with defunct ball-point pens struck me as a useful way of exploring with pre-service teachers the kinds of cognitive demands that different discourse functions make on student writers. With this in mind I conducted an experiment in "invisible writing" in an English education graduate class of teaching assistants and student-teachers. My intention was to examine how different kinds of writing tasks may differ in their cognitive demands and how the need for scanning in composing may be an index of the cognitive difficulty of a task.

For my in-class experiment I asked my students to write with spent ball-point pens on blank paper over a piece of carbon paper backed by another blank sheet. They wrote in roughly the same modes Britton identifies in his experiment: first, a piece of descriptive prose detailing the writer's environment, his experience in the here and now; then, a narrative telling about some recent event in the writer's life; then, an expository piece explaining one of the principles of composition we had been discussing; then an argument for changing the composition curriculum in local schools; and, finally, a poem. I expected, of course, that our experience would replicate Britton's—that as we progressed through these tasks, we would find our ability to coherently develop our ideas increasingly impeded by the absence of an ongoing visible record of what we were writing.

It didn't turn out that way. According to the participants, the absence of visual feedback from the text they were producing actually sharpened their concentration on each of the writing tasks, enhanced their fluency, and yielded texts that were more rather than less cohesive.[3] Some students reported that under the constraints of the experiment they produced better poems than they had thought themselves capable of.

I neglected in this first experiment to ask my students to turn in the results of their efforts, but I have since been able to retrieve a few samples. Here is one that disconfirms Britton's assertions about the necessity of scanning for the composition of a poem. It surprised even its own author.

Teaching
The students write
and outside
the full white moon
in a misty space
in a black heaven
hangs over the harbor.

The juxtaposition
tells me
once again
that existence precedes essence.

Maybe until those students
recognize that their experiences
can be the stuff of poetry,
they will always be
struggling with words,
while the full white moon
in a misty space
in a black heaven
hangs over the harbor.

In the discussion following our experiment, most of the writers reported that except for the fact that the invisible writing took a little getting used to, they didn't find it either an impediment or an aid in the descriptive or narrative writing tasks. When it came to the more cognitively difficult expository, persuasive, and poetic tasks, however (and a few found this true for the narrative task), many of the students found that under the experimental conditions they could engage in the composing process more productively and with greater satisfaction than usual. The invisibility of the words they were writing apparently forced the writers to give more concentrated and sustained attention to their emerging thoughts than they ordinarily gave when composing with a working pen or pencil. Some students reported that when they wrote under ordinary conditions they would usually allow their minds to wander after each sentence or pair of sentences. Rarely did they keep their attention focused undeviatingly on a single train of thought beyond the boundaries of one or two sentences.

Several students added that their usual pattern in composing was to interrupt the flow of their thought frequently to edit and amend the language, syntax, or mechanics of their developing text. The experiment suggested to them that their usual pauses obstructed their fluency and, more importantly, diluted their concentration. Under the conditions of the experiment they could neither edit, nor rewrite, nor allow their attention to stray from the line of thought they were developing.

III. Assumptions behind Britton's experiment

Britton's account of his informal experiment with his colleagues argues that writers need to pause in their writing to review what they have written in order to retain control over the content and direction of their emerging text, as well as to make corrections and improvements in the text as it develops. His experiment suggests that the control gained by scanning is increasingly necessary as the writer takes on increasingly difficult cognitive tasks. Presumably, a letter to a friend about what one has been doing or a report on a recent experience does not make cognitive demands that are so complex that a writer must constantly monitor the structure of his emerging text by checking back on what he is building upon. Neither the formal organizational demands (the discourse schema) of narrative or descriptive writing tasks nor the usual content of the thoughts that inform such pieces of writing are likely to constitute much of a cognitive load for an experienced writer.

When such a writer takes on the burden of exposition, however—particularly if it entails formulating theoretical principles (even on a familiar subject)—the difficulty of the task (the cognitive complexity of the thought and the governing discourse schema) is such that it cannot be carried out satisfactorily unless the writer is able to check his production at "the point of utterance" against the structure of his thought up to that point. The same necessity would seem to govern the writing of a poem—apparently because of the demands of its form. These, at any rate, would seem to be the assumptions informing Britton's remarks on the place of scanning. They are corroborated, too, by Britton's further observation that pauses in writing "tend to be shorter and less frequent in narrative writing than in most other kinds" and that young writers when given an expository task will often turn it into a narrative one, even if that means failing to do what is asked of them. (p. 35)[4]

IV. A conceptual framework for an experimental design

If no one has challenged Britton's experiment until now, it is probably because his findings seem so common-sensically right—so consistent with what all writers know from their own experience. My rough experiment with my students raised questions about the validity of such common-sense reasoning. What was called for was a more rigorous and systematic test of Britton's assertions about the role of re-reading in composing.

To conduct such a test, I set out to redo Britton's experiment with a more carefully constructed sequence of tasks or prompts for writing. Each step in the sequence had to mark a well-defined advance in cognitive difficulty over the previous one. The relative cognitive burden of each also had to reside in the task itself; it had to be independent of variations in the knowledge or skill of different writers.

The sequence I finally constructed derives (as did Britton's original experiment) from a theoretical framework articulated by James Moffett in *Teaching the Universe of Discourse*.[5] Moffett's theory is informed by his Piagetian view of intellectual development as a process of decentering—outward in perspective, away from the sensory perceptions of the here and now and upward in abstractness away from the fragmentary data of isolated experiences. Within this framework a discourse task may be said to be cognitively more advanced as it demands that a writer (or reader) call into play developmentally more advanced faculties (sense perception → memory → reason) in the interest of knowledge that is increasingly distant from concrete experience in the present moment.[6]

Moffett provides a memorable shorthand for schematizing his theory in a convenient set of tags marking a continuum of perspectives from "what is happening" to "what might happen." In the following adaptation of Moffett's schema, we see that each step on the continuum of perspectives is associated with a familiar discourse type and a perceptual or cognitive faculty.

Table 1 Scale of intellectual ascent for discourse

Temporal aspect	*Discourse acts*	*Informing faculties*	*Examples*
What is happening	describing recording	discourse organized by the senses	field notes love notes diary entries
What happened (or will happen)	reporting narrating (or planning)	discourse organized by memory (chronological thinking)	memoirs news reports summaries of field notes plans
What happens	generalizing (using examples) explaining analyzing classifying advising from experience	discourse organized by analogical reasoning— the capacity to recognize a basis for excluding instances from and including instances within classes and categories; i.e., generalizations	history scientific inquiry and explanation literary analysis prudential wisdom
What might happen What should happen	arguing (using reasons) advising from theory speculating theorizing disputing	discourse organized by the formal logic of argument or by the "tautologic"[7] that generates new theoretical frameworks yielding new perspectives and arguments	professional advice and speculation literary theory philosophical and scientific theories and proofs legal argumentation

While this chart may seem merely to rehearse the most conventional of all discourse taxonomies (descriptive, narrative, expository, argumentative)[8] it is itself an instance of what Moffett calls "the tautologic of transformation"—an act of theorizing by which one system of terms and assertions is cast in a new conceptual framework in order to provide a more penetrating or wider perspective on the same phenomena. The power of Moffett's transformed perspective seems evident in the degree to which it serves as a more powerful heuristic (than the traditional four categories) for generating topics or instances of discourse that might be classified according to their cognitive difficulty. I have found it, in any event, a helpful guide to constructing a sequence of writing prompts for my experiment with invisible writing.

V. The experiment

The participants in the form experiment were 25 teachers of all grades (K through college) who are Fellows in Composition and teacher/consultants of the South Coast Writing Project at the University of California, Santa Barbara. All of these teachers had participated in a five-week Summer Institute in Composition where they engaged in daily writing experiments. All of them were therefore accustomed to impromptu writing. As a group they would have to be regarded as experienced and accomplished writers and teachers, though not professional writers.

The formal experiment consisted of four writing tasks assigned in a sequence which moves in the direction of increased cognitive difficulty. In order to neutralize the effect of a particularly incompatible topic or subject for any writer, each task in the sequence poses at least three topic options at about the same level of cognitive complexity or abstraction.

Taken together, the various options (printed below) add up to eighteen possible topics for writing. Every one of these topics was selected by at least one writer. No topic was noticeably more popular than the others. The time limits shown for each task are approximate and were treated flexibly in the experiment.[9] For each task the writers were allowed to run over their allotted time by a minute or two until they seemed ready to stop. The last task, "Write a poem," derives from Britton's experiment, but has no place on the scale of cognitive difficulty shown on my chart (above). On the face of it, the formal constraints of a poem would seem to make scanning an even more essential dimension of composition than it would be for prose.

A Sequence of Writing Tasks (Do one in each category)
Task I (5 minutes) What is happening
  A. Write an account of what's going on right now around you or within you.

    B. Write a note to someone expressing your love, anger, dis-
        appointment, resentment, or appreciation.
    C. Write a diary entry focusing on a fear, hope, or regret.
Task II (7 minutes) What happened (or will happen)
    A. Write a brief memoir of a childhood romance or about
        some other childhood experience.
    B. Tell about a fight you had with someone close to you.
    C. Tell about some plan you have for the immediate or
        distant future.
    D. Write a report on a recent professional activity you
        participated in, e.g., a class you taught, a workshop you
        conducted, a meeting you attended.
Task III (10 minutes) What happens (or should happen)
    Select a topic from A *or* B
    A. Give advise to someone about to do one of the following:
        1. Get married/begin a relationship
        2. Get divorced/end a relationship
        3. Become a teacher
        4. Become a parent
        5. Begin anything you know about
    B. Write on one of the following topics:
        1. The benefits and dangers of daydreaming
        2. The wisdom and folly of reflecting on the past
        3. How we can hate the ones we most love
        4. What many people want from a relationship is what no
          one can ever give them
        5. The problems of student-writers
Task IV (7 minutes) Write a poem.

The results of this experiment were substantially those of my earlier informal trial. As a group these teachers found invisible writing a congenial method of composing. Many writers reported that they found their writing becoming increasingly satisfying and valuable for them with each successive task performed under the experimental conditions. Several writers attributed these effects to the fact that the distribution and selection of topics allowed for continuity in theme or subject from one topic level to the next. Some writers therefore found that the sequence encouraged them as they progressed through it to give increasingly more penetrating and thoughtful attention to a single problem. Others who did not pursue a single subject or theme throughout the sequence noted that they still found themselves writing with greater fluency and power as they moved up the abstrative ladder of assigned tasks. For them each task served as something of a warm-up to help their concentration for the next task.

In general, for this group of writers as for their predecessors, the experimental condition struck them at first as a slight inconvenience but no impediment or aid. It made virtually no difference in their fluency or copiousness with the descriptive task. As they progressed through the narrative, expository, and poetic tasks, however, it became for many of them a salutary, even a therapeutic device. Many found it to be a particularly powerful aid to their concentration and a spur to their creativity.

Here is what one writer—a kindergarten teacher—did with the narrative task, having decided to ignore the assigned topics in favor of one of her own, under the general heading of "What happened":

What Happened

I juggled the grocery bag with my purse in one arm, pulled Benjamin away from the hot water furnace with the other, and pushed the door from the garage into the house open with my foot. "Mom," said Ben, pulling on the bottom of my shirt, "I want a popsicle."

"Okay, honey," I replied, setting down the groceries and going to Alison's room to see if she'd gone to sleep.

"Where's Daddy?"

"I WANT A POPSICLE" yelled Ben, knocking the diapers I just folded off the dresser.

"As soon as you finish your dinner, Ben. It's still on the table."

Benjamin started to cry. I watched him head for the kitchen where the grocery bag was. I knew already it was a losing battle. How could I back down now without losing face? I went into the kitchen and, as Ben was tugging on my leg, crying, I said,

"Oh, Ben! You didn't tell me you finished your bread and milk! What color popsicle do you want?"

His face lit up and his grip on my leg loosened.

"Pink!"

"Oh, God," I thought, heading for the grocery bag. "There's only purple, orange and red." (Last pair of quotation marks added.)

The following are two pieces of exposition, the first on the difficulties of becoming a parent (Task III A 4), and the next on daydreaming (Task III B 1). In the daydreaming piece two lines are illegible because the writer—not able to see where he had written—wrote in the same linear space twice, making both lines impossible to read in the carbon copy.

Becoming a Parent

Becoming a parent involves more risk than anything I know of.
You do not know if you're succeeding or failing until it's too late

to correct the mistakes. Often your role must be negative with virtually no positive feedback. Appreciation is non-existent all during the hard work phase. For many years you will be devoid of independence. Fie some will say. It's not that bad. Think again. Until the child is independent, your life is not your own. Sure, you may have time away, but only if the babysitting arrangements work. If the babysitter gets sick who is responsible? You!

Not only does parenting require risk and responsibility, it lays tremendous loads of guilt on your shoulders. If something goes wrong, society and THE EXPERTS agree that it's due to faulty parenting. Everyone knows that the damage begins while the child is in the womb. The mother's eating, drinking, etc., influences the child. The more we learn about parenting, the heavier the guilt. Soon we'll need saints instead of parents.

Daydreaming

Daydreaming can serve a variety of purposes. When one is "understimulated" by the present surroundings, daydreaming can provide creative fantasy and rewarding escape. Daydreaming can also be a time of self-integration, a time to reflect on past experiences and plans for the future. When my oldest son was 6 and 7, he spent a great deal of time daydreaming—often not being able to finish assignments in class. His worst problem was in working on reading comprehension worksheets as homework. He would agonize for hours, sometimes on a single question. In talking with (illegible). I never knew if I was asking him to do something which was less important than his daydreaming.

Finally, here is a poem, "Corey 3," by a teacher who felt this to be the most promising poem he had produced in a long time.

Corey 3
Looking at the big number 12
on the front of his shirt
after two weeks of nose-through
the cyclone fence
backstop as Nathan 7
Eagles his way through these
first life days (spring and all)
of baseball or little leagues away
Corey asks for hotdogs and popcorn
looks at bugs in the grass
and days later climbing on the
bed where Mother will answer.

Looking at his 12 Corey says
"Is this a baseball shirt?" Yes
"Am I on a team?" He's gone
before mother and I answer
(tears in eyes)
Yes.

VI. Speculations on the experimental results

That the drafts produced under the experimental conditions were not "useless," as were the pieces produced by the British researchers, is itself a suggestive finding. Of even more compelling interest is the evidence— mainly the reports of the participants—that the experimental procedure was actually an aid to composing at the first draft stage.

The observations of the participating writers about how the invisible writing procedure served to focus their attention are consistent with what earlier research and our own experience tell us about the place of editing in the composing process. Sondra Perl has reported, for example, that one of the principal differences between the composing processes of unskilled and skilled writers is that unskilled writers begin their editing almost immediately.[10] They edit so much as they go that the progress of their thinking is impeded, if not brought to a standstill. At the stage of generating one's thought in a first draft, almost any editing can be a distraction, obstructing the writer's discovery of his own thought. It is no accident that most successful authors turn out their first drafts quite hurriedly, without much conscious attention to the stylistic or mechanical niceties that they will later attend to for the sake of a reader. First draft writing is, to use Linda Flower's terms, "writer-based" rather than "reader-based."[11]

Most of us also know from experience that the quality of our attention or concentration is partly a function of time-on-task. Just as our concentration will begin to taper off gradually at the limits of our attention span, so is there at the beginning of a task a gradual build-up in the intensity of our attention until we reach a plateau representing the most focused application of our skill and intelligence. Artists, actors, dancers, yogis, and all devotees of any discipline will warm up and gather their concentration in preparation for performing at the peak of their power. Such concentration is undoubtedly dissipated when a writer continually interrupts himself by shifting his attention in writing from the thought he is following (or pushing ahead) to the different form of intellectual activity entailed in editing or revising. The distinctive virtue of invisible writing may be that its constraints prevent shifts in attention away from what is essential for a first draft toward what is better postponed to subsequent drafts.

Among the most surprising findings to come out of my experiment are the reports of some of the writers that the invisible writing procedure felt increasingly helpful to them as they engaged in increasingly demanding writing tasks. That is the reverse of what we might expect. It makes sense, however, when we consider how invisible writing is a constraint that helps both to fix attention and to free it. It fixes attention on the writer's thought—what Vygotsky or Moffett would call his "inner-speech"[12]—at the same time that it frees the writer from attending to anything except his thought.

The invisibly composing writer cannot look back on a trail of words to mark the progress of his thinking as he writes. He must hold the already articulated portions of his thought in his mind as he continues to develop each separate thought and the flow of connected thoughts that constitute his discourse. This extra burden on the writer's memory is likely to improve the quality of his thinking by keeping him attentive to his thoughts at a level that may be deeper than the surface structure of the words he would otherwise be able to read on the page. In may be that, unable to depend on his own written sentences as cues to his thinking, the invisibly composing writer can tap something closer to the well-springs of his thought—his "inner-speech" or even what Sondra Perl has called a "felt sense" of meaning[13]—than their written sentences would give him access to.

It seems plausible to suggest that writers who cannot look back at their sentences will retain them in their minds in a form resembling a reader's memory of the sentences they have already read as they move forward through a text. Research in reading has found that a reader forgets the surface structure of each sentence within seconds after reading it, retaining its content in memory in the form of its semantic propositions—a form which may be said to represent the underlying cognitive structure of a thought—something closer to pure meaning than ordinarily realized sentences.[14] We might conjecture then, somewhat paradoxically, that invisible writing may help writers to think more deeply and purely in their composing because their words are less likely to get in the way of their thinking.

Invisible writing may purify the act of composing in another sense as well. Unable to see what they have written, invisibly composing writers may find themselves extraordinarily liberated from having to attend to the manner in which they are presenting themselves; to the sound of their voices, to the elegance of their utterances, to whether they appear intelligent or dull. They may even be relieved of having to attend, more generously, to the needs of their auditors; to the readability of their prose, to the reader's capacity to follow the line of an argument, to possible ambiguities in the meaning conveyed. In short, invisible writing may prevent writers from being both reader and writer as they write. Writing invisibly, one can only write. And only writing—writing without the self-consciousness or consciousness of an "other" that comes from reading as one writes—may make the act of writing more nearly that of pure thinking.

The cost of engaging in the conventionally double act of writing (or speaking) for oneself and for one's auditor—of writing and reading as one writes—may become increasingly obstructive to a writer's thinking as the thinking required by a topic for discourse becomes cognitively more difficult. That is because tasks that are cognitively more difficult make more exclusive demands on our attention. This is evident in the unselfconscious speech of children who, talking about topics that strain their cognitive capacity, will frequently fail to attend to the needs of their conversational partners. Talking about a more familiar or less complex topic, the same children will appear to be socially more competent. Similarly, when an adult speaker in conversation thinks through a difficult idea, he may avoid eye contact with his auditor or neglect other conventional signals of mutual affiliation. These social failures do not indicate any communicative incompetence on the part of the speakers. They merely show how our limited resources for attention in the production of language may be strained by the cognitive burden of a difficult topic for discourse.[15]

It makes sense, then, that the writers participating in my invisible writing experiment would have found the experimental procedure more helpful to their composing as they took on the more cognitively advanced discourse tasks. That is because as they progressed along the sequence of tasks, their success in responding to the assigned topics depended increasingly on their capacity to focus their thinking and to recover their thoughts as directly as possible, with as little interference as possible from the process of moving from inner speech to its external expression.

The more complicated and original and penetrating our thinking becomes, the more volatile and elusive it is likely to be—the more subject to flight before we can capture it in the grasp of our words. Our most fugitive thoughts require the most unmediated recovery. We need to capture them whole, not in pieces. If we shift our attention to mending the inelegance of our utterance, to looking for the best word instead of the word nearest at hand, or even to attending to the needs of our auditors, we may lose the last half of our emerging thought before we have netted the first. Hence if we are able to purge ourselves of our concern with the surface features of our utterance, with the impression we may be making, or even with how lucidly we are elaborating our ideas for a reader, we may be better able to make more immediate contact with the whole of our most elusive thoughts and recover them more surely in the net of our language for our subsequent examination and emendation. Invisible writing may help us purge our composing of most of the pitfalls of vanity and other-directedness. To that extent it may help us improve our access through writing to our most penetrating and subtle thoughts.

Here I must confess that even now as I write these sentences—as throughout the composition of this essay—I find myself smitten by disbelief in my own claims about the efficacy of invisible writing, especially as I begin to compose a difficult passage, to struggle to articulate an idea that I do not yet fully possess. At such moments I become convinced of the impossibility of ever managing to proceed without constantly reading back over what I have been writing. The more refractory and complex my idea, the more I find it necessary to pause and reread as I progress—circling back upon my thought in each sentence to review its beginning before I move ahead to its conclusion.

I have become so dubious about my own claims as I have written this essay, that upon occasion I have determined to test them by using the invisible writing procedure myself to compose the next passage where I find myself unsuccessfully struggling to fashion my thoughts into coherent prose. Yet when I take up my empty pen and carbon paper and use them in composing, I find I am always able to negotiate the problem passage more directly and successfully than I could before. And behold, that is how I have been composing these very words—the paragraph ending here and the one before it.[16]

VII. Some remaining questions

I find it puzzling and somewhat unsettling that James Britton and his London Institute colleagues obtained results so different from those my experiments have yielded. Is there a level of abstraction or possibly of rhetorical distance (psychological distance between the writer and reader) at which a writer's inability to scan would cause the composing process to break down? Can that explain Britton's failed experiment in writing without scanning? One of the teachers participating in my study suggested that our experimental procedure might have proved more obstructive to discourse tasks that are less personal—where the resources we had to tap, the *loci* for our arguments and the materials generated, were more external, more subject to verification, more in the domain of scientific objective knowledge than in that of our private experience. Would conventional scientific writing, for example, be possible, even in a first draft, with the invisible writing procedure? That question will have to be explored in future studies.

I am more troubled by the conditions I set in my experiment. On no occasion did I ask any of the participating writers to compose for longer than about 10 minutes on a single task. The discontinuities noted by Britton and his London colleagues might, perhaps, begin to appear after longer periods of sustained invisible composing. On the other hand, most of the writers in the experimental groups produced 160–180 words of prose on the expository tasks, knowing at the start how much time they would have. Many produced two or three paragraphs. Since pausing constitutes no problem in invisible writing—as long as you keep your pen on the spot where you stopped—I don't see why they couldn't have continued to write as much as they ever would at one sitting under ordinary writing conditions.[17] The effect of sustained invisible composing on the continuity of a writer's thought remains to be observed in future experiments.

Whether the writers in my experiment actually produced more or better prose than they do under ordinary circumstances is also not certain.[18] My suspicion (having seen many pieces produced in 10-minute sittings by these Writing Project teachers) is that they did write more copiously and at least as thoughtfully as they ever have in first drafts—and not merely as a result of the richness or sequence of the assigned topics. Many of the writers, at any rate, experienced the experimental procedure, for whatever reason, as an aid to their fluency and creativity. And most agreed that this was at least in part a function of their not being able to break their concentration during pauses, as they are likely to do when they can tinker with the surface of their utterance as they compose.[19]

Exactly what it is that writers do during pauses in invisible writing—and how it is different from what they ordinarily do—remains to be uncovered by further study. Composing-aloud tapes of writers engaged in invisible writing or videotapes of such composing (analyzed by the Matsuhashi-Cooper method[20]) should provide illuminating data for any researcher interested in the nature of pauses in the composing process and the possibilities for making those pauses more productive.

VIII. Instructional applications

The power of invisible writing to keep a writer's attention focused on his emerging thought points to what are probably its most significant potential uses for instruction. Invisible writing might, first of all, be used as a diagnostic instrument to see to what extent wandering attention or the distractions of premature editing—rather than a paucity of ideas—are impediments for writers who seem unable to produce satisfactory quantities of prose in a single sitting.

What is at first a diagnostic procedure may then become a therapeutic method for improving the fluency of student-writers who have become, in Robert Zoellner's phrase, "scribal stutterers." It seems reasonable to suppose that writers blocked by their verbal self-consciousness or by a tendency to compulsive overediting will find that invisible writing allows them to produce coherent first-draft prose more rapidly and copiously than they would otherwise have thought possible. Such a change is also likely to yield more satisfying prose—prose that retains much of the freshness and force of spontaneous speech.[21] Through practice in invisible writing blocked writers might gain the confidence and experience they need to trust the advantages (often cited by expert writers) of postponing their editing until they have discovered and expressed their thoughts in a voice recognizably their own.[22]

These classroom applications of invisible writing remain to be tested. In the meantime, I suspect that many teachers will find it useful to experiment with the procedure in basic and advanced writing classes. I would not advocate that any students use invisible writing on a regular basis, but I believe almost every writer can learn something about his own ordinary composing processes by experimenting once or twice with the invisible writing procedure.

Notes

1 "Understanding Composing," *College Composition and Communication*, 31 (December, 1980), 364. Earlier, Sharon Pianko, studying the composing processes of college freshmen, found that competent writers (N = 7) engaged in what she calls "rescanning" ("a rereading of a few words, or sentences, or a paragraph ... not a rereading of the entire script") approximately 12 times in the course of the 43 minutes it took them to complete a typical assigned essay of 400 words. This suggests that scanning occurs every three or four minutes or every 30 to 40 words. When she asked her subjects what they were doing when they rescanned, they explained that they were usually engaged in planning what to write next and that the rescanning helped them to formulate what they wanted to say. Sometimes they rescanned in order to revise their text. See "A Description of the Composing Processes of College Freshmen Writers," *Research in the Teaching of English*, 13 (February, 1979), 22–35.
2 Britton et al., *The Development of Writing Abilities, (11–18)* (London: Macmillan Education, 1975), p. 35.
3 I added the task in the persuasive mode only as an act of desperation, after my students reported that they had no trouble with exposition. I was convinced that our inability to reread should at some level of discourse seriously obstruct our capacity to compose.
4 Ann Matsuhashi's recent research findings provide empirical support for the assumption of most discourse theorists, including Britton, that narrative writing is cognitively less demanding than (and developmentally prior to) expository or persuasive. She found that writers tend to pause for longer intervals when engaged in generalizing or persuading than in narrating. She also found that a writer's pause time increases as the content of his discourse becomes more abstract. See "Pausing and Planning: The Tempo of Written Discourse Production," *Research in the Teaching of English*, 15 (May, 1981) 113–134.
5 Boston: Houghton Mifflin, 1968. See esp. pp. 14–59.
6 Current research and theory in the field of communication studies confirm almost every detail of the developmental theory Moffett articulated nearly fifteen years ago. Cf. James Applegate and Jessie Delia, "Person-Centered Speech, Psychological Development, and the Contexts of Language Usage," in *The Social and Psychological Contexts of Language*, ed. R. N. St. Clair and H. Giles (Hillsdale, NJ: Lawrence Erlbaum, 1980).
7 The terms Moffett uses to describe the progression of "logics" are not quite as obscure in the context in which he introduces them. See *Teaching the Universe of Discourse*, p. 34: "The logic of lowest verbal abstraction is *chronologic* (narrative) ... After playing historian we play scientist: we assimilate a lot of narratives into a generalization by the *analogic* of class inclusions and

exclusions. First I collect a lot of anecdotes about Harry's behavior and then I conclude he is a bum (I place his different acts into some class because I see them as analogous) ... After playing scientist, we play mathematician: by means of *tautologic* we transform general assertions into other general assertions which mean the same thing, but because they are now in another symbolic form, imply further assertions which we could not see before."

Moffett's choice of the term "tautologic" is unfortunate insofar as it suggests a form of reasoning that is circular and gratuitously repetitious. He wanted to identify speculative thinking and the logic of argument by means of a term that would be analogous to the two he had already used to characterize the thinking that informs narrative or reporting ("chronologic") and generalizing ("analogic"). Since the formal logic of argument and that of theorizing or speculating characteristically entail finding a new or different way of thinking about something already known in other terms, they may be said to represent "tautological" thinking. They involve saying the same thing in a different way. He might have done better to refer to such thinking as the "neologic" of speculation or argument.

8 Actual instances of discourse are nearly always mixed. To classify a discourse according to its level of abstraction is to identify it with its principal or superordinate function (i.e., to record, report, generalize, or speculate) within a hierarchy of functions which may be identified in the same piece of discourse. Thus, if I offer speculations about cognitive processes in composing, they will be built on generalizations drawn from instances and examples cited within the same discourse. And these—as in this essay—may be recounted in a narrative form. Similarly, most argumentative essays will include lots of exposition, narration, and even description. If a descriptive or narrative discourse contains generalizations or speculations (as in many descriptive passages in *Paradise Lost*) they are likely to represent digressions rather than steps in a progression.

9 The experiment calls for about 30 minutes of writing in total. That yields 10 minutes for the crucial expository task (the heart of the experiment), five minutes for a warm-up task for my experimental subjects to get used to the procedure, and the remaining time divided between the narrative task and the poem. Thirty minutes of writing is about as much as I can ask of my volunteer subjects under the circumstances in which I usually conduct the experiment, i.e., as part of an in-service presentation for teachers on current research in composition.

10 "The Composing Processes of Unskilled College Writers," *Research in the Teaching of English*, 13 (December, 1979), 317–336.

11 "Writer-Based Prose: A Cognitive Basis for Problems in Writing," *College English*, 41 (September, 1979), 19–37.

12 The term comes originally from Lev Vygotsky, *Thought and Language*, trans. E. Hanfmann and G. Vakar (Cambridge, MA: MIT Press, 1962). "Inner speech is ... thinking in pure meanings" (p. 149). The notion of inner speech informs much of Moffett's recent writing about composition. Cf. "Integrity and the Teaching of Writing" and "Writing, Inner Speech, and Meditation" in *Coming on Center: English Education in Evolution* (Montclair, NJ: Boynton/Cook, 1981).

13 "Understanding Composing" (cited above), pp. 363–369.

14 Walter Kintsch, *The Representation of Meaning in Memory* (Hillsdale, NJ: Lawrence Erlbaum, 1974).

15 Elinor Ochs, "Planned and Unplanned Discourse," in *Syntax and Semantics, Vol. 12: Discourse and Syntax*, ed. Talmy Givon (New York: Academic Press, 1979).

16 I am reluctant to admit, after such a flourish, that these two paragraphs are largely narrative and cannot be said to represent thinking very far advanced on the abstractive scale. I did use invisible writing successfully to compose more difficult passages, however. None of them were useless, but none survived later revisions in a form close enough to the original to allow me to show then as examples. At least two earlier paragraphs of this speculative section of my essay were drafted invisibly.

17 Gabriele Rico, a specialist in the neurophysiology of writing, recently told me that in demonstrating the efficacy of her pre-writing methods (Cf. Gabriele L. Rico and Mary Frances Claggett, *Balancing the Hemispheres: Brain Research and the Teaching of Writing* [Berkeley: Bay Area Writing Project Curriculum Publication No. 14, 1980]), she always asks writers to compose in ten-minute segments. That seems to her to be the optimum time for a writer in one sitting to develop an idea or narrative into a coherent and fairly self-contained discourse.

18 Their 160–180 words in ten minutes is faster than we might expect of skilled writers writing without artificial constraints. Sharon Pianko's competent college freshmen (see n. 1 above) seem to have composed at a rate of about 10 words per minute. Wallace Chafe cites Ann Matsuhashi's finding (unpublished) of a 13-word-per-minute average for a good writer over four discourse types. See Chafe's "Integration and Involvement in Speaking, Writing, and Oral Literature," forthcoming in Deborah Tannen, ed., *Spoken and Written Language* (Norwood, NJ: Ablex), n. 3. In studies of letter writing in a business setting, John Gould also found composition rates for writers to run about 13 words per minute. "Experiments on Composing Letters: Some Facts, Some Myths, and Some Observations," in L. W. Gregg and E. R. Steinberg, ed., *Cognitive Processes in Writing* (Hillsdale, NJ: Lawrence Erlbaum, 1980), p. 16.

19 This doesn't quite mean that they couldn't edit at all, however. A few of the papers show words and even whole lines crossed out. Yet these do not appear to represent editing work performed in the intervals between bursts of writing. They seem to be rather the evidence of false starts—words and phrases called back at the point of utterance, not to be reconsidered in search of improvement in style, but to be altered to reflect an adjustment in the writer's intention, discovered by him through his dissatisfaction with the words he was at that moment putting down on paper.

20 Cf. Ann Matsuhashi, "Pausing and Planning: The Tempo of Written Discourse Production," cited above.

21 Many teachers use free-writing exercises to achieve ends similar to those I am proposing for invisible writing. The difference is that free writing, as practiced by Elbow and others, allows no pauses for thinking. It urges the writer to follow his thoughts wherever they lead. Thus as a writer begins to struggle with a difficult idea, free writing allows and even encourages him or her to shift to a topic in which fluency is easier. Invisible writing, on the other hand, allows pauses for thinking and planning (and perhaps for what Donald Murray calls "rehearsing"); and it helps the writer to keep his or her attention focused directly on the assigned writing task. I suspect that writers who master free-writing have actually learned to compose as if they were writing invisibly, i.e., without looking back at their words as they progress, and without self-consciousness or concern about how they sound. Free writing is also more limited in its value as an experimental or therapeutic tool. You can tell a writer to free write, and he may even declare that he has done it. But the experimenter or teacher can't know who has really done it or to what extent. Invisible writing gives the writer no choice.

22 Not all of my suspicions and speculations are unequivocally supported by the research literature. Sharon Pianko's examination of the composing processes of competent and "remedial" freshman writers (cited above) might seem to favor conclusions opposite to mine. Her findings suggest not that unskilled writers scan too often, but that they don't scan enough. The more skilled writers in her study engaged in rescanning three times as often as the students from remedial classes—12 times in 40 minutes vs. 4 times (p. 13). My speculations about how scanning can break a writer's concentration need to be tested by direct comparisons of work produced through invisible writing against work produced under unconstrained circumstances.

47

NON-MAGICAL THINKING

Presenting writing developmentally in schools

J. Emig

Source: Goswami, D. and Butler, M. (eds) *The Web of Meaning: Essays on Writing, Teaching, Learning and Thinking* (1983) Upper Montclair, NJ: Boynton/Cook, 135–144

". . . the freedom to act upon the world and to construct reality is both the aim and the process of education." If we accept this bedrock developmental proposition, what are the implications for the ways in which writing is presented in schools? Writing represents, of course, powerful, if not unique, ways of constructing reality and of acting upon the world. Consequently, writing can itself serve as both an aim and a major process of education.

Presenting writing developmentally means that from the outset we put aside a belief that the cognitive psychologist Howard Gruber calls "magical thinking":

> We wish the child to grow up and in fact he does: we therefore attribute his growth to our own desires and our efforts (Piaget, 1930). This questionable causal attribution provides the main justification for adult efforts to educate children.
>
> In recent years we have become increasingly aware that adults do not teach children some of the most fundamental ideas; at best, we help to provide circumstances in which children discover what they must know.

That teachers teach and children learn no one will deny. But to believe that children learn *because* teachers teach and only what teachers explicitly teach is to engage in magical thinking, from a developmental point of view.

Most North American schools are temples to magical thinking, with the focus not only on explicit teaching but on a specific form of explicit teaching – adults performing before large groups of learners. As evidence:

99

I recently heard of a note an evaluating administrator slipped a teacher who was helping small groups of writers actively construct their reality through imaginative sequences of experiences and activities. The note read: "I'll come back when you're teaching."

Where matters of language like writing are concerned, the evidence from research is particularly compelling that, as Courtney Cazden of Harvard has observed, "... it is not certain that teaching knowledge *about* language helps us in any way." (italics mine) She continues: "... One reason, therefore, why language is such a difficult subject for curriculum planners is that we do not understand the relationship between what is in some way learned and what can be *taught*."

Perhaps the greatest irony in the back-to-basics movement is that current relentless and expensive efforts to teach writing, and reading, are so undeniably cases of magical thinking on the part of all the adults involved. (Another irony is that the success of explicit teaching, in this era of accountability, is measured by indexes of explicit learning by children on standardized tests.)

Teachers of writing, for many reasons, have come to believe that children's learning to write is the direct outcome of their explicit teaching. Perhaps, because of massive public pressure, they have been forced to become the most magical thinkers of all. But what if, as evidence from many disciplines now suggests, writing is developmentally a *natural* process? What if "it is just as natural ... to write books and to read them as it is natural to die or be born?"

Natural for this context must be quickly defined: As humans we seem to have a genetic predisposition to write as well as to speak; and, if we meet an enabling environment, one that possesses certain characteristics and presents us with certain opportunities, we will learn.

Since the late fifties and early sixties we have heard from such linguists as Chomsky and such biologists of language as Lenneberg strong arguments for the innatist position that humans have a propensity for creating language, that such special, even unique, capacities are "wired-in."

In *Programs of the Brain* (1978), the anatomist J. Z. Young goes further. Young claims that humans follow programs written in four "languages," two shared with other mammals, and two unique to humans, each "embodied in distinct media":

1 the fundamental inherited program, written in the triplets of the DNA code;
2 the structure of the brain with its units "the groups of nerve cells, so organized as to produce the various actions at the right times";
3 "speech and culture" largely embodied in the organized sounds of spoken langauge; and
4 programs that "find their physical expressions and codes not only in

100

human habits and speech sounds but also in writing and in other forms of *recorded* speech. These provide the fourth level of coding, also peculiar to man, enabling some of the information for living to be recorded outside of any living creature."

Interesting support for this possibility comes from the recent studies by Dr. William Condon of Boston who videotaped infants in a maternity ward: Condon found the seemingly random first movements of neonates, even within the first twelve to twenty-four hours of life, in fact, synchronized with the syllabic breaks in the adult speech around them. (In his Preface to *Programs of the Brain*, Young states that "a main aim of this book has been to show how various parts of the brain work together to produce a unified operating system, centered on the model or hypothesis that the most important acts of human life are responses to other people.")

Vygotsky makes the further case that the gesture is developmentally a requisite to the development of written language. In *A Prehistory of Written Language* (1934, trans. 1978), Vygotsky claims that the gesture is "the initial visual sign that contains the child's future writing as an acorn contains a future oak."

Gestures are writing in air, and written signs frequently are simply gestures that have been fixed.

Early on, children shuttle between actual gestures and scribbles on paper that "supplement this gestural representation." In fact, Vygotsky regards the child's first marks on paper developmentally as recorded gestures rather than as drawing in the true sense of the word. One thinks as well, of course, of Piaget, who posits that sensorimotor activity is the source of schemes that transform into subsequent modes of representation.

These marks on the paper go through a series of evolutionary change, from undifferentiated marks through indicatory signs and symbolizing marks and scribbles to the drawing of little figures and pictures to the moment when the child realizes that "one can draw not only things but speech." This recognition makes possible the transformation of writing from a first-order symbolic act, to a second-order symbolic act, from the "mnemotechnic" stage to the stage where one can deal with disembodied signs and symbols—to the stage, that is, of symbolic maturity.

Children's games represent the second realm that "links gestures and written language." In play children use objects in their representational gestures: a piece of wood can serve as a baby or a wand, for example:

... therefore, children's symbolic play can be understood as a very complex system of "speech" through gestures that communicate

101

and indicate the meaning of playthings. It is only on the basis of these indicatory gestures that playthings themselves gradually acquire their meaning—just as drawing, while initially supported by gesture, becomes an independent sign.

He concludes:

symbolic representation in play is essentially a particular form of speech at an earlier stage, one which leads directly to written language.

These two transformations can be represented by the following sketch:

Vygotsky's statements about the requisites of symbolic play to the development of writing in the life of the child are corroborated and extended by studies that examine the roots in childhood of gifted and creative performances in adults, particularly studies by Gardner (1973) and Singer (1973).

Benjamin Singer draws from his research into the fantasy lives of children five conditions "which are conducive to nurturing a predisposition to fantasy play":

1   An opportunity for privacy and for practice in a relatively protected setting where the external environment is reasonably redundant so that greater attention can be focused on internal activity. Naturally, such a situation exists also at the time of preparation for sleep and during sleep itself.
2   Availability of a variety of materials in the form of stories told, books, and playthings which increase the likelihood that the material presented to the child in the course of the reprocessing activity or in the course of a set toward elaboration of this material will be intersting and sufficiently novel so that the child will experience positive affect while playing make-believe games.
3   Freedom from interference by peers or adults who make demands for immediate motor or perceptual reactions...
4   The availability of adult models or older peers who encourage make-believe activity and provide examples of how this is done or provide basic story material which can be incorporated in privacy into the child's limited schemata.
5   Cultural acceptance of privacy and make-believe activities as a reasonably worthwhile form of play.

102

In *From Two to Five*, the Russian poet Kornei Chukovsky charmingly illustrates his hypothesis that between the ages of two and five all children are linguistic geniuses. Chukovsky confined his examples to the oral utterances of children. But in his recent study of metaphoric development in children, Howard Gardner extends the ages and range of art forms for the manifestation of creative genius in children. Gardner's conclusions:

> Perhaps the chief mystery confronting the student of artistic development is the relationship between the mature adult practitioner—the skilled poet, the painting master, the virtuoso instrumentalist or composer—and the young child playing with words, humming and inventing melodies, effortlessly producing sketches and paintings while engaging in many other activities that have only a tenuous relationship to the arts. Clearly there are important differences in skill, acquaintance with the artistic tradition, sensitivity to nuance between the child and the adult participants in the artistic process. But a more fundamental question for the psychologist is whether the schoolchild must pass through further, qualitatively different stages in order to become an artist (as it has been argued that he must pass through qualitatively different stages en route to becoming a practicing scientist). On this question I have arrived at an unexpected conclusion: the child of 7 or 8 has, in most respects, become a participant in the artistic process and he need not pass through any further qualitative reorganization. . . .

What are the possible implications of these research findings for the presentation of writing in schools?

1   Although writing is natural, it is activated by enabling environments.
2   These environments have the following characteristics: they are safe, structured, private, unobstrusive, and literate.
3   Adults in these environments have two especial roles: they are fellow practitioners, and they are providers of possible content, experiences and feedback.
4   Children need frequent opportunities to practice writing, many of these playful.

None of these conditions is met in our current schools; indeed, to honor them would require nothing less than a paradigm shift in the ways we present not only writing but also other major cognitive processes as well. Shifting paradigms is no easy task; in fact, developmentally, there is probably no more complex cognitive process.

As Gruber points out in a remarkable essay comparing children and scientists, notably Darwin, making a paradigm shift requires not only cognitive change but the courage to make the change. To give up one paradigm about the nature of learning and teaching for another requires that teachers undergo a particularly powerful conversion.

> ... The change in thinking means moving away from an established and perhaps hard-won set of relations with other human beings. This may be more important in the case of children than has been realized. When the child, for example, shifts his way of thought so that he restrains himself from making a judgment based on purely perceptual criteria, he is also making a serious change in life-style. He is increasing his independence from the stimulus. In that sense, he is increasing his independence more generally, and any increase in independence carries with it both a promise and a threat. We would probably discover, if we looked a little more closely at those moments when the child's thinking really seems to move, that the child experiences a sense of exhilaration. When we speak of "insight" or the "Aha Experience," it is not just seeing something new. It is feeling. And what the person is feeling is both the promise and the threat of this unknown that is just opening up. When we think new thoughts we really are changing our relations with the world around us, including our social moorings. . . .

Before specifying what in my opinion such a conversion requires, how can the two paradigms be characterized? What, first, are the tenets of the magical thinking paradigm about writing that currently dominates the schools? Here is its credo:

1   Writing is predominantly taught rather than learned.
2   Children must be taught to write atomistically, from parts to wholes. The commonplace is that children must be taught to write sentences before they can be allowed to write paragraphs before they can be permitted to attempt "whole" pieces of discourse.
3   There is essentially one process of writing that serves all writers for all their aims, modes, intents, and audiences.
4   That process is linear: all planning precedes all writing (often described in the paradigm as transcribing), as all writing precedes all revising.
5   The process of writing is also almost exclusively conscious: as evidence, a full plan or outline can be drawn up and adhered to for any piece of writing: the outline also assumes that writing is transcribing, since it can be so totally prefigured; thought exists prior to its linguistic formulation.
6   Perhaps because writing is conscious, it can be done swiftly and on order.
7   There is no community or collaboration in writing: it is exclusively a silent and solitary activity.

What, in contrast, are the findings from the developmental research into writing:

1   Writing is predominantly learned rather than taught.
2   Writers of all ages as frequently work from wholes to parts as from parts to wholes: in writing, there is a complex interplay between focal and global concerns: from an interest in what word should come next, to the shape of the total piece.
3   There is no monolithic process of writing: there are processes of writing that differ because of aim, intent, mode, and audience: although there are shared features in the ways we write, there are as well individual, even idiosyncratic, features in our processes of writing.
4   The processes of writing do not proceed in a linear sequence: rather, they are recursive—we not only plan, then write, then revise; but we also revise, then plan, then write.
5   Writing is as often a pre-conscious or unconscious roaming as it is a planned and conscious rendering of information and events.
6   The rhythms of writing are uneven—more, erratic. The pace of writing can be very slow, particularly if the writing represents significant learning. Writing is also slow since it involves what Vygotsky calls "elaborating the web of meaning," supplying the specific and explicit links to render lexical, syntactic, semantic, and rhetorical pieces into organic wholes.
7   The processes of writing can be enhanced by working in, and with, a group of other writers, perhaps especially a teacher, who give vital response, including advice.

What constitutes a conversation experience for those who present writing in schools, from the magical thinking paradigm to a developmental view? Obviously, since the shift is so great, so dramatic (and, at times, traumatic), the evidence and the experiences must be extremely powerful and, indeed, they must be developmental.

To undergo such a conversion, teachers of writing, our research strongly suggests, must:

1   write themselves in many modes, poetic and imaginative, as well as transactional and extensive, and introspect upon their own histories and processes as writers;
2   observe directly, and through such media as videotape, female and male writers of many ages and backgrounds engaging in the processes of writing; and speculate systematically with other teacher-writers about these observations and their implications for presenting writing in schools;
3   ascertain attitudes, constructs, and paradigms of those learning to

write because the evidence grows stronger that, as with any learning process, set affects, perhaps even determines, both process and performance;

4   assess growth in writing against its developmental dimensions, with perhaps the most important accomplishment a growing ability to distinguish between a mistake and what can be termed a developmental error.

To examine each of these in turn:

1. What is most powerful and persuasive, developmentally, of course, is direct, active, personal experience since only personal experience can transform into personal knowledge. And for teachers especially, personal knowledge of any process to be presented to learners is not an option; it is a requisite. Persons who don't themselves write cannot sensitively, even sensibly, help others learn to write.

Teachers of writing, then, must themselves write, frequently and widely. And they must introspect upon their writing, since without reflection there has been no experience, as philosophers from Socrates to Dewey point out.

2. To inform themselves about how they at once are like, and different from, their students, teachers of writing need to take an intensive look at actual students working through extended and systematic observation; interviews with the students, peers, former teachers, and parents—in other words, by the preparation of writing of at least two through case-studies. (Since the emerging research on writers of all ages suggests sex differences, I would recommend studying at least one writer of each sex.)

Models for case studies are available from many sources—from literary biographies to clinical analyses. Within the specific research on the composing processes, there are available in doctoral dissertations many exemplars: for young children, Graves (1973) and Sawkins (1971); for children nine to thirteen, Hale (1975) and Carducci (1979); for high school age, Emig (1969), Stallard (1972), and Sommers (1979); and for college, Rogers (1978), and Stokes and Heard (1975).

3. Teachers' own experiences as writers will provide the kinds of developmental issues they will want to examine in these case studies; but it is likely that they will formulate variants on some of the following questions:

- What are the attitudes toward literacy and the educational background of the family?
- When, and under what circumstances, did the child begin to write, and to read?
- If the child remembers these experiences, what description does she give? With what feeling tones?

- If the learner currently has difficulty writing, can the learner or someone else identify specific times and circumstances when difficulties began?
- What does the learner think writing is for? What are its functions?
- Does the learner write equally well in all modes? unevenly? In which modes, well; in which, less well or badly?
- How can his process(es) of writing be characterized? total length? length of given portions? amount and quality of prewriting including planning? amount and kind of revising, recursive and final? Is the writer self-critical, capable of reflection?
- What are the attitudes, constructs, and paradigms the student has about school, about English and the language arts, about writing?

Recent research suggests that, the older the writer, the more likely that such cumulative clusters of belief will affect the processes of writing and their outcomes (Pianko, 1978; King, 1979).

4. How can teachers learn to assess growth in students' abilities to write, with its concomitant question: how can we teach ourselves to discern the difference between mistakes and what can be termed developmental errors?

We can only make accurate assessments of growth if we have accurate characterizations of writing persons, processes, and outcomes; and thus far what we have are pastels or sketches for the whole or Wyeth-like drawings of a few tight particulars, not a fully delineated model of the developmental dimensions of writing.

A few persons have attempted to provide wide views. Perhaps because he has delineated one of the most compelling developmental sequences for modes, James Moffett has, in my opinion, also developed some major strategies as his metaphor "detecting growth" in writing suggests. These appear as Chapter 22 in the second edition of *A Student-Centered Language Arts Curriculum*, with Betty Jane Wagner, John Holt's *How Children Fail* (1964) and *How Children Learn* (1967) remain useful, readable general introductions to developmental issues.

Crucial to a developmental view of assessment is to learn to distinguish between mistakes and developmental errors. Developmental errors contrast readily with mistakes in that developmental errors forward learning while mistakes impede it. Developmental errors have two characteristics that mistakes do not: 1) they are bold, chance-taking; 2) and they are rational, intelligent.

While the making of mistakes marks a retreat into the familiar, the result of fear and anxiety, developmental errors represent a student's venturing out and taking chances as a writer, from trying a new spelling, or tying together two sentences with a fresh transition, to a first step into a mode previously unexplored.

A second characteristic of developmental errors is that they are rational and logical; unfortunately, they often happen also to be wrong. In *Errors and Expectations*, our most thorough account of errors among a given segment of writers, those she calls BW writers (Basic Writers), Mina Shaughnessy notes the "most damaging aspect" of the BW's experiences with writing:

> they have lost all confidence in the very faculties that serve all language learners: their ability to distinguish between essential and redundant features of a language left them logical but wrong; their abilities to draw analogies between what they knew of language when they began school and what they learned produced mistakes; and such was the quality of their instruction that no one saw the intelligence of their mistakes or thought to harness that intelligence in the service of learning.

Examples of invalid analogies include the over-regularizing of lexical, grammatical, or rhetorical features, as well as more globally, the illogicality of proceeding as if writing were talk written down, a belief some students hold perhaps because some of their teachers have told them it is so.

Assessing growth in writing is a far larger, more complex, more individual and more interesting matter than testing. Too many testing programs, particularly those devised and given by state and national agencies, public and private, use evidence divorced from the linguistic and human histories of the students involved, and evidence divorced from the only sensible developmental requirement that students write organic, sustained pieces of discourse, like the students themselves, with histories and with futures.

Presenting writing developmentally in schools will require major transformations: transformations from the traditional school paradigm that promulgates magical thinking; and consequently, transformations of teacher learning and development. It is quite as demanding as the ways of teaching writing traditionally—perhaps more demanding—requiring no less than that adults admit that the only way they can help others learn to write is that they themselves become learners and writers.

References

Bettelheim, B. *Paul & Mary: Two Case Histories of Truants from Life*. New York: Doubleday, Anchor, 1961.

Cazden, C. B. "Problems for Education: Language as Curriculum Content and Learning Environment," in "Language as a Human Problem." *Daedalus* (Summer, 1973), CII, 3, 135.

Chomsky, N. *Language and Mind*. New York: Harcourt Brace Jovanovich, 1972.

Chukovsky, K. *From Two to Five*. M. Morton (Ed. & Tr.), Berkeley, CA: University of California Press, 1963.

Condon, W., & Sander, L. "Neonate Movement Is Synchronized with Adult Speech: Interactional Participation and Language Acquisition." *Science*, 183 (4120), 1974, 99–101.

Duckworth, E. "The Having of Wonderful Ideas." M. Schwebel & J. Raph (Eds.), *Piaget in the Classroom*. New York: Basic Books, 21–22, 1973.

Feldenkrais, M. *Body and Mature Behavior*, New York: International Universities Press, 1949, 132. Ken Marcrorie brought this reference to my attention.

Gardner, H. *The Arts & Human Development: a Psychological Study of the Artistic Process*. New York: Wiley, 1973

Gruber, H. "Courage and Cognitive Growth in Children and Scientists," in M. Schwebel & J. Raph (Eds.), *Piaget in the Classroom*. New York: Basic Books, 1973, 74.

Lenneberg, E. *Biological Foundations of Language*. New York: Wiley, 1967.

Pianko, S. "A Description of the Composing Processes of College Freshman Writers," *Research in the Teaching of English*, (February, 1979), XIII, 1, 5–22.

Polanyi, M. *Personal Knowledge: Towards a Post-critical Philosophy*. Chicago: University of Chicago Press, 1958.

Redinger, R. V. *George Eliot: The Emergent Self*. New York: Knopf, 1975.

Report of the New Jersey Writing Project to the National Review Dissemination Panel, Washington, D.C.: (May, 1979).

Schwebel, M. & Raph, J. "Before and Beyond the Three R's," in M. Schwebel and J. Raph (Eds.), *Piaget in the Classroom*. New York: Basic Books, 1973, 21–22.

Shaughnessy, M. *Errors and Expectations: a Guide for the Teacher of Basic Writing*. New York: Oxford University Press, 1977, 10–11.

Vygotsky, L. "The Prehistory of Written Language" (1934), in S. Scribner *et al.* (Eds.), *Mind in Society: The Development of Higher Psychological Processes*, Cambridge, MA: Harvard University Press, 1978, pp 105–111.

Young, J. Z. *Programs of the Brain*. New York: Oxford University Press, 1978, 10.

48

WRITING STRATEGIES AND WRITERS' TOOLS

Daniel Chandler

Source: *English Today* (1993) 9(2): 32–38

In 1991 I conducted a survey of academic writers at the University College of Wales, Aberystwyth. One of the issues pursued was the possibility of relationships between the use of particular tools and individual composing styles. Of the 126 academics selected, 107 returned completed questionnaires: 31 from arts subjects (classified as literature, modern languages and history); 40 from science subjects; and 36 from other subjects (classified as social science). The distribution of the sexes was much less even: 98 were male and only 9 female (a sad reflection of the general distribution of academic staff). As for age-ranges: 4 were in their twenties; 25 in their thirties; 39 in their forties; 27 in their fifties; and 8 in their sixties (4 unknown).

Table 1 shows the proportion of writers from each subject background who reported frequent use of each of the writing tools (many, of course, use more than one tool). Clearly there were very few frequent users of dictation or the typewriter. The only frequent users of the typewriter were 4 writers in the arts (which is the only factor which distinguished those in the social sciences from the arts as users of the various writing tools). The largest proportion of frequent word-processor users was in the sciences and the smallest was in the arts, whilst the largest proportion of frequent users of the pen or pencil was in the arts and the smallest in the sciences.

82 of these academics reported using word processors directly to key in their own texts, another 16 indirectly, and 9 not at all. The proportion of indirect users and non-users of the word processor was 35% in the arts, 31% in the social sciences and only 8% in the sciences. The pattern of use revealed a statistically significant difference between arts and science writers ($p < 0.01$), and a slightly less significant one between science and social science writers ($p < 0.05$).

Another subject-related issue regarding the word processor was that some writers reported problems in comparing one printed draft with another. The largest proportion of those who experienced this was

Table 1 Proportions of frequent users of each tool in each subject area

Frequent use of tools	ARTS (N = 31)		SOCIAL SCIENCE (N = 36)		SCIENCE (N = 40)	
Pen/Pencil	65%	20	64%	23	53%	21
Dictation	3%	1	3%	1	5%	2
Typewriter	13%	4		0		0
Word Processor	55%	17	58%	21	80%	32

amongst the social scientists. This was in sharp contrast with only a few in the sciences. A large majority of users in the sciences rarely if ever find this a problem (the difference between scientists and arts specialists over this issue being significant at the 5% level).

Composing strategies

Through a wide-ranging review of published accounts by writers and of the research literature on written composition, I noted four basic composing strategies. These turned out to be not that dissimilar to the typifications employed by John Hayes and Linda Flower (1980). It was not my intention to use the questionnaire data to develop alternative or additional categories but rather to find out if these four common styles of composing behaviour seemed to be associated with any other attitudes or practices. The first four questions in the questionnaire simly asked writers to report how frequently they used each of the four strategies.

- *Architects* were defined as those who indicated frequent use of the 3-stage approach to writing (planning, writing and revising) who also indicated that their planning was mostly pre-planning.
- *Watercolourists* were defined as those who indicated frequent use of single drafts with minimal revision.
- *Oil Painters* were defined as those whose initial strategy was frequently that of writing down thoughts as they occur to them, organizing and revising them only later.
- *Bricklayers* were defined as those who frequently try to perfect each sentence before moving on to the next.

On this basis, of the 107 writers in the sample: 57 (53%) were Architects; 20 (19%) were Watercolourists; 33 (31%) were Oil Painters; and 38 (36%)

111

were Bricklayers. Only 15 writers (14%) were not frequent users of any of these strategies. The categories were not exclusive, of course: one writer reported frequent use of all four strategies, but 80 (75%) indicted frequent use of only one or two.

The use of a particular composing strategy is, of course, influenced by factors such as the nature, familiarity and complexity of the task, the text's stage of evolution, the time available and so on. However, there is evidence in the research literature to suggest that for many writers deeper preferences or habits (perhaps related to general cognitive styles) may also play a part. In particular, some writers seem to need to revise far more than others do: using writing as a way of thinking.

It is worth noting that although practitioners of one strategy are often intolerant of those who practice another, the reported use of each strategy (in this survey) by writers who publish regularly suggests that they are all potentially workable practices. They are described here in order of their prevalence in my sample.

The Architectural Strategy

The Architectural Strategy involves conscious pre-planning and organization and typically only limited drafting and reviewing. It is most unlike the Oil Painting Strategy. Although I have not uncovered a direct reference to the strategy as 'architectural' by writers who use it, Gertrude Stein does refer dismissively to writing which comes 'out of an architectural drawing of the thing you are doing' (Ghiselin, 1952). No such dismissiveness is of course intended here.

The novelist John Barth is a good example: 'I have a pretty good sense of where the book is going to go. By temperament I am an incorrigible formalist, not inclined to embark on a project without knowing where I am going.' Barth adds that 'I don't see how anybody starts a novel without knowing how it's going to end. I usually make detailed outlines: how many chapters it will be and so forth' (Winokur, 1988).

Analysis of the survey data suggests that several additional features may be associated with the use of the Architectural Strategy. The Architects were above all conscious strategists. Unlike the Bricklayers they showed a strong tendency to believe that they write better if they are concentrating on the topic rather than the way they are writing. And they showed a *very* strong tendency to think that it helps to leave writing and come back to it later. They showed up as less likely than others to correct as they write. They were also less likely to see writing as a way of thinking or to deny that the main reason they write is because they are expected to. This group would probably not gain much intrinsic satisfaction from writing. Unlike Watercolourists they showed some tendency to favour interlinear editing. Whilst most tended to prefer reviewing their word-processed texts on paper rather than on the screen, a substantial minority did not (unlike the Oil Painters). Unlike other word-processor users, they tended to report that they did *not* find the screen size restrictive (perhaps feeling less need to review their evolving texts).

The Bricklaying Strategy

The Bricklaying Strategy involves polishing each sentence before proceeding to the next. For writers who use only this strategy this usually means that there is only one draft which is not subjected to much revision. Those who employ it often refer to how different it is from the Watercolour Strategy, and it does seem most closely allied to the Architectural Strategy (in my sample 97% of the frequent Bricklayers were also frequent Architects). The American author William Zinnser (1983) himself uses the metaphor:

> I have to get every paragraph as nearly right as possible before I go onto the next paragraph. I'm somewhat like a bricklayer: I build very slowly, not adding a new row until I feel that the foundation is solid enough to hold up the house. I'm the exact opposite of the writer who dashes off his entire first draft, not caring how sloppy it looks or how badly it's written.

Patterns of approach associated with Bricklayers in the survey filled out the picture a little. Not unexpectedly, they tended to report that the correction of linguistic slips is done mainly as they write. They showed a tendency *not* to complete a draft in a single session, and a much weaker tendency than Architects to feel that it helps to leave a piece of writing and come back to it later. They reported usually having a clear idea of what they want to say and strongly disagree that thinking would be difficult without writing. In this they differ most clearly from the Oil Painters. They tended *not* to agree that the more they are concentrating on the topic rather than the way they are writing the better their writing is (in other words, the way they write matters to them more than with Architects).

Amongst their numbers one finds many of those who feel close to handwriting, and who prefer handwriting letters. Those in my sample tended *not* to use the word processor, but those who did were evenly divided over whether this encouraged them to improve the organization of their idea, (whereas others tended to deny this). They showed a strong tendency to find the screen size restrictive.

The Oil-Painting Strategy

The initial approach of Oil Painters involves jotting ideas down and organizing them later, reworking the text repeatedly. This is a strategy involving minimal pre-planning (quite unlike the Architectural Strategy). The novelist Kurt Vonnegut uses the metaphor in describing his own composing style:

> Usually I begin with several ideas, start playing with them. They are authentic concerns about things in life that bother me. One way of my dealing with them is in writing. I play with these ideas until they start to feel right. It's something like oil painting. You lay on paint and lay on paint. Suddenly you have something and you frame it ... It's like watching a teletype machine in a newspaper office to see what comes out.
>
> (Strickland, 1989)

Muriel Harris suggests that the first drafts of 'multi-drafters' tend to be 'writer-based' rather than 'reader-based': that is, primarily an aid to the writer's thinking rather than tailored to the needs of readers. Such writers tend to delete a large quantity of the text which they generate. They may also get lost in their evolving texts and have a strong need to re-read (Harris, 1989: 187).

In the survey, several other features were associated with those who used the Oil Painting Strategy. Many of my Oil Painters were in their 20s and 30s, and did not remember being given any guidance about how to approach composition. Nearly half of them were *not* conscious strategists. They were, of course, major revisers, often deleting a lot. They were much more likely than others to be interlinear editors, that is, to annotate drafts by adding further material between the existing lines of text. Very few of those who reported being frequent Oil Painters were also frequent Watercolourists. And frequent Oil Painters showed a clear tendency *not* to be frequent Bricklayers either.

Oil Painters who used the word processor were likely to report that they did more writing with the word processor. They showed an overwhelming tendency to review their text on a printout rather than on the screen and tended to find the screen size restrictive. Muriel Harris's comments on the Oil Painters' need to re-read may help to explain this.

The Watercolour Strategy

As in painting in watercolours, the Watercolour Strategy involves an attempt to produce a complete version relatively rapidly at the first attempt, with minimal revision. Such a precipitative approach (in contrast to writing which is more planned, and/or more extensively revised) is often associated with novice writers. Apart from inexperience, situational factors (such as deadlines or lack of motivation) can of course lead to the first draft being the final one. However, the Watercolour Strategy is also the preferred method of many accomplished writers. For literary writers this may reflect an attempt to retain 'spontaneity', 'truth to feeling', or descriptive accuracy. Other writers may simply feel a need to maintain momentum.

Some writers refer to complete texts being formed in the mind after a long period of mental 'incubation' or 'germination'. Others refer to 'unpremeditated' writing 'dictated' by an inner voice. Some writers stress the difference between this strategy and the Oil Painting Strategy. And in my survey only 4 of the frequent Watercolourists were also frequent Oil Painters.

Muriel Harris describes the preferences of 'one-drafters' for beginning with 'a developed focus', generating limited options prior to writing, settling quickly on a plan, making minimal changes to the text, and doing little re-reading. She also suggests that they tend to dislike writing (Harris, 1989). The American academic William Lutz seems a good example:

> Before I write, I write in my mind. The more difficult and complex the writing, the more time I need to think before I write. Ideas incubate in my mind. While I talk, drive, swim and exercise I am thinking, planning, writing. I think about the introduction, what examples to use, how to develop the main idea, what kind of conclusion to use. I write, revise, agonize, despair, give up, only to start all over again, and all of this before I ever begin to put words on paper ... Writing is not a process of discovery for me ... The writing process takes place in my mind. Once that process is complete the product emerges. Often I can write pages without pause and with very little, if any, revision or even minor changes.
>
> (Waldrep, 1985: I: 186–7)

For some writers the Watercolour Strategy is simply an initial strategy for producing a first draft; sometimes only for part of a text.

A few other features showed up in the survey as being associated with the use of the Watercolour Strategy. As one would expect, they reported correcting any slips mainly as they write and tended *not* to be interlinear editors. They were divided over whether it helps to leave a piece of writing and return to it later. And they also tended *not* to discuss work in progress.

Unfortunately, in this sample there were not enough Watercolourists who used word processors to show up statistically significant differences between them and other groups. However, for reference, we may consider all those issues relevant to the use of the word processor where significant differences between other groups arose and note the response patterns of the Watercolourists. Firstly, regarding frequency of use, only 8 of the 20 Watercolourists reported using a word processor frequently, 7 of those who did use the word processor reported that they did more writing with it than they had done before. They were fairly evenly divided over whether it led them to organise their ideas more effectively and whether the screen size is restrictive. As to whether they reviewed on a printout rather than on the screen, 7 reported doing so frequently, 1 sometimes and 4 rarely if ever (this follows the general pattern for most users).

Strategies and subject background

The association between strategies and subject background is shown in *Table 2* (note that writers may use more than one strategy). The main features here are that whilst the Architectural Strategy was most commonly

Table 2 Proportions of frequent users of strategies in each subject area

Use of strategies	ARTS (N = 31)		SOCIAL SCIENCE (N = 36)		SCIENCE (N = 40)	
Frequent ARCHITECTS	48%	15	44%	16	65%	26
Frequent WATERCOLOURISTS	23%	7	22%	8	13%	5
Frequent OIL PAINTERS	35%	11	36%	13	23%	9
Frequent BRICKLAYERS	39%	12	33%	12	35%	14

used in all subjects, the largest proportion of frequent users was in the sciences. We have already noted that the Watercolour Strategy is uncommon: it shows up here as the least frequently used in all subjects, but as particularly uncommon in the sciences, where the other uncommon strategy is Oil Painting. Those in the social sciences were fairly evenly split over use of the Bricklaying Strategy; those in the arts were also split, but showed some tendency *not* to use it.

The use of tools

Of the 107 writers in the sample: 39 were frequent users of the word processor but *not* of the pen or pencil; 31 were frequent users of both; and

---

Planners and Discoverers

In addition to the use of particular strategies, and any situational factors involved, writers' experiences of the use of tools may also be related to an underlying phenomenological orientation to the act of writing. At one end of a continuum, 'Discoverers' tend to see themselves as writing to find out what they want to say ('How do I know what I think until I see what I say?'). Their writing practices are characterized by extensive revision, as they try to get closer to what they mean. At the other end, 'Planners' tend to see writing primarily as the transcription of thoughts which they already have clear in their minds, sensing little dependence on writing as a way of thinking.

The difference is dramatic in the advice such writers offer to others. The 18th-century poet Matthew Prior advised:

Let him be kept from paper, pen and ink:
So may he cease to write, and learn to think.

But a Discoverer's advice is: 'Don't think and then write it down. Think on paper' (Harry Kemelman, in Winokur).

Extreme Discoverers may tend to prefer the Oil Painting Strategy, and extreme Planners may have a general preference for the Architectural Strategy or one of the others. Some Discoverers may also have a particular attachment to the use of the pen or pencil, which is often experienced as allowing the act of writing to be more 'physical', 'direct' and 'intimate' – a kind of 'bodily thinking'. Iris Murdoch dismissed the word processor because she felt that it 'separates one from one's thoughts and gives them a premature air of completeness' (Hammond, 1984). Discoverers who *do* use the word processor may feel a need to revert to handwriting at key stages of their writing.

Of course, many writers occupy the middle ground, being conscious that their writing involves both intuitive discovery and conscious planning. And particular tasks may feature one far more than the other. But gravitation towards the poles reflects the *value* which this dimension has for individuals, and reveals a basic orientation towards the experience of writing. It is a chicken-and-egg question whether this is simply a reflection of the kind of writing they do most, or whether it is what leads to them to do this. It is probably both.

---

33 were frequent users of the pen or pencil but *not* of the word processor. Only 4 were frequent users of the typewriter: 2 of these combined this with frequent use of the pen or pencil. Of the 4 who reported frequently using dictation, 3 combined this with frequent use of the word processor, and 2 with frequent use of the pen or pencil.

Table 3 shows the use of tools by the various strategists. From this data we can note in particular that the word processor was most frequently

Table 3 Frequent users of each tool as percentages of frequent users of each strategy

Tools used frequently	Architects (N = 57)		Water-colourists (N = 20)		Oil-Painters (N = 33)		Bricklayers (N = 38)	
Pen/Pencil	65%	37	70%	14	64%	21	63%	24
Dictation	4%	2	10%	2	3%	1		0
Typewriter	4%	2		0	3%	1		0
Word Processor	58%	33	40%	8	79%	26	45%	17

used by Oil Painters and least by Watercolourists. Nearly twice as large a proportion of Oil Painters as of Watercolourists reported frequent use of the word processor. And the largest proportion of frequent users of the pen or pencil was found amongst the Watercolourists. Further analysis of the survey data shows more clearly the Watercolourists (and to a lesser extent Bricklayers) tend to favour handwriting rather than the word processor, whilst Architects and Oil Painters tend to favour combining the frequent use of both handwriting and the word processor.

In this sample, attitudes to the usefulness of the word processor seemed to be more closely associated with factors other than with experience or frequency of use. One such factor is subject background (35% of social scientists and 25% of arts writers experience problems in comparing one word-processed draft with another). Far more important in attitudes to the use of the tool, however, were the strategies used, as we see most clearly when we consider the issue of the restrictiveness of the word processor screen. Bricklayers showed a tendency *not* to be frequent users of the word processor, but those who did use it showed a strong tendency to find the screen restrictive. Oil Painters also showed a tendency to experience this, despite the fact that a larger proportion of these writers than of others were frequent word-processor users. Watercolourists were evenly divided over this issue, and Architects showed a very strong tendency *not* to find the screen size restrictive. It would appear that Bricklayers and Oil Painters are more likely to experience such difficulties with the word processor than are Architects or Watercolourists. A cautionary note is required here since the range of screen sizes used varied, and the subjects involved were too small for checking how far a sense of restriction was related to physically smaller screens. However, evidence of differences amongst writers regarding a general sense of restrictiveness in using a screen has also been found in research by Christina Haas (1989) and by

Lillian Bridwell and her associates (1985). There does, therefore, seem to be some relationship between the usual composing styles of writers and the extent to which they feel comfortable in using particular writing tools.

References

Bridwell, L.S., G. Sirc, & R. Brooke. 1985. 'Revising and Computing: Case Studies of Student Writers', in S. W. Freedman, ed., *The Acquisition of Written Language*, Norwood, NJ: Ablex.

Ghiselin, B., ed. 1952. *The Creative Process: A Symposium*. Berkeley: University of California Press.

Haas, C. 1989. ' "Seeing it on the Screen Isn't Really Seeing It": Computer Writers' Reading Problems', in G.E. Hawisher & C.L. Selfe, eds, *Critical Perspectives on Computers and Composition Instruction*. New York: Teachers College Press.

Hammond, R. 1984. *The Writer and the Word Processor*. London: Coronet/Hodder & Stoughton.

Harris, M. 1989. 'Composing Behaviour of One- and Multi-Draft Writers', *College English* 51(2): 174–191.

Hayes, J.R. & L.S. Flower. 1980. 'Identifying the Organization of Writing Processes', in L.W. Gregg & E.R. Steinberg, eds, *Cognitive Processes in Writing*. Hillsdale, NJ: Lawrence Erlbaum.

Strickland, B., ed. 1989. *On Being a Writer*. Cincinnati, OH: Writer's Digest.

Waldrep, T., ed. 1985. *Writers on Writing* (2 Vols). New York: Random House.

Winokur, J., ed. 1988. *Writers on Writing*. London: Headline.

Zinnser, W. 1983. *Writing with a Word Processor*. New York: Harper & Row.

49

WHAT DO CHILDREN THINK ABOUT WRITING?

David Wray

Source: *Educational Review* (1993) 45(1):67–77

Since the pioneering work of Jesse Reid (1966) and John Downing (1970) a great deal of research has been carried out into childrens' perceptions of reading and the reading process (see Johns, 1986 for a review). Building upon Downing's 1979 'cognitive clarity' theory, it has emerged that not only are children's perceptions of reading linked in some way with their abilities in the activity (i.e. good readers tend to think of reading as a rather different process than poor readers (Johns, 1974; Schneckner, 1976)), but there is also evidence that children's perceptions of the reading process are linked to the strategies they use to approach it (Medwell, 1990). Perhaps unsurprisingly, however, this research interest in children's perceptions of reading has not been matched by interest in their perceptions of writing. This is largely explained by the general paucity of research in the writing area, which has only recently begun to attract serious interest from the research community. There certainly appears to be a need for further investigations, both small and large scale, into the perceptions and attitudes which primary children have towards an activity which, after all, seems to take up the lion's share of their attention at school. Research in progress at the University of Exeter (Wray, 1990; Medwell, 1991) is beginning to suggest that the complete environment for writing which primary teachers try to provide for their pupils is filtered through these pupils' perceptions of what they are doing when they write. Thus to understand, and perhaps improve, the context of classroom writing, it is necessary to understand pupils' perceptions. This line of thought also follows from an application of the insight of Edwards & Mercer (1987) that context itself is a socially constructed, mentalistic notion.

This article will, after reviewing the small number of relevant studies already available in this area, outline in greater detail a study recently carried out in conjunction with a group of teacher education students at the University of Exeter, which provided information about the perceptions of writing held by primary children of various ages.

Perceptions of writing: research evidence

The most substantial source of information about children's perceptions of writing is that provided during the course of the National Writing Project, and detailed in one of the several volumes finally published by this project (National Writing Project, 1990). Finding out what their pupils thought about writing emerged as a major concern for many of the teachers involved in the project and, to judge from the project's publications, especially its newsletter, the insights gained as a result of this concern were among the more influential in affecting the views about writing of these teachers. The evidence provided by the project is, however, problematic. Much of it is anecdotal and not gained under very controlled conditions, and, while this is not a difficulty when the investigations it comes from are perceived as largely awareness-enhancers for the teachers carrying them out, it does make it difficult to accept the evidence as fully indicative of a general picture.

This reservation notwithstanding, the surveys carried out under the auspices of the project did seem to reveal a fairly general picture of perceptions of writing. This is summarised in one of the project publications (NWP, 1990, p. 19) as a list of concerns identified by teachers:

- Children often judge the success of their writing by its neatness, spelling and punctuation rather than by the message it conveys.
- Children often have difficulty in talking about their own development as writers except in very broad terms.
- Children see writers as people who publish books (usually stories); writing is thus thought about in terms of end products.
- Writing is often seen as a school activity whose primary purpose is to show teachers what has been learned.
- Writing is seen as an individual activity; ideas for writing are rarely discussed and outcomes rarely shared with others.
- Writing, talking and reading are not always clearly associated with each other.

These children were therefore apparently much more concerned with writing as a product than as a process, and as such their attention seemed to concentrate upon the appearance of that product, i.e. its technical features such as spelling and punctuation. This attention to product is not terribly surprising, of course. It is only in the last decade or so that educational researchers, stimulated by the pioneering work of Emig (1971) and Graves (1973), have begun to investigate the writing process, and teachers similarly have traditionally given much more attention to writing products than to processes.

This primary attention to technical features is seen again in the results of a survey in West Cumbria primary schools reported in Martin, Waters

& Bloom (1989). A group of 429 11-year-old children were asked. "What is the first thing your teacher looks for when you hand in a piece of writing, such as a story?" The replies were as follows:

Handwriting, neatness, presentation	42.2%
Spelling	25.4%
Punctuation and grammar	15.8%
Whether it makes sense and style	6.1%
Content	5.2%
Effort	0.9%
Length	0.6%
Planning	0.3%

The emphasis on writing as a product is very noticeable but what is even more remarkable is the extreme concern (over 80% of replies) with what are referred to in the National Curriculum documents as 'secretarial skills' (DES, 1989). It is true, however, that the phrasing of the initial question in this study is such that it naturally focuses attention upon an end-product. When teachers look at completed pieces of writing, it must be difficult for children to realise that they might bear in mind the process by which this writing was produced. Also, of course, this question, and hence this study, are explicitly enquiring into what children think their teachers think about writing. This may not coincide with what the children themselves think about it.

The small-scale survey reported by Tamburrini, Willig & Butler (1984) of the perceptions of writing of 10- and 11-year-old children presents a less one-sided picture. These children were asked why they wrote stories, poems and project work in class. The responses were varied. In the case of stories, over half the sample mentioned 'developing the imagination' as the reason for the writing while a similar proportion mentioned learning skills such as spelling and handwriting. For poetry a quarter mentioned learning skills as its purpose, while over half could think of no purpose at all. As for project work, over three-quarters gave learning facts as the purpose, which does suggest a greater realisation of writing functions.

American research into this area, however, tends to confirm the picture of children preoccupied with secretarial aspects and writing products. Hogan (1980) surveyed 13,000 children aged between 8 and 14 and found that children's interest in writing appeared to decline as they got older. A similar picture emerged in the report of the National Assessment of Educational Progress (1980) with the number of children who said they enjoyed writing dropping by half between the ages of 9 and 13. Shook, Marrion & Ollila (1989) suggest a possible explanation for this is that "Students may be sacrificing self-expression while being hopelessly tangled in mechanics, because educators have unwittingly trivialised writing" (p. 133).

Shook *et al.* (1989) surveyed the concepts of writing held by over 100 children aged between six and eight. The children were asked questions relating to three general categories: their perceptions of the general purpose for writing, their personal preferences about writing, and their self-concepts as writers. The results indicated that:

- the children understood the communicative nature of writing and perceived that it was an important activity in the world outside school;
- most children reported doing more writing at home than at school and getting more help with their writing from people at home than from their teachers;
- most saw themselves as needing more practice, better equipment or neater printing in order to become better writers, i.e. mechanical aspects;
- over three-quarters, when asked why they wrote at school, responded with reasons relating to mechanical aspects, such as to learn more words and letters, to practise, because teacher says so. Only a fifth said they wrote because it was fun.

The researchers conclude, among other things, that their survey suggests a difference between children's experiences of writing at home and at school in terms of ownership. At home the children set their own purposes for writing and sought help in meeting these purposes: purposes and help both relating to writing as a means of communicating meaning. At school children tended to write because their teachers told them to and were therefore in danger of losing a sense of ownership of their writing. Following from this they tended to become concerned about aspects other than communication and the mechanics of writing began to loom larger as objects for attention.

A survey of primary children's thoughts about writing

Because of the scarcity of hard evidence concerning primary children's views about writing a study was conducted with the assistance of a group of students engaged in a Postgraduate Certificate of Education course at the University of Exeter. Each student collected written comments about writing from up to 10 children, aged between 7 and 11 years. From a group of 58 students, writing from 475 children was collected, made up as follows: Group 1, aged 7/8, 112 pieces of which 90 were useful; Group 2, aged 8/9, 105 pieces (93); Group 3, aged 9/10, 141 pieces (140); and Group 4, aged 10/11, 117 pieces (117).

In carrying out the study the first important decision to be made concerned the exact nature of the task which would be given to the children. Simply to ask them "What do you think about writing in school?" did not seem adequate for a number of reasons. Firstly, this question is fairly abstract in nature and it would therefore be difficult for them to give meaningful responses. Secondly, because the people asking these children the questions were at the time involved in teaching them, there was a danger that children would tend to tailor their responses to fit what they believed these teachers wished to hear, a not uncommon problem in teacher research. Thirdly, it was felt that asking the question in as open-ended a way as this may lead to a rather amorphous set of replies, whereas what was really needed was to tap into what these children considered the most important aspects of writing in their classes.

With these considerations in mind, it was decided to frame the task in a more concrete way. This was done by using a modified form of the task used in the International Study of Written Composition (Bauer & Purves, 1988) partly to assess the opinions about writing of students at or near the end of compulsory schooling in 14 different countries. The results of the British part of this study have been published (Gubb, Gorman & Price, 1987) and provide an interesting comparison with those from the present study, as will be discussed later. In the international study the task was phrased as follows: *Write a letter of advice to a student two years younger than you who is planning to attend your school and who has asked you to tell them how to write a composition that will be considered good by teachers in your school. Write a friendly letter and describe in it at least five specific hints as to what you think teachers in your school find important when they judge compositions.*

With somewhat younger children, the task in the present study was phrased as: *Someone in the class below yours has asked you what the writing will be like when he/she comes into your class. Write and tell him/her, and try to give him/her some useful advice about what he/she will have to do to do good writing in your class.*

All the children in the study were given the task in more or less these words, and their subsequent writing collected. In terms of producing extended statements from these children the task seemed to work very well, with only 35 pieces, mainly from the younger two age groups, being too short to give any useful information.

Results: a first look

The results of the study can be approached in either a quantitative or a qualitative way, with both giving useful information. A straight count of the features of writing mentioned by all the children in the study is given in Table I. Spelling, the most frequently mentioned feature, would usually be referred to by phrases such as, "Make sure you get your spellings right", or "Use a dictionary to spell words you don't know". Neatness would be referred to by things like, "Do your best handwriting" or "Make

Table I Total mentions (*n*) and % mentions of particular writing features

Feature	%	n
Spelling	19.88	(579)
Neatness	17.27	(503)
Length	12.77	(372)
Punctuation	10.71	(312)
Tools	5.49	(160)
Layout	1.58	(46)
Words	7.31	(213)
Ideas	12.33	(359)
Structure	4.53	(132)
Characters	3.43	(100)
Style	2.06	(60)
Secretarial	67.72	(1972)
Composition	29.67	(864)

sure it is not messy". Many children stressed that the writing had to be "long enough", although a significant number warned not to make it too long "because Miss might get bored". Both types of comment are included under Length. Under Punctuation are included mentions of the need for full stops and capital letters, commas and speech marks. The feature Tools refers to the surprisingly frequent mention of the materials with which to write, such as "make sure your pencil is sharp", or "Mr Ellis gets cross if you do not use a ruler to underline the title", while under Layout are included references to the drawing of a margin or the placing of the date, etc. Some children referred to the importance of Words as, for example, in "Don't use the same word over and over again", while others referred to Ideas as in "Try to have some funny bits", or "Stories should be interesting and exciting". A few mentioned Structure, as, for example, in "A story needs a beginning, a middle and an end", a few Characters, as in "Write about interesting people", and even fewer Style, as in "In poems you can repeat words to make it sound good", or "Don't begin sentences with 'and' ".

The figures under the heading Secretarial in the table are derived from adding those under Spelling, Neatness, Length, Punctuation, Tools and Layout, while those under Composition from the adding of Words, Ideas, Structure, Characters and Style. These give an idea of the balance of these children's preoccupations in writing.

In interpreting this table, the first thing to state is the problematic nature of the methods of enquiry. Although the task the children were asked to do is less abstract than the straight-forward question "What is writing?", it is still impossible to assume that the children's answers reflected entirely their real concepts about writing. The methodological problems involved in trying to tap children's concepts about such 'taken for granted' activities as writing are significant. It is quite possible that the children's statements reflect not what they really think about writing, but what they think their teacher wants them to think. Even at this level, however, the results may tell a good deal about what counts as important in writing in these children's classrooms, about which children are usually most perceptive.

These results, taken at face value, show an overwhelming preoccupation with the secretarial aspects of writing. Spelling is the most frequently mentioned feature followed quite closely by neatness. Features such as characters and style are barely mentioned at all. This seems like powerful confirmation of the trend noted in other research studies and suggests that, somehow or other, these children have gained the impression that what really matters in the writing they do in their classrooms are the technical aspects. This is confirmed by looking in detail at one or two of the pieces of writing produced.

The following two pieces were both produced by nine-year-olds, from different classrooms, and are reproduced in typed form (with original spellings and punctuation).

Piece 1
1   at the start of a sentence you have to put a capital letter.
2   if you are writing names you put a capital letter as well.
3   and in youre story book you do youre bets writing.
4   at the end of a sentence you put a full stop.
5   you have to write to tell storys and to tell peaple whate you have been doing
6   you can lern how to do joined-up writing like *abcdefghijklmnopqrstuvwxyz*.

Piece 2
first you put your pencle down and coppey a letter what someone put down like you are darwing
make your big letters go up to the line above.
put capitals letters at the bigan of centens and full stop at the end.
get on with your work, if you doing a story's don't let it cary on to long.
don't make to much smches and used rubbers to much
do your comers and speach mark's
do your marging
and *don't* wander about.

Here the children's major preoccupations are clearly with secretarial features. Composition barely figures at all. In Piece 2 it is almost possible

Table II Mentions of particular writing features by each age group (%)

Features	Group 1 %	Group 2 %	Group 3 %	Group 4 %
Spelling	22.99	21.56	20.56	16.43
Neatness	18.58	21.89	17.87	13.00
Length	14.56	11.44	15.89	9.77
Punctuation	13.22	10.45	9.46	10.63
Tools	7.47	12.77	5.14	
Layout	3.07	2.82	1.17	0.32
Words	6.90	4.64	6.78	9.77
Ideas	8.43	8.96	12.73	16.33
Structure	1.15	1.99	4.79	7.84
Characters		1.49	2.34	7.63
Style			0.82	5.69
Secretarial	79.89	80.93	70.09	50.16
Composition	16.48	17.08	27.45	47.26

to hear the voice of this child's teacher, which in many ways is the chief message from this study. Whatever these children 'really' think about writing, what they have expressed are their feelings about what counts as being successful at writing in their classrooms and this, of course, is largely defined by their teachers.

Results: a more detailed look

These results seem rather an indictment of the approach to writing adopted in the classrooms from which these children were drawn. In a situation in which the assessment procedures for the National Curriculum in English place a 70% weighting on the compositional aspects of writing and only 30% on the secretarial, it seems ironic that these children's views are almost an exact reversal of these weightings. The results, however, repay a more careful look. Because the writing samples came from children in four distinct age groups, it is possible to break down the results by age. This breakdown is shown in Table II. The results now suggest a rather different picture. It seems that in Groups 1 and 2 (first and second year junior children) there was an overwhelming emphasis upon secretarial aspects, but that this imbalance lessened with the older children and Group 4 (top juniors) actually showed a balance of preoccupations. It is apparent that the concern with Spelling gradually lessened over the four groups, while that with Ideas gradually increased. Changes in prominence of these two features can be clearly seen in Fig 1.

To give detail to this shift of emphasis it is useful to compare the pieces

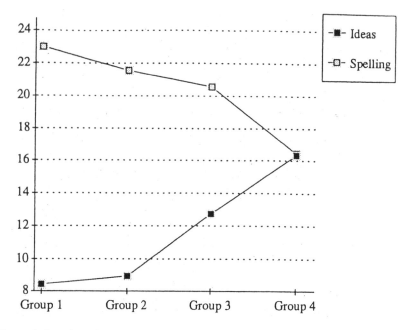

Figure 1 Graph to show the % mentions of Ideas and Spelling of the four groups.

of writing given earlier with the following piece which came from a 10-year-old girl and was, incidentally, the longest pieces of writing produced in the study.

Piece 3

In the junior class when writing it is better to express your words such as, instead of saying I saw a pretty flower, put, I saw a beautiful flower that blew from side to side in the wind. In the juniors we normally write adventure or fantasy storys about witches and wizards. When you get old enough you will be able to use big words, instead of little, very small, instead of big, enormouse. And it is a good idea before you get to old to try and write neatly joined up, it is good for letters when you are older, and may come in handy if you want to be a secretary. Example: the wind blew – > *The wind blew strongly.* When you around 2nd or third year it is old enough for you to start looking in the dictionary for to express your words, as I said at the begining. It is old enough for you to stop going to the teacher and asking for words. And a few hints for people who are just starting the juniors: If you are stuck on a word, carry on writing, write what you think instead of getting up 30 times when writing a story, let the teacher correct them when

you have finished, and if stuck on a word when reading, sound the
letters out one by one. It is fun writing in the juniors.

This piece is characterised by the very balanced views about writing
which it expresses. It certainly mentions secretarial features but these are
set firmly into an overall impression of the primacy of composition. It
begins by mentioning ideas and expression but goes on to give excellent
advice about spelling which some teachers of lower juniors would be very
grateful if their children heeded.

The results from the British (NFER) part of the international study of
writing mentioned earlier (Gubb *et al.*, 1987) provide an interesting extra
piece of evidence for the developmental trend which seems to have
emerged from the present study. In asking 15-year-olds to write some
advice about writing for younger children, the NFER study found that
40% of the responses (mentions) concerned Presentation and 58% concerned aspects of composition, including Organisation, Content, Process,
Style and Tone and Audience. The balance between Composition and
Secretarial aspects for the NFER study and each of the four groups in the
present study is shown in the graph in Fig. 2. The developmental trend
seems clear.

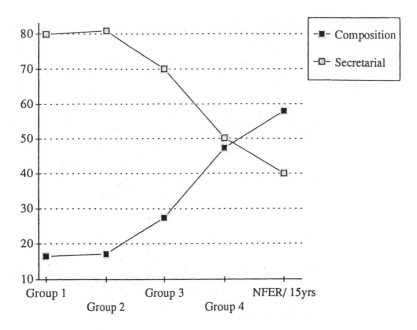

Figure 2 Graph to show the % mentions of secretarial and compositional features
of writing of Groups 1 to 4 in the present study and the 15-year-olds in
the NFER study.

Towards an explanation

Breaking down the results in this way highlights a possible developmental trend in children's views about writing. It also suggests that the simple explanation advanced earlier for the results, that is that these children have learnt what their teachers have taught them about writing and what has been taught them is a preoccupation with the technical skills, may be over harsh and over simple.

An alternative explanation might be that these children, in their advice about writing, mentioned more readily the aspects which were particularly bothering them at the time. As an aspect became less bothersome, that is, they felt they could *do it*, they mentioned it less. There is plenty of support in the results of this study for this explanation. In, for example, the dimensions of Neatness and Tools, there is a significant peaking in terms of the proportion of mentions in Group 2 (second year juniors). From personal experience it is at this age that children often get asked to change from using pencil to using pens to write with, and also are taught to produce cursive (joined up) handwriting. Concern with these aspects virtually fades in Group 4 (fourth year juniors) by which age most children have mastered both the new writing tools and the new writing style.

In the dimension of Characters there is a sudden peaking of mention in Group 4. This coincides with the argument of Fox (1990) that it is around the age of 10 years that children begin to be able to get beyond the stereotypical 'goody' and 'baddy' type characters who are described more in terms of action than in terms of inner thoughts and feelings. Similarly in the dimensions of Structure and Style there is quite a peak of attention in Group 4. This would fit with Perera's assertion (1984) that children around 10 years old begin to be able to differentiate more clearly writing from speech in terms of structure and style. The pattern of mentions in these dimensions supports a suggestion that children focus upon certain elements in their descriptions of writing because they are at that time actively engaging with these elements in their doing of writing.

If this explanation is accepted it may also help to shed light upon an issue which has occasioned fierce debate in the literature on literacy development. The cognitive clarity/confusion theory of Downing, mentioned at the beginning of this article has been seriously challenged by researchers working from an emergent literacy perspective (Hall, 1987; Harste, Woodward & Burke, 1984) who have argued that young children, brought up into a literate society, were not at all confused about the functions of literacy within this society. Yet studies of children at school have consistently shown, both in the reading and writing areas, that these children tend to have very particular, and limited, views about the processes of literacy. In reading this emerges as an over-concern with decoding and in writing, as described earlier, as a concentration on the secretarial skills. The results of this present study suggest that these views might gain prominence in children's descriptions of literacy processes because, at a particular stage of development, these are the areas which seem difficult to the children. It may be that children before the age of about five or six do not include in their descriptions of literacy references to the technical aspects (letters and sounds in reading; spelling and handwriting in writing) because they are not aware that these are problematic. When they *do* become aware that these things are difficult, they come to the forefront of children's attention and hence get mentioned most in their descriptions of the processes. Later, when the technical aspects become mastered and therefore less of a problem, mention of them fades in these descriptions.

Conclusion

This article, in reporting what was initially conceived as a rather simple study to try to produce a little more evidence about an under-researched phenomenon, has suggested that the issues uncovered in the study are anything but simple. In putting forward a possible alternative explanation for the seeming prevalence of rather limited concepts about writing in junior school children it has suggested a need to question the 'obvious' explanation, that is, that children simply respond to their teachers' over-emphasis upon the technical aspects of writing. This is not to deny, of course, that this might partially explain what children think about writing. But teachers may only be drawing attention to what would be foremost in children's minds anyway. If this is true, it suggests a real challenge to teachers of junior children.

These teachers clearly do have to ensure that children master the technical aspects of writing and, therefore, must give these some attention in their teaching. The challenge is to make sure that this attention does not lead to the children in their care thinking that these aspects are *all* they have to think about in writing. When children, because of the nature of their path towards learning to be writers, are focusing themselves upon the technical aspects, it could be vital for teachers to help them bear in mind the other, arguably more important, dimensions to the writing process.

References

BAUER, B. & PURVES, A. (1988) A letter about success in writing, in: T. GORMAN, A. PURVES & R. DEGENHART (Eds) *The IEA Study of Written Composition 1: The International Writing Tasks and Scoring Scales* (Oxford, Pergamon Press).

DEPARTMENT OF EDUCATION AND SCIENCE (1989) *English in the National Curriculum* (London, HMSO).

DOWNING, J. (1970) Children's concepts of language in learning to read, *Educational Research*, 12, pp. 106–112.

DOWNING, J. (1979) *Reading and Reasoning* (Edinburgh, Chambers).

EDWARDS, D. & MERCER, N. (1987) *Common Knowledge: The Development of Understanding in the Classroom* (London, Methuen).

EMIG, J. (1971) *The Composing Processes of Twelfth Graders* (Urbana, Ill., National Council of Teachers of English).

FOX, R. (1990) How characters become persons: the development of characterisation in children's writing, in: D. WRAY (Ed.) *Emerging Partnerships: Current Research in Language and Literacy* (Clevedon, Multilingual Matters).

GRAVES, D. (1973) *A study of the writing processes of seven year old children.* Unpublished Doctoral dissertation. State University of New York at Buffalo.

GUBB, J., GORMAN, T. & PRICE, E. (1987) *The Study of Written Composition in England and Wales* (Windsor, NFER-Nelson).

HALL, N. (1987) *The Emergence of Literacy* (Sevenoaks, Hodder & Stoughton).

HARSTE, J., WOODWARD, V. & BURKE, C. (1984) *Language Stories and Literacy Lessons* (Portsmouth, New Hampshire, Heinemann).

HOGAN, T. (1980) Students' interests in writing activities, *Research in the Teaching of English*, 14(2), pp. 119–126.

JOHNS, J. (1974) Concepts of reading among good and poor readers, *Education*, 95, pp. 58–60.

JOHNS, J. (1986) Students' perceptions of reading; thirty years of enquiry, in: D. YADEN & S. TEMPLETON (Eds) *Metalinguistic Awareness and Beginning Literacy* (Portsmouth, New Hampshire, Heinemann).

MARTIN, T., WATERS, M. & BLOOM, W. (1989) *Managing Writing* (London, Mary Glasgow).

MEDWELL, J. (1990) *An investigation of the relationship between perceptions of the reading process and reading strategies of eight year old children.* Unpublished M.Ed. Dissertation, University of Wales.

MEDWELL, J. (1991) *Contexts for Writing.* Paper presented at the European Conference on Reading. Edinburgh.

NATIONAL ASSESSMENT OF EDUCATIONAL PROGRESS (1980) *Writing Achievement 1969–79. Results from the third national writing assessment, Vol. 111: 9 year olds* (Denver, Colorado, National Assessment of Educational Progress).

NATIONAL WRITING PROJECT (1990) *Perceptions of Writing* (Edinburgh, Nelson).

PERERA, K. (1984) *Children's Reading and Writing* (London, Blackwell).

REID, J. (1966) Learning to think about reading. *Educational Research*, 9, pp. 56–62.

SCHNECKNER, P. (1976) *The concepts of reading of selected first and third grade children and the relation of these concepts to the children's intelligence and reading achievement.* Unpublished doctoral dissertation, University of North Colorado.

SHOOK, S., MARRION, L. & OLLILA, L. (1989) Primary children's concepts about writing, *Journal of Educational Research*, 82(3), pp. 133–138.

TAMBURRINI, J., WILLIG, J. & BUTLER, C. (1984) Children's conceptions of writing, in: H. COWIE (Ed.) *The Development of Children's Imaginative Writing* (London, Croom Helm).

WRAY, D. (1990) *Theoretical insights into contexts for writing.* Paper presented at the 1990 World Congress on Reading. Stockholm.

132

50

RESEARCH ON THE COMPOSING PROCESS*

Ann Hume

Source: *Review of Educational Research* (1983) 53(2): 201–216

Researchers have long been more interested in students' ability to read than in their ability to write. Recently, however, the research community has finally turned its attention to writing. Although the amount of writing research is still relatively meager, it has, during the past few years, vastly increased knowledge of the composing process. Furthermore, writing research has undergone a transformation: Research techniques have expanded beyond the classical experimental paradigm. Now other methods are also considered appropriate for investigating the cognitive processes involved in composing texts.

This paper first discusses methodologies employed in recent research on the composing process. It then presents results of that research in terms of the process and subprocesses of writing. It closes by discussing limitations of the methodologies and conclusions about the results.

Methodology

Compared with what is known about human perception activities, relatively little is understood about human production activities such as writing (Gould, 1980). This lack of knowledge results partially from a corresponding lack of valid and reliable strategies and methodologies for studying production tasks.

Until the last decade, the methodology was dominated by the experimental method, which emphasizes what is quantifiable. Consequently, research focused on measurable aspects of written products rather than on the elusive behavior of the producers of those products. Recently, however, research interest in the cognitive processes of writers has burgeoned (Emig, 1982). Now the research methodologies include laboratory case studies of the composing process, naturalistic studies, quasi-product studies that interpret results in terms of process, and studies that use unique procedures. These studies are the focus of this paper.

Case studies

The roots of laboratory case studies of the composing process are usually traced to the seminal work of Janet Emig (1971). Emig studied the composing processes of eight high school seniors, selected by their teachers as good writers. The subjects met four times with the investigator and composed orally while composing on paper. Emig observed them during their writing, making notes and recording the oral composing. All eight subjects were interviewed also.

Subjects of laboratory case studies vary in number from 1 (e.g., Mischel, 1974) to 84 (e.g., Van Bruggen, 1946). However, following Emig's model, researchers generally limit their subjects to fewer than 20 because of the complexities of data collection and analysis. Subjects most frequently compose alone in a writing area theoretically free from distraction (e.g., Matsuhashi, 1981; Perl, 1979). These subjects occasionally have been elementary students (e.g., Sawkins, 1975) or junior high students (e.g., Van Bruggen, 1946), but more often they are high school students (e.g., Emig, 1971; Matsuhashi, 1981; Mischel, 1974; Stallard, 1974), college students (e.g., Flower & Hayes, 1981b; Perl, 1979), or experienced adults (e.g., Gould, 1980). Sometimes experts and relatively inexperienced writers are compared (e.g., Flower & Hayes, 1981b; Gould, 1980).

In some studies, the researcher is in the same room with the writer, observing within the writer's view (e.g., Emig, 1971) or through a one-way screen (e.g., Van Bruggen, 1946). In other studies, the researcher observes outside the room on a videotape monitor (e.g., Matsuhashi, 1981).

Researchers make notes about the writer's behavior during composing (e.g., Emig, 1971; Matsuhashi, 1981; Perl, 1979), recording such activities as energetic spurts of writing or revising. These notes often guide interviews with the writers to stimulate their memories of the reasons for a particular composing behavior (e.g., Pianko, 1979). Interviews usually take place immediately after composing so that subjects can give accurate information (e.g., Pianko, 1979; Stallard, 1974), and often include questions about subjects' writing activities and attitudes toward writing (e.g., Emig, 1971; Pianko, 1979).

Some researchers either assign or let writers select topics ahead of time, encouraging subjects to rehearse and plan (e.g., Emig, 1971; Matsuhashi, 1981; Sommers, 1980). Other researchers assign topics at the time subjects are to write, so these writers are unable to prepare for composing (e.g., Flower & Hayes, 1981b; Gould, 1980).

Several researchers time behaviors such as reading and revising (e.g., Glassner, 1980; Matsuhashi, 1981; Perl, 1979; Pianko, 1979). Another behavior frequently investigated by timing methods is the pause phenomenon. Writers' pauses comprise an important area for composing-process research, because pausing consumes more than half the writer's composing time (e.g., Gould, 1980; Matsuhashi, 1981).

Some researchers examine the lengths of pauses between individual words, syntactic structures, or units of meaning (e.g., Flower & Hayes, 1981b; Matsuhashi, 1981). Others investigate the total length of time that writers pause while composing a whole piece of discourse (e.g., Gould, 1980). Researchers claim that

> the *lengths* of pauses ... and their location in the text ... provide a temporal taxonomy or description of the real-time aspects of written language production from which inferences about planning and decision-making can be made.
>
> (Matsuhashi, 1981, p. 114)

Still other case studies require subjects to talk while composing. Some subjects say only the words that they are writing (e.g., Emig, 1971), and others report on what they are thinking (e.g., Berkenkotter, 1982; Flower & Hayes, 1981b). This oral composing is tape-recorded. The audio recordings (and, when available, concomitant video recordings; e.g., Flower & Hayes, 1981b) are often subjected to protocol analysis, which, according to cognitive psychologists, is a powerful tool for identifying psychological processes (Flower & Hayes, 1980a).

A protocol is a detailed, time-ordered record of a subject's writing behavior, including a transcript of the tape-recording of the writer's verbalizing during composing, as well as all the written material he or she produces (Flower & Hayes, 1980a). For a protocol, "subjects are asked to say aloud everything they think and everything that occurs to them while performing the task" (Hayes & Flower, 1980, p. 4). In analyzing protocols, the researcher infers the underlying psychological processes by which the subject performs the task (Hayes & Flower, 1980). Writing processes are "identified by matching the verbal protocol word for word with the writer's notes and text" (p. 21).

The works of Flower and Hayes and of Perl are particularly significant for their contributions to protocol analysis. Flower and Hayes (1980a) have collected and analyzed many protocols in recent years. They report that a typical protocol from a 1-hour session includes 4–5 pages of a writer's notes and text as well as a 15-page manuscript typed from the tape recording. Perl's (1979) major contribution is an elaborate, effective coding system for protocol analysis. The system divides writers' behavior into 16 major categories and 15 subcategories. The coding system is complemented by Perl's numbering system for a time line, which allows her to measure the time of each writing behavior.

A far less complex protocol technique is used by Bridwell, who calls her procedure "the poor woman's protocol analysis" (Bridwell, 1981b). Bridwell asks writers to make notes, in the margins of their compositions, on what they are thinking about as they compose.

135

Naturalistic studies

In sharp contrast to studies dealing with subjects who compose in a laboratory, naturalistic studies take place within the subject's usual setting for
writing, whether that setting is the professional writer's context for composing (Berkenkotter, 1982) or the classroom (e.g., Edelsberg, 1981;
Graves, in Gentry, 1980a). In most naturalistic studies, the investigator is a
participant-observer.

In the study of one professional writer (Berkenkotter, 1982), the subject
composed in his usual environment for writing, making no adjustments in
writing time, topic, or procedures. The investigator collected data on his
behavior, analyzed his notes and texts, and talked with him about his
processes.[1]

Classroom studies are designated as participant-observer studies
(Edelsberg, 1981; Emig, 1982). In these studies, the investigator functions
within a classroom, where he or she records the events occurring in that
setting. The participant-observer may also assist the teacher and/or the
students.

A typical and the most famous participant-observer research project is
the 2-year study by Donald Graves (in Gentry, 1980a). In the Graves
project, children were observed before, during, and after writing episodes,
and the researchers kept detailed records of the students' writing process.
Some of the writing episodes were also videotaped. During videotaping,
the student writer wore a small microphone so that the researchers could
capture any vocal or subvocal behavior. Narratives reporting the behavior
of the young writers in the Graves project provide a rich source of data on
the composing process.

Quasi-product studies

Quasi-product studies provide information about one element of the composing process: revising activities. Typically, subjects compose on a topic
during the first session, making changes in their text on that day; the essays
are collected, photocopied, and analyzed. At the next session, the compositions are returned to the writers, who revise by marking on their original
drafts; then they compose a second draft. Both drafts are collected (e.g.,
Faigley & Witte, 1981). Drafts are analyzed for changes to determine, for
example, (a) whether the writers decided to add new information to the
text or to remove old information, and (b) where and why they made these
changes (e.g., Bridwell, 1980; Faigley & Witte, 1981).

In consonance with case studies, these projects may compare capable
and remedial or novice writers (Faigley & Witte, 1981; Sommers, 1980)
and elicit or infer information about their thinking processes (e.g., Beach,
1981; Bridwell, 1980; Sommers, 1980); usually few subjects are studied

(e.g., Faigley & Witte, 1981; Sommers, 1980), and the subjects are generally older students and adults (e.g., Bridwell, 1980; Faigley & Witte, 1981; Sommers, 1980). In contrast to case studies, the product is analyzed rather than observations and/or protocols of the writers (e.g., Bridwell, 1980).

Unique procedures

Occasionally, a somewhat unique procedure is used to investigate a particular facet of the composing process. One such technique is "blind writing," which is implemented to study what happens when the writer is unable to read the text that he or she is composing. In one study, the subjects composed on special paper that does not take an imprint on the first page, only on the carbon copy (Atwell, 1981). In another study, the subjects composed with a wooden stylus so that an imprint appears only on the carbon copy of the draft (Gould, 1980). In a third study, subjects used invisible ink (Hull, Arnowitz, & Smith, 1981). Consequently, only the researcher can read what is written.

Another unique procedure involves the use of an electroencephalograph to scan the activity of the left and right hemispheres of the writer's brain as he or she composes (Glassner, 1980). During scanning, the device also provides timing information on when the activity levels of the hemispheres vary. The right brain is active when a person is processing spatial, global concepts; the left brain is active when the person is processing linearly. A baseline rate is first established by recording 5 minutes of hemispheric activity with the subject's eyes closed and 5 minutes with the subject's eyes open. Then the subject composes with electrodes attached to the right and left temporal lobes.

The laboratory case studies, naturalistic studies, quasi-product studies, and unique procedures have begun to produce some results. These results have already modified the established, scholarly view of the composing process.

Results

Information derived from projects using the new methodologies to study writing has discredited the linear model of the composing process— prewriting, writing, and postwriting—as an appropriate model for research purposes.[2] The linear model is inappropriate for research purposes because it describes "the growth of the written product, not ... the inner process of the person producing the product" (Flower & Hayes, 1981b, p. 369).

As a process, writing does not move in a straight line from conception to completion: All planning is not done before words are put on paper; all the words are not on paper before writers review and revise. Writers move back and forth among these subprocesses. For example, after text has been composed on paper, the writer may notice a gap for which new content must be planned.

Although researchers variously describe the recursive subprocesses of composing (e.g., Flower & Hayes, 1981a: planning, translating, reviewing; Nold, 1979b: planning, transcribing, reviewing; Gould, 1980: planning, generating, reviewing, accessing other information), the results of the research on composing are described in this paper under these subprocess headings: planning, translating, reviewing, and revising.[3] After a detailed account of each subprocess is presented, the research results are summarized.

Planning

Research reveals that planning is a thinking process that writers engage in throughout composing—before, during, and after the time spent in putting words on a page. During planning, "writers form an internal representation of knowledge that will be used in writing" (Flower & Hayes, 1981a, p. 372). More research results are available on planning than on any other subprocess of composing. The research focuses on (a) the elements of planning, (b) the time spent in planning, (c) the kinds of planning done before and during composing, and (d) the differences between competent and remedial writers' planning activities.

Planning elements include generating and organizing content, and setting goals (Flower & Hayes, 1981a). Generating entails gathering information to write about, whether that information is material from external sources or is content discovered within the writer's mind.

Organizing is ordering content; it contributes structure to a final product. Organizing may involve deleting content when more content has been generated than is needed for the specific purpose and/or arrangement. In actual practice, plans for organizing content rarely include formal outlines (Emig, 1971; Mischel, 1974; Stallard, 1974).

Setting goals involves mentally planning the individual en-route tactics for completing the writing task. Writers may set a number of such goals while developing a complete discourse. Protocols show that goals may be as complex as "Conform to the rules of a genre," as specific as "I'll include an illustration," or as simple as "Write down what I can remember" (Flower & Hayes, 1980b, p. 18).

Writers set two kinds of goals: content goals that govern what to say (e.g., "I'll describe the character"), and process goals that direct the writer's own behavior (e.g., "I think I'll review that part") (Flower & Hayes, 1981a). Some goals specify both content and process, such as "I want to open with a statement about political views" (Flower & Hayes, 1981a, p. 377). The boundaries of a goal are evidenced in a writer's protocol when he or she describes the starting point of the goal, for example,

"Write an introduction" (Flower & Hayes, 1981a, p. 377), and evaluates the success or completeness of the goal, for example, "That's banal—that's awful" (p. 378).

The quantity and quality of goals that are set differentiate good and poor writers (Flower & Hayes, 1980a). Good writers create a rich and elaborate network of goals and subgoals that help them generate content, while poor writers concern themselves with statements about the subject (Flower & Hayes, 1981b).

In addition to setting goals and to generating and organizing content, planning includes such diverse "prewriting" or rehearsal activities as making notes about the topic, drawing (Graves & Murray, 1980) and eating or waiting for a bus (Perl, 1979) while ideas incubate. When researchers measure prewriting activities as indicators of planning time, they find that writers do little of their planning before they translate mental images into words on a page (e.g., Emig, 1971; Mischel, 1974; Perl, 1979; Pianko, 1979). In one study comparing prewriting time and total writing time for high school students, researchers found that subjects spent only 1 to 4 minutes of their composing time in prewriting planning (Stallard, 1974). In a study with college students, subjects spent only about 4 minutes in planning during the prewriting period (Perl, 1979).

These results on planning time as measured during the prewriting period contrast sharply with findings from other studies that suggest planning time is a constant high proportion of total composing time (e.g., Berkenkotter, 1982; Gould, 1980). In these latter studies, planning required more time than any other subprocess (i.e., translating, reviewing, and revising); planning may consume as much as 65 percent (Gould, 1980) to 85 percent (Berkenkotter, 1982) of total composing time. These latter studies have high totals for planning time because they count not just the time spent in planning during the prewriting period, but also the time spent on planning as composing progresses.

Differences are evident between before-writing and during-writing planning. Before words are put on the page, planning usually entails setting some general parameters. This global planning also occurs during translating (i.e., putting mental images into words on a page) when writers additionally make paragraph-, sentence-, and word-level decisions (e.g., Flower & Hayes, 1981b; Pianko, 1979). Most in-process planning (as well as some prewriting planning) is mental (Pianko, 1979). When writers do significant amounts of such unrehearsed, in-process planning, they evidence "great right hemisphere" activity (Glassner, 1980, p. 87).

These in-process planning activities, either global or local, usually occur when writers pause (Flower & Hayes, 1981b). Consequently, research on the pause phenomenon provides considerable data on planning. Pause research reveals that short pauses occur when writers are planning their next words or phrases (Matsuhashi, 1981); longer pauses transpire when

139

writers are planning sentences (Matsuhashi, 1981) and global elements (Flower & Hayes, 1981b).

Pause research also suggests that planning time may vary according to the purpose of the discourse: Generalizing and persuading have been shown to require more time than reporting (Matsuhashi, 1981). This same study has shown that planning highly abstract sentences (superordinates) requires more time than planning sentences that add supporting details (subordinates). The opposite is true for individual lexical items: Writers pause for less time before superordinate (general) terms than before subordinate (specific) terms (Matsuhashi, 1981). Writers also pause longer to plan predicates than to plan modifiers, which appear to pour out in a rapid string (Matsuhashi & Spittle, 1982), and they pause most frequently before conjunctions (Caufer, 1982).

The importance of extensive planning is supported by reports that good writers spend more time in planning than either average or remedial writers (e.g., Stallard, 1974). Good writers also appear to spend more time in global planning than in local, sentence-, and word-level planning; the opposite appears true for remedial writers—they spend more time in local planning (e.g., Atwell, 1981).

These findings are corroborated by pause research, which reveals that good writers spend more time in long planning pauses, while remedial writers pause for shorter time periods (Flower & Hayes, 1981b; Van Bruggen, 1946). Additionally, good writers pause more before they write in thought units (i.e., episodes devoted to communicating concepts or carrying out goals), while remedial writers pause more before sentence-level tasks (Atwell, 1981; Flower & Hayes, 1981b; Van Bruggen, 1946).

Translating

Terms other than "translating" have been used to label this component of the composing process; these synonyms are cited here because they help define this subprocess. The terms include "writing," "recording," "implementing," "drafting," "articulating," and "transcribing." The term "translating" was selected from the various options as an appropriate label here for the process of transforming meaning from one form of symbolization (thought) into another form of symbolization (graphic representation).

Discussions of research results on translating most frequently deal with the need to make translating skills automatic and with the difference that this "automaticity" makes in writers' ability to focus their attention on global issues rather than on word-level problems during composing.

Translating makes huge demands on writers' cognitive processes because translating is so complex: Writers must put ideas into written language while they are also dealing with problems of discourse coherence and structure:

Even a casual analysis makes it clear that the number of things that must be dealt with simultaneously is stupendous: handwriting, spelling, punctuation, word choice, syntax, textual connections, purpose, organization, clarity, rhythm, euphony, the possible reactions of various possible readers, and so on. To pay conscious attention to all of these would overload the information processing capacity of the most towering intellects.

(Scardamalia, in Bereiter, 1979, p. 152)

This mental load imposed on translating becomes lighter as an increasing number of writing skills become automatic rather than consciously driven. "As writers become more sophisticated, they may devote less conscious attention to such concerns as orthography, spelling, and basic sentence construction."

(Bridwell, 1981a, p. 96)

Being able to "devote less conscious attention" to the skills of translating requires years of practice with handwriting, spelling, language usage, word choice, capitalization, and punctuation; then these skills may become somewhat automatic. Relative automaticity may also be possible for some higher level skills such as sentence variation and figures of speech (Gould, 1980).

Studies have provided evidence that when skills become automatic, differences appear in the writing process during translating. In one study (Glassner, 1980), marked changes in cognitive processes were measured when writers engaged in a type of automatic translating. The design for this study allowed the subjects to select their topics for writing. Some subjects chose familiar topics that did not pose either global or local planning challenges because the subjects had rehearsed the topic, either mentally or in spoken discourse, until they could compose without consciously attending to such aspects as order, word choice, or sentence structure. Under these conditions, an electroencephalograph measured higher levels of activity in writers' left brains than in their right brains. Interviews with the subjects verified the automatic nature of their writing at the time of their heavier left-brain activity. One writer, who wrote about an automobile accident she had been involved in, reported,

I knew the words that I would say as I have said them before to insurance investigators, lawyers, my family, and friends. It was as if a record was in my head that kept repeating itself.

(Glassner, 1980, p. 88)

Another study (Van Bruggen, 1946) evidenced a difference in translating speed when skills were more nearly automatic. In this study, subjects

141

who had mastered translating skills, as measured by high scores on usage tests, wrote at a rapid rate between pauses. Conversely, subjects who had not mastered translating skills wrote slowly. Furthermore, the speed of translating between pauses increased with the increasing age of the subjects, a finding that supports the assumption that older writers are likely to have made more translating skills automatic than have their younger counterparts.

In an apparent, but not real, contradiction of these results, some researchers have discovered that good writers write almost half as many words per minute as their randomly chosen counterparts (Flower & Hayes, 1981b). The reason for this apparent discrepancy is that the data is based on the ratio of total words to total composing time. Since good writers pause for a long time to plan between episodes of rapid translating, they may write fewer total words. Poor writers, however, pause for shorter intervals during translating. One reason for their frequent, short pauses is that they must stop to think about the mechanics of writing. They have so many mechanical problems that they must "attend to surface matters in order to write out their ideas the first time" (Bridwell, 1980, p. 214).

Interestingly, subjects who have difficulty with skills used in translating often evidence oral mastery of them. Their skill mastery is verified by studies that compare transcripts of oral composing with the subjects' written products. These protocols reveal both what subjects *say* they are writing and what they actually do write; they use skills in their oral composing that are not reflected in their written compositions. For example, a subject might say he or she is writing "walked," but the word he or she actually writes is "walk" (Perl, 1979).

Reviewing

Reviewing is characterized by backward movements to read and assess "whether or not the words on the page capture the original sense intended" (Perl, 1979, p. 331). It includes scanning to determine where one is in relation to the discourse plan and to refamiliarize oneself with the already translated text; it also includes judging whether to do further planning and translating or to stop writing because the discourse is complete. Writers also review their texts to proofread for the conventions of written language, to decide on a conclusion, and to determine needed revisions (Pianko, 1979).

Reviewing may be intentional or spontaneous (Gentry, 1980b). Some writers review after every few phrases; however, writers more frequently review after they have composed a group of sentences. These "chunks" of information are then reviewed as a piece of discourse (Perl, 1979).

Studies have shown that most writers review, whatever their level of expertise (e.g., Atwell, 1981; Pianko, 1979). Even young writers spend some of their composing time in reviewing their texts (Graves & Murray, 1980).

Most research findings on reviewing deal with the differences between capable and remedial writers. This research shows that when poor writers review, they often do not rethink their compositions as competent writers do. Furthermore, remedial writers do not review much for elements of style, purpose, and audience. Rather, remedial writers frequently review for errors (Pianko, 1979).

When remedial writers review for errors, they are often ineffective because they do not notice their errors; they often read what they intended to write rather than what they actually did write (Daiute, 1981). Protocols that include transcripts of subjects reading their compositions aloud expose this miscue behavior. For example, a subject may read aloud words that are not actually in the composition (Perl, 1979).

Studies suggest that capable writers may review their texts more often than remedial writers do (e.g., Atwell, 1981; Stallard, 1974), yet remedial writers appear more dependent on reviewing. This dependency is evidenced in Atwell's (1981) research, which included a blind-reading condition. This research discloses that remedial writers stray further from the text than do traditional writers (i.e., both good and average writers) when they cannot review. Under blind-reading conditions, the traditional students maintained their high degrees of textual coherence, while the remedial writers wrote somewhat less coherent texts. Atwell explains that the difference occurred because her remedial writers did not have a clear mental plan. "They were, indeed, text-bound and needed to read their texts in order to keep the process moving. In contrast, traditional writers ... could rely on mental text to keep the composing process recursive and stable" (p. 9). However, even traditional writers deviated slightly from their original plans when they could not review.

Revising

Definitions for revising have suffered from the linear model of writing that portrays revising as "what the writer does after a draft is completed" (Murray, 1978, p. 87). However, revising is not merely the last stage in a process. Rather, it is a cognitive and physical activity that occurs "continually throughout the writing of a work" (Sommers, 1980, p. 380).

Thus revising is comprised of behavior that entails changing one's mind as well as changing the text. According to Nold (1979a),

Revising ... is ... (1) changing the meaning of the text in response to a realization that the original intended meaning is somehow faulty or false or weak ..., (2) adding or substituting meaning to clarify the originally intended meaning or to follow more closely the intended form or genre of the text ..., (3) making grammatical sentences more readable by deleting, reordering and restating ..., as well as (4) correcting errors of diction, transcription and syntax that nearly obscure intended meaning or that are otherwise unacceptable in the grapholect.

(pp. 105–106)

Thus revising covers editing tasks (e.g., fixing spelling and punctuation, substituting synonyms) as well as major reformulations (e.g., reorganizing blocks of discourse, adding whole sections of content). These changes are made when the writer, in reviewing the text, sees mismatches between his or her intention and the actual product. This dissonance between intention and actualization creates tension that must be resolved by revising the text (Della-Piana, 1978; Sommers, 1980). Since the writer reviews throughout composing, he or she also encounters revision-inducing dissonance throughout the process.

Revising is the most accessible component of the composing process; it "provides a window into the cognitive operations which occur when a writer writes" (Bridwell, 1980, p. 220). Surprising then is the paucity of research on revising. The most significant studies on revising have been completed by only a few researchers: Beach (1976), Bridwell (1980), Faigley and Witte (1981), Sommers (1980), and Stallard (1974). Most of the research deals with (a) when subjects revise, (b) what kinds of revisions they make, and (c) what differences occur among writers who have varying levels of expertise.

Research has revealed that writers often make more revisions while writing the first draft than they make on the draft after it is completed (e.g., Bridwell, 1980; Faigley & Witte, 1981). Writers also make many changes in subsequent drafts.

Unfortunately, first-draft revisions are often premature editing attempts, sometimes by good writers (Stallard, 1974), but more often by writers who are overly concerned with the surface features of composing (e.g., punctuation, spelling, word choice). Consequently, their concern about surface features causes these writers to interrupt the flow of composing (Perl, 1979). Correspondingly, they don't use important operations like reorganization and addition (Sommers, 1980). Rather, they try to "clean up speech" (p. 381), so they approach revision with a "thesaurus philosophy of writing" (p. 381).

Often, however, concern with surface features reflects the developmental level of the writer, for a developmental difference in the ability to revise is indicated by the research (Bridwell, 1980). Young writers are at first reluctant to mar a page of writing for any kind of change. When they overcome this resistance, they begin to see the draft as temporary. The young writer then gradually extends his or her revision skills (Calkins, in

Gentry, 1980a). Even choosing one topic while excluding others is an effective developmental step in acquiring mature revising strategies (Graves & Murray, 1980).

As writers become more experienced and competent, they view revising as a process of structuring and shaping their discourse (e.g., Sommers, 1979; Stallard, 1974). They begin to see a first draft as an attempt to "define the territory" (Sommers, 1980, p. 384), so they keep writing that first draft until they decide what they want it to say. As writers develop, they also become concerned with audience considerations, so they start reviewing and thus revising their work for its effect on their audience (Sommers, 1980). The differences between mature and developing writers are supported by one study that examined differences between the kinds of revisions made by students and experienced writers. Students made more word-and phrase-level changes than did the adults. Adults, however, made more sentence-level and theme-level changes (Sommers, 1980).

In another study (Faigley & Witte, 1981), developmental differences in writers' revising strategies were examined across three groups: inexperienced student writers, advanced student writers, and expert adults. Inexperienced students primarily corrected errors and made meaning-preserving changes of the synonym-substitution type. Advanced student writers also made many meaning-preserving changes, both substitutions and deletions; however, they also made many changes affecting the meaning in the first and second drafts. Expert adults made few corrections, a substantial number of meaning-preserving changes, and more changes in meaning than either group of students.

High school students' view of revision appears similar to that of inexperienced college writers: surface and word-level revisions accounted for over half their revisions in one study (Bridwell, 1980). Results divided the poor writers into two distinct groups—those who revised extensively for surface-level changes, and those who merely recopied their first drafts.

Summary

The composing-process research has demonstrated that planning occurs throughout composing. During planning, writers set composing goals and generate and organize their ideas. Planning consumes a high proportion of composing time, but writers plan only for brief periods before they start translating their ideas on paper. This planning that occurs before translating defines some general parameters, while in-process planning entails global as well as paragraph-, sentence-, and word-level decisions. When writers pause, they are usually planning, and the length of their pauses corresponds with the type of planning that is engaging them. Because it is such a significant element of the composing process, differences in planning behavior separate good from poor writers, with good writers spending not only more time in overall planning than poor writers do, but also more time in global rather than local planning.

Translating, which is synonymous with terms like "drafting" and "articulating," is the subprocess of transforming thought into its graphic representation. Writers deal with a heavy mental load during translating. Consequently, writers translate more easily as the requisite skills become more nearly automatic. Correspondingly, writers for whom these skills have become somewhat automatic can translate relatively rapidly and can also devote more conscious attention to global issues during composing.

Reviewing occurs throughout the composing of a piece of discourse. Writers review their texts to appraise what has been done and what needs to be done. Good writers review to rethink their texts and to attend to elements of style, purpose, and audience. Poor writers, who are more dependent on reviewing, search for errors. Yet these same writers often miss errors because they read into the text what they intended to write rather than what they actually did write.

Revising is behavior that entails changing one's mind about the content and structure of the discourse as well as changing the actual, translated text. This subprocess covers a range of behavior from simple editing to substantially reformulating whole texts, and these behaviors occur before, during, and after composing a draft. Writers evidence developmental differences in the ability to revise. In early stages of development, they concentrate on correcting errors and changing surface features in their texts. As they mature, writers progressively concentrate on restructuring and shaping their discourse, redefining their ideas as they compose, and adjusting their writing to meet their audience's needs.

Limitations and conclusions

Much important information has been derived from a small body of research because new methodologies for investigating the composing process produced results not attainable by older, more traditional strategies. However, even researchers within the field express uneasiness about the validity of the overall designs of the new research. Criticism has also been leveled at specific features of the designs and the concomitant assumptions that are made.

Proponents of the naturalistic method challenge results from both classical research and laboratory case studies because the designs of these methods do not consider the context for writing; researchers provide no descriptions of contexts and assume that writing in a laboratory and writing in a naturalistic setting are similar (Edelsberg, 1981; Emig, 1982). Both naturalistic-study proponents and case-study people are skeptical about the product-examination designs of researchers who investigate revising; they contend that researchers cannot make assumptions about the process by counting features in the product.

Numerous specific features and assumptions of the new research are also challenged. One such feature is the occasional disregard for situational variables, such as the purpose for the task and writers' familiarity with the task, subject, and audience; processes vary significantly "with changes in assignment, context, audience, and purpose for writing" (Bridwell, 1980, p. 218). A related concern is that the researchers rather than the writers often select the writing task. Under this circumstance, writers deal with a process different from the one implemented to transform "experience into self-chosen writing problems" (Newkirk, 1982, p. 86). Furthermore, the writing is often timed, yet timing constraints do not allow subjects to become involved and committed to the writing task; subjects need time to plan and develop their ideas and to shape the structure of their texts.

Many critics have reservations about the subjects in the studies. The sample population is frequently too small to allow generalizable conclusions; yet they are made. Additionally, the subjects in most studies are high school seniors, college students, and adults; few studies deal with younger writers, but the processes of young and mature writers are obviously different. Furthermore, the validity of subjects' responses during their interviews is questionable: Writers may not accurately report on their current practices because of individual sensitivity; they may not remember well enough to answer questions about past writing behavior; they may tell the investigator what they think he or she wants to hear. Finally, economic status, ethnicity, and mental age are not discussed as influential; however, these factors should be part of the data on the subjects (Gentry, 1980a).

The strongest criticism, however, is directed toward the oral-composing feature in many studies. Writing situations that require subjects to compose aloud for an audience (either an investigator or a tape recorder) are unnatural, despite reassurances by one professional writer that the composer quickly becomes at ease (Murray, 1982). The requirement places additional demands on the writing and distorts the process—it transforms the writing process into a different process, a hybrid of writing and speaking. Furthermore, many writing activities occur simultaneously, from "unconscious processes such as ordering the words in a noun phrase to conscious processes ... such as planning and monitoring" (Faigley & Witte, 1981, p. 412). Much goes on that writers cannot verbalize. Finally, researchers implement a selection process when they search for subjects who can do adequate oral reporting while composing. This selection factor alone distorts the research results because the sample population is not random.

Despite such limitations, the new methodologies have produced important findings without which we would have no authoritative knowledge about the composing process. We are at least indebted to the new methodologies for shifting the focus of research attention more toward the process and away from the product of writing. More substantively, they have enabled us to verify what most competent writers know intuitively about the recursiveness of the process and about the subprocesses of composing. We have been able to note patterns that have credibility because they appear consistently across studies. One important pattern shows that the composing process of successful writers is different from that of poor writers. Successful writers plan more and at a higher level. They review for global aspects of discourse and work more on these higher level elements when they revise. Such findings are certain to be significant for the teaching of writing.

To help all writers become good writers, researchers from many methodologies must continue to investigate the composing process, for only by using a variety of techniques can researchers explore the various facets of this complex behavior. We already know much more than we did nearly 20 years ago when, in 1963, Braddock, Lloyd-Jones, and Schoer compared research on composition to "chemical research as it emerged from the period of alchemy" (p. 5). We are no longer alchemists; although as teachers and researchers in composition, we have not lost our interest in producing gold.

Note

* This paper was presented at the Conference on Writing: Policies, Problems, and Possibilities, Los Alamitos, California, May 1982. It was prepared under Contract No. 400-80-0108 with the National Institute of Education, Department of Education. Its contents do not necessarily reflect the views of the National Institute of Education or of any other agency of the United States Government.
1 The researcher collected protocols for some episodes of writing; this procedure is not typical of naturalistic studies. However, the study is classified here as naturalistic because of other features of the project and because the writer contended that talking aloud quickly became natural.
2 For pedagogical purposes, however, the linear model is still viable because the activities of each subprocess are more easily presented in separate stages. For example, teaching students to reorder text is easier when a completed text is available to cut and paste.
3 Choice of these labels does not imply disagreement with any researcher's categories. Rather, this division represents a practical organization for discussing what is now known about the process of composing written discourse.

References

Atwell, M. A. *The evolution of text: The inter-relationship of reading and writing in the composing process.* Paper presented at the meeting of the National Council of Teachers of English, Boston, November 1981.

Beach, R. Self-evaluation strategies of extensive revisers. *College Composition and Communication*, 1976, 27, 160–164.

Beach, R. *The relationship between freshmen students' self-assessing and revising.*

Paper presented at Conference of College Composition and Communication, Dallas, March 1981.

Bereiter, C. Development in writing. In R. W. Tyler & S. H. White (Chairmen), *Testing, teaching, and learning*. Washington, D.C.: National Institute of Education, 1979.

Berkenkotter, C. *A writer and a researcher talk about composing*. Paper presented at the Conference of College Composition and Communication, San Francisco, March 1982.

Braddock, R., Lloyd-Jones, R., & Schoer, L. *Research in written composition*. Champaign, Ill.: National Council of Teachers of English, 1963.

Bridwell, L. S. Revising strategies in twelfth grade students' transactional writing. *Research in the Teaching of English*, 1980, *14*, 197–222.

Bridwell, L. S. Rethinking composing. *English Journal*, 1981, *70*(7), 96–99. (a)

Bridwell, L. *They can't change what they don't see: Students' perception of structure and their revisions*. Paper presented at the Conference of College Composition and Communication, Dallas, March 1981. (b)

Caufer, D. *A production grammar for written sentences*. Paper presented at the Conference of College Composition and Communication, San Francisco, March 1982.

Daiute, C. A. Psycholinguistic foundations of the writing process. *Research in the Teaching of English*, 1981, *15*, 5–22.

Della-Piana, G. M. Research strategies for the study of revision processes in writing poetry. In C. R. Cooper & L. Odell (Eds.), *Research on composing: Points of departures*. Urbana, Ill.: National Council of Teachers of English, 1978.

Edelsberg, C. M. *Interrelationships of students' perceptions and the revision mode*. Paper presented at the Conference of College Composition and Communication, Dallas, March 1981.

Emig, J. *The composing processes of twelfth graders*. Research Rep. No. 13. Urbana, Ill.: National Council of Teachers of English, 1971.

Emig, J. Inquiry paradigms and writing. *College Communication and Composition*, 1982, *33*, 64–75.

Faigley, L., & Witte, S. Analyzing revision. *College Composition and Communication*, 1981, *32*, 400–414.

Flower, L., & Hayes, J. R. The cognition of discovery: Defining a rhetorical problem. *College Composition and Communication*, 1980, *30*, 21–32. (a)

Flower, L., & Hayes, J. R. *A cognitive process theory of writing*. Paper presented at the Conference of College Composition and Communication, Washington, D.C., March 1980. (b)

Flower, L., & Hayes, J. R. A cognitive process theory of writing. *College Composition and Communication*, 1981, *32*, 365–387. (a)

Flower, L., & Hayes, J. R. The pregnant pause: An inquiry into the nature of planning. *Research in the Teaching of English*, 1981, *15*, 229–243. (b)

Gentry, L. A. *A new look at young writers: The writing-process research of Donald Graves* (Technical Note No. 2–80/07). Los Alamitos, Calif.: Southwest Regional Laboratory for Educational Research and Development, 1980. (ERIC Document Reproduction Service No. ED 192 354) (a)

Gentry, L. A. *Textual revision: A review of the research* (Technical Note

No. 2-80/11). Los Alamitos, Calif.: Southwest Regional Laboratory for Educational Research and Development, 1980. (ERIC Document Reproduction Service No. ED 192 355) (b)

Glassner, B. J. Preliminary report: Hemispheric relationships in composing. *Journal of Education*, 1980, *162*, 74–95.

Gould, J. D. Experiments on composing letters: Some facts, some myths, and some observations. In L. W. Gregg & E. R. Steinberg (Eds.), *Cognitive processes in writing*. Hillsdale, N.J.: Lawrence Erlbaum Associates, 1980.

Graves, D. H., & Murray, D. M. Revision: In the writer's workshop and in the classroom. *Journal of Education*, 1980, *162*, 38–56.

Hayes, J. R., & Flower, L. S. Identifying the organization of writing processes. In L. W. Gregg & E. R. Steinberg (Eds.), *Cognitive processes in writing*. Hillsdale, N.J.: Lawrence Erlbaum Associates, 1980.

Hull, G., Arnowitz, D., & Smith, W. *Interrupting visual feedback in writing*. Paper presented at the meeting of the National Council of Teachers of English, Boston, November 1981.

Matsuhashi, A. Pausing and planning: The tempo of written discourse production. *Research in the Teaching of English*, 1981, *15*, 113–134.

Matsuhashi, A., & Spittle, K. B. *Writing in real time: Is there any other way?* Paper presented at the Conference of College Composition and Communication, San Francisco, March 1982.

Mischel, T. A case study of a twelfth-grade writer. *Research in the Teaching of English*, 1974, *8*, 303–314.

Murray, D. M. Internal revision: A process of discovery. In C. R. Cooper & L. Odell (Eds.), *Research on composing: Points of departure*. Urbana, Ill.: National Council of Teachers of English, 1978.

Murray, D. M. *A laboratory rat reports—A writer is protocolled*. Paper presented at the Conference of College Composition and Communication, San Francisco, March 1982.

Newkirk, T. A review of *Cognitive Processes in Writing*. *Harvard Educational Review*, 1982, *52*, 84–89.

Nold, E. W. Alternatives to mad-hatterism. In D. McQuade (Ed.), *Linguistics, stylistics, and the teaching of composition*. Akron, Ohio: University of Akron, 1979. (a)

Nold, E. W. *Revising: Toward a theory*. Paper presented at the Conference on College Composition and Communication, Minneapolis, Minn., March 1979. (b)

Perl, S. The composing process of unskilled college writers. *Research in the Teaching of English*, 1979, *13*, 317–336.

Pianko, S. A description of the composing processes of college freshman writers. *Research in the Teaching of English*, 1979, *13*, 5–22.

Sawkins, M. W. What children say about writing. In W. T. Petty & P. Finn (Eds.), *The writing processes of students: Report of the first annual conference on language arts*. Buffalo: State University of New York, 1975.

Sommers, N. *Revision in the composing process: A case study of college freshmen and experienced adult writers* (Doctoral dissertation, Boston University, 1978). (University Microfilms, 1979, No. 79-05,022)

Sommers, N. Revision strategies of student writers and experienced adult writers. *College Composition and Communication*, 1980, *31*, 378–388.

Stallard, C. K. An analysis of the behavior of good student writers. *Research in the Teaching of English*, 1974, *8*, 206–218.

Van Bruggen, J. A. Factors affecting regularity of the flow of words during written composition. *Journal of Experimental Education*, 1946, *15*(2), 133–155.

51

RESEARCH ON REVISION IN WRITING

Jill Fitzgerald

Source: *Review of Educational Research* (1987) 57(4): 481–506

Revision is commonly regarded as a central and important part of writing (Lowenthal, 1980; Murray, 1978a; Scardamalia & Bereiter, 1986). Revision is significant partly because under certain circumstances it may enhance quality of final written work (Ash, 1983; Bamberg, 1978; Bracewell, Scardamalia, & Bereiter, 1978; Bridwell, 1980) and partly because, when writers use revision to rework thoughts and ideas, it may powerfully affect writers' knowledge. Revision enables writers to muddle through and organize what they know in order to find a line of argument, to learn anew, and to discover what was not known before (Sommers, 1980).

Although the amount of research on revision is still relatively meager, a growing body of knowledge accumulated from a set of diverse methodologies is beginning to inform us about the process of revision and about writers' revision efforts. This paper presents a brief historical perspective on the development of the meaning of revision, presents findings from research on revision, and, finally, discusses limitations of the research.

Perspectives on revision

Historical trends in perspectives on revision provide a necessary framework for understanding research on revision. Traditionally, practitioners have claimed that revision is an important part of writing (Hodges, 1982), and analyses of famous authors' revision efforts support the notion that good writing entails considerable revision (Hildick, 1965). As Hodges carefully demonstrates, however, theory has not always mirrored the practitioner's belief that revision has a central role in writing. Early views of revision were theoretically dry and uninteresting. Aristotle's *Rhetoric* (1984), for example, focused on finding and structuring, rather than creating, content. De-emphasis on creativity allowed little opportunity for revision. Consequently, for Aristotle, alterations were confined to sentence-level polishing, or what today might be termed editing, and were seen as only one aspect of revision. The conception of revision as error correction lingered for many centuries (Lyman, 1929; Tressler, 1912).

It was not until the 1970s that fuller theoretical attention to revision emerged. Even in the 1970s and 1980s, revision was rarely defined in the literature. But among the rare discussions of revision that do appear, shifts in perspectives over the last 15 years are immediately evident. The shifts in perspectives reflect changes in thinking about writing in general. Until the 1970s, writing was viewed predominantly as a linear model consisting of prewriting, writing, and postwriting (Britton, Burgess, Martin, McLeod, & Rosen, 1975; Rohman, 1965; Rohman & Wlecke, 1964). Murray (1978a) recast the three components as prevision, vision, and revision. Perhaps among the first to point to and study the importance of revision, Murray (1978a) defined revision as "what the writer does after a draft is completed to understand and communicate what has begun to appear on the page" (p. 87). Murray (1978a) talked about revision as "seeing again," and he discussed two principal forms of revision: internal revision, or "everything writers do to discover and develop what they have to say," and external revision, or "what writers do to communicate what they have found" (p. 91). The specification of internal and external revision was a forerunner to later explorations of the process of revision (i.e., the mental workings) and the product of revision (i.e., the marks made on the page). Murray's (1978a, 1978b) focus on "seeing again" and on internal mental formulations was central among his contributions to the development of an understanding of revision. Though Murray's work on revision was embedded in a linear or stage model of writing, his work can be seen as a transition (a) from a time when revision received little or no theoretical attention to a time when the meaning of revision began to take shape, (b) from a long-standing view of alterations in text as relatively minor editorial changes to a new view of text changes as including reflections of major and/or meaty reconceptualizations of ideas and meanings, and (c) from a product-focused view of revision to an increasingly process-oriented one.

In the 1970s, several factors converged to dramatically affect the study of writing (Scardamalia & Bereiter, 1986). The public and the educational community were increasingly concerned about writing skills, and cognitive psychology and the study of psycholinguistic processes were rapidly expanding. Also a methodological turning point occurred in writing research. Prior to the 1970s, experimental research dominated the writing field. Its quantitative emphasis tended to bind researchers to the study of written products (Humes, 1983). Marrying other methodologies (such as case studies and naturalistic inquiry) with the ever-growing interest in cognition probably both engendered and allowed more research on the process of writing. The upshot was that ensuing research "discredited the linear model of the composing process" (Humes, 1983, p. 205) and supported a dynamic hierarchical cognitive theory of writing, involving planning, transcribing, and reviewing. The new model had potential for recursiveness (Flower & Hayes, 1981b). That is, writers could move back and forth among subprocesses, subprocesses could be embedded in other processes, and some processes might be embedded as parts of themselves (e.g., editing is a subprocess of writing, but writing may interrupt editing).

The effects of the predominant contemporary perspective of writing on views of revision were to stir things up in at least three ways. First, if sub-processes could be hierarchically embedded, then revision could occur at any time in the composing process, before, during, and after putting pen to paper (cf., Lowenthal, 1980). As Scardamalia & Bereiter (1986) asserted, "It makes little psychological sense to treat changing a sentence after it is written down as a different process from changing it before it is written" (p. 783).

Second, thinking of revision as something that could be embedded in other subprocesses of writing, such as planning, helped build the notion that revision means more than making minor editorial changes. Consistent with Murray's (1978a) thinking, revision was now viewed as both surface- and meaning-based, and both microstructure- and macrostructure-related (Kintsch & van Dijk, 1978; van Dijk, 1980). Nold (1979), for example, said that it

> is not just correcting the lexicographic and syntactic infelicities of written prose.... It also includes (1) changing the meaning of the text in response to a realization that the original intended meaning is somehow faulty or false or weak ..., (2) adding or sub-stituting meaning to clarify the originally intended meaning or following more closely the intended form or genre of the text ..., (3) making grammatical sentences more readable by deleting, reordering, and restating ..., as well as (4) correcting errors of diction, transcription and syntax that nearly obscure intended meaning or that are otherwise unacceptable in the grapholect.
>
> (pp. 105–106)

Third, some researchers invested energy in detailing the process of revi-sion, that is, what goes on in an author's mind as revisions occur. However, as interest in the process of revision increased, it also became significantly more difficult to interpret what was meant by the term "revision." Researchers of the early 1980s seemed to disagree about whether the term "revision" referred to the product, that is, the changes that are made, or to the process authors go through in their minds, or to both. Sommers (1980), for example, may have believed it was both. She said that revision is bring-ing the writing into line with the writer's intentions. Likewise, Beach's (1984) problem-solving model and Bridwell's (1980) model of revision appear to include both the mental process and the actual changes made. Scardamalia and Bereiter (1983), on the other hand, preferred to separate revision process and products, saying that their model of the process of making textual changes was not called a model of revision because revision refers to something that happens to a text. However, their model included actually making the change, that is, it included "something that happens to a text," a product. Most recently, Scardamalia and Bereiter (1986) coined the term "reprocessing" to refer to the mental aspects of revision, saying that "reprocessing is a more suitable theoretical term than revision because it refers to what goes on mentally rather than being tied to differences in surface behavior" (p. 790). Reprocessing "spans everything from editing for mistakes to reformulating goals. Revision is a special case of reprocessing, applied to actual text" (p. 790). Again, the term "revision" was reserved for making the actual change (a product), but it was embedded in or subsumed under the mental operation (a process). Similarly, Hayes and Flower (1983) used the term "reviewing" to refer to "the act of evaluating either what has been written or what has been planned" (p. 209), adding that reviewing could lead to revisions. Reviewing seemed to refer to the mental process and revision to the product, that is, the actual changes.

Though the variations in labeling created confusion, some consensus about how revision occurs can be gleaned from Bridwell's (1979, 1980) view of revision, Beach's (1984) problem-solving model of revision, Scardamalia and Bereiter's (1983) compare/diagnose/operate (CDO) part of the composing process, and Flower, Hayes, Carey, Schriver, and Stratman's (1986) working model of revision. Each model is related to or grew out of Flower and Hayes's (1981a) problem-solving view of writing and their discussion of reviewing, evaluating, revising, and editing (Bartlett, 1982; Hayes & Flower, 1980a, 1980b, 1983). The problem-solving view of revision may also be rooted in or related to some researchers' stress on the role of dissonance in revision, that is, the recognition of incongruities between goals and instantiated text (Della-Piana, 1978; Faigley & Skinner, 1982; Flower & Hayes, 1981a; Perl, 1980; Sommers, 1980).

Details of the views vary slightly, but a characterization can be drawn that captures the essence of each.

1   Writers identify discrepancies between intended and instantiated text. (Though most researchers do not specify it, presumably "text" can refer to text in the writer's mind before setting pen to paper.) For writing to be judged successful or high in quality by others, identification of discrepancies most likely requires knowledge of characteristics of "good" writing, ability to recall and represent relevant knowledge, and ability to write/read one's own writing from a reader's perspective (Bartlett, 1982).

2   Writers diagnose; when problems are identified, authors determine what changes can be or need to be made, as well as alternatives for how the changes can be made.
3   Writers operate; actual changes are carried out.

Explicit, detailed written definitions of revision rarely exist in the literature. However, the following paragraph gives an implicit contemporary definition of revision, broadly conceived to encompass both process and product:

Revision means making any changes at any point in the writing process. It involves identifying discrepancies between intended and instantiated text, deciding what could or should be changed in the text and how to make desired changes, and operating, that is, making the desired changes. Changes may or may not affect meaning of the text, and they may be major or minor. Also, changes may be made in the writer's mind before being instantiated in written text, at the time text is first written, and/or after text is first written (Beach, 1984; Bridwell, 1980; Faigley & Witte, 1981; Flower & Hayes, 1981a; Flower et al., 1986; Nold, 1981; Scardamalia & Bereiter, 1983, 1986).

This definition guided the work of the present review. Any research that explored the mental or the pen-to-paper aspects of revision as defined immediately above was included, regardless of whether the concept was labeled "revision," "editing," "reprocessing," or something else.

Measuring and revealing revision

Until the late 1970s, revelation of revision and revision processes was limited to personal testimonies of how revision occurs and what it means (e.g., Cowley, 1958; Dembo & Pondrom, 1972; Murray, 1978a; Plimpton, 1963, 1967, 1976; van Gelder, 1946) and to analyses of famous authors' revisions made over drafts of their own works (Hildick, 1965). Over the last decade, particularly during the last few years, methods of revealing individuals' knowledge of revision, as well as actual revisions made on paper, proliferated. The development of methodology mirrored the 1970s' and 1980s' reconceptualization of revision as potentially major and significant in nature, not just editorial, as both process and product, and as a subprocess that could occur at any point in the writing process. Five clusters of research methods emerged: coding systems for categorizing revisions; process-tracing methods, including think-aloud techniques, questionnaires, interviews, and taped self-evaluations; a participant-observer method; a simulation by intervention method; and an error detection method.

Coding systems for categorizing revisions

Coding systems and accompanying procedures for collecting evidence of revisions gradually developed during the 1970s and 1980s. Their development paralleled the evolution of the theoretical perspective on revision except that they focused solely on written products, revealing much about when and what revisions were made, but little about process.

Though some earlier analysts of revisions of well-known writers used global classifications for revisions, such as "tidying up changes" and "structural alterations" (Hildick, 1965), Stallard's (1974) work and a National Assessment of Educational Progress (NAEP) (1977) report were among the landmark pieces that initiated the growth of coding schemes. In Stallard's seminal study, 12th graders wrote one essay and were asked not to erase, but to draw a line through anything they wanted to change. Stallard classified marks according to six types (spelling, syntax, multiple-word, paragraph, punctuation, and single-word changes). In the NAEP study of revision, 9-, 13-, and 17-year-olds were given 15 to 18 minutes to write (in pencil) a report or a letter of complaint, followed by an additional 13 minutes to make the work better, using a pen. They could mark on the original draft and were given the opportunity to redo the work in a clean space. Changes were coded into nine categories ranging from cosmetic to informational and organizational.

Several problems were associated with the early coding schemes. One problem was that the schemes seemed to lack well-developed theoretical bases. Second, the categories within each scheme were not mutually exclusive. For example, changes involving syntax might also be changes of multiple words. Third, meaning and surface changes were not clearly distinguished. Fourth, some kinds of revision operations, such as adding and deleting, were not accounted for.

The next set of coding schemes and their accompanying procedures addressed some of the limitations in earlier work. Bridwell (1979, 1980) had 12th graders write and revise one explanatory essay (but with some choice in topic) over a 3-day period. On Day 1, the assignment was given and prewriting or note making was done; on Day 2, the students wrote with blue pens. On Day 3, using black pens, they could revise on the first draft and write a second draft. Three stages of revisions were then analyzed: in-process revisions while writing the first draft, between-draft revisions (i.e., changes made in the draft written in black that were not noted in the draft written in blue), and in-process revisions while writing the last draft in black ink. Sommers (1980) used a similar procedure.

Advancements noted in Bridwell's (1979, 1980) and Sommers's (1980) coding schemes were that revision operations and linguistic levels were distinguished, and revision categories were mutually exclusive. Also, a procedure emerged for analyzing revisions at several points in the writing process (Bridwell, 1980).

The most recently developed coding system captured many of the advantages of preceding ones and transcended them. Using Bridwell's (1980) procedures for data collection, but building on research in discourse analysis (Clark, 1977; Crothers, 1978, 1979; Halliday & Hasan, 1976; Kintsch, 1974; Meyer, 1975; van Dijk, 1980), Faigley and Witte (1981, 1984) devised the first taxonomy of revisions that would account for revisions related to the semantic structure of text, not just syntactic aspects. The taxonomy distinguished characteristics of changes such as surface and meaning and microstructure and macrostructure features. Also, six types of operations (such as adding or deleting) and six linguistic levels (such as graphic or lexical changes) were coded.

Clearly the most comprehensive of the coding schemes available to date, the taxonomy and the accompanying procedure for data coding seemed to have one salient drawback, namely, they were used to analyze only in-process and between-draft changes once pen has met paper. Changes made before pen meets paper probably cannot be coded using the taxonomy (Witte, 1985).

Process-tracing methods

Process-tracing methods allow researchers to gain insight into writers' thinking by observing them and recording their behaviors and by asking them in either a general or a directed way about their performance and/or about decisions or thoughts. At least four main types of process-tracing techniques have emerged in research on revision: asking individuals to think aloud while writing, questionnaires, interviews, and asking individuals to tape evaluations of their work after each draft.

Typically, in a think-aloud study, writers are asked to verbalize their thinking process while they write for about 60 to 90 minutes during one to four sessions (Hayes & Flower, 1980a; Perl, 1979). Their thoughts are tape recorded and later transcribed. The transcriptions are referred to as "think-aloud protocols." The protocols are analyzed descriptively and/or quantitatively using indexes such as counts of interjections and content ideas. Hayes and Flower (1980a) give a thorough and clear description of protocol analysis, complete with a detailed example.

Although the think-aloud technique still holds promise as a useful means of determining how revision occurs, to date, revision has been only a peripheral focus in such studies, documenting that thinking about revision does occur and that revision appears to be a goal-directed process that can take precedence over and interrupt all other writing processes at any time (Hayes & Flower, 1980a, 1980b; Perl, 1978, 1979). More specific information about how revision happens has not so far emerged from think-aloud research.

Beach (1979, 1984) and Beach and Eaton (1984) used a type of questionnaire called a "guided self-assessing form" to determine facets of writers' goals and strategies that precipitated revision. The form was used as an intervention technique (Beach, 1979; Beach & Eaton, 1984) and as an outcome measure (Beach, 1984), but in each case it was also used to reveal writers' thoughts. After completing prewriting and a draft, students filled out the form, which asked them first to define their overall goal and audience. Next they divided their drafts into sections by paragraphs. For each section, they had to describe what they were trying to say, the strategies they used, and audience characteristics. Finally, they listed questions or problems they had in each section. In one study (Beach & Eaton), responses were then analyzed into categories of strategies such as thesis, back-grounding, and lexical items. Each strategy category was divided into inferences that described (e.g., "I am giving some background") versus ones that judged (e.g., "I didn't give enough examples to support my point") the use of a strategy type. In another study (Beach, 1984), responses regarding students' intentions, problems in fulfilling intentions, and predicted revision inferences were rated using a 3-point degree-of-specificity scale.

Interviews have occasionally been used to gain insight into thoughts about revision. Stallard (1974) and Sommers (1980) used retrospective interviews. Stallard interviewed senior high school writers immediately after observing them while they write. She asked about things they remembered consciously attending to and feeling concerned about while writing, such as if they thought about the intended reader. Data were categorized and analyzed descriptively and by percentages (e.g., 40% of the good writers said they made a mental outline before beginning to write). Sommers interviewed writers about revisions after their first, second, and third drafts of three essays. From transcriptions of the taped interviews, Sommers developed a scale of writers' primary, secondary, and tertiary concerns.

Fitzgerald and Markham (1987) used a prospective interview with sixth graders after a first session of writing and before a second session providing opportunity to revise. First, students identified specific spots where something could or should be changed. For each spot identified, students were asked about reasons or goals for the change and about how the change could or should be made. Data were coded in a variety of ways, such as the degree to which goals were specific and what types of changes were suggested.

A final process-tracing method used in studies of revision is "taped self-evaluation." Beach (1976) asked college students to write, tape their evaluation of the draft, and then to write as many drafts as necessary, taping their evaluations after each draft. Responses were analyzed descriptively to determine characteristics such as conceptions of the revision process.

A participant-observer method

Participant-observer research that yielded information about the development of revision was fashioned mainly by Graves and his associates (Calkins, 1979, 1980a, 1980b, 1982; Gentry, 1980a, 1980b; Graves, 1981b, 1983; Graves & Murray, 1980). In participant-observer research, typically, the investigator works in a classroom, observing and recording through notes and tapes, and videotapes events, sometimes also helping the teacher and/or the students. Anecdotes and rich and detailed narrative accounts written by the investigator constitute the mainstay data. Results are summarized descriptively.

Simulation-by-intervention methods

A recent and innovative method called "simulation by intervention" was designed to investigate composing strategies or abilities by structuring tasks to simulate common writing situations or processes (Bereiter & Scardamalia, 1983; Cattani, Scardamalia, & Bereiter, 1981; Scardamalia & Bereiter, 1983; Scardamalia, Bereiter, Gartshore, & Cattani, 1980). Though sometimes cumbersome and painstaking for subjects, the simulation-by-intervention method is unique and imaginative and holds promise for revealing new perspectives on how writers think about revising.

In one simulation-by-intervention technique, researchers postulated a model of the mental process involved in revision and then developed an intervention sequence called "procedural facilitation" to ease writers' use of the hypothesized process. The hypothesized model was the earlier mentioned CDO model proposed by Scardamalia and Bereiter (1983). During procedural facilitation, writers were required to implement a compare/diagnose/operate process, but the process was simplified for them through an opportunity to choose, from sets of standard evaluative and diagnostic statements (such as "People won't see why this is important," "I think this could be said more clearly," and "I'd better say more"), statement that they thought best characterized the sentences. In two examples, students wrote and were stopped periodically and asked to select evaluative, diagnostic, and tactic statements, and then to carry out any desired revisions (Scardamalia & Bereiter, 1983, 1985).

While simulating the CDO process, the routine decreased demands on students' attentional resources, yet permitted the rest of the composing process to remain essentially intact and allowed underlying competencies to appear. Thus, difficulties in each of the three aspects of the CDO process, as well as in the integration of them, could be ascertained.

Another structured simulation task was used by Lehrer and Comeaux (1987). Students read a paragraph on a familiar topic, read a list of 11 details, and were asked to insert at least 4 of the details into the paragraph.

Some of the details could be inserted without violating either the local coherence between individual sentences or the global coherence (the gist of the paragraph), some were globally incoherent (irrelevant to the topic or gist of the paragraph), and some were locally incoherent (relevant to the general topic, but not relevant in the particular paragraph). Because they carefully manipulated features of details presented in the list, the researchers could analyze students' choices to gain insight into which levels of textual constraints (global and/or local) guided students' revision choices.

To examine students' ability to manipulate surface-level features of text (syntax) so as to better reflect intended meaning, Bracewell (1987) used a structured simulation task in which students wrote compositions and then met individually with the investigator, who underlined parts of sentences and asked the students to paraphrase them, beginning with the underlined part. Students then decided whether the original or revised version was better and justified their choices. The revisions, in conjunction with thoughtful experimenter sentence selection and student explanation for choices, helped to provide insight into (a) what revisions writers *could* carry out with external support and (b) ability to coordinate written and intended texts.

An error-detection method

To gain insight into writers' identification of spots or ideas for revision and their choices of how to make revisions, Hull (1984) and Lehrer and Comeaux (1987) used an error-detection-and-correction paradigm. Students read self-written and/or rigged passages that had surface-level errors (such as incorrect spelling or misplaced transitions like "however") or global-level errors that needed to be deleted or moved. Students were told to make changes or corrections. Hull also asked students to explain aloud why they made the change. Quantitative and descriptive data then provided insight into the students' abilities to notice problem spots, as well their reasoning about making changes.

Findings

Research on cognitive aspects of the current problem-solving view of the revision process

Research on cognitive aspects of the problem-solving view of revision has focused on reasons for breakdowns. Several reasons are plausible. First, one breakdown may occur if a writer does not clearly establish intentions for text. Beach and Eaton (1984) did find that college students had considerable difficulty specifying intentions for their writing.

161

Intentions may be for content or for form or presentation (Bracewell, 1980), so writers may have difficulty establishing intentions because of lack of knowledge about what to say (i.e., about content-related goals) and/or because of lack of knowledge about how to say it (i.e., about presentation-related goals such as structure, style, format, etc.). On the other hand, writers may actually have the requisite knowledge, but may have difficulty recalling and/or representing the knowledge (Bartlett, 1982; Flower et al., 1986).

Little research has been done to sort out the possibilities. One study suggested that lack of presentation-related knowledge at the discourse level (or ability to recall it) may be an inhibiting factor. Bracewell, Bereiter, and Scardamalia (1980) supported 9- and 11-year-old writers by pointing out structural features of their compositions which could be revised while allowing the writers to supply their own content. Children were able to improve the content when the discourse-level knowledge was provided for them.

Second, simultaneously juggling presentation- and content-related goals may affect revision. Results of one case study of a dissertation writer suggest that the revision process actually may be blocked when presentation-related goals are in conflict with, or take precedence over, expression-of-content goals (Galbraith, 1980). Similarly, when writing brief persuasive documents, college freshmen contending with more presentation-related facets of text tend to make fewer content-related revisions from first to last drafts (Glynn, Britton, Muth, & Dogan, 1982).

Third, to create texts judged readable by others, establishment of intentions and identification of discrepancies between intended and instantiated text require ability to write/read one's own writing from a reader's perspective. Bartlett (1982) and Flower et al. (1986), for example, discussed the crucial importance of an author's ability to inhibit interpretations of the text based on one's own intentions while taking on the reader's nonprivileged view.

Egocentrism is often suggested as a reason for an inability to establish intentions and identify discrepancies between intended and actual text (Flower, 1979; Graves, 1981a; Kroll, 1978). Research findings are limited and mixed on this point. Bartlett (1982) found that elementary school children detected problems and revised substantially more when they worked with texts written by others, indicating that egocentrism does seem to be a plausible contributing factor to a breakdown in the revision process. However, Bracewell, Bereiter, and Scardamalia (1979) found that when children revised texts written by themselves and by others, the only difference was that they identified more spelling errors in the texts of others.

Fourth, limited evidence suggests that children may be aware that discrepancies between intended and actual text exist, but they have difficulty determining what/where changes need to be made. Scardamalia and Ber-

162

eiter (1983) found that children did not agree with experts about the source of perceived difficulties, often focusing on overly specific details, whereas experts dealt more with issues at the text level.

Fifth, limited evidence suggests that children have difficulty knowing how to make desired changes, but competence may improve from fourth grade through eighth grade. Scardamalia and Bereiter (1983) found that when students' indications of how to make changes were rated by an expert as high-probability or low-probability choices for dealing with the identified problem, high-probability choices increased from 50% at grade 4 to 74% at grade 8.

Sixth, a writer may have trouble carrying out the desired operations. However, inability to execute desired operations does not appear to be highly supported in the literature. Writers do appear to carry out more revision and more appropriate revision when revising texts of others (Bartlett, 1982), high school students revise more when teachers evaluate their work than when students evaluate their own pieces (Beach, 1979), and sixth grades can make syntactical revisions when spots for the revisions are located for them (Bracewell, 1987).

Seventh, a writer may possess all or most of the separate knowledge and abilities, but may have difficulty managing the entire process, that is, there may be a breakdown in executive control over the components involved in the revision process (Scardamalia & Bereiter, 1983). This hypothesis is heavily supported in a series of simulation-by-intervention studies by Scardamalia and Bereiter and colleagues (Cohen & Scardamalia, 1983; Scardamalia & Bereiter, 1983, 1985, 1986; Scardamalia, Bereiter, Gartshore, & Cattani, 1980). Results showed that when possible problems with executive control were minimized through a supportive routine, students performed revisions at higher linguistic levels than is typical.

In sum, although research so far supports the problem-solving view of revision, speculation about reasons for breakdowns in the process is only beginning, and research on cognitive aspects of the problem-solving view is in its infancy.

How much, when, and what kinds of revision: effects of expertise and age

Most revision research has addressed how much revision occurs, when it occurs, and what kinds of revisions are made. Conclusions about each of the three issues are somewhat dependent on writers' expertise or ages. Some children do begin revising when they begin to write (Calkins, 1980b; Graves, 1975, 1979; Smith, 1982), but, generally, beginning writers do not revise very much (Calkins, cited in Gentry, 1980a; Graves & Murray, 1980). Younger students, and even many older students, do very little revision without peer group or teacher support (Butler-Nalin, 1984; Emig, 1971; Freedman & Pringle, 1980; Gould, 1980; Graves, 1979; Markham, 1983; NAEP, 1977; Nold, 1981; Scardamalia & Bereiter, 1986). Though there is marked individual variation (Faigley & Witte, 1981; NAEP & Educational Testing Service [ETS], 1986), revision behavior tends to change with age and/or competence.

Most of the studies on how much and when to revise and what kind of revisions are made have focused on revision products that appear on paper, though a few have investigated changes writers make in their minds between drafts. Virtually no attention has been given to changes made in the mind before pen meets paper.

It is important to recognize that although counts of overall amount of revision and of types of revision do tell that revision is occurring, they do not tell whether it is a lot, a little, or enough, or even if it is the "right" kind. To address such an issue, researchers would need to examine revisions in light of "what's needed." Very few studies have attempted to do so, and no clear patterns emerge as yet. One way to examine the issue is to compare writers' choices and decisions to those of experts. Faigley and Witte (1981), for example, found little correspondence in revision operations between expert adult writers and inexperienced adult writers when both groups revised the inexperienced writers' first drafts. On the other hand, Scardamalia and Bereiter (1983) found that although fourth graders' choices of revision tactics did not match those of a semiprofessional writer very well, sixth graders' choices matched better, and eighth graders' choices matched quite well. Also, the students' sentence-by-sentence evaluations of their texts corresponded closely to the semiprofessional writer's, but justifications of their evaluations did not.

Another way to examine the relationship between revisions and "what's needed" is to estimate the quality of each revision. Scardamalia and Bereiter (1983), for example, found more of fourth, sixth, and eighth grade students' changes were judged to be for the better rather than the worse, though results should be interpreted cautiously since the reliability estimate for the judgments was very low.

How much revision. The recent NAEP and ETS (1986) summary surprisingly indicates that students at least believe that they do a fair amount of revising. Of the fourth graders surveyed, for example, 60% reported that they made changes in their last paper before handing it in, and 69% said that they regularly revised papers. When interpreting these data, it is important to remember that they were unverified self-reports.

Averages reported for older students, adults, and one group of sixth graders for amounts of revisions made on paper ranged from 14 to 34 revisions per 100 words (Bridwell, 1980; Faigley & Witte, 1981; Fitzgerald & Markham, 1987), though Stallard (1974) reported a much lower figure of 4.26 revisions per paper for a randomly selected group of 12th graders, and

Pianko (1977) reported 3.03 changes per 100 words for college freshmen. Some variability in results across studies may be due to different ways of counting revisions.

There is considerable variation in the amount of revision that goes on within both expert and inexpert (or younger) groups of writers (Bridwell, 1980; Della-Piana, 1978; Dembo & Pondrom, 1972; Emig, 1971; Faigley & Witte, 1981; Scardamalia & Bereiter, 1986; Wason, 1980). However, at the high school level and beyond there is a tendency for more competent writers to make more revisions, up to twice as many as less competent ones or slightly younger ones (Maynor, 1982; Monahan, 1982; Stallard), although exceptions to this generalization have been noted (Ash, 1983; Faigley & Witte, 1981). Counts of revisions for younger writers are scarce.

When revision occurs. Research with both elementary and university students supports the belief that certain kinds of revision go on before pen meets paper. Spontaneous changes have been documented between words students say they are about to write and words they do write (de Beaugrande, 1984; Scardamalia & Bereiter, 1986; Scardamalia, Bereiter, & Goelman, 1982), and between changes students say could or should be made on a following draft and changes actually made (Fitzgerald & Markham, 1987). Both youngsters (as young as 10) and older competent and less competent writers make major changes in their minds between plans and eventual written texts (Burtis, Bereiter, Scardamalia, & Tetroe, 1983). Similarly, there is evidence of revision while writing (Bridwell, 1980; Faigley & Witte, 1981; Fitzgerald & Markham, Stallard, 1974) and between written drafts (Bridwell, 1980; Faigley & Witte, 1981; Fitzgerald & Markham).

Some limited evidence suggests that for older individuals, more competent writers do more revising while composing a first draft than do less competent writers (Bridwell, 1980; Faigley & Witte, 1981). Similarly, 4th-, 8th-, and 11th-grade students tend to report that they do more revising while writing than after having completed a draft (NAEP & ETS, 1986). Also, Bridwell (1980) found that 12th graders made more changes while writing than between-draft changes. However, others found that older expert and inexpert individuals and 6th graders made more between-draft changes than in-process ones (Faigley & Witte, 1981; Fitzgerald & Markham, 1987). Reasons for some discrepant results could again be attributed to different methods of counting.

What kinds of revisions are made. Overwhelming evidence supports the belief that writers at various ages and various levels of competence mainly make surface and mechanical revisions, often revealing a view of revision as proofreading (Bridwell, 1980; Crowley, 1977; Faigley & Witte, 1981; Fitzgerald & Markham, 1987; Freedman & Pringle, 1980; Graves, 1979; Kane, 1983; Monahan, 1982; NAEP, 1977; NAEP & ETS, 1986; Ramig, 1982; Scardamalia & Bereiter, 1986; Sommers, 1980). Only two contradictory reports were found. Ash (1983) reported that fewer than one third of the revisions made by 8th, 10th, and 12th graders were surface changes, and Hawisher (1987) found advanced college freshmen made slightly fewer surface than meaning changes.

Surface revisions predominate, but there is also a plethora of evidence that suggests that older and/or more competent writers tend to do more revising for meaning and make more sentence- and theme-level changes than do younger and/or less competent writers (Ash, 1983; Butler-Nalin, 1984; Crowhurst, 1983; Faigley & Witte, 1981; Lehrer & Comeaux, 1987; Levin, Riel, Rowe, & Boruta, 1985; Monahan, 1983; NAEP & ETS, 1986; Sommers, 1980; Stallard, 1974). A striking example of the age-related increasing focus on meaning-related revision was reported by Faigley and Witte (1981). Expert professional writers made one meaning-related revision for every two surface changes; advanced college student writers made one for every three; and inexperienced college student writers made one for every seven.

Finally, limited evidence suggests that writers make different kinds of changes when they revise their own texts than when they revise others' texts. Bartlett (1982) found, for example, that children in fourth through seventh grades detected syntactic problems and referential ambiguities more often in others' texts.

The relationship of revision to quality of writing

Generally, for high school age and older or more skilled writers, revisions appear to improve the quality of compositions (Ash, 1983; Bamberg, 1978; Bracewell, Scardamalia, & Bereiter, 1978; Bridwell, 1980). Similarly, students judged higher in writing achievement tend to report that they do more revising (NAEP & ETS, 1986). Two exceptions were found where no relationship emerged between degree of revision or amount of revision and quality for high school and college freshman writers (Beach, 1979; Hawisher, 1987). Also, for older writers, higher quality writing tends to be associated with a wider variety of types of revisions (Bridwell, 1980), revisions beyond the word level (Maynor, 1982), and macrostructure changes (Hawisher).

In contrast, some limited evidence suggests that for younger or less competent college writers, revision may not have a positive effect on quality. Bracewell, Scardamalia, and Bereiter (1978) found no relationship for fourth graders, and eighth graders' changes *reduced* the quality of drafts. Perl (1978) found that revisions of unskilled college writers often resulted in worse drafts.

Some intervention research suggests that instructional support or feedback may enhance the link between revision and quality. Buxton (1959) found that a group of college freshman who received feedback and then revised outscored others on grades on their essays; and two other sets of researchers (Cohen & Scardamalia, 1983; Fitzgerald & Markham, 1987) reported that after instruction designed to enhance revision efforts, sixth-grade students' second drafts were judged higher in quality than first drafts. One other intervention study (Scardamalia & Bereiter, 1983), however, found no improvement in overall quality.

Intervention research

As a preface to a synthesis of findings of intervention research, it is perhaps useful to note that some research indicates that little emphasis is placed on revision in writing in American public schools. Results of several studies suggest that high school students are seldom asked to revise their work (Applebee, 1981; Hoetker & Brossell, 1979; Pipman, 1984; Shaw, Pettigrew, & van Nostrand, 1983; Squire & Applebee, 1968). Squire and Applebee, for example, found, in a survey of 106 high schools of good reputation, that only about 12% of the high schools had students revise their writing completely. Applebee (1981) found that just under 30% of 134 high school teachers (participating in a national survey) reported they regularly required students to write more than one draft of a writing assignment; most of the 30% were English teachers. Similarly, in a sample of 1,129 college freshmen, more than 75% said they had seldom or never been asked to revise papers in their high school English classes (Hoetker & Brossell, 1979). Two reports indicated that in elementary and secondary English classrooms, only from 3% to 6% of the writing time and class time, respectively, was allocated to revision. In contrast, Carter (1983) found considerably more emphasis placed on revision in advanced college composition classes, with faculty reporting 10% to 30% of class time devoted to revision.

The total number of intervention studies is small. However, several different types of interventions have been designed to enhance revision efforts. Broad categories of interventions are: procedural support, direct instruction in the process of revision, teacher or peer feedback, and giving directions. These broad categories do overlap somewhat. For example, procedural support may include teacher or peer feedback and/or directions to revise. In the present review, studies have been grouped according to the predominant paradigm used.

Research on procedural support and direct instruction mainly involves younger students, whereas research on feedback and directions to revise mainly invovles older students. On the whole, procedural support, direct instruction, and feedback from others (particularly peers) have tended to produce positive results, whereas giving directions to revise has yielded mixed findings.

Effects of procedural support. Procedural support scaffolds writers by cuing them about their products or about aspects of revision. Four types of

167

facilitation may be identified: procedural facilitation, naturalistic class-room support, student self-assessment, and microcomputer prompting.

Procedural facilitation, developed by Scardamalia and Bereiter (1983, 1985) (defined earlier in this paper in the section "Simulation-by-intervention Method"), has been effective in (a) helping elementary grade children to make appropriate evaluations of their work as compared to evaluations made by professionals (Scardamalia & Bereiter, 1983, 1985), (b) eliciting higher level revisions than normal from elementary grade chil-dren (Scardamalia & Bereiter, 1983, 1985), and (c), in at least one case, enhancing overall quality of children's texts, as well as quality of individual revisions (Cohen & Scardamalia, 1983).

Naturalistic classroom support refers to intervention procedures such as questioning, conferencing, having dialogues, and providing lots of opportunity to write and revise. It is summed up well by Calkins (1980a): "Learning to revise is an organic, personal process. It is not unlike learning to think, question, and research. Children will grow into the writing process if given the opportunity to experiment and the encouragement to fail and try again" (p. 44). Reports of effects of naturalistic classroom activities in primary grades suggest that such external support can substan-tially enhance children's revision activity (Calkins, 1979, 1980a, 1980b; Graves, 1978).

Student self-assessment intervention was used by Beach and Eaton (1984). They developed a self-assessment form listing questions about goals and problems in achieving goals for specific parts of students' drafts. Engineered as a device to help students learn to think about revising as a problem-solving process, training and practice in using the form affected college freshmen's judgments of problems but did not affect their ability to describe strategies for revisions.

Finally, microcomputer programs designed to prompt or enhance revi-sion activity may be useful for helping children, technical writers, and college students to learn about aspects of revision (Daiute, 1983, 1985, 1986; Daiute & Kruidenier, 1985; Frase, Kiefer, Smith, & Fox, 1985; Kiefer & Smith, 1984; McCutchen, Hull, & Smith, 1987). Prompting programs may increase revision activity and efficiency over writing with word processors or pens with no prompts (Daiute, 1985, 1986; Daiute & Kruide-nier; McCutchen et al.), and they may lead to more substitution, consoli-dation, and meaningful changes (Daiute, 1985; Daiute & Kruidenier). However, there is variability in the effectiveness of prompting programs. Case studies of two 11- and 12-year-olds hint that computer prompting may facilitate revision for less skilled writers but inhibit certain types of revision activity for better writers (Daiute, 1985). Such a finding, albeit tentative, leads to the speculation that the effectiveness of word processing prompting programs may lie not so much in facilitation of physical factors involved in revision, that is, in carrying out desired operations, as in facilitation of cognitive factors, such as identifying problem spots. Better writers may be more capable of problem identification than poorer writers; prompting, therefore, might not help them much, or could even be a hindrance to an already smooth-running revision routine.

At least two studies showed evidence of transfer of learning about revision or editing from microcomputer programs to pen-and-paper writing (Kiefer & Smith, 1984; Woodruff, Bereiter, & Scardamalia, 1981). However, learning the skills from microcomputer programs may have no advantage over learning them from regular classroom instruction (Kiefer & Smith, 1984).

A limited amount of research suggests that children and adult users prefer prompting or text analysis programs which aid word- and sentence-level changes, rather than ones that aid revision of larger text features such as organization (Daiute, 1983; Gingrich, 1982).

Effects of direct instruction. Direct instruction attempts to tell about, and show writers, what the revision process is and how to revise. Direct instruction in revision research appears to be rare, but at least one study revealed beneficial effects of teaching sixth graders about the compare/diagnose/operate process of revision (Fitzgerald & Markham, 1987). The instruction enhanced children's ability to identify discrepancies between goals and intentions, their knowledge of what could be changed in their texts, their knowledge of how to make desired changes, and their ability to make actual changes. Also, quality of revised compositions was judged higher than first drafts.

Effects of teacher or peer feedback and effects of directions to revise. Some studies investigate both feedback and directions to revise (i.e., simply telling students to revise [e.g., Buxton, 1959; Hillocks, 1982]), and some combine these two variables with others (e.g., Hillocks). To simplify presentation, effects of feedback and of directions to revise are separated here as much as possible.

Several general conclusions may be drawn about feedback:

1   Findings tend to suggest that feedback can enhance revision. Although Vukelich (1986) found only a weak relationship between peer sharing and 7-year-olds' text revisions, a handful of reports indicate that teacher or peer feedback can enhance revision for writers in the primary grades through high school, especially if the feedback is focused and part of a wider instructional program (Benson, 1979; Gere & Stevens, 1985; Graves, 1979; Hillocks, 1982; Kamler, 1980; Sperling & Freedman, 1987).

2   Research with high school and older students suggests that feedback to writers from others, followed by subsequent revision, also positively affects quality of writing (Dudenhefer, 1976; Maize, 1952; McColly & Remstad, 1963).

3   For high school writers, peer feedback may be more effective than teacher feedback for improving quality (Karegianes, Pascarella, & Pflaum, 1980), and teacher feedback may be better than self-evaluation or no evaluation (Beach, 1979).

Results of research on effectiveness of giving instructions to high school and college students to revise are mixed and may be summarized as follows:

1   Though Hillocks (1982) found that practice in revising can affect performance on subsequent new writing tasks, Hansen (1978) and Newman (1982a, 1982b) found no such effects.
2   Similarly, Matsuhashi and Gordon (1985) found that specific cues to revise (e.g., directions to add material) affected revision efforts, whereas Newman (1982a, 1982b) found no effect of directions to revise on revision skills.

Finally, teacher feedback, comments, and/or suggestions combined with requests to revise may enhance revision efforts (Arnold, 1963; Buxton, 1959; West, 1967).

Miscellaneous findings

A few studies have addressed notable issues not subsumed under topics summarized so far. The issues are gender effects, genre or topic effects, the relationship between reading ability and revision, and effects of using word processors (with no accompanying prompting or text evaluation program). Briefly, the studies found the following:

1   Females tend to revise more extensively than males (Beach, 1979; Bridwell, 1980; NAEP, 1977).
2   Effects of genre or topic are unclear. Crowhurst (1983) found, for 14 good and 14 average writers in grades 5, 7, and 11, that neither amount nor type of revision varied across expressive and persuasive compositions. But Butler-Nalin (1984) reported that 15 9th- and 11th-grade students revised more for topics that required theorizing or analysis than for topics that required reporting or summarizing. The students revised social science papers more than science papers, and English papers most of all.
3   Some evidence supports a relationship between reading ability and selected aspects of the revision process. Beach (1984) found a significant positive relationship between students' reading ability and the degree of students' specificity regarding their goals and intentions for the composition. No relationships existed between reading ability and

students' specificity regarding problems in fulfilling their intentions, students' specificity regarding their own predictions for revisions on a future draft, or the degree of revision actually carried out.

4 Whether using word processors (with no accompanying prompting or text evaluation program) affects amount of revision is unclear. Some reports indicate that junior high students and adults revise more with word processors than with pens or typewriters (Bridwell, Sirc, & Brooke, 1985; Collier, 1983; Daiute, 1986; Gould, 1980; Levin, Riel, Rowe, & Boruta, 1985), and some indicate less revision with word processors (Harris, 1985; Hawisher, 1987). More consistent results emerge, however, for effects of using word processors on the kind of revisions made; more surface revisions tend to be made with word processors, as compared with conventional methods (Bridwell, Sirc, & Brooke, 1985; Daiute, 1986; Gould, 1980), and more expanded revising may occur with pens (Daiute, 1986; Harris, 1985). Only one study showed no effect on type of revisions made (Hawisher, 1987). Furthermore, a few researchers studying revision with word processors report no simultaneous effect on quality of writing (Collier, 1983; Gould; Hawisher). Only Daiute (1986) found slight improvement in quality from the first to the last drafts written using word processors.

Conclusions, limitations, and recommendations

Research on revision in writing is at a pivotal point. A view of revision that begins to capture its potential complexity is developing. Research has documented the recursive and problem-solving nature of revision and has described how much writers revise, when they revise, and what kinds of revision operations they make. However, work on the cognitive aspects of the revision process is scant. Issues of how and when writers learn through revision remain virtually unexplored. Little is known about the circumstances under which the revision process is related to judgments of quality of writing, and intervention studies are just beginning to provide insight into ways of nurturing the development of revision knowledge and abilities.

One key factor in the productiveness of new research is the extent to which future studies center on a common detailed definition of revision. Though tacit consensus has been gained about views of revision, to date stated definitions are rare. A widely used, broad, and clear definition of revision is essential for the development of research and theory.

A second factor in the productiveness of new research is the degree to which researchers can invent new methodologies and research designs, or better utilize existing ones to tap the cognitive aspects of revision. At least six features of research methodology and design might be especially important to consider in future studies.

171

1   A crucial design factor is likely to be the extent to which new research examines revision in a broader context than it has in the past. Two earlier findings suggest one way in which revision research might take on more breadth. One is the glimmer of a developmental pattern in the relationship between revision and quality of writing, with revision activity of older and/or more competent writers tending to be positively associated with quality of compositions, but revision activity of younger and/or less competent writers having no relationship (or a negative one) with quality. The other finding is that older, more competent writers make more substantive and meaning changes than do younger, less competent ones. When the two findings are linked, it appears possible that the relationship between revision activity and quality may be mediated by the types of revision that are made. Most likely, the critical aspect of revision with regard to quality is not merely how much is done or how many revisions are made, but what is done or which revisions are made. The inescapable conclusion is that more research might be shaped to enlighten our knowledge about writers' revisions in relation to "what's needed," rather than merely describing revision operations that are done.

Similarly, many revision studies have attempted to investigate revision activity without significant regard for the integration of the revision process into the total act of writing. A few investigators, for example, have attempted either to ease aspects of the writing/revision process or to teach a way to think about revising without specification of the writers' knowledge of formal characteristics of writing (such as sentence structure or syntax). The revision process itself is embedded in other subprocesses of writing and cannot be divorced from such features as knowledge of the content of what is being written and knowledge of characteristics of what makes a text a "good" text. Our understanding of revision might be dramatically enhanced if studies could be formulated that could account for and/or examine revision as it is encased in, or linked to, such knowledge.

2   Few studies have examined revisions of adult writers other than college students, professional writers, or English teachers. Revision activity of other adults—especially adults in occupations where functional writing is prevalent—would be enlightening.

3   The predominant method used so far to study revision has been coding schemes, which have most often focused on revision operations or products, though sometimes they have been used to gain insight into writers' minds. To gain a fuller understanding of revision, other procedures might be further explored, or new procedures developed, to provide more insight into how and when the revision process happens and how and when it breaks down (Faigley, Cherry, Jolliffe, & Skinner, 1985).

4 Methodologies have so far restricted insights to revision as it occurs while or after the pen meets paper (Witte, 1985). Techniques should be explored which hold potential for garnering information about revision that occurs before pen meets paper.

5 No studies that were located used multiple samples of writing in the same genre, and effects of genre are often ignored. Revision is likely to be linked to content of the composition. It will be important to raise further questions about the generalizability of findings about revision across multiple samples and genres (Clark, 1973; Fulkerson, 1978).

6 Many studies that counted revision operations did not take length of writing sample into account and/or ignored issues of reliability and validity of the variables investigated. Length of writing sample may be correlated with both amount and kind of revision operations and with writers' ability to deploy revision (Fisher, 1981). Also, high reliability is essential to establishing the veracity of findings.

A third, and perhaps most important, factor in the long-range significance of research on revision may be tied to researchers' ability to raise questions about how revision helps people to learn. Expert and well-known authors testify that they learn what they are trying to say as they write and revise (Lowenthal, 1980; Murray, 1978a, 1978b; Odell, 1980). Revision may be a powerful tool for mental development (Freedman, 1985), but today very little is known about how or when revision aids learning.

Two theoretical outlooks, currently being developed by reading and writing researchers and by psychologists interested in knowledge acquisition, may inspire new directions in thinking about the role of revision in learning. One outlook involves exploration of the parallels between revision in writing and revision in reading (Kucer, 1985; Tierney & Pearson, 1985). Revision in reading refers to mental rebuilding or reconstruction of models of meaning and can entail activities such as rereading, annotating texts with comments, and questioning while reading. An important contribution of identification of parallels in revision processes in reading and writing may be that it can lead researchers to identification of a common research space. For example, current problem-solving models of writing appear to be similar to, but more extensively developed than, earlier problem-solving views of reading (cf. Olshavsky, 1976–1977); new problem-solving models of revision in writing might more fully inform understanding of revision processes in reading. Separate communities of researchers may learn from each other and may begin to pursue more generic research issues, such as identification of the conditions under which reconstructive thought takes place, which in turn can inform the specific domains of reading and writing.

A second outlook addresses how knowledge is acquired or changed. Vosniadou and Brewer (1987) recently proposed several mechanisms for knowledge restructuring. At least one of them seems especially relevant to learning through revision in writing, that is, Socratic dialogue. Socratic dialogue, Vosniadou and Brewer say, is likely to enhance individuals' awareness of inconsistencies or anomalies in their knowledge change. Notice that the language used to discuss the restructuring phenomenon, that is, *inconsistencies* and *anomalies*, is reminiscent of language used by writing researchers to explain aspects of a problem-solving model of revision, that is, revisers identify *discrepancies* between intentions and instantiated text. Perhaps something like an internal Socratic dialogue occurs when writers learn or reconstruct meaning through writing. Maybe teachers and peers who support writers through questioning and commenting on their written pieces are sometimes actually engaging in Socratic-like dialogue which leads the writer to new visions. The study of how knowledge is restructured might inform theories of how revision in writing may shape writers' insights.

Many new lines of inquiry could be developed by linking revision in writing research with other theoretical developments. Perhaps such inquiry could lead to a better understanding of the revision process, the circumstances under which revision aids learning, and ways we might better cultivate the development of revision abilities.

Acknowledgements

I would like to thank Lynda Markham (Alma College, Michigan) and two anonymous reviewers for comments on earlier drafts of this paper.

References

Applebee, A. N. (1981). *Writing in the secondary school: English and the content areas*. Urbana, IL: National Council of Teachers of English.

Aristotle. (1984). (W. Rhye Roberts, Trans.). *Rhetoric*. New York: Modern Library.

Arnold, L. V. (1963). Effects of frequency of writing and intensity of teacher evaluation upon performance in written composition of tenth grade students. *Dissertation Abstracts, 24*, 1021A.

Ash, B. H. (1983). Selected effects of elapsed time and grade level on the revisions in eighth, tenth, and twelfth graders' writing. *Dissertation Abstracts, 43*(12), 3830A.

Bamberg, B. (1978). Composition instruction does make a difference: A comparison of college freshmen in regular and remedial English courses. *Research in the Teaching of English, 12*, 47–59.

Bartlett, E. J. (1982). Learning to revise. In M. Nystrand (Ed.), *What writers know* (pp. 345–363). New York: Academic Press.

Beach, R. (1976). Self-evaluation strategies of extensive revisers. *College Composition and Communication, 27*, 160–164.

Beach, R. (1979). The effects of between-draft teacher evaluation versus student self-evaluation on high school students' revision of rough drafts. *Research in the Teaching of English, 13*, 111–119.

Beach, R. (1984, April). *The effect of reading ability on seventh graders' narrative writing*. Paper presented at the annual meeting of the American Educational Research Association, New Orleans.

Beach, R., & Eaton, S. (1984). Factors influencing self-assessing and revising by college freshmen. In R. Beach & L. Bridwell (Eds.), *New directions in composition research* (pp. 149–170). New York: Guilford Press.

Benson, N. L. (1979). The effects of peer feedback during the writing process on writing performance, revision behavior, and attitude toward writing. *Dissertation Abstracts, 40* (04), 1987a.

Bereiter, C., & Scardamalia, M. (1983). Levels of inquiry in writing research. In P. Mosenthal, L. Tamor, & S. A. Walmsley (Eds.), *Research on writing: Principles and methods* (3–25). New York: Longman.

Bracewell, R. J. (1980, April). *The ability of primary school students to manipulate language form when writing*. Paper presented at the annual meeting of the American Educational Research Association, Boston.

Bracewell, R. J. (1987, April). *Semantic and textual constraints students use in revising their writing*. Paper presented at the annual meeting of the American Educational Research Association, Washington, DC.

Bracewell, R. J., Bereiter, C., & Scardamalia, M. (1979, April). *A test of two myths about revision*. Paper presented at the annual meeting of the American Educational Research Association, San Francisco.

Bracewell, R. J., Bereiter, C., & Scardamalia, M. (1980, April). *How beginning writers succeed and fail in making written arguments more convincing*. Paper presented at the annual meeting of the American Educational Research Association, Boston.

Bracewell, R. J., Scardamalia, M., & Bereiter, C. (1978). *The development of audience awareness in writing*. (ERIC Document Reproduction Service No. ED 154 433)

Bridwell, L. (1979). Revising processes in twelfth grade students' transactional writing. *Dissertation Abstracts, 40*(11), 5765 A.

Bridwell, L. S. (1980). Revising strategies in twelfth grade students' transactional writing. *Research in the Teaching of English, 14*, 197–222.

Bridwell, L., Sirc, G., & Brooke, R. (1985). Revising and computing: Case studies of student writers. In S. W. Freedman (Ed.), *The acquisition of written language: Response and revision* (pp. 172–194). Norwood, NJ: Ablex.

Britton, J., Burgess, T., Martin, N., McLeod, A., & Rosen, H. (1975). *The development of writing abilities (11–18)*. London: Macmillan Education.

Burtis, P. J., Bereiter, C., Scardamalia, M., & Tetroe, J. (1983). The development of planning in writing. In G. Wells & B. M. Kroll (Eds.), *Explorations in the development of writing* (pp. 153–174). Chichester, England: Wiley.

Butler-Nalin, K. (1984). Revision patterns in students' writing. In Arthur N. Applebee (Ed.), *Contexts for learning to write: Studies for secondary school instruction* (pp. 121–215). Norwood, NJ: Ablex.

Buxton, E. W. (1959). An experiment to test the effects of writing frequency and guided practice upon student mechanics skill in writing expression. *Alberta Journal of Educational Research, 5*, 91–99.

175

Calkins, L. M. (1979). Andrea learns to make writing hard. *Language Arts, 56,* 569–576.

Calkins, L. M. (1980a). The craft of writing. *Teacher, 98,* 41–44.

Calkins, L. M. (1980b). Notes and comments: Children's rewriting strategies. *Research in the Teaching of English, 14,* 331–341.

Calkins, L. M. (1982). *A study of children's rewriting.* Final Report for NCTE Research Foundation Project No. 80:11, (ERIC Document Reproduction Service No. ED 229 750).

Carter, R. D. (1983, March). *A survey of revision practices in today's advanced composition course.* Paper presented at the annual meeting of the Conference on College Composition and Communication, Detroit. (ERIC Document Reproduction Service No. ED 229 794)

Cattani, C., Scardamalia, M., & Bereiter, C. (1981). *Facilitating diagnosis in student writing.* Unpublished manuscript, Ontario Institute for Studies in Education, Toronto.

Clark, H. H. (1973). The language-as-fixed-effect fallacy: A critique of language statistics in psychological research. *Journal of Verbal Learning and Verbal Behavior, 12,* 335–359.

Clark, H. H. (1977). Inferences in comprehension. In D. LaBerge & S. J. Samuels (Eds.), *Basic processes in reading: Perception and comprehension* (pp. 243–262). Hillsdale, NJ: Erlbaum.

Cohen, E., & Scardamalia, M. (1983, April). *The effects of instructional intervention in the revision of essays by grade six children.* Paper presented at the annual meeting of the American Educational Research Association, Montreal.

Collier, R. M. (1983, May). The word processor and revision strategies. *College Composition and Communication, 34*(2), 149–155.

Cowley, M. (Ed.). (1958). *Writers at work: The Paris Review interview* (Vol. 1). New York: Viking.

Crothers, E. J. (1978). Inference and coherence. *Discourse Processes, 1,* 51–71.

Crothers, E. J. (1979). *Paragraph structure inference.* Norwood, NJ: Ablex.

Crowhurst, M. (1983). *Revision strategies of students at three grade levels: Final report.* Vancouver: Educational Research Institute of British Columbia. (ERIC Document Reproduction Service No. ED 283 009).

Crowley, S. (1977). Components of the composing process. *College Composition and Communication, 28*(2), 166–169.

Daiute, C. (1983, April). *The effects of automatic prompting on young writers.* Paper presented at the annual meeting of the American Educational Research Association, Montreal.

Daiute, C. (1985). Do writers talk to themselves? In S. Freedman (Ed.), *The acquisition of written language: Response and revision* (pp. 133–139). Norwood, NJ: Ablex.

Daiute, C. (1986, May). Physical and cognitive factors in revising: Insights from studies with computers. *Research in the Teaching of English, 20*(2), 141–159.

Daiute, C., & Kruidenier, J. (1985). A self-questioning strategy to increase young writers' revising processes. *Applied Psycholinguistics, 6,* 307–318.

de Beaugrande, R. (1984). *Text production: Toward a science of composition.* Norwood, NJ: Ablex.

Della-Piana, G. (1978). Research strategies for the study of revisions processes in writing poetry. In C. R. Cooper & L. Odell (Eds.), *Research on composing: Points of departure* (pp. 105–134). Urbana, IL: National Council of Teachers of English.

Dembo, L. S., & Pondrom, C. M. (1972). *The contemporary writer: Interviews with sixteen novelists and poets.* Madison: University of Wisconsin Press.

Dudenhefer, J. P., Jr. (1976). An experimental study of two techniques of composition revision in a developmental English course for technical students. *Dissertation Abstracts, 36*(11), 7230A.

Emig, J. (1971). *The composing processes of twelfth graders.* (NCTE Research Report No. 13.X). Urbana, IL: National Council of Teachers of English.

Faigley, L., Cherry, R. D., Jolliffe, D. A., & Skinner, A. M. (1985). *Assessing writers' knowledge and processes of composing.* Norwood, NJ: Ablex.

Faigley, L., & Skinner, A. (1982). *Writer's processes and writer's knowledge: A review of research.* (Tech. Rep. No. 6). Austin: University of Texas.

Faigley, L., & Witte, S. (1981). Analyzing revision. *College Composition and Communication, 32,* 400–414.

Faigley, L., & Witte, S. P. (1984). Measuring the effects of revisions on text structure. In R. Beach & L. Bridwell (Eds.), *New directions in composition research* (pp. 95–108). New York: Guilford Press.

Fisher, J. E. (1981). *The interference of mechanical errors in the revision of compositions by grade six children.* Unpublished master's thesis, Ontario Institute for Studies in Education, Toronto.

Fitzgerald, J., & Markham, L. (1987). Teaching children about revision in writing. *Cognition and Instruction, 4*(1), 3–24.

Flower, L. S. (1979). Writer-based prose: A cognitive basis for problems in writing. *College English, 41,* 19–37.

Flower, L., & Hayes, J. A. (1981a). A cognitive process theory of writing. *College Composition and Communication, 32,* 365–387.

Flower, L., & Hayes, J. R. (1981b). Plans that guide the composing process. In C. H. Frederiksen & J. F. Dominic (Eds.), *Writing: The nature, development, and teaching of written communication: Volume 2. Writing: Process, development & communication.* Hillsdale, NJ: Erlbaum.

Flower, L., Hayes, J. R., Carey, L., Schriver, K., & Stratman, J. (1986). Detection, diagnosis, and the strategies of revision. *College Composition and Communication, 37*(1), 16–55.

Frase, L. T., Kiefer, K. E., Smith C. R., & Fox, M. L. (1985). Theory and practice in computer-aided composition. In S. W. Freedman (Ed.), *The acquisition of written language: Response and revision* (pp. 195–212). Norwood, NJ: Ablex.

Freedman, A., & Pringle, I. (1980). *The writing abilities of a representative sample of grade 5, 8, and 12 students: The Carleton Writing Project, Part II* (Final Report). Carleton (Ontario) Board of Education. (ERIC Document Reproduction Service No. ED 217 413)

Freedman, S. W. (Ed.). (1985). *The acquisition of written language: Response and revision.* Norwood, NJ: Ablex.

Fulkerson, R. (1978). Some cautions about pedagogical research. *College English, 40,* 463–466.

Galbraith, David. (1980). The effect of conflicting goals on writing: A case study. *Visible Language, 14*(4), 364–375.

Gentry, L. A. (1980a). *A new look at young writers: The writing-process research of Donald Graves* (Technical Note No. 2–80/07). Los Alamitos, CA: Southwest Regional Laboratory for Educational Research and Development. (ERIC Document Reproduction Service No. ED 192 354)

Gentry, L. A. (1980b). *Textual revision: A review of the research* (Technical Note No. 2–80/11). Los Alamitos, CA: Southwest Regional Laboratory for Educational Research and Development. (ERIC Document Reproduction Service No. ED 192 355)

Gere, A. R., & Stevens, R. S. (1985). The language of writing groups: How oral response shapes revision. In S. W. Freedman (Ed.), *The acquisition of written language: Response and revision* (pp. 85–105). Norwood, NJ: Ablex.

Gingrich, P. (1982). Writer's Workbench: Studies of users. *29th International Technical Communications conference proceedings.* Piscataway, NJ: Bell Laboratories.

Glynn, S. M., Britton, B. K., Muth, D. K., & Dogan, N. (1982). Writing and revising persuasive documents: Cognitive demands. *Journal of Educational Psychology, 74,* 557–567.

Gould, J. D. (1980). Experiments on composing letters: Some facts, some myths, and some observations. In L. W. Gregg & E. R. Steinberg (Eds.), *Cognitive process in writing* (pp. 97–127). Hillsdale, NJ: Erlbaum.

Graves, D. H. (1975). An examination of the writing processes of seven year old children. *Research in the Teaching of English, 9,* 227–241.

Graves, D. H. (1978). *Balance the basics: Let them write.* New York: Ford Foundation.

Graves, D. H. (1979, March). What children show us about revision. *Language Arts, 56,* 312–319.

Graves, D. H. (Ed.). (1981a). *A case study observing the development of primary children's composing, spelling, and motor behaviors during the writing process report.* (NIE Grant No. G–78–0174). Durham: University of New Hampshire. (ERIC Document Reproduction Service ED 218 653)

Graves, D. H. (1981b). Research update: Writing research for the eighties: What is needed. *Language Arts, 58,* 197–206.

Graves, D. H. (1983). *Writing: Teachers and children at work.* Exeter, NH: Hernemann.

Graves, D. H., & Murray, D. M. (1980). Revision: In the writer's workshop and in the classroom. *Journal of Education, 162,* 38–56.

Halliday, M. A. K., & Hasan, R. (1976). *Cohesion in English.* London: Longman.

Hansen, B. (1978). Rewriting is a waste of time. *College English, 39,* 956–960.

Harris, J. (1985). Student writers and word processing: A preliminary evaluation. *College Composition and Communication, 36,* 323–330.

Hawisher, G. E. (1987). The effects of word processing on the revision strategies of college freshmen. *Research in the Teaching of English, 21*(2), 145–159.

Hayes, J. R., & Flower, L. S. (1980a). Identifying the organization of writing processes. In L. W. Gregg & E. R. Steinberg (Eds.), *Cognitive processes in writing* (pp. 4–30). Hillsdale, NJ: Erlbaum.

Hayes, J. R., & Flower, L. S. (1980b). Writing as problem solving. *Visible Language, 14,* 388–399.

Hayes, J. R., & Flower, L. S. (1983). Uncovering cognitive processes in writing: An introduction to protocol analysis. In P. Mosenthal, L. Tamor, & S. A. Walmsley (Eds.), *Research on writing: Principles and methods* (pp. 207–220). New York: Longman.

Hildick, E. W. (1965). *Word for word: The rewriting of fiction*. London: Faber and Faber.

Hillocks, G. (1982, October). The interaction of instruction, teacher comment, and revision in teaching the composing process. *Research in the Teaching of English, 16*, 261–278.

Hodges, K. (1982). A history of revision: Theory versus practice. In R. A. Sudol (Ed.), *Revising: New essays for teachers of writing* (pp. 24–42). Urbana, IL: ERIC Clearinghouse on Reading and Communication Skills, National Institute of Education and National Council of Teachers of English.

Hoetker, J., & Brossell, G. (1979). Who (if anyone) is teaching them writing and how? *English Journal, 68*, 19–25.

Hull, G. A. (1984, April). *The editing process in writing: A performance study of experts and novices*. Paper presented at the annual meeting of the American Educational Research Association, New Orleans.

Humes, A. (1983). Research on the composing process. *Review of Educational Research, 53*(2), 201–216.

Kamler, B. (1980). One child, one teacher, one class: The story of one piece of writing. *Language Arts, 57*, 680–693.

Kane, J. H. (1983, April). *Computers for composing*. Paper presented at the annual meeting of the American Educational Research Association, Montreal. (ERIC Document Reproduction Service No. ED 230 978)

Karegianes, M. L., Pascarella, E. T., & Pflaum, S. W. (1980). The effects of peer editing on the writing proficiency of low-achieving tenth grade students. *Journal of Educational Research, 73*(2), 203–207.

Kiefer, K., & Smith, C. (1984). Improving students' revising and editing: The Writer's Workbench system at Colorado State University. In W. Wresch (Ed.), *A writer's tool: The computer in composition instructions* (pp. 65–82). Urbana, IL: National Council of Teachers of English.

Kintsch, W. (1974). *The representation of meaning in memory*. Hillsdale, NJ: Erlbaum.

Kintsch, W., & van Dijk, T. A. (1978). Toward a model of text comprehension and production. *Psychological Review, 85*, 363–394.

Kroll, B. M. (1978). Cognitive egocentrism and the problem of audience awareness in written discourse. *Research in the Teaching of English, 12*, 269–281.

Kucer, S. (1985, December). *The parallel role of revision in reading and writing*. Paper presented at the annual meeting of the National Reading Conference, San Diego, CA.

Lehrer, R., & Comeaux, M. (1987, April). *A developmental study of the effects of goal constraints on composition*. Paper presented at the annual meeting of the American Educational Research Association, Washington, DC.

Levin, J. A., Riel, M. M., Rowe, R. D., & Boruta, M. J. (1985). Muktuk meets Jacuzzi: Computer networks and elementary school writers. In S. W. Freedman (Ed.), *The acquisition of written language: Response and revision* (pp. 160–171). Norwood, NJ: Ablex.

Lowenthal, D. (1980). Mixing levels of revision. *Visible Language, 14*(4), 383–387.

179

Lyman, R. L. (1929). *Summary of investigations relating to grammar, language, and composition.* Chicago: The University of Chicago.

Maize, R. C. (1952). *A study of two methods of teaching English composition to retarded college freshman.* Unpublished doctoral dissertation, Purdue University, West Lafayette, IN.

Markham, L. R. (1983, November). *Revision in first graders' writing: Learning to communicate with yourself.* Paper presented at the annual meeting of the National Council of Teachers of English, Denver.

Matsuhashi, A., & Gordon, E. (1985). Revision, addition, and the power of the unseen text. In S. Freedman (Ed.), *The acquisition of written language: Response and revision* (pp. 226–249). Norwood, NJ: Ablex.

Maynor, L. C. (1982). An investigation of the revising practices of college freshman writers. *Dissertation Abstracts, 43*(8), 2543A.

McColly, W., & Remstad, R. (1963). *Comparative effectiveness of composition skills learning activities in the secondary school.* U.S. Educational Resources Information Center. (ERIC Document Reproduction Service No. ED 003 279)

McCutchen, D., Hull, G. A., & Smith, W. L. (1987). Editing strategies and error correction in basic writing. *Written Communication, 4*(2), 139–154.

Meyer, B. (1975). *The organization of prose and its effect upon memory.* Amsterdam: North Holland.

Monahan, B. D. (1982). *Revision strategies of basic and competent writers as they write for different audiences.* (ERIC Document Reproduction Service No. ED 229 756).

Murray, D. (1978a). Internal revision: A process of discovery. In C. Cooper and L. Odell (Eds.), *Research on composing: Points of departure* (pp. 85–103). Urbana, IL: National Council of Teachers of English.

Murray, D. M. (1978b, October). Teach the motivating force of revision. *English Journal, 67*, 56–60.

National Assessment of Educational Progress. (1977). *Write/rewrite: An assessment of revision skills: Selected results from the second national assessment of writing.* (ERIC Document Reproduction Service No. ED 141 826)

National Assessment of Educational Progress & Educational Testing Service. (1986). *The writing report card: Writing achievement in American schools.* Princeton, NJ: National Assessment of Educational Progress.

Newman, J. M. (1982a). The effects of formal revision in an enriched composing environment on composing improvement of college-bound high school seniors. *Dissertation Abstracts, 43*(11), 3575A.

Newman, J. M. (1982b). *The effect of formal revision on improving writing skills.* (ERIC Document Reproduction Service No. ED 234 380).

Nold, E. W. (1979). Alternatives to mad-hatterism. In D. McQuade (Ed.), *Linguistics, stylistics, and the teaching of composition* (pp. 103–117). Akron, OH: University of Akron.

Nold, E. W. (1981). Revising. In C. H. Frederiksen & J. F. Dominic (Eds.), *Writing: The nature, development and teaching of written communication* (pp. 67–79). Hillsdale, NJ: Erlbaum.

Odell, L. (1980). Business writing: Observations and implications for teaching composition. *Theory Into Practice, 19*(3), 225–232.

Olshavsky, J. E. (1976–1977). Reading as problem solving: An investigation of strategies. *Reading Research Quarterly, 12*, 654–674.

Perl, S. (1978). Five writers writing: Case studies of the composing processes of unskilled college writers. *Dissertation Abstracts, 39*(8), 4788A.

Perl, S. (1979). The composing processes of unskilled college writers. *Research in the Teaching of English, 13*(4), 317–336.

Perl, S. (1980, December). Understanding composing. *College Composition and Communication, 31*, 363–369.

Pianko, S. (1977). The composing acts of college freshman writers: A description. *Dissertation Abstracts, 38*(7), 3983A.

Pipman, M. H. (1984, August). The amount and nature of composition instruction in two secondary English classrooms. *Dissertation Abstracts, 45*(2), 486A.

Plimpton, G. G. (1963). *Writers at work: The Paris Review interviews* (2nd series). New York: Viking.

Plimpton, G. G. (Ed.). (1967). *Writers at work: The Paris Review interviews* (3rd series). New York: Viking.

Plimpton, G. G. (Ed.). (1976). *Writers at work: The Paris Review interviews* (4th series). New York: Viking.

Ramig, J. R. D. (1982). An investigation of the revision practices of competent student writers writing research papers in a freshman composition course at a community college. *Dissertation Abstracts, 43*(10), 3208A.

Rohman, D. G. (1965). Pre-writing: The stages of discovery in the writing process. *College Composition and Communication, 16*, 106–112.

Rohman, D. G., & Wlecke, A. O. (1964). *Pre-writing: The construction and application of models for concept formation in writing.* East Lansing: Michigan State University. (Eric Document Reproduction Service No. ED 001 273)

Scardamalia, M., & Bereiter, C. (1983). The development of evaluative, diagnostic, and remedial capabilities in children's composing. In M. Martlew (Ed.), *The psychology of written language: A developmental approach* (pp. 67–95). London: Wiley.

Scardamalia, M., & Bereiter, C. (1985). The development of dialectical processes in writing. In D. Olson, N. Terrance, & A. Hildyard (Eds.), *Literacy, language and learning: The nature and consequences of reading and writing.* Cambridge, England: Cambridge University Press.

Scardamalia, M., & Bereiter, C. (1986). Research on written composition. In C. Wittrock (Ed.), *Handbook of research on teaching* (3rd ed., pp. 778–803). New York: Macmillan.

Scardamalia, M., Bereiter, C., Gartshore, S., & Cattani, C. (1980, April). *Locating the source of children's revision difficulties.* Paper presented at the annual meeting of the American Educational Research Association, Boston.

Scardamalia, M., Bereiter, C., & Goelman, H. (1982). The role of production factors in writing ability. In M. Nystrand (Ed.), *What writers know: The language, process, and structure of written discourse* (pp. 113–210). New York: Academic Press.

Shaw, R. A., Pettigrew, J., & van Nostrand, A. D. (1983). Tactical planning of writing instruction. *The Elementary School Journal, 84*, 45–51.

Smith, G. L. (1982). Revision and improvement: Making the connection. In R. A. Sudol (Ed.), *Revising: New essays for teachers of writing* (pp. 132–139). Urbana, IL: ERIC Clearinghouse on Reading and Communication Skills, National Institute of Education, and National Council of Teachers of English.

Sommers, N. (1980). Revision strategies of student writers and experienced adult writers. *College Composition and Communication, 31*, 378–388.

Sperling, M., & Freedman, S. W. (1987). *A good girl writes like a good girl: Written response and clues to the teaching/learning process*. (Tech. Rep. No. 3). Berkeley: University of California and Pittsburgh, PA: Carnegie Mellon University.

Squire, J., & Applebee, R. (1968). *High school English instruction today: The national study of high school English programs*. New York: Appleton-Century-Crofts.

Stallard, C. K. (1974). An analysis of the behavior of good student writers. *Research in the Teaching of English, 8*, 206–218.

Tierney, R. J., & Pearson, P. D. (1985). Toward a composing model of reading. In C. N. Hedley & A. N. Baratta (Eds.), *Contexts of reading* (pp. 63–77). Norwood, NJ: Ablex.

Tressler, J. C. (1912). The efficiency of student correction of composition. *English Journal, 1*, 405–411.

van Dijk, T. A. (1980). *Macrostructures: An interdisciplinary study of global structures in discourse, interaction, and cognition*. Hillsdale, NJ: Erlbaum.

van Gelder, R. (1946). *Writers and writing*. New York: Charles Scribner's Sons.

Vosniadou, S., & Brewer, W. F. (1987). Theories of knowledge of restructuring in development. *Review of Educational Research, 57*, 51–67.

Vukelich, C. (1986). The relationship between peer sharing and seven-year-olds' text revisions. In J. A. Niles & R. V. Lalik (Eds.), *Solving problems in literacy: Learners, teachers and researchers. Thirty-fifth Yearbook of the National Reading Conference* (pp. 300–305). Rochester, NY: National Reading Conference.

Wason, P. C. (1980). Specific thoughts on the writing process. In L. W. Gregg & E. R. Steinberg (Eds.), *Cognitive processes in writing* (pp. 129–137). Hillsdale, NJ: Erlbaum.

West, W. W. (1967). Written composition. *Review of Educational Research, 37*, 159–167.

Witte, S. P. (1985). Revising, composing theory, and research design. In S. Freedman (Ed.), *The acquisition of written language: Response and revision* (pp. 250–284). Norwood, NJ: Ablex.

Woodruff, E., Bereiter, C., & Scardamalia, M. (1981). On the road to computer assisted compositions. *Journal of Educational Technology Systems, 10*(2), 133–148.

52

THE REVISING PROCESSES OF SIXTH-GRADE WRITERS WITH AND WITHOUT PEER FEEDBACK

Vicki L. Brakel Olson

Source: *Journal of Educational Research* (1990) 84(1): 23–29

The process approach to teaching writing has gone beyond being a new and breaking trend as school districts and textbooks attempt to institute its major principles. Research that initially brought the ideas of process writing to our attention is also completing a cycle. Case study research of the early 1980s showed in great detail the writing process of selected children (Calkins, 1983; Graves, 1981, 1983). The richness of information provided by those studies obscured their descriptive nature. Recent critics of that research (Barr, 1983; Smagorinsky, 1987) have questioned the generalizations resulting from those case studies. One critic argued that Graves's research is reportage rather than proof of successful use of process writing instruction because only the side that has worked is seen (Smagorinsky, 1987).

By contrast, this study reflects an attempt to systematically manipulate components of process writing under controlled classroom conditions (as controlled as normal classrooms will allow) and in the mode of whole group instruction. Revision was chosen as a major focus of the study because of recent interest in writing process instruction at the elementary school level (Applebee, 1986). That kind of instruction holds at its core a writing process that includes multiple drafting, with the expectation that revision across drafts will improve writing quality (Barr, 1983). Because of this focus, the immediate question becomes "Can and do elementary-aged children revise their writing?"

Revising as part of the writing process

The case study research of Graves (1981, 1983, 1984) and Calkins (1980, 1983) described in detail the revision behavior of child writers. By the time that those researchers' subjects were in the midelementary grades, the children were using many of the same revision techniques as older writers. Those children added information to their personal narratives, rearranged portions of their stories, and deleted sections that they no longer wanted.

Experimental studies indicated that across Grades 4 through 12, the predominant revision behaviors were mechanical revisions (spelling, punctuation, capitalization, usage) and word-level content revisions (additions, deletions, substitutions, rearrangements) (Bridwell, 1980; Crowhurst, 1983; NAEP, 1978). However, within each grade level, the number and kind of revisions per individual paper varied widely (Bridwell; Crowhurst, 1982). The willingness to revise and the ability to determine when revision was necessary fluctuated among students in Grade 5 (Crowhurst, 1982) and continued to do so in Grades 11 and 12 (Bridwell, 1980; Crowhurst, 1982). Those studies suggested that revision behavior cannot be succinctly "pigeonholed" and described by grade level. Some students at all levels revised prolifically, whereas others made minimal changes.

But evidence of revision does not necessarily mean mature and practiced application. Bartlett (1982) concluded that children have two obvious difficulties that set their revising apart from older (adult) writers: (a) They are not always able to recognize problems in their own writing. (b) They are not always able to improve writing even when they recognize problems.

Audience awareness: What will present problems for my readers? Every writer has difficulty at one time or another determining what to say and how to say it effectively. Young writers have even greater hurdles to clear than more experienced writers. The young writers have to figure out not only what to say but also how to write it. Many skills that are automatic for experienced writers require the conscious attention of young ones (Graves, 1983a). Only after the young writers gain automatic control over fluency and mechanical conventions are they able to consciously consider the needs of an audience as they write (Bereiter, 1980). However, young writers have less difficulty locating problems of content and syntax in the writing of others (Bartlett, 1982). This finding suggests the potential helpfulness of peer response during the writing process.

Peer response has appeared as a positive and helpful part of writing workshops at the high school and college level for several years (Carter, 1982; Healy, 1983; Lewes, 1981; Ziv, 1983). Case study results of peer response at the elementary level also are reported as positive (Calkins, 1983; Crowhurst, 1979; Weeks & White, 1982). However, despite the many benefits cited for peer response, attempts to link peer response to improved writing quality at a statistically significant level have been less successful (Carter, 1982; Lewes, 1981; Stevens, Madden, Slavin, & Farnish, 1987; Ziv, 1983).

Conscious control over language: How can I fix problematic text? Sophisticated language behaviors occasionally appear in the language output of young writers, but such behaviors do not appear consistently. Consistency requires more cognitive maturity and conscious control over language processes than is possessed by the young (Burtis, Bereiter, Scardamalia, & Tetroe, 1983). Birnbaum (1982) suggested that "If we can specify what [language] behaviors are associated with production of better text, we may be able to promote them through instruction" (p. 257).

Cohen and Scardamalia (1983), operating from the aforementioned assumption in a revision training study of students in Grade 6, asked: Can sixth graders be trained to revise their own text at the idea (content) level? The results of those authors showed that students who received direct instruction in several specific revision strategies did make significantly more idea-level revisions which, in turn, improved the quality of their writing.

In this study I assumed that young writers will have revision problems that are unique to their developmental and experiential levels. Specifically, those writers will have difficulty recognizing audience need and consciously controlling their use of revision strategies. The research just reported suggested two instructional strategies for use in the elementary classroom to increase revision behaviors and improve quality of writing: (a) peer feedback and (b) direct instruction in specific revision strategies.

Overview of study

Purpose

Classroom teachers, being pragmatists, recognize revision as a potential ally in their struggle to help children become successful writers. In the upper elementary grades where expectations for quality are often high, revision becomes an especially attractive skill.

This study explored the effects of two instructional strategies on the revision behavior and quality of writing of sixth-grade students. Research questions guiding this investigation were as follows:

1   Will type and amount of revision behavior vary significantly across four different instructional situations?
2   Will quality of writing vary significantly across instructional situations?
3   Will quality of writing vary significantly between rough and final drafts within each instructional situation?

Subjects

The subjects in this study were 93 sixth graders from four different schools within the same middle-class suburban school district. Of the 93 students,

49 were girls and 44 were boys. The subjects were members of four hetero-geneous instructional groups, one group per school—each group being an intact classroom. Each classroom was informally grouped by classroom teachers at the beginning of the school year to include the existing range of abilities represented in each school; no attempt was made to isolate spe-cific ability groups within the classrooms. All the students within each class received process writing instruction, but not all the students were part of the final analysis. I eliminated some students because they were either fifth-grade children in a combination classroom, or they were sixth-grade students with incomplete sets of writing samples.

Teachers

All of the participating teachers volunteered to be a part of the study. The teachers had a special interest in improving their own writing instruction and were motivated to try the materials used in this study. All were veteran teachers with between 13 and 24 years of experience at the time of the study.

Materials

Writing lessons. Six autobiographical writing lessons were developed for this study. Each lesson incorporated a prewriting, drafting, and sharing component similar to the precomposing, composing, and postcomposing components described by Graves (1984). Formal focus on revision occurred during the drafting phase and was structured differently for each of the four instructional groups. As is apparent, I developed those lessons within a linear framework. While recognizing the recursive nature of the writing process (Flower & Hayes, 1981), I operated from the philosophy stated by Humes (1983): "Although these processes are recursive rather than linear, for pedagogical purposes the activities of planning and revis-ing are easier to present separately.... As students begin to understand the processes, they can be taught to function recursively" (p. 10).

In all ways but revision, the lessons were the same for each group. I designed the lessons to be taught by classroom teachers in whole group instructional settings. Lesson plans were developed in detail and contained step-by-step directions as well as comments and rationale.

In order to assess revision behavior under optimum conditions, I created writing experiences in which students would have an investment in their stories. The importance of writing from topics of personal interest has been documented forcefully and frequently by Graves (1983, 1984). Thus, the writing lessons used in this study were autobiographical in nature. When all of the students completed each of their six stories, the final copies were collected into autobiographical booklets for each child to take home as a keepsake of sixth grade.

Revision lessons. Five direct-instruction lessons were used with two of the four treatment groups. Those lessons focused on specific revision tactics of adding, deleting, substituting, paraphrasing, and rearranging information within a text. All five lessons were designed to be taught prior to the autobiographical writing lessons.

The purpose behind the revision instruction was two-fold—to develop and support the idea that text can be revised once it is written and to help students gain conscious control over specific strategies for revising text. The guiding philosophy behind the instruction was that "children [who do not often revise] do not necessarily suffer from a lack of competence but rather a lack of understanding of processes relevant to revision" (Cohen & Scardamalia, 1983).

Unlike some lessons that use highly directive instructions, those revision lessons encouraged divergent responses. The lesson plans included several reminders to teachers that divergent responses were to be modeled, discussed, and valued as long as the revisions fit and improved the text.

Procedures

Instruction. This study was conducted over $4\frac{1}{2}$ months under routine classroom conditions. Classroom teachers carried out the prescribed instruction. Students in two of the groups received direct instruction in the use of the five revision tactics prior to starting the autobiographical writing lessons. That instruction occurred approximately twice a week for about 1 month. During that time, the other groups continued with their prescribed language arts program, which focused on grammar and combining sentences. Then all students participated in the six process-based writing lessons. Instruction during the writing lessons varied only at the point of revision. The four instructional situations can be summarized as follows:

Revision instruction/peer partners (RI/PP): Instruction in specific revision strategies was given prior to the use of six process-based writing lessons. During the writing lessons, students met with peer partners to respond to and revise rough drafts.

Peer partner only (PP): No revision instruction was given. During the writing lessons, the students met with peer partners to respond to and revise rough drafts.

Revision instruction only (RI): Instruction in specific revision strategies was given prior to the writing lessons. During the writing lessons, students worked alone to evaluate and revise their rough drafts.

Control: Those students completed the same writing lessons, but they did not receive revision instruction nor did they work with a peer partner to revise their rough drafts. Those participants were given time but no help in revising during the writing lessons.

Because peer collaboration was integral to two of the treatment groups and because of the duration of the study, I attempted to assign treatments on the basis of how the participating teachers normally structured their classrooms. Those teachers who regularly used peer collaboration as a part of their instruction were assigned to instructional situations that incorporated peer collaboration. Treatments not requiring peer collaboration were assigned to teachers who tended to use whole group discussion techniques rather than peer collaboration. So that each treatment was given the best possible chance to succeed, I overruled random assignment of treatment in favor of my more pragmatic method. I hoped that by my action teacher cooperation and enthusiasm would be maintained throughout the course of the study.

Data collection. Data consisted of the rough drafts of lesson 6, collected and copied before and after the formal revising session and the final drafts of the same lesson. Those drafts were used in the analysis of revision behavior and writing quality. I kept session 6 as similar to the previous sessions as possible and returned all original work to the students after copying.

Analysis

Revision behavior. The revision category system in this study was adapted from a system used by Bridwell (1980). That system considered the syntactic levels of revision behavior affecting content of text:

- *Single-word level* ("Run" is changed to "race.")
- *Multiple-word level* ("In front of my house" is deleted from a sentence.)
- *Sentence level* ("I loved my horse very much" is added to a paragraph.)
- *Multiple-sentence level* ("Grandma and Grandpa were waiting for us when we arrived. They had supper ready and our beds all made. Boy were we glad to see them" are rearranged from the beginning of the story to a spot near the middle.)

That system also considered types of revision behavior—mechanics, spelling, additions, deletions, substitutions, and rearrangements (referred to as an "order shift" by Bridwell, 1980). All revision types (except mechanics and spelling) could occur at any of the syntactic levels.

Revision categorization was done twice for each student. First, the revised rough draft was read, and all apparent revisions were classified as to type and syntactic level. Second, the rough and final drafts of each paper were compared, word by word. All changes between rough and final drafts were classified and tallied by category. The revision behaviors for each set of rough and final drafts were counted and recorded. Following this procedure, I calculated revisions per 100 words by category for each student. The numbers of students falling within specific ranges of revisions per 100 words were determined. Chi-square tests were then used to analyze each type of revision behavior.

As a cross-check on rater reliability, a random sample of 10% of the papers was categorized by a second rater trained to use the category system. Of 344 total revisions, both raters noted 266 revisions, a result of 77% agreement. Of the 266 revisions noted by both raters, 242 were categorized by them in the same way for 91% agreement. Failing to note revision behaviors was a problem for both raters. Those results indicated that numbers of revisions were likely to be underestimated in the analysis of revision behavior but that the categorization system itself could be consistently applied.

Quality of writing. The scale used in this study to analyze writing quality was an adaptation of Cooper's (1977) Personal Narrative Writing Scale. Because the current study involved the writing of students younger than those for whom this scale was originally developed, minor modifications were necessary.

The Personal Narrative Writing Scale considers both rhetorical and surface structure qualities. Rhetorical quality is divided into six subcategories: audience considerations, voice, central figure, setting/background, overall organization, and theme/topic. Surface structure quality is also divided into six subcategories: wording, syntax, usage, punctuation/capitalization, spelling, and appearance. Internal consistency of this scale was evaluated using Cronbach's alpha (Mehrens & Lehmann, 1973). The results, shown in Table 1, suggest that the rhetorical quality and total quality portions of that scale are reliable as measures of writing quality.

The Personal Narrative Writing Scale was used to evaluate all three writing samples. The preinstructional sample was analyzed first, and each paper was evaluated by two raters. Interrater reliability, as measured by Pearson's r, was relatively low ($r = .58$). That result prompted a second training session for the raters. Their subsequent efforts produced slightly higher correlations ($r = .69$) when their results on the postinstructional

Table 1 Interitem consistency of quality scale by treatment group

Treatment groups	All items	Rhetorical items	Surface structure items
RI/PP	.88	.95	.86
PP	.91	.90	.77
RI	.90	.96	.77
C	.89	.93	.67

Table 2 ANOVA of preinstructional writing sample quality scores

Source	SS	df	MS	F	p
Among	4,906.09	3	1,635.36	3.35	.02*
Within	39,554.90	81	488.33		
Total	44,460.99	84			

Note
Group means: RI/PP = 107.79; PP = 94.04; RI = 113.58; C = 109.05.
* Judged significant at *p* <.05.

sample were compared. A third rater evaluated those postinstructional papers that showed two or more subcategories discrepant by more than 2 points (points ranged from 1 to 4, with 4 being high). The third rating was compared with the other two ratings, and the most discrepant of the three was discarded. That process resulted in quality scores that correlated more closely than those obtained by the initial rating process ($r = .85$), and those scores were used in subsequent quality analyses.

Scores from the preinstructional writing samples were compared across groups using a one-way ANOVA. The results of this analysis as reported in Table 2 indicated statistically significant differences among groups prior to instruction, $F = 3.35$, $p < .02$. An objective test of language skills also showed differences among groups that approached statistical significance, $F = 2.44$, $p < .07$ (Group means: RI/PP = 38.17; PP = 35.87; RI = 34.28; C = 34.04). Those results indicated the use of analysis of covariance to assess across-group differences for postinstructional samples. The scores from the preinstructional, objective test of language skills correlated most strongly with final quality scores and thus were used as the covariate, $N = 89$, $r = .39$, $p < .002$.

Within-group analysis involved assessing the differences in quality between rough and final drafts of each student. A dependent *t* test was applied to total quality scores within each group. This same test was also used to compare the rhetorical quality scores within each group.

Results

Revision behavior

Amount. Chi-square analysis of all content revisions (additions, deletions, substitutions, rearrangements) made on rough and final drafts indicated significant differences across groups. The majority of students who worked with peer partners revised the content 9 or fewer times per 100 words, whereas the majority of students who worked without peer partners

Table 3 Revision behavior per 100 words

Groups	Content			Surface structure		
	1–9	*10 or more*	n	*1–9*	*10 or more*	n
RI/PP	16	7	23	17	6	23
PP	16	8	24	15	11	26
RI	4	20	24	19	5	24
C	7	11	18	7	11	18

Note
$\chi^2 = 17.66$; $df = 3$; $p < .05$ for content. $\chi^2 = 8.72$; $df = 3$; $p < .03$ for surface structure. p judged significant at $p < .05$.

revised content 10 or more times per 100 words (see Table 3). Students in the RI group seemed most discrepant because considerably more students than expected fell into the upper range of revisions per 100 words (see Table 3).

The results for surface structure revision (mechanics, spelling) showed only the C group to have the majority of its students in the upper range of revisions per 100 words (see Table 3). Thus, the majority of the students who worked without peer partners claimed the upper frequency range of revisions per 100 words, whereas RI students dominated in content revisions and C students led in surface structure revisions. Students in both peer-partner groups were striking for their consistent tendency to fall into the lower frequency ranges of revisions per 100 words across all types of revision behavior.

Type. All groups showed a majority of students making more content revisions than surface structure revisions, but the RI group showed this pattern most strongly (see Table 4). Across all groups, the predominant syntactic level for content revisions was word level (67% of all content revisions).

The most frequently used revision types for RI/PP, PP, and C students

Table 4 Revision behavior compared by frequency of use

Groups	Content	Surface structure	n
RI/PP	13	10	23
PP	15	9	24
RI	22	1	23
C	11	6	17

Note
$\chi^2 = 10.09$, $df = 3$, $p < .02$. p judged significant at $p < .05$.

Table 5 Comparison of time of revising

Groups	Rough draft	Final draft	n
RI/PP	7	14	21
PP	6	19	25
RI	20	4	24
C	8	8	16

Note
$\chi^2 = 19.62$, $df = 3$, $p < .01$. p judged significant at $p < .05$.

were mechanical revisions and substitutions. For RI students, substitutions and additions predominated. Between 92 to 99% of all students, regardless of group, made substitutions, additions, and deletions in their stories. Frequency of use seemed to be affected by instructional situation, but the ability to revise using those tactics existed—with or without instruction.

Time of revising. The instructional groups also were contrasted by predominant time of revising, that is, between drafts or during final drafting (see Table 5). Once again, the RI group stood apart from the rest with only that group showing a majority of students revising more often between drafts than during final drafting. All other groups showed the majority of students making most of their revisions on the final draft.

Discussion

The first research question asked: Will type and amount of revision behavior vary significantly across four different instructional situations? From the results just reported, three points can be made in answer to that question. First, the two groups revising with peer partners (RI/PP and PP) were more similar than the two groups receiving revision instruction (RI/PP and RI). This result suggests that type and amount of revision behavior may have been influenced more by the use of peer partners than by the revision lessons used in this study.

Second, the groups revising without peer partners (RI and C) revised more often than those who had peer partners (RI/PP and PP). RI students revised content more often, whereas C students revised surface structure more often.

Third, revision instruction of the type used in this study was not needed to elicit substitution, addition, and deletion tactics. Students used those tactics regardless of instructional situation, leading one to conclude that revision instruction used in this study did not build skills that were unique to those students receiving instruction. However, the emphasis that those tactics received may have caused the RI students to revise content more frequently than the other students did.

Writing quality

Across-group effects. Analysis of covariance indicated significant differences across groups in quality of writing scores on both rough and final drafts. For total quality scores, students in the RI/PP groups wrote rough and final drafts of significantly higher quality than all other groups (see Tables 6 and 7). Students in the PP group wrote rough and final drafts that ranked second in quality.

When rhetorical quality scores were considered separately, rough and final drafts of the RI/PP groups were again significantly superior to those of all other groups (see Table 8). Although the remaining groups showed

Table 6 ANCOVA of total quality scores

Source	SS	df	MS	F	p
		Rough draft			
Among	10,387.62	3	3,462.54	9.62	.01
Within	29,875.58	83	359.95		
Total	40,263.20	86			
		Final draft			
Among	8,784.80	3	2,928.27	8.96	.01
Within	27,114.10	83	326.68		
Total	35,898.90	86			

Note
Multiple comparison of group means in rough draft: Set 1: RI/PP; Set 2: PP, RI; Set 3: RI, C.
Multiple comparison of group means in final draft: Set 1: RI/PP; Set. 2: PP, C: Set. 3: RI, C.

Table 7 Covariate, dependent, and adjusted means and standard deviations

Groups	Covariate		Dependent		Adjusted
	M	SD	M	SD	M
			Rough draft		
RI/PP	34.65	5.40	112.87	18.16	114.61
PP	35.87	5.81	98.78	26.81	98.76
RI	38.17	5.31	94.63	17.08	91.26
C	34.28	6.18	82.78	18.41	85.07
			Final draft		
RI/PP	34.65	5.40	117.26	21.74	119.71
PP	35.87	5.81	106.83	19.09	106.79
RI	38.17	5.31	97.13	21.56	92.40
C	34.28	6.18	97.94	23.25	101.16

Table 8 Summary of ANCOVA results of partial quality scores

Draft	df	F	p	Post hoc multiple comparisons *(adjusted means)*
				Rhetorical quality
Rough	3, 83	8.39	.02	Set 1: RI/PP (75.75)
				Set 2: PP (62.68); RI (56.30); C (55.05)
Final	3, 83	12.24	.01	Set 1: RI/PP (78.85)
				Set 2: PP (68.32); C (62.92)
				Set 3: C; RI (54.76)
				Surface structure quality
Rough	3, 83	7.61	.03	Set 1: RI/PP (38.87); PP (36.08)
				Set 2: PP; RI (34.96)
				Set 3: C (30.02)
Final	3, 83	1.11	.35	NSD[a]

Note
p judged significant at $p < .05$.
[a] Adjusted group means: RI/PP = 40.83; PP = 38.47; RI = 37.68; C = 37.76.

no significant differences in rough-draft rhetorical quality, by final drafts the PP group was significantly superior to the RI group.

On the rough draft, the C group scored significantly lower than all other groups on surface structure quality, and the RI group scored significantly lower than the RI/PP group (see Table 8). But by the final draft, no significant differences were found in surface structure quality.

Within-group effects. Rough and final draft quality scores for students in each instructional group were compared using dependent *t* tests. The results of those *t* tests are summarized in Table 9.

Those results confirmed that students in all groups were able to significantly improve the surface structure quality of their stories across drafts. According to that finding, the multiple-draft process, where overt concern for surface structure issues is postponed until later in the drafting process, was comfortable for those students regardless of group.

In contrast to surface structure revising, only the PP group was able to significantly improve rhetorical quality. Analysis of revision behavior showed that those students consistently fell in the lower range of revisions per 100 words for all types of revision. Yet, their revising must have been purposeful, targeting with some success the portions of text that needed revising the most.

RI/PP students did not significantly improve rhetorical quality. At least two factors may have been operating in this study. First, the RI/PP teacher evaluated each story as heavily for mechanical accuracy as for communica-

Table 9 Summary of within-group quality comparisons

Group	df	t	p
RI/PP			
Total	22	1.58	.06
Rhetorical	22	1.11	.14
Surface structure	22	1.77	.04*
PP			
Total	25	2.20	.02*
Rhetorical	25	1.81	.04*
Surface structure	25	2.22	.02*
RI			
Total	23	.71	.25
Rhetorical	23	−.14	.44
Surface structure	23	2.29	.02*
C			
Total	18	2.2	.02*
Rhetorical	18	1.16	.13
Surface structure	18	4.13	.05*

Note
* Judged significant at $p < .05$.

tive quality. Students, accustomed to the teacher's high expectations for accuracy, may have focused more attention on perfecting surface structure and less on improving content as they revised. Second, RI/PP students had already written stories of superior quality. The content of their stories may not have needed as much revising, and thus significant growth did not occur.

The second and third research questions asked: "Will quality of writing vary significantly across instructional situations?" and "Will quality of writing vary significantly between rough and final drafts within each instructional situation?"

After considering the effects of instructional situation on quality of writing both within and across groups, the following conclusions seem fair. First, peer feedback did seem to have positive effects on quality of writing. The groups receiving peer feedback ranked first and second in terms of writing quality. The PP group improved rhetorical quality scores significantly between rough and final drafts; the RI/PP group did not, but their stories initially were significantly superior. Peer response may have helped those students anticipate audience need as well as maintain enthusiasm for the task of writing six autobiographical stories in the full-process mode. This study cannot describe how peer partners helped each other, but it does indicate that help was given and received.

Second, a situation not conducive to productive revising was isolated. The results of the RI instructional situation strongly suggest that students should not be systematically prompted to apply revision strategies to rough drafts without the benefit of peer feedback. Without feedback, students revised more, but the quality of writing did not improve; in fact, for the group as a whole, rhetorical quality declined between rough and final drafts. Students may have regarded revision as an end in itself rather than as a means to improve writing for an audience of peers.

Third, for the sixth-grade students in the current study, frequent revising had mixed effects. RI students tended to make more content revisions on both drafts than did students in other groups. The RI participants also had final drafts of significantly lower quality than did members of either of the peer-partner groups. By contrast, students in the C group tended to make more surface structure revisions than did students in all other groups. But in this study, the frequent revisions were warranted by the C group's low surface-structure quality scores on the rough drafts. Frequent revisions by the C group allowed them to raise their surface structure quality scores enough to place them on par with other students. Evidently, students in sixth grade who revise alone have greater success in detecting and correcting surface structure problems than content problems. This finding substantiates Bartlett's (1982) earlier conclusions to the same effect.

Finally, one can conclude from these results that sixth-grade students are able to significantly improve surface structure quality within a multiple-draft process both with and without the benefit of peer feedback. All groups showed significant growth in surface structure quality between drafts, although the C group students improved their papers the most. Peer response did not seem to be absolutely essential for significant improvement of text-based problems of punctuation, capitalization, spelling, usage, and handwriting in the writing of those sixth-grade students.

Summary of conclusions

Several of the findings of the current study substantiate results from previous studies.

1   All groups in this study did most revising of content at the word level (Bridwell, 1980; Crowhurst, 1982; NAEP, 1978).
2   The RI/PP, PP, and C groups made surface structure revisions and substitutions more often than any other revision type (Mullis, 1985; NAEP, 1978).
3   Those same groups revised more often while drafting than they did between drafts (Bridwell, 1980).
4   Students in the RI group were induced through training and prompting to do more revising of content than was expected (Cohen & Scardamalia, 1983; Matsuhashi & Gordon, 1985).

Results of this study also suggest that direct instruction in specific revision strategies does not result in improved quality of writing when students revise in isolation. The group that received revision instruction but revised alone (RI) made more content revisions than other groups did but showed a decline in rhetorical quality between rough and final drafts.

Suggestions for future research

This study did not include observations of and interviews with students as they revised. As such, one cannot state with certainty why students responded as they did to the various instructional situations. Additional research with this focus is warranted. A question to consider might be: Do students focus their revision efforts on problems specified by other students, or do they use a more personal, internally guided system of evaluation to focus their revision?

References

Applebee, A. N. (1986). Problems in process approaches: Toward a reconceptualization of process instruction. In A. R. Petrosky & C. Bartholomae (Eds.), *The teaching of writing: 85th Yearbook of the National Society for the Study of Education. Part II*, Chicago, IL: NSSE.

Barr, M. (1983). The new orthodoxy about writing: Confusing process and pedagogy. *Language Arts, 60*(7). 829–840.

Bartlett, E. J. (1982). Learning to revise: Some component processes. In Martin Nystrand (Ed.). *What writers know*. New York: Academic Press.

Bereiter, C. (1980). Development in writing. In L. W. Gregg & E. R. Steinberg (Eds.), *Cognitive processes in writing*. Hillsdale, NJ: Lawrence Erlbaum Associates.

Birnbaum, J. C. (1982). The reading and composing behavior of selected fourth and seventh grade students. *Research in the Teaching of English, 16*(3), 241–260.

Bridwell, L. (1980). Revising strategies in twelfth grade students' transactional writing. *Research in the Teaching of English, 14*(3), 197–222.

Burtis, P. J., Bereiter, C., Scardamalia, M., Stero, J. (1983). The development of planning in writing. In B. Kroll & G. Wells (Eds.), *Explorations in the development of writing*. New York: Wiley.

Calkins, L. (1980). Children's rewriting strategies. *Research in the Teaching of English, 14*(6).

Calkins, L. (1983). *Lessons from a child*. Exeter, NH: Heinemann.

Carter, R. (1982). By itself, peer group revision has no power. ERIC Document Reproduction Service No. 226 350

Cohen, E., & Scardamalia, M. (1983). The effects of instructional intervention in the revision of essays by grade six children. Paper presented at the annual meeting of the American Educational Research Association, Montreal.

Cooper, C. R. (1977). Holistic evaluation of writing. In C. Cooper & L. Odell (Eds.), *Evaluating writing: Describing measuring, judging*. Urbana, IL: National Council of Teachers of English.

Crowhurst, M. (1979). Writing workshop: An experience in peer response to writing. *Language Arts, 56*, 757–762.

Crowhurst, M. (1983). Revision strategies of students at three grade levels. Education Research Institute of British Columbia. (ERIC Document Reproduction Service No. 238 009)

Flower, L., & Hayes, J. R. (1981). A cognitive process theory of writing. *College Composition and Communication, 32*, 365–387.

Graves, D. (1981). What children show us about revision. In R. Walshe (Ed.), *Donald Graves in Australia*. Rozelle, NSW: Australia Primary English Teachers' Association.

Graves, D. (1983). *Writing: Teachers and Children at Work*. Exeter, NH: Heinemann.

Graves, D. (1984). The child, the writing process, and the role of the professional. In *A researcher learns to write*. Exeter, NH: Heinemann.

Healy, M. K. (1983). Using student writing response groups in the classroom. In M. Myers & J. Gray (Eds.), *Theory and practice in teaching of composition: Processing, distancing and modeling*. (ERIC Document Reproduction Service No. 277 515)

Humes, A. (1983). Putting writing research into practice. *The Elementary School Journal, 84*(1), 3–17.

Lewes, U. E. (1981). Peer evaluation in a writing seminar. (ERIC Document Reproduction Service 226 355)

Matsuhashi, A., & Gordon, E. (1985). Revision, addition, and the power of the unseen text. In S. Freedman (Ed.), *The acquisition of written language: Response and revision*. Norwood, NJ: Ablex.

Mehrens, W. A., & Lehmann, I. (1973). *Measurement and evaluation in education and psychology*. New York: Holt, Rinehart and Winston.

Mullis I. V. (1985, May). Writing achievement and instruction results from the 1983–1984 NAEP writing assessment. Paper presented at the annual meeting of the International Reading Association, New Orleans.

National Assessment of Educational Progress, (1978). *An assessment of revision skills*. (ERIC Document Reproduction Service No. 141 826)

Smagorinsky, P. (1987). Graves revisited: A look at the methods and conclusions of the New Hampshire study. *Written Communication, 9*(9), 331–342.

Stevens, R., Madden, N., Slavin, R., & Farnish, A. M. (1987). Cooperative integrated reading and composition: Two field experiments. *Reading Research Quarterly, 22*(4), 433–454.

Weeks, J. O., & White, M. B. (1982). Peer editing vs. teacher editing: Does it make a difference? (ERIC Document Reproduction Service No. 224 014)

Ziv, N. (1983). Peer groups in the composition classroom: A Case study. (ERIC Document Reproduction Service No. 229 799)

53

STUDENTS' METACOGNITIVE KNOWLEDGE ABOUT WRITING

Taffy E. Raphael, Carol Sue Englert and Becky W. Kirschner

Source: *Research in the Teaching of English* (1989) 23(4): 343–379

Interest in understanding and describing the writing process has risen dramatically in the past decade (Applebee, 1986; Bouchard, 1983; Hairston, 1982; Hillocks, 1984; Murray, 1982). An integral part of studying the writing process has involved examining what skilled writers know about writing, and how they engage in writing activities (e.g., Berkenkotter, 1983; Nystrand, 1982). Additional research has involved examining and manipulating the writing curriculum in classrooms from elementary to secondary schools (e.g., Applebee, 1984; Calkins, 1983; Florio & Clark, 1982; Giacobbi, 1986; Graves, 1983). While some literature exists describing students' understanding of the writing process, and how this understanding affects their writing ability (e.g., Hansen, 1983), most research has focused primarily on the writing of narratives (e.g., Gordon & Braun, 1985). The study presented in this report examines fifth and sixth grade students' metacognitive knowledge of the writing process for both narrative and expository writing, and represents one data set from a line of research conducted within the Cognitive Strategy Instruction in Writing Project at the Institute for Research on Teaching, Michigan State University.

Students' metacognitive knowledge was examined prior to, during, and following their participation in one of four writing programs implemented over the course of an academic year. Three of the programs were based on introducing students to the process of writing, though each program stressed different aspects of the process. A fourth control group in which instruction proceeded as usual was also included. Two areas of research contributed to the development of the writing programs. The first area considered was research on the writing process. The second area was research on metacognitive knowledge in general, and specifically as it relates to students' metacognitive knowledge about text structures, audience, and purpose in writing.

Process of writing

Research on the process of writing has detailed nonlinear cognitive behaviors that occur as prewriting, drafting, revising, and editing (Flower & Hayes, 1981). Throughout this process, writers focus with varying degrees of attention on the subject or topic about which they are writing, their audience, their reasons for writing, and the form in which they present their writing (Britton, 1978; Kinneavy, 1971; Moffet, 1968). During prewriting, for example, writers engage in activities designed to help them generate ideas. These activities can include brainstorming, uninterrupted sustained writing for several minutes, or imaging previous experiences. Writers also consider their audience, such as the teacher only or a wider audience of classmates, family members, and other readers. They consider their reasons for writing, both general (e.g., to communicate a feeling) and specific (e.g., to tell about what it felt like to win the relay race; to explain how to play a game). Finally, they consider how to organize their paper and select a form to best present their ideas. Though there are several ways to inform students about the writing process, two lines of inquiry in the research literature—one examining social context and the other examining text structure—suggest factors that seem particularly likely to affect students' assumptions about writing and their activities within the writing process.

Social context

Research has indicated that the social context in which students learn to write has a major effect on the type of writing they produce (DeFord, 1986) and on their control of prewriting, drafting, revising, and editing activities (Calkins, 1983; Graves, 1983; Hansen, 1983; Rubin & Bruce, 1986). One aspect of the social context that has been stressed is the importance of audience. Audience provides a forum for the expression of one's ideas, and it communicates to children the purpose of prewriting, revising, and editing activities. Several authors have recommended ways in which audience can be created, such as sharing finished products within a single classroom (Graves & Hansen, 1983), peer-conferencing and publishing written work (Graves, 1983), or transmitting work via microcomputer networks (Rubin & Bruce, 1986). Audience has a critical impact on how children construe the functions of writing. For example, when the audience is solely the teacher, students may come to view writing as a way that teachers test knowledge, and consider revision activities as punishment for sloppiness or inexactitude. When children write for an expanded audience that includes peers and others, they may arrive at a view of writing as that of communication, and consider revision activities as essential to the communication process.

A second important aspect of the social context is the purpose for writing. Purpose affects the ideas generated during writing and how those ideas are communicated. Purpose can be established in different ways. Bruce and Rubin (in preparation) describe a writing project in a community in Alaska in which elementary school students published a brochure used by the department of tourism. Purpose can also be established by publishing class or individual books for placement in the school and classroom libraries (DeFord, 1986) or by sharing ideas with teachers in the form of dialogue journals (Atwell, 1983). When both purpose and audience are emphasized in the writing curriculum, students are more likely to be aware of the social and communicative purpose of writing. These aspects enter the writing process at the points when children brainstorm topics during prewriting, decide on details to include during drafting, and insure that information is clear and organized during revising and editing. In practice, audience and purpose are two aspects of the social context that are thoroughly interrelated and critical to the development of skilled writers.

Text structure

Another aspect of writing that influences students' perceptions of what to do during the writing process is text structure. Research on text structures suggests that a number of structures exist such as problem/solution and comparison/contrast (Meyer, 1975), and that the different structures are used by writers to address different sets of questions. For example, writers using a comparison/contrast structure include information answering questions such as "What is being compared and contrasted? On what? How are they alike? different?" In contrast, writers using a problem/solution text structure include information that addresses "What is the problem? What caused it? What is/are possible solution(s)?" Authors use key words and phrases that signal the reader about the type of structure and information contained. Words such as "similarly" or "in contrast" signal comparison/contrast, while words such as "first" or "next" signal explanations or other chronology-based text structures. Research on the role of text structures in writing suggests that there is a positive relationship between text structure knowledge and writing ability (Dunn & Bridwell, 1980; Hillocks, 1986), and that teaching about text structures improves students' writing (Englert, Raphael, & Kirschner, 1985; Gordon & Braun, 1985; Raphael & Kirschner, 1985).

Knowledge about text structures appears to enter at several points in the writing process. During prewriting, writers consider how to present information to their audience, the questions that they plan to answer, and the text structure that best conveys their ideas. During drafting, writers consider the information to include throughout their paper, and those key words and phrases to include as text structure signals to their readers. During editing and revising, writers examine their papers to insure that the information is sufficiently clear and organized. Throughout this process, an understanding of the types of information and questions that different text structures address plays a decided role. Langer (1985, 1986) conducted developmental research examining high achieving students' awareness of differences in organizational patterns in stories and reports, and the relationship of this awareness to their ability to produce papers within the two general genres. She found that as young as third grade, students differentiated between the two, and improved over time in their ability to produce such texts. She suggests that developmental differences may be better understood through the study of children as they learn to elaborate upon known genres, and as they use them in relationship to specific goals.

Metacognition and the writing process

In addition to the literature on the process of writing, another area of research that influenced the development of this research program was the study of metacognition in general, and specifically as it applies to the development of writing abilities. The term, metacognition, has met with criticisms such as its having become an "abused concept" (Garner, 1987, p. 15), a "fuzzy concept" (Flavell, 1981, p. 37), or a term that has "amounted to almost 'buzzword' proportions" (Gavelek & Raphel, 1985, p. 103). Yet its popularity may be attributed to how well the concept resonates to at least two issues fundamental to both cognitive and instructional psychology. First, metacognition describes the control processes in which active learners engage as they perform various cognitive activities. Second, metacognitive or executive control processes may underlie the very important processes of generalization and transfer of strategies learned. It is hard to imagine skilled writers who are not actively engaged in applying their knowledge about the writing process, text structures, purposes, audiences, and so forth as they regulate their use of strategies throughout the writing process. Thus, the study of writers' metacognitive knowledge may help to identify those areas of instruction which might be particularly valuable in the development of skilled writers.

A number of researchers have suggested definitions for metacognition. Flavell suggests that "metacognition refers to one's knowledge concerning one's own cognitive processes and products or anything related to them" (Flavell, 1976, p. 232), and further that, "metacognitive knowledge consists primarily of knowledge or beliefs about what factors or variables act and interact in what ways to affect the course and outcome of cognitive enterprises" (Flavell, 1979, p. 907). Paris, Lipson, and Wixson (1983) elaborate on the elements subsumed under metacognitive knowledge, suggesting three types of knowledge: declarative, procedural, and conditional.

Declarative knowledge includes information about task structure and task goals. For example, declarative knowledge about writing includes knowledge that writing includes prewriting activities such as considering audience and purpose, drafting and revising, and copy-editing. Procedural knowledge includes information about how the various actions or strategies are implemented. In other words, procedural knowledge includes the repertoire of behavior available from which the learner selects the one(s) best able to help reach a particular goal. In writing, procedural knowledge includes the writers' knowledge that there are strategies to use such as inserting key words and phrases to signal potential readers about location of information, or that writers can revise by taking out or adding information to their papers. Most definitions of metacognition distinguish only between declarative and procedural knowledge, often identifying the former as "knowing that" and the latter as "knowing how." However, Paris et al. (1983) suggest a third category, conditional knowledge. It is conditional knowledge that addresses the conditions under which one elects to use a particular strategy, suggesting that "an expert with full procedural knowledge could not adjust behavior to changing task demands without conditional knowledge" (Paris, 1986, p. 119). That is, conditional knowledge involves "knowing when and why." While procedural knowledge may be in evidence as a child describes addition and deletion as potential revision strategies, conditional knowledge can only be verified if such strategies are used appropriately in the context of revision. Thus, conditional knowledge is perhaps best identified as those strategies actually implemented during the writing process, as opposed to strategies talked about in the abstract. In this study of metacognitive knowledge about writing, declarative, procedural, and conditional knowledge were examined.

Research questions

The purpose of this study was to examine changes in students' metacognitive knowledge as a result of participating in instructional programs emphasizing a communicative context for writing, or emphasizing the role of text structure knowledge in writing. The instructional programs in which the students participated can be characterized as "environmental" in scope (vis a vis Hillocks, 1984) in that they emphasized clear and specific objectives (e.g., learning of questions related to different text structures; learning questions to ask prior to writing), and they contained materials and problems that were selected "to engage students with each other in specifiable processes important to some particular aspect of writing" (Hillocks, p. 144) "and to minimize teacher lecture while increasing student involvement as 'generator of ideas.'" The instructional programs also were similar in their emphasis on prewriting, drafting, revising, and editing activities within the writing process.

What differed across the instructional programs, however, was the type of activities in which the students engaged, and the focus of the instruction on the communicative context or on text structure in prewriting, drafting, revising, and editing activities. Four groups were created to examine the influence of such instruction on students' metacognitive knowledge: (1) a Communicative Context group that learned and practiced writing within an environment that emphasized the writing process with a particular stress on audience and purposes for writing; (2) a Communicative Context/Text Structure group that received text structure instruction embedded within a program that emphasized the communicative context (i.e., audience and purpose) for writing; (3) a Text Structure group that received text structure instruction as part of the writing process, but in the absence of an environment stressing audience and purpose; and (4) a no treatment Control group that received neither text structure instruction nor the defined communicative context, but participated in the traditional language arts curriculum of the school. The Control group more generally fit the pattern Hillocks (1984) described as presentational, using primarily teacher-led discussion and individual skill activities or writing assignments generally prompted by the district-adopted language arts textbook.

Three types of metacognitive knowledge were examined: (1) declarative knowledge concerning audience, purpose, and text structure, (2) procedural knowledge concerning steps in the writing process, and (3) conditional knowledge concerning how procedures vary under different writing conditions and during revisions. In analyzing this data, a general description of strategies was synthesized from group questionnaire data, with specific data and in-depth profiles of students' responses selected from individual interviews and writing samples.

Methods

Participants

Participating in the study were 140 heterogeneously grouped students from 7 upper elementary classrooms (i.e., 4 fifth and 3 sixth grades). The students were from a lower SES neighborhood, with an approximately equal mix of Caucasian, Hispanic, and Black ethnic groups. Students had been assigned randomly to classrooms at the beginning of the academic year by school personnel. Students then were assigned by classroom within grade levels to one of the three treatment groups or to the control group (Communicative Context $n = 41$; Text Structure $n = 41$; Communicative Context/Text Structure $n = 44$; Control $n = 14$). A subset of 12 students (6 per classroom) from each treatment group was identified by the teachers for participation in in-depth individual interviews (n interviewed = 48). Criteria used to select the students were that they represent a range of

204

ability levels from low-average to high-average, based on a combination of teacher judgment and standardized test scores. To insure that treatment groups were of comparable ability, an analysis of variance was performed on students' language achievement scores on the subtest of the Stanford Achievement Test administered in the spring. The results showed no significant differences ($p > .05$) between groups.

Materials

Materials used for the assessment of metacognitive knowledge included group questionnaires, individual interviews, and writing packets. Metacognitive knowledge (i.e., declarative and procedural) was formally assessed at three points in the study: pretreatment, at the end of Phase I (i.e., mid-point), and at the end of Phase II (i.e., posttreatment). Pre-and posttreatment assessments of declarative, procedural, and conditional knowledge included both questionnaires and interviews, while the mid-point assessment included only questionnaires. In addition, materials that were used both in assessment and during instruction included writing packets consisting of think-sheets that guided students through the prewriting, drafting, and revising activities in the writing process. The think-sheet packets allowed the examination of students' strategy use in the context of writing, providing information about conditional knowledge of the writing process. These materials are described below.

Group questionnaires

The group questionnaire was developed for administration prior to training, midway through the programs, and following training, assessing students' declarative and procedural knowledge. Declarative knowledge was assessed in terms of students' awareness of audience and purpose in writing. Sample questions include, "Who reads your writing?" (audience) and "What reasons do you have for writing?" (purpose). To examine students' procedural knowledge about writing, questions asked included "What do you do when you write a paper? What do you do first? second? third? fourth?"

Individual interviews

The individual interviews focused on students' declarative knowledge of audience and purposes for writing, and differences between reading and writing expository and narrative texts. Procedural knowledge was examined in terms of knowledge of steps in the writing process, and how writing varies across different text structures. Questions were similar to those asked on the group questionnaire regarding audience, purpose, and steps in writing. Additionally, to further tap awareness of the audience and of the writing process, students were asked, "Why is editing useful?" "Why would you revise a paper?" To assess knowledge of text structure, two question sets were used. First, students were asked to discuss differences between writing stories and reports, including purposes, audience, and sources for ideas. Second, they were presented with the titles of three articles in a fictitious magazine about dogs. The titles ("Choosing a Dog for You: Labrador Retriever, Poodle, and Cocker Spaniel"; "Puppy's First Year"; and "Breaking a Puppy's Bad Habits") were designed to elicit students' knowledge of what information would be expected for three different text structures: comparison/contrast, narration, and problem/solution, respectively.

Think-sheets

During the instructional program, students completed writing packets that consisted of a series of think-sheets for each paper. The think-sheets included questions and prompts adapted from Kirschner and Yates (1983) to guide prewriting, drafting, editing, and revising. Think sheets were consonant with the objectives and foci of the individual programs. Think-sheets for the Communicative Context group focused on audience (e.g., Who will read your paper? What will they think is interesting about your paper?) and purpose (e.g., How do you want your reader(s) to feel when they read your paper? Why are you writing about this topic?) in planning, peer-editing, and revising drafts. Think sheets for the Text Structure group focused on organization (e.g., What is the problem? Causes? Steps of the solution? Circle the part that tells about the problem.) and key words (e.g., Circle the key words that tell there is a problem.) in planning and revising drafts. Think-sheets for the Communicative Context/Text Structure group focused on a combination of text structure and communicative context emphases. For example, students in the Communicative Context/Text Structure group used an editing sheet that emphasized audience through prompts that led them to consider parts of the authors' paper that they liked best, parts that were confusing, and information that could be added to make it more interesting to the reader or easier for the reader to follow. These questions were present on the editing think-sheet regardless of the text structure. Also present were questions that focused the editors' attention on whether or not the author had included information invited by the structure of the text.

These think-sheets plus first and second drafts were used to examine the students' conditional knowledge; that is, their selection and implementation of strategies during their production and revision of text. Students completed approximately 10 writing packets (i.e., think-sheets, first drafts, second drafts) over the course of the academic year.

Treatment groups

Students in three experimental treatment groups and one control group participated in the study. Each treatment group received a two-phase instructional program, each phase lasting approximately eight to ten weeks. A detailed description of the four groups follows.

Communicative context

During Phase I, instruction for students in the Communicative Context group focused on creating a social context, emphasizing purposes for writing, and encouraging participation in the process of writing including prewriting activities, drafting, self- and peer-editing, revision, copy-editing, and publication of students' papers into class books. Social context was emphasized on the think-sheets in terms of prompts focusing on audience and purpose during prewriting, drafting, editing, and revising. Further, students in these classrooms published their papers in class books which were available in the classroom library. Though these students were not formally introduced to text structures (i.e., the questions different texts are designed to answer, the key words and phrases used to signal readers about information), they completed writing packets for six different papers (i.e., one narration, one explanation, two comparison/contrast, and two problem/solution papers) with topics drawn from their personal experiences (e.g., explaining how to play a particular game, comparing/contrasting two restaurants, two friends). Each cycle of think-sheets took approximately two weeks. Students were introduced to the different strategies and activities appropriate to various aspects of writing, with instruction and modeling guided by prompts and questions on the think-sheets. Teachers used instructional strategies such as placing a transparency of the prewriting think-sheet on an overhead projector and modeling how it could be used to prompt appropriate prewriting activities or to remind writers about what to consider before they begin to write.

When think-sheets for all six papers had been completed, students then selected their favorite paper for publication in the class book. These drafts were then peer-edited and revised a final time prior to publication in the book. This signaled the end of the first phase. Students then completed individual copies of the group questionnaire.

In Phase II, Communicative context students repeated the same type of instructional and writing activities as they had in Phase I, with a focus on topics related to their social studies class. For example, in one classroom where students were studying states of the United States, they composed brief reports about different aspects of the states (e.g., comparing/contrasting two amusement parks within a state; describing a problem in their state related to polluting factories and how the problem was solved).

During Phase II, students completed four sets of think-sheets related to social studies topics, one each for narration, explanation, comparison/contrast, and problem/solution.

Text structure

Students in the Text Structure group also wrote six papers during Phase I, to provide a control on the midpoint questionnaire for practice effects. However, they did not receive think-sheets, nor did they participate in any aspect of the peer-editing or publishing of their papers. In fact, the writing of these papers was embedded within assignments in the language arts textbook used in the classroom. Typically, students produced first drafts of papers, each week writing a paper that invited use of a different structure (e.g., explaining about a favorite game). Similar to the Communicative Context group, they completed six papers (one each narration and explanation, two each comparison/contrast and problem/solution). At the end of this phase, they completed the group questionnaire. Since this group did not receive any instruction emphasizing the communicative context, but did write the papers, they served as the control group for Phase I.

In Phase II, text structure instruction was introduced in the Text Structure classrooms. The instruction consisted of seven steps. First, using an overhead projector, teachers presented one good example of each text type written by students during Phase I. The students worked in large groups to identify the structure of each paper and the characteristics (i.e., key words and phrases; questions answered in the text) that led to the identification of the dominant structure. Second, students repeated this activity using their own papers. Responding individually to their own six papers from Phase I, they identified the text structure type, the questions answered in the text, and any key words and phrases. Third, teachers reviewed with them the generic questions answered in each text type (for a sample of generic questions for narration, see Singer & Donlan, 1982), and related key words and phrases. Fourth, students revised one of their Phase I papers, focusing on the questions, the organization of ideas, clarity, and use of key words and phrases. Fifth, teachers presented good examples of well-structured social studies passages; students again identified the structure, generic questions answered, and key words and phrases. Sixth, they repeated this activity with less clear examples taken directly from their social studies books. Finally, over the course of eight weeks they used the think-sheets to focus on text structures in planning, drafting, and editing four papers on social studies topics, one each for narration, explanation, comparison/contrast, and problem/solution. Sources of information for the content of the papers were their social studies books, tradebooks, and reference materials. However, students planned, drafted, and revised their papers without peer editing (audience) or publishing their papers (purpose and audience).

Communicative Context/Text Structure

In Phase I, students in the Communicative Context/Text Structure group participated in the instruction that focused on creating a social context and purpose for writing (see description for Communicative Context treatment), then completed the group questionnaire. In Phase II, students in the Communicative Context/Text Structure classrooms were introduced to the instruction provided students in the text structure classrooms (see instruction for Text Structure treatment). However, students in the Communicative Context/Text Structure group continued to peer-edit and publish their papers about social studies topics.

Control

The Control group participated in those language arts and social studies assignments suggested by their textbooks, but without instruction that focused on specific topics, structure, or the writing process. That is, control group students received the instruction their teachers normally provided in both language arts and social studies. Questionnaires were administered to the Control group prior to Phase I and at the conclusion of Phase II.

Procedures

Students had been randomly assigned to classrooms by the school administrator prior to the opening day of school, forming heterogenous groups of students. Teachers were interviewed in early fall to determine the treatment group most appropriate to their goals of instruction (e.g., a teacher who was using journals and some peer-editing was placed in one of the social context conditions; a teacher who indicated that she was uncomfortable with allowing students to share their papers was placed in a group without the social context treatment). Once teachers were assigned to treatment groups, pretests were administered to students in their classrooms. Pre-treatment assessment included the questionnaires and interviews.

Following the administration of pretests, the two-phase training program began, with students receiving instruction from their classroom teachers (see Table 1). During Phase I, there were two types of activities engaged in by the groups: they either participated in activities related to the establishment of a social context for writing, or they practiced writing in the absence of such an environment. Thus, in half the classrooms a social context was established with an emphasis on the writing process including peer editing and publishing. Teachers in these classrooms participated in inservice sessions held weekly after school to provide them with information related to the instructional program. After one month,

Table 1 Instructional groups

	Phase I	Phase II
Communicative Context	Process writing introduced, emphasis on purpose and audience	Continue Phase I instruction using social studies topics
Communicative Context/ Text Structure	Process writing introduced, emphasis on purpose and audience	Text structure instruction for four structures, continued emphasis on purpose and audience
Text Structure	Weekly writing assignments	Text structure instruction for four structures, emphasis on writing process, but without stress on purpose or audience
Control	Traditional focus of language arts textbook driven lessons	

these sessions were held on a bi-weekly basis as teachers began to feel comfortable with the instructional techniques. The biweekly meetings became a time for sharing ideas for program implementation and modification, for asking questions of the researchers, and for monitoring the progress of the instruction.

In the other half of the classrooms during Phase I, teachers had their students practice writing, either using the same types of papers (e.g., an explanation) or an assignment that naturally occurred through language arts or social studies, but focusing on the production of first drafts without the opportunity for peer editing or publishing (i.e., the Communicative Context "Absent" classrooms in Phase I). Researchers stopped in to visit these classroom teachers and to provide a resource for questions about writing, but did not offer formal suggestions related to writing instruction.

At the end of the first phase, students completed the group midpoint questionnaire, designed to assess the effects of participation in a general writing environment emphasizing process, purpose, and audience, versus participation in a language arts textbook-driven writing program.

During Phase II, the Communicative Context group continued to receive instruction focusing on audience and purpose. The Communicative Context/Text Structure students continued to receive emphasis on the writing process, but it was embedded within instruction that emphasized the role of text structure knowledge during all aspects of the writing process. Text Structure classrooms who had merely practiced writing during Phase I were also introduced to text structure instruction within the writing process, but without an emphasis on purpose or audience through peer editing and publication. Control classrooms continued with their writing programs, driven by the content of the district-adopted language arts textbook.

Inservice activity continued in Phase II. Teachers in the text structure groups (Text Structure, Communicative Context/Text Structure) attended weekly after-school meetings to discuss implementation of the instructional program, but met separately to prevent teachers from becoming biased from learning details of the other program. The teachers in the Communicative Context classroom continued to meet biweeky. To ensure fidelity to the instructional program, researchers visited each classroom at least once a week. Feedback to teachers was offered on an individual basis within classrooms, and more generally during the weekly and biweekly inservice meetings within treatment groups.

Thus, during Phase I, there were two basic groups, a Communicative Context treatment group, and a Control group to evaluate the effects of a communicative context on students' declarative and procedural knowledge of writing. During Phase II, four groups were formed with the introduction of text structure instruction to examine potential additive effects: Communicative Context, Communicative Context/Text Structure, Text Structure, and Control.

Scoring procedures

Questionnaires were examined by two adult judges who categorized students' responses for each question. These schemes then were verified by a third adult judge. To allow the examination of patterns of responses across treatment groups, students' responses were converted to percentage of students responding in each category. These patterns then provided a basis for an initial examination of the data prior to indepth analysis of the individual interviews. Significance of response variations across groups was tested using a Chi-square analysis.

The *individual interviews* were examined in two phases. First, two judges who were blind to the treatment group and hypotheses of the study administered the interviews. These two judges then read each interview and wrote a description characterizing the type of knowledge students in different classrooms displayed. Judges did not know which classrooms received which treatment so were not subject to preconceived views of how the students should have responded. Second, based upon the characterizations of the different classrooms from the overall analysis of individual interviews and the group questionnaire data, the interviews were further analyzed to identify illustrative examples that supported the general characterizations and trends.

The *writing packets* of think-sheets were analyzed as follows. First, comparisons of students' first and second drafts were made in terms of types of revisions (e.g., mechanical, overall organization, additions, and deletions).

General patterns were observed within and across the three treatment conditions. Second, target students who appeared to best characterize the patterns in each group were selected for further examination. For each of these students, the changes made from first to second draft were compared to their plans as outlined on their prewriting/planning, editing, and revising think-sheets. The focus of this analysis was on students' conditional knowledge, how their awareness of audience and their knowledge of the writing process influenced their composition.

Results and discussion

Results are discussed separately for students' declarative knowledge, procedural knowledge, and conditional knowledge. Students' declarative knowledge data focused on knowledge of audience, purpose, and text structure and were derived from students' responses on the group questionnaires and individual interviews. Procedural knowledge data focused on knowledge about steps in the writing process, and how these may vary as a function of narrative versus expository writing, again derived from questionnaires and interviews. Conditional knowledge data were derived from students' responses to the questions about prewriting, editing, and revising on think-sheet packets, as well as from their revisions from first to second drafts.

Declarative knowledge about writing

Audience awareness

To assess the extent to which creating a communicative context affects students' perceptions of audience, students were asked, "Who reads your writing?". Results on the midpoint group questionnaire administered at the end of Phase I revealed that students' awareness of audience changed significantly for students in classrooms in which the defined communicative context was present in contrast to those in which such a context was absent, $\chi^2 (1) = 4.30, p < .038$ (see Table 2). No other contrasts were statistically significant ($p > .05$). In classrooms where the focus was on the communicative functions of writing, response patterns indicate that students increasingly viewed peers as their primary audience. Significant is the fact that while the number of students identifying "teacher" as one type of audience does not change from the pretest to the midpoint at the end of Phase I, there is a dramatic increase in the students who add "peers" as another potential audience. Family as audience was mentioned by less than half of these students. In contrast, in control classrooms where such a focus was not emphasized, family and teacher accounted for the most common responses at pretest and midpoint, with peers infrequently men-

Table 2 Percentage of students giving each response type for audience on pretest and midpoint group questionnaire

Who reads your writing?				
	Communicative pretest (n = 81)	*Context present midpoint* (n = 81)	*Communicative pretest* (n = 40)	*Context absent midpoint* (n = 40)
Response type (percentage)				
Teachers	74	73	65	67
Family	62	40	75	85
Peers	19	69	35	13

Chi-square analyses of differences between context-present and context-absent groups at midpoint

Response Type	χ^2	p
Teachers	.46	.496
Family	.85	.356
Peers	4.30	.038

tioned at either time. In fact, there is a significant *decrease* of 22 percent from pretest to midpoint in the students' identification of peers as one potential audience. In most cases, when family was mentioned as audience, it related to the parents reading the students' homework assignments, rather than serving as audience for compositions.

Students' responses on the posttreatment questionnaire, administered at the end of Phase II, were consistent with those obtained at the end of Phase I. Significant changes were found in the percent of students selecting peers as their audience, $\chi^2(1) = 8.25$, $p < .016$ with no other statistically significant changes, $p > .05$. Table 3 provides patterns of responses from pre- to posttreatment within the four treatment groups, separating the Communicative Context Present students' responses into Communicative Context and Communicative Context/Text Structure, and the Communicative Context Absent students' responses into Text Structure and Control groups.

Again, the most notable differences were in the responses of students in the Communicatice Context groups, who increasingly mentioned peers as their audience. For example, on the posttreatment questionnaire, peers were cited as an audience by 93 percent and 68 percent of the Communicative Context and Communicative Context/Text Structure students, respectively, whereas only 20 percent and 17 percent of the Text Structure and Control students, respectively, cited peers. On the other hand, the teacher and family were the primary audience for children's writing in the Text Structure and Control groups, although consistent with the data from individual interviews, family was often cited as it related to reading homework.

Table 3 Percentage of students giving each response type for audience on pretest and posttest group questionnaires

	Communicative Context present				Communicative Context absent			
	Communicative Context		Communicative Context/ Text Structure		Text Structure		Control	
	(n = 41)		(n = 44)		(n = 41)		(n = 14)	
	pre	post	pre	post	pre	post	pre	post
Who reads your writing? (percentage)								
Teacher	59	63	86	86	66	68	100	93%
Family	73	68	50	50	73	61	57	50%
Peers	34	93	9	68	32	20	21	17%

Chi-square analyses of differences between context-present and context-absent groups at posttest

	χ^2	p
Response type		
Teachers	3.96	.138
Family	1.04	.593
Peers	8.25	.016

The following typical comments from students' individual interviews provide insight into the differences seen from pre to post and across treatments. Jenny is a student in the Communicative Context group. Her pre- and posttreatment responses comments about audience were:

> PRE: Sometimes my parents read my reports. Every once in a while I'll have a friend or two of mine get to read it and you swap. And my teacher reads it to. If nobody important is going to read it, it doesn't matter the way you do it.
> POST: If there is just a score, probably my teacher, and if I got a good grade on it, my parents would see it, and maybe a couple of friends, if we were doing the same thing and want to check out each other. For a story, I guess almost anybody, we've been putting them into books and stuff.

Following participation in the Communicative Context group, she identified audience based on the purpose of the writing, and greatly expanded her audience from "a friend or two" to "almost anybody," apparently because of the influence of the publishing process.

A similar change was noted in Dawn's comments prior to and following her participation in the Communicative Context/Text Structure group. Initially she indicated that only "Mr. V" (her teacher) would read her paper. At the end of the year, she noted that, "My teacher, my mom, my grandparents, my aunt and uncle, and most of my family would read it: my editor, Ms. K., my friends if it was published."

These two examples contrast with those from students in the Text Structure and Control groups. Yolanda, prior to receiving text structure instruction, described her audience as follows: "If homework, my mom would read it first; in school, my teacher; if I could take it home, my sister. If a story, my teacher, my mother, one of my friends." At the end of the year, she responded, "Teacher or a friend." In the absence of a communicative context for writing, her range of audience actually decreased. Ray, from the Control group, shows minimal change. In the fall, he responded, "My teacher, or me." During posttreatment, he said, "Me, and the teacher. For a story I'd take it home and my parents would read it." Without the presence of the writing environment as created in the two Communicative Context groups, students tended to be limited in their view of audience or reader. The teacher, themselves, and perhaps their parents were the only audiences for their compositions.

Knowledge about purpose in writing

Students' response patterns in terms of knowledge about purposes varied somewhat between students in communicative context present and those in communicative context absent classrooms at the end of Phase I (see Table 4) and in individual interviews. Responses for this analysis were categorized into three broad purposes: (1) writing to learn or to inform, (2) writing as a school task, including skills practice, assessment, or general teacher-made assignments, and (3) writing to communicate or for personal

Table 4 Purposes in writing, end of Phase I group questionnaire

What reasons do you have for writing?	Communicative Context present		Communicative Context absent	
	pretest (n = 81)	midpoint (n = 81)	pretest (n = 40)	midpoint (n = 40)
Response type (percentage)				
Learn/inform	5	17	00	00
School task	62	52	50	65
Communication	60	51	73	45

Chi-square analyses of differences between context-present and context absent groups at midpoint

	χ^2	p
Learn/inform	13.21	.001
School Task	1.70	.192
Communication	.27	.603

reasons. The chi-square analysis revealed significant changes in pattern of responses from pre- to midpoint in the writing to learn category, χ^2 (1) = 13.21, $p < .001$. Students in the Communicative Context groups maintained their view of writing for the purposes of school tasks and communication, but increased in the extent to which they also saw writing's function as part of learning and informing. Students who had not experienced this environment showed no significant changes, though it is interesting to note the shift in their patterns of response. These students showed a drop from 73 percent to 45 percent in their identification of communication as a purpose for writing, while increasing in the frequency with which they identified writing's purpose as school-task related.

When such patterns of responses are examined from pre- to posttreatment across the four treatment groups, the differences are less dramatic. Table 5 provides percentage of responses in each category for the pre/post comparison. The variation in response pattern is seen in responses that fall in the category, "writing to learn," which was significant, χ^2 (1) = 17.38, $p < .001$. After students received text structure instruction (Text Structure & Communicative Context/Text Structure) they showed pretest-posttest increases (2 percent and 20 percent, respectively) in viewing learning as one purpose for writing. This suggests that the text structure treatment, at least when part of a general writing-as-communication environment, did

Table 5 Purpose in writing, pretreatment and end of phase II group questionnaires

	Communicative Context present				Communicative Context absent			
	Communicative Context		Communicative Context/ Text Structure		Text Structure		Control	
	(n = 41)		(n = 44)		(n = 41)		(n = 14)	
	pre	post	pre	post	pre	post	pre	post
What reasons do you have for writing? (percentage)								
Learn/ Inform	7	5	2	32	0	2	14	7
School Task	39	54	82	39	49	61	50	57
Communica- tion	66	75	39	30	66	51	50	43

Chi-square analyses of differences between context-present and context absent groups at posttest

	χ^2	p
Learn/inform	17.37	.001
School task	1.47	.477
Communication	.76	.684

impart a belief that writing was a means to gather information and learn from expository materials. Students in the Communicative Context and Control groups, who received instruction focusing on audience and purpose, but not on how to gather information from expository materials, showed the opposite trend (decreases of 2 percent and 7 percent, respectively). Apparently, students who were not taught strategies for gathering information from expository materials did not feel confident in their ability to write to learn.

The following comments from students' individual interviews provide further information about differences from pre- to posttreatment in their views of purposes for writing. Note in particular the change in view from writing as schoolwork and a means for teachers to evaluate understanding, to writing as a student tool for learning and for enjoyment. Also note their finer distinctions in purpose depending on type of text (narrative versus expository).

Ridgely, a student from the Communicative Context group, stated reasons for writing at the pretreatment interview, "(For stories) they want to find out what I read to see if I know it ... (For a report, I) learn about other cultures, like how families lived." While aware of differences between the two text types, Ridgely predicted that stories were for assessment. He also tended to provide a single reason for writing each type of text. Note the expanded number of reasons, and their appropriateness in his posttreatment comments.

> (Writing stories is) for pleasure mostly, and it helps people remember if you write a story about something, and all of a sudden somebody tells you to write a story about a certain place and you've been there before, you remember about it. To keep our imagination going. (Writing reports), well if it is a kid like me, then the teacher might try to teach them something; also grammar we might be studying that; and I know you are going to have to write later, so you should learn how to do it before you have to do it.

Devonna was a student in the Communicative Context/Text Structure group. Like Ridgely, she began the year viewing the purpose of writing as a means for teacher evaluation of her skills, or for practicing skills, stating for reports, "to see if I read the book good, the pages, and to see if I understand what she was saying," and for stories, "to get practice on writing and to learn more about the guy. To see how much I know" Following her participation in the instructional program, she shifted to a view of writing as a form of recreation and for learning, stating for reports, "So we can get information from our reports or learn about the state that we want to learn about," and for stories, "So you won't be bored or so you have something to read."

Another interesting aspect of her answer is her view of her own writing as something she and others would read, which is consistent with the fact that her writing had, in fact, been published in the class book.

Keith was a student in the Text Structure group. His pre/post responses clearly indicated a change from assessment at pretreatment, "(For stories) to see if I know what I was supposed to do. (For reports) to see if I read it over carefully," to an orientation combining learning and assessment at posttreatment, "(for stories) to see if you really learned anything. (For reports) to let us know about the cities and things because we've read about them; see what you've learned." Unlike Devonna or Ridgely, he did not address purposes such as pleasure or communication, except in terms of communication with the teacher. This was not surprising given the absence of this emphasis in his treatment group.

Stacy, a student in the Control group, actually seemed to regress. At pretreatment she indicated the teacher was the dominant factor for writing, but also indicated interest as another factor. She stated, "(For stories) she (the teacher) thinks that it would be a good story to write. (For reports) because it is probably interesting to her and she wants to see if it is interesting to us." At the end of the year, she suggests stories are "so people could get information from it." When asked about the purpose of writing reports, she stated, "I don't know." The interviewer then asked, "Do you have any ideas (about why you would write a report) at all?" Stacy replied, "No."

Knowledge about text structure

Text structure instruction should clarify students' views of how narrative and expository texts differ on critical features. It should also help them distinguish between the questions different types of texts are designed to answer. To assess the extent to which the former effects occurred, students were asked to describe how writing stories and writing reports differed. To assess the latter, students were asked to predict the content and organization of a text when given only the title.

In their interviews, students addressed differences between narrative and expository text writing. A major difference cited by most students was the creative, imaginary aspect of story writing in contrast to the factual, informative nature of report writing. For example, Ridgely, from the Communicative Context group, stated in his posttreatment interview, "if it is a fiction story, you don't have to research it. In a report, you have to do research so you can get everything right." Roy, from the Control group, stated, "Because a story, you get all the information that you want. But a report you've got to get information that is true. A story you can write anything you want." Roy's sense of the difference is that stories give the author complete and absolute freedom. Ridgely focuses more specifically on the need to be accurate in reports. In contrast, two students who received text structure instruction focused more specifically on the different text structure features of expository writing (e.g., questions answered and keywords) versus narrative writing (e.g., characters) and on the type of information appropriate for each type. Stacy, from the Text Structure group, suggested the difference is that "You have different questions and key words. The report has more information that the story (hasn't) ... (I) use my imagination ... when writing a story." Dawn, from the Communicative Context/Text Structure group, articulated the need for character information in stories versus structural or comparison information in a report, stating, "Because a story you have characters, but with a report, you've got like comparing two states, and states aren't characters ... (also) a report you have research in a story you can just have fantasy."

To examine students' awareness of the questions that different text types might address, students were asked to predict the content and organization of articles based upon three titles in a fictitious magazine about dogs. Students in the Communicative Context and Control groups showed relatively little change over time, and their pretreatment responses looked much like those in the structure groups (Text Structure and Communicative Context/Text Structure) on the pretreatment interviews. Prior to text structure instruction, students tended to suggest content that related in a general way to the title, but they were unable to provide consistently relevant information. For example, Dawn indicated that the Choosing a Dog article would be about "If you like poodles, you might want to find out where you can go to get their hair curled and get some shampoo ... how to pick a dog." Her relevant content related to picking the dog is somewhat offset by the irrelevant details about shampooing. For the title, Puppy's First Year, she suggested that it "probably tells you how to give him a bath and what age he has to be ... how to tell if he's sick ... because at a year old he might be able to take a bath." She indicated no awareness of the likelihood of explanation or narration about the events in the puppy's life, again focusing on the less relevant information about bathing. Her answers below after Communicative Context/Text Structure instruction were in marked contrast. She differentiates clearly between the type of text structure used in each article, comparison/contrast, narration, or problem/solution articles. Notice how clear she is about the type of information to be included in each article, how the information might be organized, and the questions each one might answer.

CHOOSING A DOG ... I would include how good they are at protecting your home, how good pets are with children, and what their size is, how big they get. A compare/contrast because you might be comparing two dogs and find one that you like ... comparing the characters(istics).

PUPPY'S FIRST YEAR ... probably how old you have to be to give it a bath because you have to be a certain age, how much they have to eat so that don't get full or if they don't have enough. (It is) a narrative because it would be talking about his first year, where does it take place? Who's in the story? And when does it take place?

BREAKING A PUPPY'S BAD HABITS ... How to break the bad habits, what the habits are. How you solved it. (It is) a problem solution. What was the problem? How did you solve it? ... Clues were "bad habits."

Bill, another student in the Communicative Context/Text Structure group, showed similar gains. For example, during the pretreatment interview he indicated that the article, Breaking a Puppy's Bad Habits, "could be about the puppy likes to nibble on things and you might have him on the furniture, and you might want to break him off the furniture and stuff." His details were relevant and he identified problems, but he did not mention the type of text or questions it might answer. During the posttreatment interview, he was more specific, stating the following: "(In this article,) the kind of questions the text should answer should be what's the problem? What's the solution? and probably what order?" Like Dawn, his answer suggests a clear understanding of what elements to include and how they should be organized.

In summary, students' declarative knowledge about writing was notably influenced by the type of instruction they received. Students who participated actively in a communicative context stressing audience and purpose in writing focused on writing as a way of sharing ideas to be read by many different readers. Students who received text structure instruction discussed such knowledge as it related to presenting ideas and organizing them.

Procedural knowledge about writing

The writing process

Students described the activities they use in the writing process at the end of Phase I and during their posttreatment interviews. In addition to asking for specific procedures, the interviews also focused on the editor's role and the role of revision in the writing process.

On the Phase I questionnaire, students were asked to explain four different types of activities in which they engage as they write. Student's responses were rated on a 0–3 scale based on a combination of their appropriateness as strategies in general, and based on the aspect of writing in which students suggested the strategy be used. For example, during

Table 6 Activities in the writing process, end of Phase I group questionnaire

	n	Pretest		Posttest	
		M	*S.D.*	*M*	*S.D.*
Communicative Context	41	1.16	.42	2.02	.95
Communicative Context/Text Structure	44	1.00	.00	1.52	.91
Text Structure	41	1.16	.37	1.77	.78
Control	14	1.00	.00	1.07	.25

prewriting or planning, highly ranked strategies included brainstorming or drawing pictures to gather ideas, since research indicated that both activities are appropriate and useful (Graves, 1983). Lower-ranked strategies included drafting or titling the paper, since these activities are aspects of writing, but are not activities designed to generate ideas. The lowest ranked strategies were those that did not contribute to the generation of ideas, such as writing the date, looking up words, or checking spelling. Table 6 presents the means and standard deviations for each group, with the between subjects factor of group (Communicative Context, Text Structure, Communicative Context/Text Structure, Control), and the within-subjects factor of time (Pretest, Midpoint).

The results of the analysis variance on the ratings revealed statistically significant main effects for Time, $F(1,334) = 71.56$, $p < .01$, and Group, $F(3,334) = 16.93$, $p < .01$, and a significant Group × Time interaction, $F(3,334) = 4.70$, $p < .01$. When Scheffe's post hoc procedure was performed on the pre- and posttreatment scores, the results revealed no significant differences between the four groups at pretreatment ($p > .05$), but at posttreatment, Communicative Context and Text Structure groups significantly ($p < .05$) surpassed the Control group in their knowledge of activities used during the writing process, and the Communicative Context group significantly ($p < .05$) outperformed the Communicative Context/Text Structure group. No other group differences were statistically significant ($p > .05$).

These data are supported and further explained by students' responses on the posttreatment individual interviews. Sample responses from each of the four treatment groups are found in Table 7. The differences across groups are seen in students' descriptions of the general writing process, and in specific information they provided regarding the roles of audience and editors, the questions texts answer, and key words and phrases in different types of text (e.g., comparison/contrast).

For example, Jenny and Dawn were both from classrooms emphasizing

Table 7 Activities in the writing process, individual interviews: posttreatment

Jenny (CC):	First you write down what kinds of things you're going to be doing, and just get all you ideas out on the page. And then you try to make the first draft and you get as much stuff in as you can. Then, what we are doing in our class is, we check them over with editors. They read your paper and they say, well this doesn't sound right and maybe you should try to change this to so and so. Before that I start thinking about my first draft, and then ... do (the) editorial. Then you just do a revision form where you decide what things you want to change, and then you put it all together in a final copy.
Keith (TS):	If you want to do a compare/contrast, you got to tell what you are comparing it with, and contrasting about. See what would go first, second, put them in a certain order. See if there is any misspelled words or something and try to fix it up. If there is something you have to add or take away, then you put that on a different piece of paper and then you'd go into (the) final draft. (If a friend were writing a story) I would tell him where does this take place, what is this about, and who is it about, and what came first, second, and third. Gather information if he has to, then he would write it down for his first draft, then check for misspelled words and take stuff out and add stuff, then go onto final draft.
Dawn (CC/TS):	(To write a compare/contrast), I would look at two people, find their alike and different points. Like if I was comparing my friend Stacy and my friend Tracy, I would say that Tracy is shorter than Stacy or Tracy has real dark hair and Stacy has a little light hair. (If I didn't know them), I'd have to go to the library and do some research on them. I sit down and write the first draft. Before that I do brainstorming, ... like if I was doing George Washington and Abraham Lincoln I'd have to write (about) both Presidents ... no full sentences, only words. Before our first draft we do prewriting and preplanning. (Interviewer asks, what is that?) Prewriting is like in a compare and contrast, who or what is being compared on? What are they being compared on? How are they alike and how are they different? (Interviewer asks: Then the first draft?) Yea, then we get these sheets with a friend, and we write, what do you think your editor said about your paper? What will you do to change the things with your editor suggestions? Your editor reads your story, and on the pink sheet they tell you what you should do to get it in better shape for your final draft or what you should take out. And what you should put in. (And then?) If it was published, my family would be reading it and my friends.
Terry (C):	I never head of it (compare/contrast). When I write a story this is how I first start off, write the title and then write the beginning of it. First step I do is write the major story. And then I go all the way through and stop at periods and when I ask a question I write a question mark. And if it's exciting, I put an exclamation mark. Put a period (at the end).

a communicative context, and their answers reflected an awareness of the steps in the writing process and the role of an editor prior to revision. While students in the Communicative Context/Text Structure group performed at the lowest level of students in the three treatment groups on the group questionnaire, responses on the individual interviews revealed a growing knowledge of text structure and audience. Dawn, from the Communicative Context/Text Structure group, suggested that part of the process was considering what questions should be answered. Notice how much more organized and specific Dawn's answer is relative to Jenny's, from the Communicative Context group, in detailing information to include and how it will be organized. Keith, a student in the Text Structure treatment, also mentioned the questions one should answer in a story, suggested an organization for comparing and contrasting, and identified other aspects of the writing process, but mentioned nothing about sharing the paper with friends or other readers. When he mentions a friend, it is in the context of *telling* the friend what steps to follow rather than to communicate with, share with, and learn from friends. Terry, one of the control group students, indicated first that he had never heard of compare/contrast (when given a prompt by the interviewer), then described a process that largely centered around global statements (e.g., "write the major story") and punctuation.

Students' comments also suggest differences among groups in terms of the salience of an editor in the writing process. Table 8 provides further elaboration of their views of the role of an editor.

What is most striking is that many students in the communicative context groups focused on the role of sense-making and reader interest in the editorial process. For example, 7 of the 12 students interviewed from the Communicative Context group specifically mentioned that the editor helps their story make sense, or helps make it more interesting, yet none of the Text Structure students mentioned those aspects in their description of the editor's role. The emphasis on sense-making in the editorial process suggested that peer editors were serving as external monitors for comprehension breakdowns in the communication process. As one student commented, "I write something down and I can't explain it right, and I can't give it thoughts or write it in sentences, maybe he can help me;" another student similarly noted, "An editor is useful because sometimes your brain misses something." In addition, peer-editing seemed to provide opportunities for peer-mediated coaching and learning. The students mentioned that an editor helps them "think about what you wrote," "helps you learn because when you wrote it you just had your ideas ... but someone else gives you more ideas," and "helps me write better and make my story make sense ... (If I can't explain it right) maybe he can help me."

In summary, communicative context students viewed the author-editor relationship as one in which they got ideas from or learned from their

Table 8 Sample responses about students' knowledge of editor's role from posttreatment individual interviews

GROUP	SAMPLES OF STUDENTS' COMMENTS
Communicative Context	(Jenny) It makes me think about what you wrote and like what things you need to change and work on. (Oudone) It helps you to learn because when you wrote it you just had your ideas but when someone else helps you or edits it, you have more ideas and then it gets more interesting. (Melissa) Editor can help me write better and make my story make sense, correct my spelling, and stuff like that. (Daryl) My editor checks and sees if it makes sense. They see if it makes sense and look for run-on sentences and checks spelling. Sees what I should add or what I should drop. (Richard) He can go through the paper and find out like things that you did wrong and then he'll tell you his ideas, and what he thinks. (Alex) Editor tells me how he likes it and how he doesn't like it. I write something down, and I can't explain it right, and I con't give it thoughts or write it in sentences, maybe he can help me.
Text Structure	(Yolanda) To make people understand it better … get a better grade. (Jennifer) It's the same as revising. (Jim) Editing helps you get a job. (Kelly) To look it over and add anything possible like key words and stuff. Check spelling. (Salome) Puts an "x" where you should, put a key word so that you know on your final copy to put a key word there. Or circle things so that if you want to add things on to it or take things out.
Communicative Context/Text Structure	(DeVonna) Change or add punctuation, she would give me her ideas. An editor is useful because sometimes times your brain misses something … easier to hear mistakes from a friend than your teacher. (Bill) The best thing … my editor helped me organize the paper. (Robert) He corrects spelling and fixes up the story and makes it (make) more sense. (Dawn) Your editor reads your story and on the pink sheet they tell you what you should do to get it in better shape for your final draft, or what you should take and what you should put in … (Tamara) So that you know what the other person would like to see to make it more interesting … if she liked it or not. (Mark) Because you might have your own opinions and think this paper is the best think, somebody else, they don't like it. Try some of their ideas, you might want to change it.

editor, and that it was a thoughtful interchange that led them to reflect on and extend their writing. Peer-conferencing and peer-editing helped these writers understand the importance of making sense in writing, and it provided the response that turned them back onto their topics in a reflective way. They had a vivid understanding of the purpose and utility of editing as one in which they further tried out, extended, and refined their ideas.

In contrast, students in the Text Structure classrooms focused largely on mechanics in the editing process. Even when students used text structure to find errors, it was primarily a mechanical process with little attention to the importance of making the paper more understandable or interesting to the reader. In fact, only one writer mentioned that the editor helped make people understand it (the paper) better, and even then, the goal was for the purpose of getting a better grade. Their comments suggest that they are not reflecting on their topic, or even considering new ideas during the editing phase. For students not engaged in peer-editing and peer-conferencing, there is little point to editing beyond copy-editing, and there is no understanding of how to read their own paper for their potential readers' perspective.

Conditional knowledge

Students' revisions from first to second draft were examined for general patterns within and across treatment groups in the quantity and types of changes made in their papers. Then three students were selected as best characterizing the strategies implemented by students in each group: Rachel from the Communicative Context group, Mike from the Text Structure group, and Mark from the Communicative Context/Text Structure group. Conditional knowledge is described in terms of the relationship between plans made on their think-sheets and writing samples from first and second drafts. A description of evidence of general patterns within the three treatment groups is presented first, followed by illustrative examples from Rachel's, Mike's, and Mark's writing packets.

In general, students in the Communicative Context group showed growth in their ability to develop a revision plan based on their editors' comments, but they tended to be vague both in their peer-editing think-sheet comments and in the specifics of their revision plan. They showed an increasing sensitivity to audience over the course of the program and asked questions of their reader to promote author/reader interactions. However, they indicated some frustration over the lack of specific suggestions from their editors, as evidenced by comments on revision think-sheets about editors who did not provide needed assistance. In contrast, students in the Text Structure group were quite specific in their revision plans and carried out their plans in revising their paper. Their plans focused on adding key words, inserting missing information based on questions specific texts should answer, but showed little awareness of sensitivity to their audience. Finally, students in the Communicative Context/Text Structure group initially showed an increasing concern for their readers, and some frustration in not knowing how to improve their paper. As did students in the Text Structure group, they used the text structure information learned during Phase II in their revisions. However, they seemed to keep audience concerns and involvement as a primary goal.

Illustrative examples of these patterns can be found in students' writing packets. One area in which students' conditional knowledge was examined was in their plans for revision, either prior to or following an editing session. In early fall, Rachel, in the Communicative Context group, showed little concept of how to develop questions for her editor. (Note that in all writing samples that follow, students' spelling, grammar, and punctuation are presented without editing). She writes, in fact, "I don't have no questions (for my editor)" or similar statements on several of her early editing session preparation sheets. Though she initially took no control of the editing process, she did indicate that she expected assistance, stating, "(no questions) because she (her editor) will tell me in the paper I am getting." As she began to take control of the writing process, she made requests of her editor, and her questions showed increasing recognition of audience, asking "How do you like it? Do I need to change anything around? Do I need an opening sentence?" By spring, she also expressed frustration at a peer-editor's lack of substantive feedback, stating, "(she had a problem with) the end, but didn't tell me why!" Her solution to "take the end and make it longer" suggested that she as well as her editor may be able to recognize problems (e.g., weak ending), but did not have strategies available for solving them, other than to add on by writing an additional word or two. Her initial ending was "If I hadn't of writ this no one would know what our name means." She expanded it to say, "If I hadn't wrote this paper no one would know what my point of view is on being a hunter" (the class nickname).

Students in the Communicative Context group tended to have a well-developed sense of author/reader relationships. This was illustrated in their tendency to bring in personal experiences or anecdotes even in expository papers. Rachel's compare/contrast papers from fall to spring illustrate this sense of reader. In the fall, Rachel's compare/contrast paper consisted of two definitions, one for each of two emotions. In the spring, she compared and contrasted living in the mountains of Colorado versus living in the plains. She described the geography, jobs, getting clothes and food, and ended by asking her readers where they would rather live. Her sense that writing communicates information to readers is illustrated by the sentence above describing why she wrote about being called a "hunter." Her concern for the reader and her personal involvement with the topic enhanced her ability to write more complete papers that were both interesting and informative.

Students in the Text Structure group made their greatest gains in their understanding of text structure forms. In the early fall, Mike from this group showed little concept of text structure in expository writing. For example, in writing a problem/solution paper, he wrote:

> Once I was at a lake and I fell and bumped my head. I cried a lot. That night, when I was asleep, I started to yell. My mom and dad came running. Then I said "My nose needs cleaning".

Missing from Mike's paper are the text structure clues that signal the reader what organizational structure to expect and what information will be included (e.g., problem, causes, and solution). Even within the paper, Mike fails to explicitly convey the relationship among ideas such as falling and bumping his head, starting to yell at night, and nose needing cleaning.

In the spring, Mike clearly shows a greater understanding of text structure. When planning a first draft, he states that he is comparing languages on grammar, sounds, and words. In fact, his first draft contains these structural elements, as well as keywords and phrases that signal the relationship among these ideas. He writes, "Sounds are another thing I'm comparing language on. Each language has sounds. For example English has 43 sounds and Spanish has 24." When revising this draft, Mike shows his deepening awareness of the importance of keywords. Note how his revised paragraph includes more keywords that precisely convey the likenesses and differences between languages:

> Another thing languages can be compared on is sound. Like grammar, every language has sound. Some of these are similar, but most of them are different. Not all languages has the same amount of sounds. For example, english has about 43 different sounds, and Spanish has only 24 sounds.

On the other hand, Mike is less concerned with audience in his writing. When asked what he could do to make his paper even more interesting, he writes that he will add more information about "... most languages have 20–60 sounds, Russian has 50." Yet his revision does not contain any reference to the Russian language, suggesting that his plans for maintaining reader interest in the topic are less important than his plans for conveying text structure cues through the addition of conventions such as keywords and questions.

In contrast to Rachel and Mike, Mark in the Communicative Context/Text Structure group shows an increasing awareness of both audience and form in planning and revising his drafts. In the fall, when purpose and audience is introduced, Mark shows a concern for the reader, but is unsure how to structure his writing to communicate the text structure. For example, in the following excerpt from a paper, he tells his reader to have fun, but does not have a clear picture of the parallel attributes on which he is comparing and contrasting his topics (spelling and punctuation errors are as they were written in the draft):

> Kickball and baseball are alot a like and different. In kickball, you kick the red rubber ball then run on base and in baseball you hit then run to the ball. In Kickball if the ball goes to a side its fowl and baseball if you miss the ball its a strike. If you kick a ball and its caught you're out, so if your on base don't run unless they miss the ball. Things that are the same are 3 outs, 3 strikes, if they catch it your out and 1 base for an over throw. That's how you play so have fun!

Like many students in context classrooms, Mark even senses that something is wrong with the organization. On his revision plan, he states that he needs to "put it (the ideas) in better order." However, Mark doesn't have the tools for reorganizing his ideas, and his final draft varies little from his initial draft. In fact, most of his changes involve minor word changes and insertions.

After text structure instruction, Mark shows a better grasp of what information to include and how to organize it. In writing a problem/ solution paper, for example, Marks' revisions provide greater detail about the causes of the problem and how specific actions are solutions to the problem. Furthermore, his concern for the reader remains foremost in his mind. One strategy that Mark uses quite often to make his expository papers more interesting to his readers is to introduce main characters as a focal point for providing information about the topic to his audience. The paper below illustrates how he combines foci on text structure and audience in a comparison/contrast paper.

> As Bill Robinson landed in Brazil he said "all those mountains over there, do people live in them". "Yes" said the tour guide. Now today I am going to tell you how the Aztecs and Brazil are alike and different. One way their alike is they both live near alot of mountains. And one thing how there different is the Aztecs live in homes they built and here in Brazil people live in shacks in the mountains. "How do they get food"? asked Bill. "Well one way their alike in getting food is they both grow food and there different because the Aztecs built crops of rafts because they didn't have enough land and Brazil grow coffee on land..."

These examples and others based on an examination of the students' writing packets provides information about their implementation of the strategies they described during their interviews and on their questionnaires. What is apparent is that (1) there is a general consistency between what students say they do and what they actually do, though (2) the correlation is not perfect. There were instances where students' descriptions were able to specify strategies that they did not use during the writing, as well as instances in which students applied strategies that they were not able to describe. The point to be stressed is that there is a strong relationship between the types of instruction students received and the strategies they were able to both discuss and use during writing.

Conclusion

In summary, students in the Communicative Context and Communicative Context/Text Structure groups showed a heightened awareness of the range of people who constituted their audience and could articulate the processes involved in writing, particularly those during editing and publishing of papers. Students in the Text Structure and Communicative Context/Text Structure groups showed an increased sense of ways to present information in an organized manner. They also showed greater sensitivity to different types of texts and to the questions these texts are able to answer. The awareness of questions appeared during discussions of planning and editing phases. All three treatments had a positive effect on students' knowledge about the writing process and awareness of writing strategies. However, an important question remains, the question of the impact of such training on students' performance on different writing assignments. Data from a companion study (Englert et al., 1985) suggest that students' performance does improve as a result of participation in the three different treatment groups. To illustrate the nature of changes in students' writing performance, three pre- and postintervention samples are presented, one set from each of the three treatment groups.

Rachel had participated in the Communicative Context treatment group. Her papers were written in response to directions requesting students to write a story about anything they wish. Students were told to think about who they were writing the story for, and to think in terms of sending the story to a friend to read. Her pretest sample clearly indicates the salience of the part of the directions that indicated the story would be sent to a friend, as she ends with a request to the friend to write back. It also reflects the salience of the upcoming Halloween holiday.

I wish I went into the hunted house. The way Tammy describe it,
it mush of been fun. Speicely when you walk. When they said

(here comes some more meat) that is when I ran out. When I hear
screams it gets me scared. Why did you all the suden get scared?
P.S. Please write back.

On the pretest, she indicates a sense of audience and a desire to interact
with that audience. However, she shows little notion of setting or character development, and leaves the audience with much to infer. What is
particularly impressive in terms of her growth is her ability to maintain
voice and the ability to impact her audience, while at the same time presenting a more organized paper. Her moving account of a childhood
experience is representative of her own growth as a writer and her sense of
writing to communicate personal experiences.

> When I was little my dad would come home with a box of donuts.
> He would only give them to me and I couldn't share with my
> brothers. One day I gave them both one. My dad saw me and give
> me a wippen and put me up in my room. The next day he didn't
> give me some donuts. I felt like he didn't love me. When I was 2
> years old my dad told me and my mom that he was to good for us.
> When he went out the door I thought he was going to come back.
> I waited near the door a lot. I never seen him again. When I
> turned 3 years old I moved out of that house.
> Now I am 11 years old I still go by that house looking for him, but
> there is no hope.
> One day I siad to my self, I am going to look for him when I get
> older.
> I don't know if he alive. All the other kids make ... in front of me
> when I am at school. They don't under stand what my problem is.
> I know there are alot of kids without a father.
> It seems like he taught me how not to share.
> That is why I act kind of strange.
> Now evertime I eat a donut I think of him.

As a footnote, the student was aware that only adults from the university
would read the posttest. It is not likely that such a paper would have been
written for the other students in her class, and in fact her other papers do
not present such personal information. Her papers suggest that the impact
of audience awareness cannot be underestimated.

Mike participated in the Text Structure treatment group, and his
problem/solution pre- and postintervention papers indicate the effect of
such instruction on writing. One concern of teaching students about text
structures in the absence of a general writing environment is that students'
writing may become formulaic. Mike's works suggest that such fears may
be unfounded. He indicates an awareness of audience, and both his papers

contain his underlying voice as he describes different problems. Notice the greater detail, however, in his posttest, as he writes to answer questions concerning his problem's causes and potential solution. His pretest focuses on a problem with his sister.

> Dear Randy,
> I have a question for you. I've been having trouble with my sister lately. She's always bugging me, and then when I yell at her she gos of and cries. I know you've been through all of this with Joe, so I was wondering if you could give me some advice. I'll wait for your letter.
> Your cousin,
> Mike

Mike literally takes the notion of writing for a friend or relative, and presents his problem to his cousin. However, the reader is left to infer what has led to the problem in the first place, and there is no sense of solutions that have been tried. In contrast, his posttest contains such information, at no loss of voice or audience awareness.

> A problem I have right now is I don't have enough money to buy a radio cassete recorder, also called a "box". The one that I want is $100.00. Right now I only have $60.00. It has a radio, a cassette deck, a song tracer, and two built in speakers. It's got a handle so you can take it any were. I didn't now how I could get one.
> Then my aunt called and asked me if I wanted to mow her lawn for five dollars. I said yes. Then my mom asked me if I would mow our lawn. I said yes again. Since it costs $100.00, I'm only eight lawns away from getting it.

It is clear that Mike has internalized the questions, What is the problem? What caused it? What is the solution? He addresses each in this first draft. Yet, in answering these questions, he maintains a sense of text and does not fall into a pattern of translating the assignment into a series of questions and answers. One gets a sense of who the writer is, his personality and ingenuity.

A comparison/contrast written by Bill, a student in the Communicative Context/Text Structure group, indicates the impact of the combined intervention. In his pretest, Bill compares/contrasts two schools and indicates an initial awareness of text structure. However, there is no context-setting statement, nor does he provide the audience with information about the few parallel traits included. While his topic may have personal relevance, it is not clear what his purpose is (e.g., whether one school is preferred, whether he has attended both).

> I like both of the schools. They are nice. Oak Park don't have bathrooms in the classrooms. It don't have a playground. We eat in the gym. The teacher I had was nice. Grand River has bathrooms in the classrooms. It does have a playground. We eat in the gym. The teacher is nice. The classrooms are a lot different.

On his posttest, he shows slightly more sensitivity to audience by informing them of what he plans to write about, and picks a topic—his friends—that has personal relevance. While he could improve this first draft by expanding upon his themes (e.g., why they are good friends, how they differ in their ability to show this friendship), he has a well organized initial draft from which he can work.

> I'm comparing Kemie and David. I'm comparing them on how good of a friend they are. How good they are in pinball and basketball. How smart they are.
>
> I'm going to tell how they're alike. They both are my friend. They're both smart. They both like to play pinball and basketball. That's how they're alike.
>
> Now I'm going to tell how they're different. Kemie is a better friend than David. David can only have one friend at a time. Kemie is better in pinball and basketball.

In summary, these data suggest that students did improve in their writing as well as show enhanced metacognitive awareness. The changes generally were in areas focused upon in their instructional programs. Furthermore, observations made while researchers visited classrooms during the year indicated students used this knowledge in other curriculum areas. For example, Darryl, a Communicative Context student, created his own think-sheets for a writing assignment required by his teacher (taken from the language arts textbook). Rose, a Communicative Context/Text Structure student, told her teacher, with a great deal of excitement, that "I just figured it out! This is an explanation question, isn't it? (pointing to her social studies book). Now I know how to do this!"

Future research is needed to examine direct correlations between students' metacognitive knowledge and their writing performance, and clearly more information is needed on how to best enlighten students to specific strategies used during writing. Finally, research is needed delineating the relationship between the nature of the instructional environment and teaching strategies used to convey to students the knowledge and strategies relevant to skilled writing and subsequent writing performance. In terms of the effects of this study, perhaps Freddy, a low-achieving Communicative Context student, sums the benefits best in a note written at the end of his posttreatment group questionnaire to one of the researchers who visited his classroom:

To Dr. R,
I don't like to write but when you came along I begane to write. I
thank you four helping me to starte liking to writting.
  from you best friend
  Frederick   Thank you!

References

Applebee, A. N. (1984). *Contexts for learning to write: Studies of secondary school instruction.* Norwood, NJ: Ablex.

Applebee, A. N. (1986). Problems in process approaches. Toward a reconceptualization of process instruction. In A. R. Petrosky & D. Bartholomae (Eds.), *Teaching of writing: Eighty-fifth Yearbook of the National Society for the Study of Education* (pp. 95–113). Chicago: University of Chicago Press.

Atwell, N. (1983). Writing and reading literature from the inside out. *Language Arts, 61,* 240–252.

Bouchard, L. (1983). The teaching of writing in the United States. *Prospects,* 13(1), 107–115.

Berkenkotter, C. (1983). Decisions and revisions: The planning strategies of a publishing writer. *College Composition and Communication, 34,* 156–169.

Britton, J. (1978). The composing process and the function of writing. In C. Cooper & L. Odell (Eds.), *Research on composing: Points of departure (pp. 13–28). Urbana, IL: National Council of Teachers of English.*

Bruce, B. C., & Rubin, A. (in preparation). *Electronic quills.* Hillsdale, NJ: Erlbaum.

Calkins, L. M. (1983). *Lessons from a child.* Exeter, NH: Heinemann Educational Books.

DeFord, D. E. (1986). Classroom contexts for literacy learning. In T. E. Raphael (Ed.), *Contexts of school-based literacy,* (pp. 163–180). NY: Random House.

Dunn, A., & Bridwell, L. S. (1980). *Discourse competence: Evidence from written products, reading and composing processes, and cognitive-developmental stage of college freshman.* Paper presented at a meeting of National Council of Teachers of English, Cincinnati, OH.

Englert, C. S., Raphael, T. E., & Kirschner, B. W. (1985). *The impact of text structure instruction and process writing on students' comprehension and composition of expository text.* Paper presented at National Reading Conference, San Diego, CA.

Flavell, J. H. (1976). Metacognitive aspects of problem-solving. In L. B. Resnick (Ed.), *The nature of intelligence* (pp. 231–235). Hillsdale, NJ: Erlbaum.

Flavell, J. H. (1979). Metacognition and cognitive monitoring: A new area of cognitive-developmental inquiry. *American Psychologist, 34,* 906–911.

Florio, S., & Clark, C. (1982). The functions of writing in an elementary classroom. *Research in the Teaching of English, 15*(2), 115–130.

Flower, L. S., & Hayes, J. R. (1981). Problem-solving and the cognitive process of writing. In C. H. Frederiksen & J. F. Dominic (Eds.), *Writing: The nature, development and teaching of written communication* (pp. 39–58). Hillsdale, NJ: Lawrence Erlbaum.

233

Garner, R. (1987). *Metacognition and reading comprehension*. Norwood, NJ: Ablex Publishing Corporation.

Gavelek, J. R., & Raphael, T. E. (1985). Metacognition, instruction, and the role of questioning activities. In D. L. Forrest-Pressley, G. E. MacKinnon, & T. Gary Waller (Eds.), *Metacognition, cognition and human performance* (vol. 2). (pp. 103–136).

Giacobbe, M. E. (1986). Learning to write and writing to learn in the elementary school. In A. K. Petrosky & D. Bartholomae (Eds.), *Teaching of writing: Eighty-fifth Yearbook of the National Society for the Study of Education* (pp. 131–147). Chicago: University of Chicago Press.

Gordon, C. J., & Braun, C. (1985). Metacognitive processes: Reading and writing narrative discussion. In D. L. Forrest-Pressley, G. E. MacKinnon, & T. G. Waller (Eds.), *Metacognition, cognition, and human performance* (vol 2) (pp. 1–75), NY: Academic Press.

Graves, D. H. (1983). *Writing: Teachers and children at work*. Exeter, NH: Heinemann Educational Books.

Graves, D. H., & Hansen, J. (1983). The author's chair. *Language Arts, 60*(2), 176–183.

Hairston, M. (1982). The winds of change: Thomas Kuhn and the revolution in the teaching of writing. *College composition and communication, 33*, 76–88.

Hansen, J. (1983). Authors respond to authors. *Language Arts, 60*, 970–977.

Hillocks, G. Jr. (1984). What works in teaching composition: A meta-analysis of experimental treatment studies. *American Journal of Education, 93*(1), 107–132.

Hillocks, G. Jr. (1986). The writer's knowledge: Theory, research, and implications for practice. In *NSSE Yearbook* (pp. 71–93). Chicago: University of Chicago Press.

Kinneavy, J. (1971). *Theory of discourse*. New York, NY: N. W. Norton & Co.

Kirschner, B. W., & Yates, J. M. (1983). *Discovery to discourse*. NY: Macmillan.

Langer, J. A. (1985). Children's sense of genre: A study of performance on parallel reading and writing tasks. *Written Communication, 2*, 157–187.

Langer, J. A. (1986). *Children reading and writing: Structure and strategies*. Norwood, NJ: Ablex.

Moffett, J. (1968). *Teaching the universe of discourse*. Boston, MA: Houghton Mifflin Co.

Murray, D. M. (1982). *Learning by teaching*. Montclair, NJ: Boynton/Cook.

Nystrand, M. (1982). *What writers know*. NY: Academic Press.

Paris, S. G. (1986). Teaching children to guide their reading and learning. In T. E. Raphael (Ed.), *The contexts of school-based literacy*. NY: Random House.

Paris, S. G., Lipson, M. Y., & Wixson, K. K. (1983). Becoming a strategic reader. *Contemporary Educational Psychology, 8*, 293–316.

Raphel, T. E., & Kirschner, B. W. (August, 1985). *The effects of instruction in compare/contrast text structure on sixth-grade students' reading comprehension and writing products* (Research series No. 161). Michigan State University: Institute for Research on Teaching.

Rubin, A., & Bruce, B. C. (1986). Learning With QUILL: Lessons for students, teachers, and software designers. In T. E. Raphel (Ed.), *Contexts of school-based literacy* (pp. 217–230). NY: Random House.

Singer, H., & Donlan, D. (1982). Active comprehension: Problem-solving schema with question generation for comprehension of complex short stories. *Reading Research Quarterly, 17*, 166–186.

Taylor, B. M., & Beach, R. W. (1984). The effects of text structure instruction on middle grade students' comprehension and production of expository text. *Reading Research Quarterly, 19* 134–146.

54

AN ANALYSIS OF DEVELOPMENTAL SPELLING IN *GNYS AT WRK*

J. Richard Gentry

Source: *The Reading Teacher* (1982) 36(2): 192–200

Teachers who understand that spelling is a complex developmental process can help students acquire spelling competency. Initially, the teacher must recognize five stages of spelling development. Once the stages are identified, the teacher can provide opportunities for children to develop cognitive strategies for dealing with English orthography, and assess the pupils' development. This article demonstrates a scheme for categorizing spelling development and shows ways to foster pupils' spelling competency. In doing so, it integrates important work by Bissex (1980), spelling researchers, and reading/language researchers over the past decade.

GNYS AT WRK, an account of a case study conducted by Glenda Bissex (1980), contributes much understanding to how children may develop reading, writing, and oral language skills. In addition, it provides an excellent data base for this focus on spelling development. Bissex traces her son Paul's written language development from his first writing as a 4 year old through productions typical of fourth graders whose reading, writing, and spelling development has progressed normally up through the ages of 9 or 10 years.

This article applies a developmental spelling classification system to the Bissex case study, revealing developmental stages that researchers (Beers and Henderson, 1977; Gentry, 1977; Henderson and Beers, 1980; Read, 1975) have discovered in children's early spelling and writing. Such preexisting form suggests "that learning to spell is not simply a matter of memorizing words but in large measure a consequence of developing cognitive strategies for dealing with English orthography ..." (Read and Hodges, in press). Further, the article outlines the developmental process and provides suggestions for how spelling development may be nurtured in the classroom.

As children discover the intricacies of printed English, they progress

236

through five levels of spelling, with each representing a different conceptualization of English orthography; precommunicative spelling, semiphonetic spelling, phonetic spelling, transitional spelling, and correct spelling
(Gentry, 1978). A progressive differentiation of orthographic knowledge
may be observed which, over time, enables the competent speller to rely
on multiple strategies, including visual, phonological, and lexical or morphological information accrued not from rote memory but from extensive
experience with written language (Read and Hodges, in press). The classification system applied here to the Bissex case study focuses on an analysis
of spelling miscues and observation of the strategies used to spell words.
Classification is based primarily on studies reported by Read (1975) and
Henderson and Beers (1980).

Precommunicative stage

Developmental spelling studies (Gentry, 1977; Henderson and Beers,
1980) have identified the earliest level of spelling development as the level
where a child first uses symbols from the alphabet to represent words.
[Note, however, that writing development begins much earlier, with pencil
or pen handling and scribbling as early as 18 months of age (Gibson and
Levin, 1975).] Paul, before the formal observation of the Bissex case study
began, had clearly been a precommunicative speller. Bissex provides two
examples of Paul's productions at this earliest spelling level which, for
Paul, appeared while he was still 4 years old. She describes the first
example as a "welcome home" banner that took the following form
(actual size 1 by 4 feet, 30 by 120 cm);

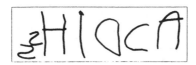

Bissex (1980, p. 4) reports other incidences of precommunicative spelling:
"Next, he [Paul] typed strings of letters which he described as notes to his
friends. Then he produced a handwritten message—large, green letters to
cheer me up when I was feeling low:

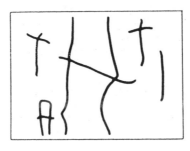

These first, occasional writings spanned several months, during which time he showed an interest in handwriting." Such instances clearly document Paul's stint as a precommunicative speller. [Illustrations from *GNYS AT WRK: A Child Learns to Write and Read*, by Glenda L. Bissex, published by Harvard University Press, reprinted by permission of the publisher.]

A speller is specifically precommunicative when his/her spelling errors are characterized by the following behaviors (Bissex, 1980; Goodman, 1980; Söderbergh, 1971; Torrey, 1973).

1   The speller demonstrates some knowledge of the alphabet through production of letter forms to represent a message.
2   The speller demonstrates *no* knowledge of letter-sound correspondence. Spelling attempts appear to be a random stringing together of letters of the alphabet which the speller is able to produce in written form.
3   The speller may or may not know the principle of left-to-right directionality for English spelling.
4   The speller may include number symbols as part of the spelling of a word.
5   The speller's level of alphabet knowledge may range from much repetition of a few known alphabetic symbols to substantial production of letters of the alphabet.
6   The speller frequently mixes uppercase and lowercase letters indiscriminately.
7   The speller generally shows a preference for uppercase letter forms in his/her earliest samples of writing.

The primary constraint under which the precommunicative speller operates is a lack of knowledge of letter-sound correspondence. As a result, precommunicative spelling attempts are not readable—hence the term "precommunicative." Though these initial attempts are purposeful productions representing the child's concept of words, at this stage spellings do not communicate language by mapping letters to sounds.

"Precommunicative" appears to be a more appropriate label for this first stage than the term "deviant," which is used in some earlier studies (Gentry, 1977; Gentry, 1978). Although precommunicative spellings deviate extensively from conventional spelling patterns, they are in no sense unnatural or uncommon, as the word "deviant" implies. Precommunicative spelling is the natural early expression of the child's initial hypotheses about how alphabetic symbols represent words.

The semiphonetic stage

The second stage of spelling development, which for Paul began at 5 years 1 month of age and lasted only a few weeks, is illustrated by productions such as: RUDF [Are you deaf?!], GABJ [garbage], BZR [buzzer], KR [car], TLEFNMBER [telephone number], PKIHER [picture], BRZ [birds], DP [dump], HAB [happy], OD [old]. These invented spellings, called semiphonetic (reported as "prephonetic" in some earlier studies), represent the child's first approximations to an alphabetic orthography.

Unlike the previous stage, semiphonetic spellings represent letter-sound correspondence. It is at this stage that a child first begins to conceptualize the alphabetic principle. The conditions of semiphonetic spelling are:

1   The speller begins to conceptualize that letters have sounds that are used to represent the sounds in words.
2   Letters used to represent words provide a partial (but not total) mapping of phonetic representation for the word being spelled. Semiphonetic spelling is abbreviated; one, two, or three letters may represent the whole word.
3   A letter name strategy is very much in evidence at the semiphonetic stage. Where possible the speller represents words, sounds, or syllables with letters that match their letter names (e.g., R [are]; U [you]; LEFT [elephant]) instead of representing the vowel and consonant sounds separately.
4   The semiphonetic speller begins to grasp the left-to-right sequential arrangement of letters in English orthography.
5   Alphabet knowledge and mastery of letter formation become more complete during the semiphonetic stage.
6   Word segmentation may or may not be in evidence in semiphonetic spelling.

Paul's rather short stint as a semiphonetic speller may be attributed to the intensity and quantity of writing during the first month after his fifth birthday and to his mother's intervention (e.g., suggestions for spacing between words, supplying letter-sound correspondences upon request, encouragement and obvious interest in Paul's invented spellings). Bissex reports "rapid flourishing and evolution of that development" (Bissex, 1980, p. 11) which is evident as Paul moved quickly from semiphonetic to complete phonetic spelling. The evolution of complete phonetic spelling from the earlier semiphonetic version is demonstrated as Paul switched from TLEFN [telephone] to TALAFON [telephone], KR [car] to KOR [car], BRZ [birds] to BRDE [birdie], and produced messages with fewer semiphonetic and more phonetic spellings, such as the message Paul typed at 5 years 2 months:

EFU KAN OPN KAZ I WIL GEV U A KN OPENR

[If you can open cans I will give you a can opener] (underlined words are phonetic spellings) (p. 11).

The phonetic stage

Paul enjoyed spurts as a prolific phonetic speller from 5 years 1 month through around 5 years 8 months to 6 years 1 month, writing in a wide variety of forms: signs, lists, notes, letters, labels and captions, stories, greeting cards, game boards, directions, and statements (Bissex, 1980, p. 15). Examples of his phonetic spelling include: IFU LEV AT THRD STRET IWEL KOM TO YOR HAWS THE ED [If you live at Third Street I will come to your house. The End] (p. 13), and PAULZ RABR SAF RABRZ KANT GT EN [Paul's robber safe. Robbers can't get in] (p. 23).

The phonetic stage has been well documented in the literature (Beers, 1974; Gentry, 1977, 1978, 1981; Gentry and Henderson, 1978; Henderson and Beers, 1980; Read, 1971, 1975, 1980; Zutell, 1975, 1978). Read's (1975) very complete documentation reports children's phonetic spellings of 80 phonetypes, some reflecting obscure details of phonetic form. Children's phonetic spelling is the ingenious and systematic invention of an orthographic system that completely represents the entire sound structure of the word being spelled. Though some of the inventive speller's letter choices do not conform to conventional English spelling for some sounds, the choices are systematic and perceptually correct. Phonetic spellings (which are quite readable) adhere to the following conditions:

1　For the first time the child is able to provide a total mapping of letter-sound correspondence; all of the surface sound features of the words being spelled are represented in the spelling.
2　Children systematically develop particular spellings for certain details of phonetic form; namely, tense vowels, lax vowels, preconsonantal nasals, syllabic sonorants, -ed endings, retroflex vowels, affricates, and intervocalic flaps (Gentry, 1978; Read, 1975).
3　Letters are assigned strictly on the basis of sound, without regard for acceptable English letter sequence or other conventions of English orthography.
4　Word segmentation and spatial orientation are generally, but not always, in evidence during the phonetic stage.

Bissex reports examples of Paul articulating an awareness of English orthography that was developing through the mental exercise employed each time he wrote. " 'With letters there's two ways of spelling some words,' he said, pointing out that 'cat' could be spelled K-A-T or C-A-T and 'baby' B-A-B-Y or B-A-B-E" (p. 10). This cognitive awareness of English orthography becomes markedly more developed in children who are allowed to invent their own spellings during their progression through the phonetic stage. As they become more and more aware of the conventions of English spelling, they emerge into the fourth stage.

Bissex correctly predicted Paul's move into "the next phase of his spelling development," the transitional stage (p. 15).

> While writing the song book, Paul observed, "You spell 'book' B-O-O-K. To write 'look' you just change one letter—take away the B and add an L." This mental spelling and word transforming continued after his writing spurt temporarily petered out: "If you took the L out of 'glass' and pushed it all together, you'd have 'gas,' " he mused while lying in bed. Such manipulation was the form that the next phase of his spelling development took. The following week (5:3) he mentally removed the L from "please," (or "peas" or "pees"), and after we had some conversation about Daedalus and Icarus, observed that "if you put an L in front of Icarus, you get "licorice.' " And "If you take the T and R off of 'trike' and put a B in front, you have 'bike.' "

The transitional stage

Most of Paul's mental rehearsal and hypothesizing about words were unrecorded. It took place, however, whenever he wrote and, as Bissex reports, sometimes when he was not writing. This kind of mental activity allowed Paul to make the discoveries necessary for moving into the transitional stage of spelling development. After 6 years 1 month, his spelling looked different from the previous phonetic spelling. A weather forecast from Newspaper # 1 said: THES AFTERNEWN IT'S GOING TO RAIN. IT'S GOING TO BE FAIR TOMORO. A news item in Newspaper # 4 read: FAKTARE'S [factories] CAN NO LONGER OFORD MAKING PLAY DOW [dough] (p. 46).

Paul was a transitional speller throughout most of his first and second grade years.

The transition stage, during which time great integration and differentiation of orthographic forms take place, marks a major move toward standard English orthography. During this stage, the speller begins to assimilate the conventional alternatives for representing sounds. The speller undergoes a transition from great reliance on phonology or sound for representing words in the printed form to much greater reliance on visual and morphological representations. During this stage, instruction in reading and spelling facilitates the move toward spelling competency, but the changes affecting the speller's conceptualization of orthography are too complex to be explained by a simple visual memorization of spelling patterns (Chomsky and Halle, 1968; Henderson and Beers, 1980; Read and Hodges, in press).

Transitional spelling exhibits the following characteristics:

1   Transitional spellers adhere to basic conventions of English orthography: vowels appear in every syllable (e.g., EGUL instead of the

241

phonetic EGL [eagle]; nasals are represented before consonants (e.g., BANGK instead of the phonetic BAK [bank]); both vowels and consonants are employed instead of a letter name strategy (e.g., EL rather than L for the first syllable of ELEFANT [elephant]); a vowel is represented before syllabic *r* even though it is not heard or felt as a separate sound (e.g., MONSTUR instead of the phonetic MOSTR [monster]); common English letter sequences are used in spelling (e.g., YOUNITED [united], STINGKS [stinks]; especially liberal use of vowel digraphs like *ai, ea, ay, ee*, and *ow* appears; silent *e* pattern becomes fixed as an alternative for spelling long vowel sounds (e.g., TIPE in place of the phonetic TIP [type]; inflectional endings like *s, 's, ing*, and *est* are spelled conventionally.

2   Transitional spellers present the first evidence of a new visual strategy; the child moves from phonological to morphological and visual spelling (e.g., EIGHTEE instead of the phonetic ATE [eighty]).

3   Due to the child's new visual strategy, transitional spellers may include all appropriate letters, but they may reverse some letters (e.g., TAOD [toad], HUOSE [house], OPNE [open]. Bissex (p. 44) attributes this phenomenon to interference. The new visual strategy, though in use, is not yet integrated to the point that the speller recognizes what "looks right."

4   Transitional spellers have not fully developed the use of factors identified by researchers that contribute to spelling competency: graphemic environment of the unit, position in the word, stress, morpheme boundaries, and phonological influences (Bissex, 1980; Gibson and Levin, 1975; Venezky, 1970).

5   Transitional spellers differentiate alternate spellings for the same sound. A long *a* sound, for example, may be spelled the following ways by a transitional speller: EIGHTE [eighty], ABUL [able], LASEE [lazy], RANE [rain], and SAIL [sale]. However, as indicated above in condition number 4, the conditions governing particular alternatives for representing a sound are only partially understood at the transitional stage.

6   Transitional spellers generally use learned words (correctly spelled words) in greater abundance in their writing.

Thus far, this analysis of developmental spelling has focused on information obtained from misspelled words. Early in development, semiphonetic and even some precommunicative spellers may have "learned" or "automatic" spellings for certain words like C-A-T or their names. These correct spellings offer no clues to the speller's notion of how English orthography works and are interspersed with developmental forms in varying degrees. For example, correct forms may account for from 0 to 50% or more of the words in semiphonetic writing, depending largely upon the writer's exposure to reading and the amount and type of instructional intervention experienced. Developmental spelling levels may be determined only by observing spelling miscues, not by observation of words spelled correctly. As in reading miscue analysis, the miscues are "the windows into the mind" (Goodman, 1979, p. 3) that allow the observer to determine the speller's level of development. Beyond the transitional stage, the child reaches a stage where miscues are relatively infrequent.

The correct stage

Correct spelling, though easily identified, may exist at different levels. Instructionally, a second grader is a "correct speller" after mastering a certain corpus of words that has been designated as "second grade level." Likewise, a sixth grade level speller has mastered the designated sixth grade level corpus. "Correct spelling" is usually viewed from the instructional scheme rather than the developmental scheme because developmental spelling research beyond the ages of 8 or 9 is limited to a few research studies (Juola et al., 1978; Marsh et al., 1980; Templeton, 1979).

It may be that the major cognitive changes necessary for spelling competency are accomplished by the end of the transitional stage and that further growth is an extension of existing strategies. Research suggests that formal spelling instruction facilitates spelling growth once the child gets into the transitional stage (Allen and Ager, 1965). In addition to formal instruction, the child continues to learn from being attentive and interested in spelling through writing experiences. Beyond the transitional stage, frequent writing experiences with some formal instruction enables children to attain spelling competency over a period of time (usually 5 or 6 years).

Developmentally, Paul was a "correct" speller by the time he was 8 years old. At that time he knew the English orthographic system and its basic rules. (At 8, Paul's spelling achievement was superior to the average development for children his age.) Further experience with words would result in finer discrimination and an extension of orthographic knowledge, but Paul had entered the correct stage, where the basis of his knowledge of English orthography was firmly set. His spelling matched well the characteristics of the developmentally correct speller:

1   The speller's knowledge of the English orthographic system and its basic rules is firmly established.
2   The correct speller extends his/her knowledge of word environmental constraints (i.e., graphemic environment in the word, position in word, and stress).
3   The correct speller shows an extended knowledge of word structure

including accurate spelling of prefixes, suffixes, contractions, and compound words, and ability to distinguish homonyms.

4   The correct speller demonstrates growing accuracy in using silent consonants and in doubling consonants appropriately.
5   The correct speller is able to think of alternative spellings and employ visual identification of misspelled words as a correction strategy. He/she recognizes when "words don't look right."
6   The correct speller continues to master uncommon alternative patterns (e.g., *ie* and *ei*) and words with irregular spellings.
7   The correct speller masters Latinate forms and other morphological structures.
8   The child accumulates a large corpus of learned words.

The developmental spelling scheme presented here has progressed through precommunicative, semiphonetic, phonetic, transitional, to correct spelling. Change from one spelling stage to the next is more or less gradual; samples of more than one stage may co-exist in a particular sample of writing as the child moves from one stage to the next.

Development, however, is continuous. Children do not fluctuate between stages, passing from phonetic back into semiphonetic spelling or from transitional back to phonetic (Gentry, 1977). As spelling develops, children draw increasingly from alternative strategies – phonological, visual, and morphological. Development proceeds from simple to more complex, from concrete to more abstract form, toward differentiation and integration. Teachers can nurture this process in the classroom by providing opportunities for children to develop cognitive strategies for dealing with English orthography.

Fostering spelling competency in the classroom

The following guidelines enable primary teachers to help children acquire foundations for spelling competency.

1   Provide purposeful writing experiences in the classroom. Purposeful writing is the key to cognitive growth in spelling. As pupils hypothesize and mentally rehearse printed representations for words, they engage in the cognitive activity needed for developmental growth. This activity is most frequent and natural when children write for a purpose, that is, enjoy a meaningful experience of sharing information in print. This occurs whenever children write stories, songs, lists, plans, messages, recipes, letters, and signs. It occurs when writing is both functional and fun.
2   Have pupils write frequently. Pupils should add something new to their creative writing folders each week. Writing (integrated with all

aspects of the curriculum and with all classroom activity), should be a natural part of the daily classroom routine. As in learning any complex cognitive process, practice and frequency of occurrence are important. Frequent application of spelling knowledge while writing moves spelling forward developmentally.

3 De-emphasize correctness, writing mechanics, and memorization. The primary school teacher's main job is to set the foundations for spelling growth. When frequent purposeful writing in the classroom takes precedence, focus on correctness, mechanics, and memorization must be secondary. Early overemphasis on mechanical aspects of spelling inhibits natural developmental spelling competency and growth. This is not to suggest eliminating mechanics altogether. Proofreading and editing should begin early. Handwriting should be taught. Models of correct writing, patterns of written form, and teacher edited and typed versions of children's work should be a part of the classroom. The core of this activity, however, should be children's purposeful writing. Teacher expectations for correctness should be adjusted to fit the pupils' level of development.

4 Help pupils develop spelling consciousness. An environment of frequent purposeful writing provides numerous opportunities for teachers to help students discover more about spelling words. In responding to children's writing, teachers build pupil interest in words, make word study fun, answer questions, and teach skills. Pupils become conscious of English spelling without being overwhelmed by its complexity.

5 Observe and assess pupil progress. Guidelines 1 through 4 suggest ways the teacher may teach spelling as a cognitive activity. Knowing how to intervene and what instructional skills to address hinge upon teacher knowledge of the developmental process, teacher observation, and assessment. Teachers may begin by applying stage descriptions (provided) in this article) to samples of the child's writing to determine the child's developmental level. Level of development and observation provide clues for instruction. For precommunicative and semiphonetic spellers, instruction may focus on alphabet knowledge, directionality of print and its spatial orientation, children's concept of words, matching oral language to print, and representing sounds with letters. Phonetic spellers are ready for introduction to the conventions of English orthography: word families, spelling patterns, phonics, and word structure. Word study is extended for the transitional speller, who is ready for a spelling textbook and formal spelling instruction. Even after formal spelling instruction begins, the pupil must maintain a vigorous program of independent writing. All writing is collected in a writing folder which becomes the focal point for assessment. The teacher analyzes the writing samples, noting changes in spelling

strategies, application of skills taught, and general progress toward spelling competency.

In summary, learning to spell must be treated as a complex developmental process that begins at the preschool and primary school levels. As teachers observe spelling skills unfold, they must engage pupils in the kinds of cognitive activity that lead to spelling competency.

References

Allen, D., and J. Ager. "A Factor Analytic Study of the Ability to Spell." *Educational and Psychological Measurement*, vol. 25 (1965), pp. 153–61.

Beers, James W. "First and Second Grade Children's Developing Orthographic Concepts of Tense and Lax Vowels." Doctoral dissertation, University of Virginia, Charlottesville, 1974.

Beers, James W., and Edmund H. Henderson. "A Study of Developing Orthographic Concepts among First Grade Children." *Research in the Teaching of English*, vol. 11 (Fall 1977), pp. 133–48.

Bissex, Glenda L. *GNYS AT WRK: A Child Learns to Write and Read.* Cambridge, Mass.: Harvard University Press, 1980.

Chomsky, Noam, and Morris Halle. *The Sound Pattern of English.* New York, N.Y.: Harper and Row, 1968.

Gentry, J. Richard. "A Study of the Orthographic Strategies of Beginning Readers." Doctoral dissertation, University of Virginia, Charlottesville, 1977.

Gentry, J. Richard. "Early Scalling Strategies." *The Elementary School Journal*, vol. 79 (November 1978), pp. 88–92.

Gentry, J. Richard. "Learning to Spell Developmentally." *The Reading Teacher*, vol. 34 (January 1981), pp. 378–81.

Gentry, J. Richard, and Edmund H. Henderson. "Three Steps to Teaching Beginning Readers to Spell." *The Reading Teacher*, vol. 31 (March 1970), pp. 632–37.

Gibson, Eleanor, and Harry Levin. *The Psychology of Reading*, Cambridge, Mass.: The MIT Press, 1975.

Goodman, Kenneth S., ed. *Miscue Analysis: Applications to Reading Instruction.* Urbana, Ill.: National Council of Teachers of English, 1979.

Goodman, Yetta M. "The Roots of Literacy." In *Claremont Reading Conference: Forty-fourth Yearbook*, edited by Malcolm P. Douglas. Claremont, Calif.: Claremont Reading Conference, 1980.

Henderson, Edmund, and James W. Beers. *Developmental and Cognitive Aspects of Learning to Spell.* Newark, Del.: International Reading Association, 1980.

Juola, J.F., M. Schadler, R.J. Chalot, and M.W. McCaughey. "The Development of Visual Information Processing Skills Related to Reading," *Journal of Experimental Child Psychology*, vol. 25 (1978), pp. 459–76.

Marsh, G., M. Friedman, V. Welch, and P. Desberg. "The Development of Strategies in Spelling." In *Cognitive Processes in Spelling*, edited by Uta Frith. London, England: Academic Press, 1980.

Read, Charles. "Preschool Children's Knowledge of English Phonology." *Harvard Educational Review*, vol. 41 (1971), pp. 1–34.

Read, Charles. *Children's Categorizations of Speech Sounds in English*. Urbana, Ill.: National Council of Teachers of English, 1975.

Read, Charles. "Creative Spelling by Young Children." In *Standards and Dialects in English*, edited by T. Shopen and J.M. Williams. Cambridge, Mass.: Winthrop Publishers, 1980.

Read, Charles, and Richard E. Hodges. "Spelling." In *Encyclopedia of Educational Research*, 5th ed. New York, N.Y.: Macmillan, In press.

Söderbergh, R. *Reading in Early Childhood*. Stockholm, Sweden: Almqvist and Wiksell, 1971.

Templeton, Shane. "Spelling First. Sound Later: The Relationship between Orthography and Higher Order Phonological Knowledge in Older Students." *Research in the Teaching of English*, vol. 13 (1979), pp. 255–64.

Torrey, Jane. "Learning to Read without a Teacher: A Case Study." In *Psycholinguistics and Reading*, edited by Frank Smith. New York, N.Y.: Holt, Rinhart, and Winston, 1973.

Venezky, Richard. *The Structure of English Orthography*. The Hague, Netherlands: Mouton, 1970.

Zutell, Jerry B., Jr. "Spelling Strategies of Primary School No. 1 Children and Their Relationship to the Piagetian Concept of Decentration." Doctoral dissertation, University of Virginia, Charlottesville, 1975.

Zutell, Jerry B., Jr. "Some Psycholinguistic Perspectives on Children's Spelling." *Language Arts*, vol. 55 (1978), pp. 844–50.

55

GRAVES REVISITED

A look at the methods and conclusions of the New Hampshire study

Peter Smagorinsky

Source: *Written Communication* (1987) 4(4): 331–342

A number of writing process researchers who have become prominent in the last decade disdain experimental research. Such studies, they say, describe the conditions and behaviors of a specific time and place, and their findings can not be extrapolated to other contexts. These critics contend that the methods of scientific inquiry are inapplicable in social situations, because people do not behave as predictably as chemicals or elements. Rather, individuals are unique, and so are the different settings in which they find themselves. The fact that a group of people responds in a particular way in one setting does not mean that we can declare their behavior to be law and generalize that other people in other situations responding to different variables will behave similarly. These critics believe that if we are to study the behavior of children in classrooms, we must find some method of inquiry other than that borrowed from experimental science.

One such researcher is Donald H. Graves of the University of New Hampshire. Graves claims that his major research project, a study of sixteen elementary school students in rural New Hampshire, is a form of the case study method, because of its intensive focus on a limited population. Only this type of study, he feels, can conclusively provide information about classrooms. In "A New Look at Writing Research" (1980), Graves refers to the "sad figures" that have characterized elementary school studies because of the distortions resulting from the experimental designs that had dominated educational research until the early 1970s, and declares that this older, experimental research "wasn't readable and was of limited value. It couldn't help [teachers] in the classroom. They could not see their schools, classrooms, or children in the data. *Context* had been ignored" (p. 914). He goes on to elaborate on context: the child's behavior as he or she writes, his or her interests that inspire the writing, the manner in which he or she has been taught up to the point of observation, the arrangement and tone of his or her classroom, and the interests and priorities of his or her parents, teachers, and school administrators.

Graves suggests that we abandon the traditional method of experimental inquiry as a means of studying classrooms, and, in particular, of studying students' composing processes. "We need," he says "more information on child behaviors and decisions *during* the process, rather than through speculation on child activity during writing from written products alone" (p. 915). Not merely, he says, is the teeming quality of the classroom impossible to analyze experimentally, but the phenomenon of writing itself is far too complicated a process to be broken down and analyzed by a researcher.

Graves feels that by conducting investigations based on case study methodology, researchers need not confine their observations to behaviors that they can record only according to their codability, and that relate only to the researcher's hypotheses; rather, they may observe all of the subjects' behaviors and record them in a narrative fashion that allows them to "describe in detail the full context of data gathering and the processes of learning and teaching" (p. 918). The major assumption behind this contention is that such a means of study will account fully for the educational context in which learning occurs. An examination of the research reports filed by Graves and his associates reveals, however, that they do not in fact give good account of the educational context. Their studies focus on certain students and observe them intensely, recording their behavior in a narrative string of anecdotes. Yet the researchers do not report every behavior and thought of the child and record them categorically; instead, the data consist of the researcher's own narration of particular behaviors of the child, giving us a limited view of the whole range of behaviors the child exhibits, and leaving open the possibility that the selection of what is recorded as data might be biased by the researcher's anticipated findings.

One might argue that, rather than being researchers, Graves and his colleagues are simply excellent demonstrators of instructional techniques that work well. The great number of elementary school teachers who implement their ideas and attend their conference presentations should easily attest to the effectiveness of many of their ideas. The purpose of this article is not to dispute whether or not Graves deserves his reputation as an innovative and sensitive educator. We can, however, question his claim that the conclusions that he draws from his classroom observations serve as a research basis for his instructional ideas. What he and his followers call "research" is, I propose, instead reportage.

Let us start with a look at some of the claims that the Graves team makes in their publications. They maintain that their role as researchers is to observe, rather than control, student behavior, and to draw their conclusions about the writing process by watching and recording how young writers develop naturally. Graves (1979a, p. 78) says, "Children give us information in the way they write, solve problems, and conceive of the writing process. This information falls in an order that tells us where and how to teach. . . . We speak of letting the child lead for effective learning to take place." He further maintains that his observations of this emerging process will allow him to describe, without influencing them, children's stages of writing development.

Other evidence in the reports published by the Graves team indicate, however, that the writing of these students does not in fact develop naturally, but is highly influenced by the biases and interventions of the researchers. Although he generally maintains that a benign teaching approach is best, he also says that children "occasionally lose control of their writing and help is needed" (Graves, 1983b, p. 843). He does not specify here the point at which they lose this control; the examples he gives indicate that it comes only when a writer is blocked. However, the other published research from this project indicates that intervention occurs when the students' processes deviate from those preferred by the researchers and teachers.

One such form of intervention is for the teacher to direct students to write several "leads," or openings to pieces of writing, until the student arrives at one that the teacher finds satisfactory. For instances, in "What Children Show Us about Revision" (1979b), Graves describes the progress of Brian: "Brian's teacher was responsible for the change. Noting Brian's level of fluency, yet lack of revision, she stressed two new approaches to the writing process. One required Brian to write about a personal experience, the other to write three leads before beginning to write the main paper" (p. 315). We will examine the researchers' emphasis on personal experience writing later. For now, let us look at a typical session, reported by Calkins, in which a teacher directs students to write leads (Barrs, 1983):

> A few weeks later Becky brought a carefully penned article beginning to her teacher. They read it together.
>
> I walked up to the pond. I wanted to catch something like a catfish, or something, I went to the other side of the pond. . . .
> "This is a good try, Becky," Mrs. Howard said. Then, with a magic marker, she drew a dark green line under Becky's opening. "Try another beginning, O.K.?" Becky's mouth gaped open. "But, but . . ." she started to say. Mrs. Howard had moved on. Becky scowled to see her perfect, neat paper ruined by a dark slash of green. Then, shrugging her shoulders, she wrote another beginning.
>
> I sat down on the rock. I put my hand in the water. Fish gathered around. The catfish charged at my bait. He bit it, and swam

away. Becky read what she had written out loud, "It's better," she said smiling. Mrs. Howard agreed. Hugging Becky warmly, she drew another dark green line across the page. "See if you can do another one," and she cheerfully left the dismayed child to discover for herself the process professional writers experience.

Becky reread her two openings, numbering them as she finished each one. Then she slowly drew a number three.

3. I felt a tug! It was a catfish "I'm going to use this lead as my opening," Becky said to the teacher. Back at her seat, Becky shared her paper with Amy. Soon Amy was writing leads, while Becky encouragingly slashed green lines under each. The concept of leads spread quickly, as children helped each other.

(pp. 834–835)

Here, the teacher has intervened until the child has exhibited "the process professional writers experience," which is clearly the optimal writing process in the eyes of the observer both from the tone of the description and the fact that it is a form of behavior of which the teacher ultimately approves. In this case, the teacher has instructed Becky to write new leads until she arrives at the type we frequently find in Calkins's own writing, that of *in medias res*. In three of the articles she wrote for this research project, Calkins begins with this approach. Here is the way in which she opens her "Case Study of a Nine Year Old Writer" (1981):

The classroom door squeaked. The circle of third graders looked up as the visitor came into the room. "Shhh," one child said, beckoning him to join the circle. "Andrea's about to share her final draft."

Andrea smiled, then ducked her pale blue eyes behind her paper. The nine year old glanced up. "It's not very long," she apologized. "I had much more in my third draft, but ... here's what I kept."

I snuggled deeper in the blanket. I felt uneasy. Something big was missing. Then Daddy came and lay down with me. He made a pocket with his legs and I crawled in. He patted my head. I felt happy. Nothing was missing anymore. The visitor's pleased eyes met mine. "I got here just in time," he said.

I thought of the drafts and redrafts Andrea had made over the last three weeks. He'd heard the final draft, but he'd missed the process of creating it.

"I guess we see it differently," I said to the visitor. "I'd say you got here just too late."

Through a grant from the National Institute of Education, Donald Graves, Susan Sowers and I aren't too late. On a day to day basis, we watch the writing process of eleven school aged children.

(p. 240)

I would suggest that Calkin's frequent use of this form of opening indicates that she regards it as a highly desirable, and possibly a highly developed way to write. (See Hillocks, 1986, for a further development of this argument.) The teacher here seems influenced by Calkins's preference; only when Andrea begins *in medias res* does she avoid the green line. With such instruction, we should not be surprised that these students develop as Graves predicts they will.

Another writing behavior favored by the researchers is for students to write about personal experiences. The comments from both teachers and researchers, as reported in their articles, indicate that it is the only form of writing they regard as legitimate for children. Graves (1979b) lauds the teacher who encourages writing about personal experiences. "Brian's teacher," he relates, "believed that revision is easiest when it relates to writing about personal experience. It is easier to confirm the truth of personal experience than the stories of fantasies" (p. 315). Graves praises the teacher for encouraging Brian to abandon his natural impulse for writing fiction, and turn instead to writing about personal experience. After Brian begins to produce such text spontaneously, Graves says that "once children like Brian feel control of the writing process from the choice of topic, selecting the best lead to the clarification of experience through several drafts, a Copernican revolution has taken place. The center of control is more in the child's hands than in the teacher's" (p. 316). The evidence is stronger, however, that Brian's natural path of development has been thrown off course, and that his behavior is being carefully shaped by the researchers and his teachers. He is simply following his teacher's explicit instructions and trying to satisfy her to the best of his ability. Nowhere in Graves's publications do we find a reason for believing that personal experience writing is a superior and highly developed form of expression; rather, we simply have the claim that it is so, followed by the evidence that children can produce it when so directed.

Another unproven claim permeating the writing of this research group is that the highest stage of writing resembles the writing processes of "professional writers," such as William Faulkner and Rumer Godden; in other words, people who have earned reputations for publishing fiction. Godden, for instance, is quoted by Sowers (1979, p.834) as saying, "Of course one never knows in draft if it is going to turn out, even with my age and experience," a statement she used to encourage spontaneous rather than planned writing. She also gives Faulkner's description of his writing process: "It begins with a character, usually, and once he stands up on his feet and begins to move, all I do is trot along behind him with a paper and pencil trying to keep up long enough to put down what he says and does" (p. 834). This nebulous sense of the writing process is praised by Calkins (1981, p. 253) in her descriptions of Andrea: "Once she selects her subject, the story seems to write itself." On the other end of the spectrum we have Chris, who "is scornful of this [spontaneous] process, not realizing it is the process most professional writers experience" (Calkins, 1980a, p. 12).

This continual reference to the authority of "professional writers" is bothersome for a number of reasons. First of all, their definition for "professional writers" is very narrow, excluding journalists, researchers who must publish to further their careers, essayists, and other wordsmiths who do not go trotting around after characters but rather produce text that is highly structured, usually planned, and clearly focused. It is also often written for pay and very real and meaningful to them.

Also questionable is the manner in which these educators present this "professional" writing process as the ultimate style without giving any reasons for why they have made this determination. Instead, they assume that the weighty reference to the authority of literary greats such as Faulkner makes it a legitimate claim, in the process committing the logical fallacy of the argument *ad verecundiam*, an appeal "to awe," which seeks the acceptance of a conclusion based on its endorsement by those who are highly respected. The teachers in the study even use this to influence the children. Here is an exchange reported by Graves (1981a, pp. 185–186) between teacher and student:

Teacher: How could you show [that these ideas] were connected?
Chris: I could put an arrow down here pointing to the part that's at the top.
Teacher: Good, but you'll need to connect the arrow with the top. This is what writers do when they are getting their books ready for the publisher.

With his teacher, a researcher, and the mystique and authority of a professional writer behind this approach, Chris has little alternative but to develop in this fashion. Later in this article, Graves says that "It is natural to want children to progress. But our anxieties about child growth lead us to take control of the writing away from children" (p. 188). Yet, through their interventions, this is precisely what this research team has done.

The possibility also exists that Graves and his colleagues have, in addition to their use of direct instruction, influenced student behavior in subtle and unconscious ways. I am reminded of Clever Hans, the turn-of-the-century European horse who performed in public and seemingly had human consciousness, apparently being able to solve arithmetical problems, spell and define words, identify musical notes and intervals, and display powers of abstract reasoning. He could answer almost any question put to him in German, his responses coming in the form of tapping his hoof, shaking his head, or walking over and pointing to letters on a board or objects on a rack. He performed these feats not only for his trainer, a man found to be of scrupulous integrity, but to the unqualified satisfaction of an elite panel of skeptical experts who studied him.

Finally, psychologist Oskar Pfungst (1911) carried out a serious and scientific investigation of the horse's behaviour. At first Pfungst was amazed to find that, although he was not coaching or cuing the horse, Clever Hans could answer any question he put to him, even in the absence of his trainer. Through controlled experiments, though, he found that Hans could answer questions only when the questioner knew the answer; he found further that Hans could not answer questions when he could not see his questioner. Considerable research led him to conclude that a questioner, when watching Hans answer a question, would pay close attention and thus produce a tenseness that resulted in an extremely subtle slouching of the head. This would cue Hans to begin tapping, or whatever behavior would answer the question. When Hans had given the correct number of taps in response to the question, the questioner, sensing that the horse should stop, would subtly raise his head and straighten up. Pfungst determined that the horse was reading these involuntary cues on the part of the questioners. In all of Pfungst's experiments, the questioners denied knowledge of giving these cues; yet extensive research revealed that they were responsible for the illusion of the horse's (and, in some of Pfungst's experiments, trained human subjects') ability to read minds and answer questions and perform in the manner expected of them.

In Graves's studies, the researchers claim that students arrive at certain decisions about their writing with no guidance (aside from the interventions) from the teachers or researchers. Yet the conclusions that the children come to are always those predicted by the researchers. Is it possible that the researchers, and the teachers in the classrooms they are studying, are providing subtle and unconscious approval of certain decisions made by their students, and disapproval of undesirable decisions? Graves and his colleagues maintain that they are observing students without influencing or leading them in any direction; says Graves (1981b, p. 113), the teachers in his study "have placed the responsibility for writing where it belongs, with the children. They believe that it is the child's responsibility to teach them about what they know."

Yet an analysis of their reports reveals a distinct bias for certain writing styles and processes that the researchers praise in certain children, and critically note the absence of in others. Graves notes that in this study the teachers and researchers were working very closely together: "Over coffee, at lunch, at breaks when gym, art, and music were taught, teachers asked questions about their children and the relation of the data to their teaching. ... In a short time the mystique of 'research and researcher' were removed," and the teachers and researchers were able to collaborate on the research effort. Under such intimate conditions, the biases of the researchers could easily be transmitted to the teachers, creating an atmosphere encouraging certain behaviors. Operating, then, under the impression that a "developmental scale" exists in which the best students write in the manner of "professional writers," following spontaneous renderings of personal experiences rather than planned efforts or fiction, these teachers and the researchers who are constantly in attendance and even occasionally participating in the instruction, could be offering subtle signs of encouragement for some behaviors, and subtle discouragement for undesirable behaviors. I would not suggest that this is deliberate, for we will recall that in Pfungst's experiments, the questioners were never aware that they were issuing what Pfungst (and Hans) saw to be clear signals identifying the correct or anticipated response.

I was not in these classrooms, so I can hardly make any claims as to what actually was happening. I do offer this, though, as an alternate interpretation of the results of their research. Since their studies do not control for this possibility, we can not say for certain. I would be interested to see how these children would respond, however, if the study were repeated with teachers and researchers of a different bias. Indeed, this is a major problem with regarding Graves's work as research: He and his colleagues do not look for negative evidence for their hypotheses. All of their reported results give an enthusiastic endorsement of the theories that they are testing; nowhere do we see them raising questions about whether the evidence does in fact support their hypotheses. The purpose of this article is to ask some of those questions.

Ironically, Graves maintains that his intensive study is the only way to get a fair picture of context. However, with such a heavy concentration on certain individuals, we do not in fact get an accurate view of the educational context at all. In the New Hampshire study, we get a restricted view of the whole classroom, receiving instead accounts of the activities of certain students. A scan of 11 articles written by the Graves team, covering 137 pages, reveals that 30 different children were referred to; Andrea is mentioned on 41 pages, and only one other student is referred to on more than 10 (Sarah, 15 pages). The 29 students other than Andrea are mentioned on a total of 92 pages, an average of just over 3 per student. Graves finds the rigor and difficulty with his research in the selection of significant and representative behaviors, and his ability to interpret them and extrapolate their meaning to all other learning situations. In accepting his research, then, we must have faith in: (1) the significance of the behaviors he reports; (2) the insignificance of the behaviors he does not report, and/or those that he reports but dismisses as insignificant; (3) the reliability of his interpretations of the immediate behavior; and (4) the reliability of his extrapolations to all situations. We must wonder, though, how representative the behaviors he reports are when he concentrates so heavily on a few individuals, particularly such a talented child as Andrea.

My point in this article is not that "the Graves method" is without merit; the legions of teachers who employ it would no doubt scoff at such a suggestion. My concern is that he and his colleagues have represented, seemingly without challenge, their classroom observations as research, when they more resemble journalism about ideas that work well under favorable circumstances, particularly when the instructors have such great enthusiasm for their work that it positively affects their students' attitudes. Indeed, the inspirational tone in which their reports are written, and that no doubt had existed in the classrooms where the instruction took place, may account to some extent for the success of the methods they report. Before we can attribute their success to solid research findings that describe general human behavior, we must test them under conditions that have better controls to rule out the many alternative explanations for the performance of the children in Graves's study.

References

Barrs, M. (1983). The new orthodoxy about writing: Confusing process and pedagogy. *Language Arts, 60*, 829–840.

Becker, H. (1968). Social observation and social case studies. In D. L. Sills (Ed.), *International encyclopedia of the social sciences* (pp. 232–238). New York: Macmillan.

Calkins, L. (1979). Andrea learns to make writing hard. *Language Arts, 56*, 569–576.

Calkins, L. (1980a). Children learn the writer's craft. *Language Arts, 57*, 207–213.

Calkins, L. (1980b). Children's rewriting strategies. *Research in the Teaching of English, 14*, 331–341.

Calkins, L. (1981). Case study of a nine year old writer. In D. H. Graves (Ed.), *A case study observing the development of primary children's composing, spelling, and motor behaviors during the writing process, final report* (pp. 239–262). Durham: University of New Hampshire.

Graves, D. (1979a). Research doesn't have to be boring. *Language Arts, 56*, 76–80.

Graves, D. (1979b). What children show us about revision. *Language Arts, 56*, 312–319.

Graves, D. (1979c). Andrea learns to make writing hard. *Language Arts, 56*, 569–576.

Graves, D. (1980). A new look at writing research. *Language Arts, 57*, 913–919.

Graves, D. (1981a). Patterns of child control of the writing process. In D. H. Graves (Ed.). *A case study observing the development of primary children's composing, spelling, and motor behaviors during the writing process, final report* (pp. 177–188). Durham: University of New Hampshire.

Graves, D. (1981b). A new look at research on writing. In S. Haley James (Ed.), *Perspectives on writing in grades 1–8* (pp. 93–116). Urbana, IL: NCTE.

Graves, D. (1983a). *Writing: Teachers and children at work*. Exeter, NH: Heinemann Educational Books.

Graves, D. (1983b). Teacher intervention in children's writing: A response to Myra Barrs. *Language Arts, 60,* 841–846.

Graves, D., & Murray, D. (1982). Revision: In the writers' workshop and in the classroom. In R. D. Walshe (Ed.), *Donald Graves in Australia.* Exeter, NH: Heinemann Educational Books.

Hillocks, G. (1986). The writer's knowledge: Theory, research, and implications for practice. In A. R. Petrosky & D. Bartholamae (Eds.), *The teaching of writing.* Chicago: University of Chicago Press.

Kamler, B. (1980). One child, one teacher, one classroom: The story of one piece of writing. *Language Arts, 57,* 680–693.

Pfungst, O. (1911). *Clever Hans.* New York: Henry Holt.

Smagorinsky, P. (1986). An apology for structured composition instruction. *Written Communication, 3*(1), 105–121.

Sowers, S. (1979). A six-year-old's writing process: The first half of first grade. *Language Arts, 56,* 829–835.

56

SUBJECT-SPECIFIC LITERACY AND SCHOOL LEARNING

A focus on writing

Bill Green

Source: *Australian Journal of Education* (1988) 32(2): 156–179

Introduction

The central proposition of this paper is twofold: first, that curriculum developers, teacher educators and teachers generally, regardless of subject area and level of schooling, are profitably informed by current developments in writing and literacy research; and secondly, that increased and more informed attention to writing throughout schooling is likely to have a positive effect on the development of literacy, as well as on the quality of classroom learning. Writing and schooling are closely linked practices. This is so, right across the curriculum. However a major assumption of the present situation in schools is that writing as such—and, more generally, literacy—is more properly the concern of, on the one hand, English teachers and, on the other, the junior primary school. This is not only quite erroneous but also, importantly, harmful, based as it is on an incorrect view of writing and of literacy which, when perpetuated in this manner, has a quite negative and deleterious effect on the development of literacy generally. From the perspective of this paper, the focus of which is the notion of literacy and the manner in which an across-the-curriculum emphasis contributes to its overall development and enhancement, attention to writing as an active means of learning is likely to have a particularly positive and beneficial effect on students' writing abilities and their literacy as well as on their learning generally.

The specific concern here is with the nature of school literacy and more particularly subject-specific literacy. This, it is argued, has a significant relation to general literacy. Such a concern is, in the first instance, a pragmatic emphasis in that it acknowledges the manner in which knowledge, information and experience are organised, classified and (re)produced in

258

schools, either implicitly or explicitly. It is also theoretically motivated, acknowledging and affirming the importance of context when considering literacy. In the highly specific social settings of schools, learning and literacy development largely proceed in the context of the school subjects. For present purposes, literacy will be defined flexibly and operationally as a situation-specific competency with regard to written language. The main concept to be introduced is the notion of subject-specific literacy—that is, the particular literacy, or set of literacy competencies, that is inextricably part of the operation of specific subject areas as contexts for learning and meaning.

Understanding literacy

A major problem in adequately conceptualising literacy involves its relation to thinking and cognition, as opposed to a more restricted view of literacy as concerned with written language in the most narrow, materialistic sense. Moffett (1981) sees literacy as tied hierarchically and developmentally to what he asserts are the more significant and problematical levels of verbalisation and conceptualisation (Figure 1).

In this formulation, speaking and thinking are the real basics of the literacy issue, not spelling, punctuation and grammar, as is far too commonly believed. These he describes as 'surface features'. Clearly they are important and necessary aspects of the written communication process, but they must be seen emphatically in relation to thinking and effective and meaningful communication, not as sufficient and self-contained in themselves.

Moffett's model is useful, relating best to the manner in which literacy in the fullest sense develops, and also having specific relevance to those individuals who have not successfully made what he calls the 'media shift' from spoken to written language and hence have not developed competence with specific regard to the written language system. But it does not, in itself, fully allow for a more appropriate view of the literacy process which emphasises its character as *thinking*. Literacy is not simply a matter of speech written down; speaking is not a necessary intermediary. Reading

LITERACY
(speech into print)
↑
VERBALISATION
(thought into speech)
↑
CONCEPTUALISATION
(experience into thought)

Figure 1 Formulation of literacy (Moffett, 1981)

does not necessarily involve, for the mature fluent reader, decoding written symbols into sounds, and similarly writing does not necessarily involve moving from sound into symbol. The written language system and the spoken language system, although they are related developmentally and historically, differ significantly in their structure and function, and it must be emphasised that speech and writing are in fact different and alternative language systems (Harste, 1984; Kress, 1982; Vygotsky, 1962). Hence a better formulation, based on but adapting Moffett's model, is shown in Figure 2.

This enables us to view literacy directly in relation to thinking and meaning which can be now seen as the real basics. In one sense, literacy is simply a problem of expressing meaning in and through written language. In other circumstances, it might just as well have been expressed in and through spoken language, in which case there would have been other kinds of problems for the individual. It is important to recognise that the term 'meaning' is linked to verbalisation. Meaning is employed here as a verb analogous to thinking. This usage is consistent with Halliday's perspective on language as behaviour and as action; emphasis here is on the verb 'to mean' (Halliday, 1975). In such a view, meaning and thinking are activities underpinning and impelling an individual's usage of the written language system. Literacy in the fullest sense involves using written language for thinking and meaning.

It needs to be stressed that the terms 'thinking' and 'meaning', as employed in this argument, need to be understood in a semiotic sense, and not psychologistically as is too often the case in literacy research. This means seeing them as matters of semiosis—that is, as involving the production, consumption and circulation of signs and sign systems, with reference to specific contexts and context types. This certainly includes the inner speech of cognitive processes (Moffet, 1981; Vygotsky, 1962) and it suggests that there is likely to be particular value in reconceptualising so-called mental operations in explicit (psycho)semiotic terms (Walkerdine, 1982).

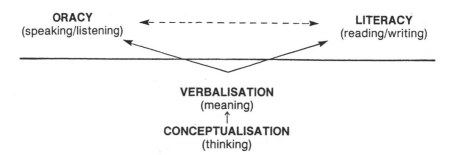

Figure 2 Formulation of literacy (adapted from Moffett, 1981)

The following quotation captures something of the complexity and rich implication of the view of literacy that is espoused here:

> Reading and writing are complexly constituted and potentially enabling competencies that develop only when they are practised; literacy that is worthy of the name ... develops only through the productive exercise of available and developing competencies with language—through the use of such competencies in composing and comprehending texts, through the use of language to make meanings that count for something in contexts where learning and sharing what is learned counts for something. Literacy is an outcome, not a skill, and not (even) a competency. It is something that is achieved when competencies are enabled through exercise of the human capacity to make meaning.
>
> (Robinson, 1985, p. 485)

This statement indicates the importance and even the necessity of embedding an appropriate literacy consideration in curriculum generally, as an integral and organic part of teaching/learning and not in any sense an adjunct or an optional extra. The implications for both teacher education and curriculum development are obvious.

Two points must be made here. First, it is not the case that such a view de-emphasises and undervalues the surface features of language usage. Such a stance would involve a totally inadequate theory of language and meaning. Language is social behaviour. One aspect of this is that an individual's use of language must conform to accepted standards, in contexts where such conformity is required. This is always a matter of convention, in several senses of that term. Secondly, it is not the case that the written language system is a neutral transmitter of meaning, a mere receptacle for meaning. Rather the system both constrains and enables the kinds of meaning that can be made, and feeds back into the verbalisation process— in significant although often subtle ways thereby changing and influencing it. Writing is not simply the transcription of meaning but very often works actively, in various ways and in varying degrees, as the discovery and production of meaning. While part of the literacy process certainly has to do with the practical and material problems of written language as a separate and distinct symbol system, it is important to view literacy in relation to thinking, as a thinking skill and so a tool for learning and meaning.

At the same time, care must be taken to view literacy in the larger context of language generally—that is, in terms of the interrelated systems of spoken and written language. This is depicted in Figure 3.

The point to recognise is that it is difficult, and finally unprofitable, to work with too sharp a distinction between the two systems, since they are so closely and necessarily related, albeit in ways rather different from the

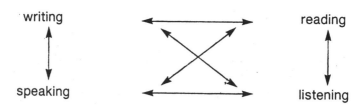

Figure 3 Interrelation of spoken and written language

conventional wisdom of recent literacy pedagogy. What is important to note is the effect and significance of written language (and related to this, the invention of print) on language generally and hence on thinking itself (Olson, 1977). This is of particular significance in the context of schooling. Much classroom practice involves the teacher presenting information orally, more or less in monological terms. This is sometimes described as 'recitation' (Henry, 1984). A common feature of such speech is its proximity, in significant ways, to written language, and very often it is more or less direct transformation of a written text, whether that be in the form of a textbook or the teacher's own writing. More often than not, it is a combination of these. This phenomenon—the shaping influence of writing on speech—has been described as 'secondary orality' (Ong, 1982, p. 3), and clearly account needs to be taken of it in any adequate discussion of literacy, certainly in the school context. It is relevant, however, not only in the context of the school, since it is a feature also of much media language and political text.

Dimensions of literacy

A further consideration, and an important step in viewing literacy more holistically, is the need to see literacy in terms of three related dimensions: the operational, the cultural and the critical. These are sometimes presented as alternatives; it is more productive and adequate to the issue at hand to see them as significantly interrelated dimensions.[1] The first, the operational dimension, refers to the means of literacy in the sense that it is in and through the medium of language that the literacy event happens. It involves, in essence, competency with regard to the language system. To refer to the operational dimension of literacy is to point to the manner in which individuals use language in literacy tasks, in order to operate effectively in specific contexts. The emphasis is on the written language system and how adequately it is handled. From this perspective, it is a question of individuals being able to read and write in a range of contexts, in an appropriate and adequate manner. This is to focus on the language aspect of literacy.

The cultural dimension involves what may be called the meaning aspect of literacy. It involves, by contrast, competency with regard to the meaning system (Lemke, 1984). This is to take more emphatic account of the notion that literacy acts and events are not only *context* specific but also entail a specific *content*. It is never simply a case of being literate in and of itself but of being literate with regard to something, some aspect of knowledge or experience. This is an important point. A person may be said to be literate in the more significant sense if he or she has competence with regard to a sufficiently wide repertoire of contexts and written registers, in accordance with a relatively arbitrary and socially determined standard. As Margaret Spencer (1980) has observed, the literate individual is someone who knows that he or she does not have to be and, further, cannot be literate with regard to everything. Importantly, however, literate individuals are not rendered powerless in circumstances outside their immediate competence; they know what to do and who to see in order to achieve their purposes.

The term 'cultural' is employed here in order to invoke the notion of cultural learning, which is to say, the learning of culture. This formulation is based upon the work of Halliday (1975, 1978). He asserts that learning language involves learning culture—that is, being socialised into the culture. Language learning is, therefore, enculturation. Conversely, to learn culture and to become an effective, functioning participant in the culture involves learning the language and becoming competent with regard to using it as a resource for meaning. It is in this sense that there is a complementary and mutually informing relationship between the language system and the meaning system, and so between the operational and the cultural dimensions of literacy. Cultural learning involves language learning, and vice versa. The two are bound together necessarily in a reciprocal, mutually enriching relationship.

Halliday's work focuses mainly on early language development and its relation broadly to cultural learning; mature and relatively achieved language competence is closely related to effective participation in the adult culture. Schooling has a particularly significant role to play in the process that this involves; indeed, in Bernstein's phrase, schooling must be regarded as a 'critical socializing agency' (1971). What is involved here is the combined operation of language learning and cultural learning. Towards the lower end of schooling, it is more clearly a matter of language learning, particularly with regard to the written language system; that is, literacy learning. But it must also be seen as cultural learning, albeit less formally conceived. As the child moves up through the school, the situation is gradually reversed, or seems to be. Whereas in the earlier stages cultural learning is more implicit and informal, and hence less visible, it becomes more and more explicit and formal, and so more visible, in the movement from kindergarten to Year 12. At the same time and in the same movement, language learning becomes less visible and more implicit and even taken for granted (a notional exception here being subject English). This is reflected in the commonplace assumption that language (and literacy) learning is the province of the junior primary school, after which basic competence may be assumed and the emphasis consequently placed on what is called here cultural learning.

The point that must be stressed is that cultural learning as organised and formalised in the school context involves subject-area learning. The organisation of school knowledge, and hence school learning, in terms of more or less distinct subject areas or disciplines is not a natural or inevitable occurrence but, rather, cultural and conventional. Just as curriculum generally involves a culturally specific selection from the culture, so too do the various school subjects involve culturally specific selections. They represent intermediary meaning systems significant in themselves and in their interrelation in the socialisation and learning process of the school. Knowledge is socially constructed and classified, and the organisation of the school curriculum into an array of distinct subject areas, in a specific sense every bit as arbitrary as the school curriculum as a whole, serves specific social functions (Young, 1971). It is a significant means of access to the culture generally, conceived as a structured system of meanings.

Subject-area learning is cultural learning; in learning the subject, one is also learning the culture. In a sense, of course, one is learning only part of it: the specific meaning system of the subject in relation to the larger meaning system of the culture. But individual subjects are defined in part by their difference from other subjects in the array; one learns not only through what is said via the subject but also through what is not said. Partly this 'not said' is said elsewhere in other subjects, albeit differently. Partly it is said outside the context of the formal school curriculum, in a range of quite different ways. The main point here is to recognise that individual subjects are themselves matters of selection, interpretation and perspective. Therefore, while there is certainly a significant degree of explicit teaching and learning involved in engaging with a particular subject, there is as much if not more learnt and taught implicitly. Learning a subject inevitably involves being socialised into the subject. This can be expressed as socialisation into the culture, or subculture, of the subject (the specific meaning system of the subject), which in turn is socialisation into the culture generally. It is in this sense that subject-area learning can be described as cultural learning.

Since school learning is highly dependent on and closely related to literacy (Wells, 1981), there is similarly a close and reciprocal relation between cultural learning and literacy learning. Such a proposition permits a clearer sense of the relation between subject-area learning and, specifically, the development and enhancement of reading and writing abilities. To speak of the cultural dimension of literacy is to point to the notion of subject-specific literacy and in particular it is to emphasise subject-specific learning. Thus the operational and cultural dimensions of subject-specific literacy are clearly and closely related. The former involves literacy learning, the specific use and development of literacy competencies (with regard to reading and writing); the latter involves cultural learning, developing specific competency with regard to the subject area in question.

The third dimension of literacy, the critical, similarly has to do with the social construction of knowledge and the notion of schooling as socialisation. A socially critical perspective on literacy, culture and schooling recognises that these are not and cannot be neutral concepts (Giroux, 1983; Kemmis, Cole, & Suggett, 1983). Contending definitions and intentions are evident wherever they are discussed, suggesting a struggle over meaning and between sectional interests. Cultural and subject-specific learning involves socialisation into the dominant culture (Cherryholmes, 1983; Lemke, 1982). This is an important and necessary process and a significant aspect of schooling. Individuals need to gain access to the meaning system of the culture in order to function in it effectively and productively. But meaning systems are always selective and sectional; they represent particular interpretations and classifications. Unless individuals are also given access to the grounds for selection and the principles of interpretation (and hence given more critical insight into the processes and possibilities of knowledge production, their own and that of the culture), they are merely socialised into the dominant meaning system and lack the capacity to take an active role in its transformation. It is in this sense that literacy, and in particular subject-specific literacy, can operate as a means of social control. Implicit in the most significant sense of literacy, there must be a critical dimension: one that enables the individual not simply to participate in the culture but also, in various ways, to transform and actively produce it.

This has the following implication. Subject-area learning is not just about the reproduction of knowledge and information within the boundaries of the subject, although clearly it does involve that to some degree. It is also about the production of knowledge and the making of personal meanings, with a significant bearing on the maintenance and transformation of culture. A socially critical stance on subject-specific literacy means providing individuals, at any level of schooling, with the means to reflect critically on what is being learned and taught in classrooms and to take an active role in the production of knowledge and meaning. It involves giving individuals the capacity to recognise the socially constructed and conventional nature of school knowledge, and to work collaboratively and constructively towards informed personal meanings. Rather than the single, authorised version of the textbook, for instance, students should have the capacity and be given the opportunity to consult different and sometimes conflicting sources of information, in order to arrive at personal understandings. The literate individual is someone who knows that there is more than one version available, and that what one is reading, or is given to read, represents both a selection and an abstraction from a larger context. Similarly, with writing, the individual is able to personalise and synthesise information, making significant connections between what is new and what is familiar, such that learning becomes more meaningful and 'school knowledge' is transformed into 'action knowledge' (Barnes, 1976). Writing is particularly and uniquely suitable for this, and an active means of making it happen.

Clearly this is a controversial issue: crucial, indeed, to the most adequate and significant understanding of the literacy process and the literacy debate. There comes a point where questions about the relevance and function of schooling and literacy become important. At that point it is surely justifiable to ask: literacy and schooling for what? While it is more likely that schools will accept the argument for the operational and cultural dimensions of subject-specific literacy and learning than for the critical dimension, all three dimensions, as they interrelate, need to be considered in understanding literacy in the fullest sense.

Literacy and learning: a writing focus

There is now considerable research consensus about the significance of literacy in learning and schooling. In addition to the administrative and regulative role that it plays in schools, literacy has a specific cognitive and intellectual role at the same time as it is a powerful enabling mechanism for thinking and learning. Wells (1981) suggests that literacy is particularly significant in terms of the contribution that schooling makes to the development of higher order cognitive skills associated with symbolic activities. 'It is in and through the acquisition of the skills of literacy that the individual's command of language reaches the stage where it is available for deliberate and conscious exploitation' (p. 267). This is an important point. It links up to the now firmly established argument that there is a close and necessary relation between language and learning (Britton, 1970; Christie, 1985a) and indicates that what is significant in the use of written language is that it enables the user to take up a more abstract, reflexive stance towards text and so one's own thinking and processing of meaning (Bruner, 1984; Olson, 1984).[2]

Writing is of particular significance in this matter. There are several reasons for making this assertion. One reflects the nature of and rationale for this present intervention: the urgent need to redress a current imbalance of some seriousness and consequence. Much discussion of literacy tends to emphasise reading rather than, or at the expense of, writing.

When writing is considered in this view, it tends to be in the most limited, instrumental sense. Noting this, one commentator makes the following observation:

> One possibility is that being asked to stay inside the constraints of another's text, or at least a single interpretation of that text, can perhaps be a training in docility that can well serve any religious, political or aesthetic majority.
>
> (Emig, 1983, p. 174)

Such a point offers perspective on the critical dimension of literacy and its role in subject-area learning. The importance of reading in schools cannot be under-estimated or denied. Increasingly, schooling involves students gathering and engaging with information through reading, either in itself or as mediated by the teacher. An important part of the business of schooling is certainly the transmission of knowledge and the maintenance of culture. It is also more than this. The emphasis on reading and teacher recitation in schools can mean that students are customarily and too readily in a receptive, passive position with regard to school learning—remaining 'inside the constraints of another's text', whether it be the text-book writer's or the teacher's, or more normally a combination of the two. Students need to engage as fully as possible with information and actively transform it into personal, 'internally persuasive' understandings (Rosen, 1986). They need to be active producers of their own texts, their own meanings. Certainly reading at its most significant can be an active, pro-ductive process. It certainly should be. But writing is arguably even more suited to this and results more tangibly in text, a feature that may make it particularly appropriate for learners and learning. This is to view the matter politically, as it were, placing the stress on production rather than consumption, and emphasising that students should be more actively engaged in learning.[3]

To emphasise writing in this fashion is not simply a matter of politics; it also has a cognitive aspect. This is effectively expressed by Wells (1981):

> Many discussions of literacy, particularly of the early stages, give most of their attention to reading. But it is in the process of com-position—in 'wrestling with words and meanings'—whether to render subtleties of feeling, to convey precise observations of objects, or to develop a coherent line of reasoning, that one ulti-mately becomes most fully aware of the power and limitations of the written language ... It is also through writing in various models that one is most called upon to develop those skills of lit-eracy which are associated with higher levels of cognitive activity.
>
> (p. 274)

Two points may be made here. The first involves the manner in which writing enables the learner to grasp more powerfully the significance of language as a medium for thinking and reasoning. The palpability and materiality of language as a medium is particularly evident in and heightened by the activity of writing, and this is significant because such an awareness would appear crucial to the development of 'disembedded' thinking (Brandt, 1985; Pattison, 1982). One is not tied to the immediate context but, increasingly, able to use language to generate an appropriate contextualisation; this greatly enlarges the scope of one's meaning potential. Writing enables the learner to put his or her thinking at a distance and then to work on it; this is an enormous advantage in terms of being able to elaborate one's thinking. The Russian psychologist Vygotsky (1968) has expressed this as 'deliberate semantics—the deliberate structuring of the web of meaning' (p. 100). The use of written language enables the learner to focus deliberately on his or her thinking and work on it so as to develop it further. This feeds back on to language generally, and it is in this sense that the development of writing abilities, and of literacy, is instrumental in the development of higher-order cognitive skills.

The second point involves the notion of text. It is important to recognise a close and necessary relation between meaning and text; meanings are realised in and only in text, and different kinds of text realise different kinds of meaning. In Halliday's (1978) terms, text is a basic semantic unit (p. 135)—the actualisation of meaning potential and the process of semantic choice. This means, furthermore, that text is the basic unit of literacy (Harste, 1983, p. 34). Unless a student is actively producing text, in the fullest sense, he or she is not going through the process of producing meaning. If no sense is being made, if no learning is happening through the literacy event, then the individual concerned cannot rightfully be said to be literate with regard to that event, nor indeed can he/she be said to be really learning.[4] The emphasis must at all times be on meaning making. To be actively involved in the construction of text specific to a given situation is to be engaged in a specific kind of organisation and articulation of information and knowledge, in the course of which the individual is not only discovering and producing meaning but also learning how to make meaning. This applies to both reading and writing. In reading, understood in its most active sense, one is not simply taking meaning from text and realising it in another form; rather one is actively constructing text or meaning for oneself, on the basis of the 'text potential' that one is engaged with and also that which one brings to the literacy encounter (Harste, Woodward & Burke, 1984). The reader makes something new and specific to him or herself, bringing together a personal history and the meaning potential of what is being read. Reading in itself produces what may be called a 'virtual' text; it remains essentially a subjective experience, unless transformed into written or some other graphic form. In contrast, writing involves very tangibly and materially a text production.

Emig (1983) expresses this distinction in the following terms: 'Writing is originating and creating a unique verbal construct that is graphically recorded. Reading is creating or re-creating but *not* originating a verbal construct that is graphically recorded' (p. 124). In the case of reading, one's meaning making (and hence one's construction of text) is framed by a pre-existent text, that which is being read. At least some of the cognitive work involved in meaning making is already done, in that the reader has a frame of reference tangibly and ready at hand. In part the act of meaning making is structured by something that already exists. This is not the case with writing. The writer does not have a pre-existent frame of reference in the same tangible way that the reader does. In a quite specific sense, in writing one is generating a frame of reference, or context, as one goes along. Hence there is arguably more cognitive work involved in writing, in that one is originating text and increasingly taking responsibility for the generation of context. This is surely Wells's implication in stressing that it is in the act of composition that the cognitive significance of literacy is most evident.

Taken together, these points support the contention that there is particular value in putting the emphasis on writing in considering subject-specific literacy and how it might be enhanced, bearing in mind the links that have been suggested already between subject-specific literacy and general literacy, and between literacy and learning. At the very least, it is imperative that the role of writing with relation to subject-area learning, and school learning generally, be reassessed and reconceptualised.

Learning literacy/learning through literacy

A particularly important consideration is the relationship between the notions of learning literacy and learning through literacy. The first involves the development of reading and writing abilities, or literacy competency—how children become literate. The second concerns the notion of literacy as a specific tool for learning. On the one hand, literacy is conceived as the goal of schooling; on the other, it is the means of schooling. This does not mean that there is no reciprocal relation between the two. On the contrary, it is likely that literacy learning and learning through literacy are interdependent and mutually informing. Literacy develops in use, in the course of learning; that is, literacy is learned in use. Similarly learning in schools proceeds significantly on the basis of literacy.

It is important to recognise differing emphases here. This present discussion is concerned first and foremost with the enhancement of literacy. Teachers, particularly those in the content areas, may understandably see as their primary concern the promotion and enhancement of learning in their own areas; for them, literacy will be more of a subsidiary concern, as an end in itself. This will tend to be the case also towards the upper end of the primary school, although such a distinction is certainly less clear. It can be argued, however, that such a shift in emphasis is a general tendency in schooling, becoming all the more strong as one moves up the school, from kindergarten to Year 12. It is important therefore to affirm and insist that there is a particularly significant link between literacy and learning throughout schooling; one is constantly learning literacy and one is constantly learning through literacy. It is important to recognise that, in focusing on school or subject-specific literacy, there is a twofold emphasis: on literacy and on learning as they interrelate and inform one another.

It is useful, further, to consider the distinction referred to previously between literacy as the goal of schooling and literacy as the means of schooling. In the former case, an important intended outcome of the schooling process is a literate individual and a literate society—that is, what may correctly be described as an educated individual and an educated society. One significant motivation for the development of compulsory mass schooling was, and remains, a recognition of the need for 'universal literacy' (Donald, 1983). From this perspective, it is clear that schooling generally, across the whole curriculum, has a contribution to make to the development of literacy, understood in these terms.

A shift in position is required to focus on literacy as the means of schooling—as a means to the achievement of the aims of schooling (including, notably, literacy as an end in itself). This involves consideration of the role and significance of literacy in and for learning, or as a means and an instrument of learning. The question becomes one of deciding how best to enhance students' opportunities for learning and also the quality of their learning. This requires specific attention to language, both spoken and written (Christie, 1985a). In such a view, a concern for literacy on the part of teachers, regardless of subject area or teaching level, is a necessary factor in the achievement of the most effective student learning. Further it is likely to be the most effective means of contributing to the general task of schooling, conceived as the achievement of a full and appropriate literacy. Although the links between these perspectives are clear, the distinction is an important and useful one to make in order to clarify discussion and decision making.

Finally reference needs to be made to the notion of general literacy— that is, a general competency regardless of, or abstracted from, circumstance and context. It may in fact be quite unproductive to employ such a notion at all, presenting as it does similar difficulties to the notion of education as the aim of schooling. How useful is it, for instance, to speak of an educated individual, other than rhetorically? The most that can be said is that schools must equip students with competency across a range of specific contexts, which means increasing their repertoire of competencies.

Richards (1978) argues that an important task of schooling is to increase students' range with regard to language 'repertoire', and this can be appropriated here to enable us to refer to the development of a repertoire of literacies. This involves in the first instance the specific contexts of the school—the various subject areas—and also the school itself as a specific social context. Boomer (in press) has specifically referred to the need for students to become 'literate' with regard to the school, by which he means becoming capable of 'reading the whole curriculum' as a culture in itself so as to be able to participate in it effectively. Although in one sense a metaphor, it is useful in illuminating the notion of competency in context with regard to literacy more generally.

Competency in the context of schooling does not, however, automatically and unproblematically transfer to other social contexts, for instance the workplace. To rely simply, and simplistically, on what may be called 'transfer of literacy' is, at best, naive. Again the most that can be said, albeit with some caution, is that it is likely that those individuals with larger literacy repertoires may well be able to recognise and predict certain formal features of new and different contexts. Even so, they will still need to develop specific competencies with regard to those contexts. This suggests that schools are best advised, first, to concentrate on developing what is described here as school literacy and secondly, within that particular context, to seek actively to develop and extend students' repertoires with regard to literacy. This is clearly a matter for concerted and collaborative effort on the part of all subject areas and across the school curriculum as a whole.

Conceptualising context

It is necessary at this stage to re-affirm and then investigate a point made earlier: that literacy is to be considered as a particular kind of situation-specific competency with regard to written language usage. In particular, the importance of context needs to be emphasised. Meaning making and language usage are both enabled and constrained by the contexts in which they occur. This suggests that an adequate understanding of literacy involves an explicit consideration of those contexts in which it occurs, so that we can discover to what extent different contexts shape and determine the kinds of meanings that can be and are made. This is not simply to refer to the physical environment of the language usage, although that may be and often is a factor; more to the point, context is an abstract term referring to 'a generalized social context or situation type' (Halliday, 1978, p. 122).

Consider the contexts for what is described here as school literacy. The first and perhaps most obvious one is the school itself, as a specialised and highly specific social setting. In what way do literacy operations in the context of school differ from those in other contexts? Certainly the demands of school literacy differ considerably. For many people, the major portion of their formal literacy activity happens in the school context. In the case of reading, individuals may well continue to read after they leave school but, in most instances, the situation will be quite different. They will thereafter read according to their own needs and interests and on their own volition. The majority of people are much less likely to write in any significant and intensive way after they leave school. Reading and writing are closely tied to the compulsory character of schooling, and both (but, in particular, writing) are closely associated with schooling. Writing is used for different purposes in school, but the main and overriding use traditionally has been as a means of testing and assessment (Applebee, 1981). Students tend to write in order to demonstrate to their teacher what they know or what they have learned. Furthermore what they write is highly restricted. The main point here is that school writing is highly circumscribed as a consequence of being produced in the school setting (Applebee, 1984; Bennett, 1983).

Perhaps the most striking illustration of this is provided by seeing school writing in relation to the characteristic three-part discourse structure of schooling: question–answer–evaluation (Sinclair & Coulthard, 1975). The writing that students characteristically engage in is in the form of a reply to a teacher's question or compliance with an instruction; it is entirely structured by the task that the teacher assigns. It is followed, in turn, by an evaluation by the teacher. The student's writing is entirely framed by the teacher; learning is framed and contained by teaching. This has a significant effect on the nature and quality of the writing. What is important is that the school is a highly specialised and specific discourse context, markedly affecting the writing that students produce.

The second specific kind of context that impinges on the production of school writing is the subject area. It has already been proposed that school learning is structured in terms of an array of distinct subject areas or disciplines. Following Applebee's (1981) study of writing in the secondary school, a major assumption of this present paper is that 'major subject areas represent differing universes of discourse, each with characteristic registers and differentiated writing skills' (p. 4). Understanding what is involved in this assumption is crucial to understanding and conceptualising the problem of subject-specific literacy. The subject area as a context for writing and literacy generally can be conceptualised in two ways. The first is to focus on the situational context of the subject area in question. This involves considering the language appropriate to that particular context, and so involves accounting for register. The second is to focus on the cultural context of the subject area, which means in the first instance considering the kinds of behaviour appropriate to that context, especially the kinds of speaking and writing behaviour. The most immediate concern here is the notion of genre. With regard to register, this is as employed in systemic-functional linguistics; with regard to genre, it is the notion of 'context of culture' that is being referred to (Martin, 1984). In this formulation, register and genre are directly related but distinct concepts.

Situational context: register

The term 'register' refers to the distinctive kind of language usage associated with a particular context of situation (Christie, 1984a; Halliday, 1978, 1985). Given knowledge of the context, one is able to predict how language might be used in terms of three categories: field, tenor and mode. 'Field' refers to what is going on in the social activity in question, and includes topic and subject matter; 'tenor' refers to the interpersonal relationship of those participating in the social activity; and 'mode' refers to the channel or means of the exchange. It is not only a question of the kind of language that is used in a particular situation but how it is used, and students need to acquire the appropriate register, or registers, if they are to be competent within the terms of reference of the subject area.

One way of conceptualising subject areas is as separate and distinct languages in themselves, into which students are socialised. Subject-area learning is both like language learning and, in a quite specific sense, one instance of language learning. This is not to suggest that subject-area learning is simply a matter of acquiring the appropriate language in a more or less mechanical way; rather what is involved is a much more dynamic and organic process of acquiring the meaning potential of the subject area in question.

Focusing on the science classroom, Lemke (1988) proposes a view of 'the learning of science as the mastery of a specialized system of language use', and asserts the following:

> To a greater extent than we may think, science as a thematic system is learned more as we learn the semantic system of our own native language: implicitly, by hearing, speaking, being corrected, but mostly by shaping our speech to conform to what we hear around us, inferring patterns of meaning relations between terms and longer expressions from their usage in context.

This observation may be generalised to other subject areas. One may be said to have 'learned' a subject when one is able to 'mean' in and through the subject. This is not simply a matter of saying and that alone, but of saying in association with doing and meaning. Hence one can refer to a subject area, from different perspectives, as possessing a language potential, a behaviour potential and a meaning potential. The acquisition and subsequent development of a subject register associated with learning the subject is to a significant degree a matter both of operational learning and of environmental learning; that is, one learns the language in part by using it and in part by being immersed in its context and hence exposed to models of its usage. Learning science, for instance, involves learning *how to mean in science*, and that in turn involves developing the capacity to activate the potentials of language, action and meaning with regard to subject science.

Further points to consider are, first, the need to see subject registers as, in a quite specific sense, a family of register (Lemke, 1982) and, secondly, the need to bear in mind that, by and large, subjects registers differ most significantly in terms of *field*. No subject register exists in a single, fixed form; rather each register consists of a set of registers, or subregisters, in both the spoken and written form. For example, there would be noticeable differences in the way a certain concept is handled in a textbook and how it might be handled in a classroom teaching-learning exchange. Similarly there would be a marked difference between the register of the practising scientist or literary scholar, for example, and that of science education or literary education, whatever the case may be.

In terms of considering differences between subject registers, clearly an important way in which they differ would be the kind of social activity participants are engaged in. Consequently one can refer, on the large scale, to the social activity of 'doing science' or 'doing health education' (and on the small scale, doing a topic like magnetism or eye care), in terms of which there would be noticeable differences in the kind of language used, as regards lexical, grammatical and textual items and their patterning. In the simplest sense, each subject area involves a different content and this would be marked in the language. It is not simply a problem of subject-specific or specialist terminology although that is certainly important, but of how this combines with the characteristic syntactic, semantic and pragmatic structures of the subject in the service of a student's meaning making.

Field is certainly not the only consideration, however. It is clear that mode is significant, in that there may well be significant differences between subject areas in terms of the relative and comparative status of the spoken and written modes. Furthermore, in the case of writing, it is likely that different subjects will assign different functions to writing and there may well be significant differences in terms of textualisation; that is, how a student writes in each of the subject areas and how writing in one places demands on the writer which are different from writing in another subject area. Similarly students need to learn how to handle the interpersonal component in their writing, in a manner appropriate first to schooling and secondly to specific subject areas. Indications are that the impersonal stance, with high degrees of passivisation and nominalisation (a characteristic feature of analytical writing generally, particularly in the sciences), is not something students take to naturally, nor would they be likely to develop such a skill simply because they are instructed to do so. They need precise and specific instruction in how to do so, and plenty of opportunity to engage in such activity, in appropriate contexts, in order to develop the skill by using it.

The main implication of this discussion of subject-situational context is that students' writing and hence their learning is likely to be greatly enhanced if the language environment is as rich and meaningful as possible. Hence teachers might well give more explicit attention to familiarising students with the field, tenor and mode features of their writing tasks, and they might also seek to ensure that in each instance they seek to widen students' range and flexibility with regard to them.

Cultural context: genre

The subject-cultural context involves the important notion of genre and is closely related and complementary to the subject-situational context. In particular, it involves the kinds of writing that are characteristic of particular subject areas. 'Genre' here specifically refers to distinctive kinds of forms of writing, as staged, purposeful cultural activities structured in various important ways. The terms may also be applied to distinctive and typical kinds of classroom action and interaction, as in Christie's notion of 'curriculum genre' (1984b).

It has already been suggested that subject-area learning can be conceptualised as a particular form of cultural learning. Learning to write involves, among other things, learning how to handle written genres (Kress, 1982). This is an on-going process of development and consolidation. The student in learning to write is writing to learn; that is, to make meanings and construct appropriate textualisations. In learning how to recognise and control a variety of written genres, the student is developing the capacity to mean. It is in this sense that subject-area learning may be linked up with the notion of generic literacy—that is, competency with regard to a particular set of written genres pertaining to the subject area in question.

One implication of this is that there is a need to focus more closely and deliberately on the genres characteristic of particular subject areas, and to provide students with appropriate guidance about how to handle them. This will certainly involve making finer distinctions than we are wont to do in this regard. It is likely, for instance, that there are quite significant differences in what constitutes a good essay in different subject areas. Other kinds of writing, ostensibly and more or less superficially similar across subject areas, may in practice entail significant and perhaps quite subtle differences. These need to be surfaced so as to allow for more explicit teaching and more effective learning.

Curriculum as contextualisation

In addition to the formal contexts of school and subject, consideration needs to be given to other ways of conceptualising the role and significance of context in literacy and learning. In a very particular way, teaching and learning (and meaning making generally) involve complex processes of contextualization, or the more or less systematic provision of meaningful contexts for human action (Lemke, 1984). Teaching and learning both involve perceiving patterns and making connections between old and new information and different kinds of experience, in and through the social interaction of the classroom. This involves, as Messenger (1980) notes, a recognition of 'the importance of contexts in the process of learning':

> There are the cultural contexts upon which we and the pupils draw; the specific contexts of experience they bring to the discipline; the contexts which the teacher uses in presenting the discipline; the contexts of language in which all these aspects of teaching and learning are embodied ... *Bridges have to be built from one context to another.*
>
> (p. 79) [emphasis added]

Halliday (1985) similarly observes: 'All learning is a process of contextualization: a building up of expectancies about what will happen next' (p. 49). His work and that of Lemke (1985) suggest that a significant factor in enhancing the quality of both literacy and learning involves taking into more explicit account those texts and events that precede the one presently in question, as constituting its context in an important and immediate sense; it also involves attending to those texts and events following on from and coming after the one in question. This means in the first instance actively planning ahead. What texts and events does this present one relate to, retrospectively and prospectively? Halliday refers to this as the 'intertextual context', drawing on the concept of intertextuality. A related concept, intratextuality, concerns the relations inside the text or event that is presently in focus, making for its internal coherence and cohesion, the way it hangs together and makes sense. The point to draw from all of this is the critical importance of text-context relations. For present purposes, this means in particular taking into account the relationship between curriculum contexts and written texts.

School writing and subject-specific literacy

What does this mean for writing pedagogy, particularly with reference to the concept of subject-specific literacy? First, there is a need to recognise the manner in which school writing is structured within specific discourse and genre frameworks (Kress, 1985a, 1985b). That is, school writing activity needs to be explicitly related, in and through teaching, to the cultural and semiotic resources that such activity necessarily draws on. Secondly, writing pedagogy needs to be sensitive to the notion of contextualisation, conceiving this specifically in process-developmental terms, so that adequate attention is given to writing processes and the movement in classrooms towards an effective grasp of matters of register and genre, with regard to specific instances of written text.[5] Classrooms and school subjects are specific contexts for learning and meaning, and it is likely that the quality of writing pedagogy will be greatly enhanced by more sensitive attention to these kinds of specificity.

The task lies ahead to consider the full implications for writing pedagogy of the concept of subject-specific literacy. There is clearly a need to think very carefully about the relationship between writing and learning, in the context of specific subject areas. What are the operational, cultural and critical aspects of the typical writing activities of, for instance, the science or the social studies classroom? How might teachers become more pedagogically sensitive to, for instance, the gender dimensions of the literacy demands of their classrooms, as sites of the engendering of social differences? And what might be the effects of such awareness with regard to subject-area learning generally?

Conclusion: towards a whole-curriculum perspective

The most important point to emerge from this discussion is the assertion of literacy as a situation-specific competency with particular reference to written language, within the context of language generally. This is to be regarded emphatically as competency with regard to thinking and meaning, in and through the devices and resources of written text, and applies equally to reading and writing as different but related expressions of literacy. It has been argued here that the school subjects, separately and in their array across the curriculum, provide the basic context for school learning and meaning. Since a close and necessary relation exists between literacy and learning (more broadly, language and learning), attention needs to be given to the concept of subject-specific literacy as a critical feature in the most effective and productive subject-area learning. As Christie (1985b) notes, 'Learning to understand the various school subjects, successfully interpreting the information they deal with, and the methods of reasoning and enquiry they require, is a matter of learning to use the relevant language' (p. 32). This suggests that all teachers at all levels need to have greater sensitivity to and more explicit and informed awareness of the language and literacy dimensions of their subject area. This is not in any sense ancillary to their concern for subject-area teaching and learning, but a necessary and significant part of it.

To refer in this fashion to subject-specific literacy may suggest the pertinence of this argument more for secondary teachers than for primary teachers. This is not the case, although there are institutional and organisational differences with regard to curriculum between two levels of schooling which need to be taken into account. Recent investigation indicates that, despite what might be described as the surface features of much primary schooling, emphasising integration and the blurring of subject-area boundaries, in actual practice these structures often persist, as marked in the distinctive kinds of language behaviour expected of children (Christie, 1985b; Kress, 1982; Martin, 1984). Increasingly, as they move through the primary school, children are expected to engage in appropriate and relevant ways of speaking and writing, and increasingly they are exposed to more conventional and subject-specific forms of reading and teacher talk. This may well be contrary to the best intentions and commitments of the teachers involved. Where it does not happen, or to a lesser degree than suggested here, it may still be that the children concerned are being actively disadvantaged in that they are not sufficiently prepared for the more formalised curriculum of the secondary school. At the same time, the generally fixed subject-area orientation of the secondary school needs itself to be viewed critically. There are losses as well as gains in such organisation of curriculum. It is highly likely, for instance, that the characteristic tenor of primary schooling, its emphasis on the interpersonal dimension of curriculum understood as teaching-learning experience, might to good effect be realised more actively in the secondary school context.

Equally important, however, primary teachers are potentially advantaged in this regard, in that they have access to and responsibility for a range of subject registers, in varying degrees of explicitness, and so may well be better equipped to provide a conducive environment for the active development of literacy. This suggests that, in conceptualising subject-specific literacy, attention needs to be given to the relations among the different subjects as well as to their differences and specificities.[6] This has particular implications for teacher education and teacher development, as well as for curriculum development and school policy. Richards (1978) makes the following assertion:

> If promotion in the pupil of an adequately wide repertoire range becomes the major objective of a language programme across the curriculum, it will be necessary for teachers themselves to become *acquainted* with the characteristics of subject registers other than their own and *familiar* with the characteristics of their own subject register.
>
> (p. 141) [emphasis added]

278

Above all else, this means a heightened awareness of language in teaching and learning and schooling generally. It is important, however, that it is an adequate and informed awareness of language, one that is sensitive to matters of function, context and meaning. In particular, it entails engaging with the concepts of register and genre, as outlined here.

With regard to register, teachers in different subject areas must be aware of and attentive to such matters as lexico-grammar (including but going well beyond specialist terminology) and discourse patterning, and sensitive to variation in terms of field, tenor and mode considered developmentally—that is, with regard to the necessary movement on the part of learners towards understanding and meaning. Similarly with genre: teachers must be knowledgeable, within their own disciplinary provinces, about 'schematic structure' and also the effects of 'functional tenor' (or purpose) on discourse (Martin, 1984). This is a matter, in the first instance, of identifying the various kinds of writing and purposes for writing that characterise particular subject areas, and articulating their distinctive features so that they may be shared with and made explicit for students.

What is more, the relative insularity of much teaching, more particularly in the secondary school, is not likely to be conducive to the optimal development of either literacy or learning. Students may well find themselves negotiating quite significant shifts in register and genre without any explicit guidance and assistance. This suggests that, in addition to becoming familiar with the discourse features of their own subject areas, teachers need to be aware of at least the general features of other subject registers and, where possible, work congruently with regard to those genres, such as reports and essays, which are part of normal classroom practice across subject areas.

It needs to be stressed that this argument applies right across the curriculum and in all subject areas, from kindergarten to Year 12. Subjects such as art and physical education have their own language (and literacy) dimensions which must be accounted for and properly considered with regard to the holistic development of school literacy. This becomes particularly so in the light of assertions that literacy is intimately and integrally associated with consciousness of language as such (Pattison, 1982). There can be no doubt that all subject areas and all levels of schooling contribute to students' awareness of and sensitivity to language—their constructs of and theories about language, however implicit and embedded in commonsense these may be.

At the same time, while the principle of subject-specific literacy holds for all subject areas, including subject English, attention needs to be given to the particular role of subject English in the achievement of school literacy. This has critical policy implications, on the levels of both system and school. As has been suggested, literacy is usefully regarded as 'consciousness of language as a force in human affairs', coupled with awareness of and mastery over the means of expression, the 'available technologies' (Pattison, 1982, p. vii). This is closely associated with the concept of meta-linguistic awareness (Bruner, 1984; Olson, 1984). If this is so, then the explicit focus on language which is a proper and appropriate concern for subject English is indeed a significant factor in the literacy project of schooling. This should not be seen, however, as the primary task of subject English, which has its own subject-specific concerns, including its own subject-specific literacy concerns. In the interests of enhancing school literacy, therefore, particular provision needs to be made in the case of English teaching so that it can effectively manage its dual responsibility.

Finally it is suggested that there is particular value in adopting more actively what might be called, with some caution, a 'productivist' emphasis in literacy pedagogy. This involves, among other things, re-assessing the role and significance of writing in the discourse of schooling, as a means of authentic learning, as well as, potentially at least, a means of empowerment, both personally and socially. It may well be that a writing emphasis in considerations of the culture of literacy has far-ranging political and pedagogical implications. The account presented earlier of a three-dimensional view of literacy is obviously relevant, in this and other respects. This remains a matter for further investigation.

Notes

1 In work in progress, provisionally entitled 'Literacy and Schooling: Towards a Reconceptualization', I intend to present a more extensive theorisation of the 'three-dimensional' view of literacy argued for here, from an explicitly political perspective. It will involve an account of the main discourses on literacy which are currently in circulation, which focus on concepts of 'functional literacy', 'cultural literacy' and 'critical literacy' respectively.
2 That this is no simple or straightforward matter is becoming increasingly recognised and acknowledged. See Schribner and Cole (1981) and Street (1984); also Cook-Gumperz (1986).
3 I acknowledge that reading, properly conceived (i.e. as comprehending), is equally active and productive. The emphasis here on writing is, however, at once deliberate and strategic. Notwithstanding the current state of research into both reading and literacy, I suspect that the situation at ground level, among many teachers and administrators but also among many teacher educators, especially those working in the subject areas, is quite different. For this group, I suggest that there is still a general equation between 'literacy' and 'reading'—cf. Cambourne (1985), Lemke (in press), Smith (1983).
4 Of course there is always some learning going on since, as Smith argues, learning is 'involuntary' for human beings. The point is that it may not be tied programmatically to instruction. See Smith (1983).
5 This is an important point. Recent polarisations in writing pedagogy, involving proponents of 'process' approaches and 'genre' approaches, are counter-productive. I have argued this point elsewhere (Green, 1987).
6 This argument is intended to apply equally to both primary and secondary teaching, although the emphasis here is on the secondary school context. Obvi-

ously there would need to be adjustments and qualifications made, appropriate to the characteristically more generalist nature of primary teaching.

References

APPLEBEE, A. N. (1981). *Writing in the Secondary School.* Urbana, IL: National Council for the Teaching of English.

APPLEBEE, A. N. (1984). *Contexts for learning to write: Studies of Secondary School Instruction.* Norwood, NJ: Ablex.

BARNES, D. (1976). *From Communication to Curriculum.* Harmondsworth, MX: Penguin.

BEAZLEY, K. (Chair). (1984). *Education in Western Australia: Report of the Committee of Inquiry into Education in Western Australia.* Perth: WA Education Department.

BENNETT, B. (1983). Writers and their writing, 15–17. In A. Freedman, I. Pringle, & J. Yalden (Eds.), *Learning to write: First Language/Second Language.* London: Longman.

BERNSTEIN, B. (1971). *Class, Codes and Control* (Vol. 1). London: Routledge & Kegan Paul.

BOOMER, G. (in press). Reading the whole curriculum. In B. Green (Ed.), *Metaphors and Meanings: Essays on English Teaching by Garth Boomer.* Adelaide: Australian Association for the Teaching of English.

BRANDT, D. (1985). Versions of literacy. *College English,* **47** (2), 128–38.

BRITTON, J. (1970). *Language and Learning.* Harmondsworth, MX: Penguin.

BRUNER, J. (1984). Language, mind and reading. In H. Goelman, A. Oberg, & F. Smith (Eds.), *Awakening to Literacy.* London: Heinemann Educational Books.

CAMBOURNE, B. (1985). Change and conflict in literacy education: What it's all about. *Australian Journal of Reading,* **8** (2), 77–87.

CHERRYHOLMES, C. H. (1983). Knowledge, power and discourse in social studies education. *Boston University Journal of Education,* **165** (4), 341–58.

CHRISTIE, F. (1984a). Varieties of written discourse. In *Language Studies: Children Writing, Study Guide* (ECT 418). Geelong, Vic.: Deakin University Press.

CHRISTIE, F. (1984b, August). Young children's writing development: The relationship of written genres to curriculum genres. Paper presented at the Language in Education Conference, Brisbane.

CHRISTIE, F. (1985a). Language and schooling. In S. Tchudi (Ed.), *Language, Schooling and Society.* Montclair, NJ: Boynton/Cook.

CHRISTIE, F. (1985b). Language in learning: The hidden curriculum of schooling. Deakin University, Geelong, Vic. (mimeo.)

COOK-GUMPERZ, J. Literacy and schooling: An unchanging equation? In J. Cook-Gumperz (Ed.), *The Social Construction of Literacy.* London: Cambridge University Press.

DONALD, J. (1983). How illiteracy became a problem (and literacy stopped being one). *Boston University Journal of Education,* **165** (1), 35–52.

EMIG, J. (1983). *The Web of Meaning.* Montclair, NJ: Boynton/Cook.

GIROUX, H. A. (1983). *Theory and Resistance in Education.* South Hadley, MA: Bergin & Garvey.

GREEN, B. (1987). Gender, genre and writing pedagogy. In Reid, I. (Ed.), *The Place of Genre in Learning: Current Debates* (Centre for Studies in Literary Education, Typereader Publications No. 1). Geelong, Vic.: Deakin University Press.

HALLIDAY, M. A. K. (1975). *Learning how to mean*. London: Edward Arnold.

HALLIDAY, M. A. K. (1978). *Language as Social Semiotic*. London: Edward Arnold.

HARSTE, J. (1983). Read better, write better, reason better: Literacy in transaction. In J. Anderson & K. Lovett (Eds.), *Teaching Reading and Writing to Every Child*. Adelaide: Australian Reading Association.

HARSTE J., WOODWARD, V., & BURKE, C. (1984). *Language Stories and Literacy Lessons*. Portsmouth, NH: Heinemann Educational.

HENRY J. A. (1984). Curriculum change in classrooms: What can be within the context of what is. *Curriculum Perspectives*. **4** (1), 35–42.

KEMMIS, S., COLE, P., & SUGGETT, D. (1983). *Towards the Socially Critical School*. Melbourne: Victorian Institute of Secondary Education.

KRESS, G. (1982). *Learning to write*. London: Routledge & Kegan Paul.

KRESS, G. (1985a). *Linguistic Processes in Sociocultural Practice*. Geelong, Vic.: Deakin University Press.

KRESS, G. (1985b). Socio-linguistic development and the mature language learner: Voices for different occasions. In G. Wells & J. Nicholls (Eds.), *Language and Learning: An Interactional Perspective*. London: Falmer Press.

LEMKE, J. L. (1982). Talking physics. *Physics Education*, **17** (1), 263–7.

LEMKE, J. L. (1984a) Action, context and meaning. In *Education and Semiotics* (Toronto Semiotic Circle Monograph). Toronto: University of Toronto.

LEMKE, J. L. (1984b). Making trouble. In *Education and Semiotics* (Toronto Semiotic Circle Monograph). Toronto: University of Toronto.

LEMKE, J. L. (1985). *Using Language in the Classroom*. Geelong, Vic.: Deakin University Press.

LEMKE, J. L. (1988). The language of science teaching. In C. Emihovich (Ed.), *Locating Learning across the Curriculum*. Norwood, NJ: Ablex.

LEMKE, J. L. (in press). Social semiotics: A new model for literacy education. In D. Bloome (Ed.), *Learning to use Literacy in Educational Settings*. Norwood, NJ: Ablex.

MARTIN, J. R. (1984). Language, register and genre. In *Language Studies: Children Writing (Reader)* (ECT 418). Geelong, Vic.: Deakin University Press.

MESSENGER, T. (1980). Language across the curriculum. In W. A. Gatherer & R. J. Jeffs (Eds.), *Language Skills through the Secondary Curriculum*. Edinburgh: Holmes McDougall.

MOFFETT, (1981). *Coming on Centre: English Education in Evolution*. Montclair, NJ: Boynton/Cook.

OLSON, D. R. (1984). 'See! Jumping!' Some oral language antecedents of literacy. In H. Goelman, A. Oberg, & F. Smith (Eds.), *Awakening to Literacy*. London: Heinemann Educational.

ONG, W. J. (1982). *Orality and Literacy*. London: Methuen.

PATTISON, R. (1982). *On Literacy*. New York: Oxford University Press.

RICHARDS, J. (1978). *Classroom Language: What Sort?* London: George Allen & Unwin.

ROBINSON, J. L. (1985). Literacy in the department of English. *College English*, **42** (5), 482–98.

ROSEN, H. (1986). The importance of story. *Language Arts*, **63** (3), 226–37.

SCHRIBNER, S. & COLE, M. (1981). *The Psychology of Literacy*. Cambridge, MA: Harvard University Press.

SINCLAIR, J. & COULTHARD, M. (1975). *Towards an Analysis of Discourse*. London: Oxford University Press.

SMITH, F. (1983). *Essays into Literacy*. London: Heinemann Educational.

SPENCER, M. (1980). Handing down the magic. In P. Salmon (Ed.), *Coming to know*. London: Routledge & Kegan Paul.

STREET, B. (1984). *Literacy in Theory and Practice*. London: Cambridge University Press.

VYGOTSKY, L. S. (1962). *Thought and Language*. New York: Massachusetts Institute of Technology Press & John Wiley.

WALKERDINE, V. (1982). From context to text: A psychosemiotic approach to abstract thought. In M. Beveridge (Ed.), *Children thinking through Language*. London: Edward Arnold.

WELLS, G. (1981). Language, literacy and education. In G. Wells (Ed.), *Learning through Interaction*. London: Cambridge University Press.

YOUNG, M. F. (Ed.). (1971). *Knowledge and Control*. New York: Collier Macmillan.

57

GENRE THEORY

What's it all about?

Myra Barrs

Source: *Language Matters* (1991) 1: 9–16

A writer in the American magazine *English Journal* once began an article entitled *How the British Teach Writing* with one brief sentence; "They don't". He went on to say that he had been on sabbatical leave for a year in England and that his children had attended the local primary and secondary schools during that time. He was as amazed by the fact that, throughout that year, they received no direct instruction in writing as he was by the amount of writing they actually did, and by its quality. Noone, apparently, was teaching them writing, and yet they were learning to write.

For a long time teachers in England didn't teach writing, in the sense that it has generally been taught in the USA, though they did teach spelling and punctuation and a few grammatical points. They did other things. What they chiefly did was to invite children to write and discuss their writing with them. They often put a lot of thought into the nature of the invitation to write, into the way they responded to the writing, and into the most effective ways of helping children to develop and correct their work, but they didn't systematically induct children into ways of structuring written text. American teachers, whose practice in this respect comes out of a very different tradition, were meanwhile instructing children in how to begin every paragraph with a topic sentence, how to write a three-paragraph theme and so on. But in recent years American developments in writing, and particularly the work of Donald Graves and his associates, have influenced practice in the UK, and have focused attention on aspects of the writing process, such as revision. Now, from Australia, we are beginning to learn about genre theory, and about the way Australian linguists are advocating that writing should be taught.

'Genre' is not a term that trips off the tongue, but it is a useful label for different kinds of writing that have different functions in written discourse and in society. Though genre theories generally derive themselves from the work of Michael Halliday in Australia, they began to be diffused in the

UK in the form of Gunther Kress's book *Learning to Write (1982)*. In this book Kress made the case for thinking about the large scale textual structures in writing: 'linguistic structures beyond the sentence'. He argued that children learning to write have to learn to use these large scale structures, as well as being able to control the smaller units in texts.

In many ways what Kress had to say in this book was exciting, because he was focusing attention on these larger textual structures, rather than on the smaller units of language which have sometimes dominated discussion of children's developing literacy. He was also pointing out the relationship between a particular genre and the smaller elements in text: if you are writing a report of an investigation, for instance, the genre you are writing in will affect everything from the vocabulary you use to the layout of the text on the page. We are only just beginning to realise the full importance of these larger-scale textual structures, and to appreciate how far both readers and writers draw on them.

But all the same, genre theory does present some problems, and for the last few years there has been a running debate in Australia on the application of this theory to the classroom. There is now a growing school of genre linguists based at Deakin University publishing a lengthening list of papers on all forms and aspects of genre. (The definition of genre has gradually been widened to mean 'a purposeful staged cultural activity' and 'texts' to include all forms of language use, so now there are genre linguists investigating texts of all kinds, including dinner-party conversations . . .). Some of these linguists are publishing materials for teachers to use in in-service courses; their ideas have begun to influence linguists and educationalists in this country, and are reflected in both the Cox Report and the LINC Project. For this reason it seems important for primary teachers with an interest in writing to pay them some attention.

Essentially genre theorists argue that schools fail children by not teaching them to write in 'powerful' genres; the impersonal genres of factual and expository prose. They consider that far too much emphasis is placed on personal narrative writing and story, genres which children are unlikely to use in their adult lives. Working-class children and minority groups, they think, are particularly in need of access to these socially important genres.

Writers such as Frances Christie and Joan Rothery argue that genres like this cannot be picked up by osmosis, they need to be explicitly taught. They want teachers to be more informed about the linguistics of texts so that they can teach factual genres more effectively. Their in-service writings aim to provide teachers with the skills to analyse children's writing using Hallidayan linguistics, and to look at development in terms of these linguistic categories.

The Australian genre theorists are not the only people who have suggested that story writing is overvalued, particularly in primary schools. Even in 1967 the Plowden Report was quite scathing about the amount of routine story writing that the committee found was going on in schools, and tried to shift the emphasis towards more personal writing and different kinds of writing. In America, Thomas Newkirk, in his book *More than Stories (1989)* has looked at the kinds of writing that young children spontaneously engage in and had found a tremendous range of types of texts in the writing of pre-school children. Janet White, of the APU, has suggested that there is a widespread presumption in the UK that argumentative writing is difficult for children, and that this has unnecessarily limited children's experience of writing to persuade and to argue a case (Richard Andrew's new project on Rhetoric reported elsewhere in this issue will explore this area further).

So the Australian linguists are asking us to examine important issues when they raise the question of genre, and most teachers might agree that we need to give more attention to the range of writing that children are given experience of in the primary school. Where we might begin to question the linguists' position is in the following areas:

Gunther Kress announced in *Learning to Write* that "there exists a small and fixed number of genres in any written tradition." His critics since have comprehensively questioned this assumption. They have pointed to the fact that there are different ways of categorising genres (some possible categories are narrative writing, expository writing, report writing, and so on) and that, like all other forms of language, genres are continually changing and developing. They have commented that Kress seems only to be concerned with quite a narrow range of school-based writing, and to be ignoring an enormous number of kinds of texts that exist in the world outside school and never find their way into academic discussions of writing. They have argued that 'genre' is a vague category; the loose term 'narrative' gets nowhere near defining the set of linguistic choices that a writer of narrative has to make, and there are all manner of ways of doing science writing. Kress has conceded this point, but other linguists in this field, especially those like Rothery and Christie who are involved in extensive in-service work with teachers, still operate on the assumption that most writing done in schools can be classified neatly into set genres.

Secondly, the view of learning and teaching that emerges from the work of many of the linguists concerned with genre is worrying. The children's texts quoted in their books and papers are often viewed as failed adult texts, rather than transitional forms of writing. For instance, Gunther Kress quotes the following text twice in *Learning to Write*:

> The mices enemy are cats and owls, the mices eat all kinds of things. Mices are little animals, people set traps to catch mouse; mouse live in holes at the skirting board. Baby mouse does have their eisopne, baby mouses can't see and they do not have fer. Some people are scered of mouses.

Of this text Kress remarks that "The text is not a story in the conventional sense, so the child cannot use the familiar genre of narrative. The topic is not developed in the more mature sense; that is there is no clear indication of a particular ordering of a conceptual kind, neither sequence nor any internal logic." Later he concludes that "these sentences hardly form a text at all." The reader receives the impression that he can find nothing positive to say about this writing. Yet it seems clear that this text is a list, a list of all the things that the seven year old writer knows about mice. As a list it makes sense, and reflect the writer's idea of what it is he is being asked to do (write what you know about mice). It might be seen as a step towards more mature forms of factual writing, rather than a failed attempt.

In an article called "The development of genres – primary to secondary school (1984), Joan Rothery reveals a similar inability to decentre when commenting on a text by a six year old girl. The text reads as follows:

> *I sor a bike a in the shop. My dad woot by me the bike.*
> *After school sar a big box in my bed room.*
> *A bike.*

Rothery remarks:

> *The last part of this text, 'A bike' requires some comment. This is much more like spoken than written text. It is the exclamation a child might make on seeing the present. In written language we need to expand this to 'It was a bike!'.*

The only possible response to this is "Who says?" This six year old writer seems likely to have made quite a conscious choice of words in ending her story. The words "A bike," are given a line to themselves, the capital letter, and full stop are firmly marked in the copy of the text that Rothery prints. The writer may well have intended the words to stand as they are, brief and dramatic.

In another article, Martin, Christie and Rothery (1987) comment on the following text, which is a piece of shared writing based on a set of photos:

> *All the things are on the table. We will use them to make toast. There is honey vegemite, peanut butter, bread, margarine, jam, a knife, a plate and a toaster. We are ready to make toast. Kevin is getting two slices of bread out of the packet. Then he puts the bread in the toaster. The bread goes down automatically with a spring. The element starts to get hot and red. Kevin puts his hand over the toaster to feel how hot the toaster was. The control switch makes the bread brown. Kevin watched the bread inside the toaster cooking. It*

is still white. The toast came popping out. Jean is getting the toast out of the toaster. The bread has gone brown. Jean has to be careful because of the electricity and also because the toaster was hot.

The three linguists comment:

This kind of writing is not functional in our culture. Generically speaking it is neither recount (i.e. what we did) nor procedure (i.e. how to do something) And the mode is wrong: parts of the text read like a running commentary on the photos scaffolding the field. But running commentaries are spoken, not written down.

They are particularly concerned about the mixture of tenses in the writing:

The inconsistency of tense selection is symptomatic of the lack of generic focus given by the teacher to the negotiation. The teacher had no clear social purpose in mind.

This sort of incomprehension is hard to understand. The text, despite some inconsistencies of tense, seems quite clear, it is a commentary on the photographs. *Without* the photographs the text obviously doesn't function so well, but we can presume that it is meant to be accompanied by them. (A careful reading of the text makes fairly clear how many photographs there probably were). To pronounce that 'running commentaries are spoken not written' is to reveal a lamentable lack of knowledge of many popular genres such as action comics, photo magazines, and so on, where pictures are often accompanied by just this sort of text.

What that example has demonstrated nicely is the tone frequently taken by the genre linguists. It's an authoritarian tone. Previous to reading in this literature I had never fully understood what Halliday's term 'tenor' meant, in relation to writing. It has to do with the social relations and the power relations implied in a text – Rothery glosses it:

According to our social relationships with other participants we take up roles of telling or asking as we move from one to another.

Rothery and her colleagues all too readily take up the roles of telling, asserting, pronouncing, and positively laying down the law. Some quotations from a long paper by her (1984) will illustrate this characteristic tone. She states that:

It is not good enough to tell students to do other things. They must be taught to do them.

and in another place:

> *It is quite wrong to regard imaginative writing as the product of some kind of isolated creativity.*

Teachers are frequently taken to task:

> *Teachers usually ask children to write a story though the evidence suggests they do not write stories for some years after starting school*

and:

> *An awareness of how language is used to create text would reveal to teachers that this advice is not helpful – indeed it is wrong.*

Rothery's view of language relations between adults and children is revealing:

> *Adults use language to exert power over children, to punish and to criticise.*

Linguists, one might reasonably paraphrase, given the tenor of these quotations, use their knowledge of language to exert power over teachers, to censure and to criticise.

Most of the Australian genre school really do think that most children need to be directly and explicitly taught the features of different genres. They argue that children come school with very different linguistic/generic backgrounds (Kress 1987) and that only 'bright motivated middle class children' can acquire sufficient knowledge of genres apparently without effort. (Martin, Christie and Rothery, 1987). They see some genres as being associated with social power, and want all children to have access to them because of this. Kress puts in this way:

> *In my view there are genres; they, and access to them, are unevenly distributed in society, along the lines of social structuring. Some genres – and the possibility of their use – convey more power than other genres. As a minimal goal I would wish every writer to have access to all powerful genres. That is not the position in our society now.*
>
> (1987)

There is some naivete in this. Genres in themselves are not powerful it is indeed the 'possibility of their use' that counts most. It's not only knowing how to write that matters in this world, but being in a position to ensure that your writing reaches an audience, and then is noticed and read. We could all learn how to write certain powerful genres – such as high-level memos – but this wouldn't increase our access to power by one jot.

Kress's statement is disturbing too because it demonstrates how apparently democratic arguments about access can be used to justify authoritarian practices in teaching. In this country we have increasingly seen equal opportunities arguments used by both left and right to justify moves towards what the Cox Report repeatedly called, in a phrase that has recurred in several recent inspectorial and ministerial pronouncements, 'direct and explicit teaching'. But it is hard to see how children are to be either informed or empowered by teaching approaches which are as insensitive to children's attempts, and as relentlessly didactic, as those implied in many of the writings of the genre school.

The subtext of much writing about genre is a contempt for modern approaches to language education, and actually an incomprehension of such approaches. Progressive education has failed, according to these linguists because it has ignored the formal discipline of linguistics which would enable teachers to analyse children's development as language users more closely, identify the gaps in their knowledge, and fill these gaps with explicit teaching:

> *Because it has turned its back on language, progressive education is in a very poor position to take up this challenge ... It lacks the tools to analyse and construct the curriculum genres that could be used; and it lacks the tools to monitor children's speaking and writing to see if development is taking place ... Genre theory puts language back in the picture ... It is the key to providing progressive educators with somewhere to go.*
>
> (Martin, Christie and Rothery, 1987)

Like the writers of editorials in *The Sun*, or *The Guardian*, these writers view child-centred education as laissez-faire, and progressive teaching as abandoning children to their own devices.

There is arrogance in this, and some ignorance. The members of the genre club often write about children's developing literacy, but their papers and articles reveal little knowledge of this subject. A whole literature that has grown up in recent years on early literacy, and the relationships between learning to write and learning to read, is never referred to in their bibliographies; references to reading are conspicuously absent. This apparent lack of awareness of a mass of material – including the work of Gordon Wells and Yetta Goodman, and all of the research referred to in, for example, *Awakening to Literacy* – means that it is hard to take their work seriously as a contribution to discussion in this area. There are three key points relating to learning to write which genre theorists seem not to take into account.

1   A major development in the past twenty or thirty years has been the realisation that learning to read and write has a great deal in common with learning to talk. Children begin to acquire literacy in very much the same way that they acquire spoken language, because they are members of a society where written language is omnipresent. All children when they come to school are, in Gordon Wells' phrase, 'partially literate'. To state this is not, of course, to state that children acquire literacy 'naturally', or quite on their own, or that they need no support, feedback, information, or teaching; much ongoing discussion in this field has to do with the nature of this support, and of effective intervention. But the basics parallel that is to be drawn between language development and literacy development now seems inescapable. Genre linguists, however, are unhappy with this parallel and insist that learning speech and learning writing are quite different:

> *'Why is writing essentially any more a matter of conscious learning of structures than is speech?' Part of the answer is that children cannot be expected to understand in their own spoken words what generations of scholars have interpreted in writing. Because of the differences in modes, the understandings could never be the same.*
>
> (Ibid.)

There is a strong tendency in genre theory to emphasise the differences between spoken and written language rather than the continuities.

It seems essential to recognise that the statement that children begin to acquire literacy before school is true of all children, not only well motivated middle-class children, though children from literate homes obviously do have more experience of written language. The implication we should draw from this is not, however, that working class children or children from less literate homes, need more 'direct and explicit' teaching and fewer opportunities for self-expression – but this is the conclusion that the genre linguists arrive at. Gunther Kress writes:

> *I worry that overly strong emphasis on individual creativity quite overlooks the fact that children come to school with very different linguistic/generic preparation from home. To a child from the literate middle class home the teacher's exhortation to express her/himself is no threat – she or he will implement the generic forms acquired at home. A child from the inner-city slums of Sydney cannot respond in the same way.*
>
> (1987)

This is a concern that needs to be taken seriously, but it should not lead us to lower our expectations of children from 'inner-city slums', or imagine that they learn differently or need an entirely different kind of education. What matters is that the experience of children should be recognised, built on, and extended in school. Many inner-city primary schools succeed in this, but we still need to think harder about the ways in which the access of all children to what Margaret Meek has taught us to call 'full literacy', and not any watered down or minimal substitute, can be assured. We shall not achieve this by defining learning differently, or advocating different educational programmes, for children from different social classes.

2   A second key parallel that needs to be drawn is that between learning to write and learning to read. Learning to write is one side of a two-sided process. Children learn a great deal about writing from their reading (and vice versa). Margaret Meek (once more) has demonstrated over and over again the role of the text in the process of learning to read, and has shown that many of the 'untaught lessons' which help children see what the reader has to do are learnt from books, through reading, or through being read to. In just the same way, children learn a great deal about writing from the texts they hear or read, and they use this knowledge in their own writing. When a six year old girl writes:

> The circus was coming and the animals had babies. But one animal did not have a baby. She looked high and low for a baby to suit her. But no, she could not find one.

it is clear that she is using the language of books that she has learnt from reading or from being read to.

Gunther Kress recognises that this kind of learning exists, but does not seem to value it:

> ... children pick up the requirements of the different genres by osmosis, as it were. They do, of course, have models, but these are presented as models of something else. For instance, the stories which children read are often presented as reading exercises, or else the texts for dictation are presented as relevant to dictation alone ... The children absorb together with whatever other purposes there may be, the forms and rules of the genre in which the content is presented to them.

> (1982)

This reveals some odd ideas about contemporary practice (reading exercises, dictation) but is an account which does at least recognise that something is going on when writers read. The tone, however, indicates that

Kress feels this way of learning to be a hit and miss affair. The text continues;

> *Sometimes the teacher's instruction is sufficiently detailed and directed to lead to the constructing of a text which embodies the demands of a genre.*

Kenneth Clarke and others have recently made play with the view that teachers think children learn 'by osmosis'. This kind of crude distortion of modern ideas about learning is currently being used to justify a general attack on developments in primary education over the past twenty years or more. It's sad to say that linguists working in education have sometimes provided the ammunition for these political moves. (The LINC project was an attempt to use linguistic arguments to affect practice in schools; it was intended to sharpen up teachers' ideas about language, and shift them towards more 'direct and explicit' forms of teaching. The fact that LINC did not operate in this way and did not produce the required results has resulted in the suppression of the LINC materials).

Nobody learns 'by osmosis' though much language learning is inductive in character, and learning in this area is sometimes so invisible that we fall into the error of seeing it as an almost organic process. But learning is a more active and constructive process than this. Recently, the rediscovery of Vygotsky, the work of Jerome Bruner, and developments in cognitive and constructivist psychology in the USA have begun to provide us with an adequate account of the complexity of human learning. It is interesting to see how important in the creation of that account, has been the evidence derived from studies of children learning spoken and written language. What is striking in any even partially adequate description of acts of this level of complexity – such as Michael Halliday's highly documented description of learning to talk in *Learning How to Mean (1975)* – is the interactive nature of the learning of the role of human relationships in it, and the immense amount of work that both adult and child do in the course of the learning process. Members of the 'genre school' may know a great deal about language, but seem to know little about learning, and this handicaps them when they come to advise teachers about what they should be doing.

3   Finally, the question of how children do learn written genres needs to be complicated a little. It seems likely that, as the genre theorists maintain, most children are less confident at managing factual and impersonal genres than they are in writing personal or fictional narratives. One major reason for this must be that they generally have less experience of such genres, both as readers and as writers. The question of how children can be given more experience of these important genres might be one we

could confront before getting involved in plans for the 'direct and explicit' teaching of genres.

Moreover, under some circumstances, children do seem to be able to write in the kinds of genres that genre theorists regard as socially important. It is observable, for instance, that children writing in role, either as part of a drama or in what might be termed 'drama on paper', can take on voices that they never usually use, and write as politicians, scientists, or news reporters. In the following example, a nine year old boy is writing in role as a scientist reporting on a new planet, in a piece of science fiction which strikes a deliberately detached and impersonal note:

> *The planet from space looks quite hospitable. But that is caused by its thick cloud layer. But when you have penetrated the cloud layer it is a pleasant planet, 38 degrees Centigrade, one degree over the normal body temperature. The planet is green for about 2/4, 1/4 is H2O9 C2, which is wasoter. Luckily, it is safe for people to drink. But the remaining 1/4 is red this is caused by a disease called ce-mon-frceh-he-mhars-ca-clone-fon-nash-agon. The symptoms are the patient's brain is taken over, a plant starts to grow out of the patient's head.*
> *They have to be terminated.*

The following piece is not strictly 'writing in role', but it clearly shows the nine year old girl author assuming an adult voice, the voice of an expert in this field. Her favourite television series was *Life on Earth*, and after seeing the series three times she read the book. In this piece of writing the characteristic tones of David Attenborough can clearly be heard, and the young writer, who is thoroughly acquainted with his style, is obviously trying on his voice in this piece:

> *We have not found enough proof on just how the first living thing started; it may always remain a mystery to us. This is just one of many explanations. Some time after the earth cooled, and its crust formed, after mountains had been raised and eroded over and over again, after salt seas had formed in a barren landscape of deserts and hills and volcanoes, some of the elements and simple compounds on and near the earth's surface combined to form more complicated compounds. A few of these compounds had the ability of taking material from their own body and making it the same thing as them. That is by simply breaking in two they were able to reproduce themselves.*

It may be easier for these young writers to use certain kinds of impersonal language and formal structures when they are writing in another persona than it is when they are writing in their own. In drama and dramatic play children frequently reveal that their linguistic range is wider than that which they normally use. In role they draw on hidden resources. They can assume adult voices, and show how much they have learned about different registers from listening and from reading.

Finally, any study of the way children learn to take on particular forms of language needs above all to examine not only their competence at using formal structures, but also the meanings that they are making. The genres that Kress and the genre linguists want children to learn are associated with particular ways of thinking. Children's texts differ from adult texts not merely because children have not been inducted into the use of particular linguistic forms, but because their texts express a certain level of conceptual development. We need to attend to children's 'spontaneous concepts' in order to see how we can best support and extend their thinking, and we shall find out more about their understanding if they are encouraged to write in their own voices. This was the theory behind the language across the curriculum movement, which argued for a broader range of language use in school, and against the dominance of impersonal and abstract forms of writing in the secondary curriculum.

Genre is a fascinating subject because it makes us look at the 'big shapes' in text and begin to think about how children learn these high level structures, which affect so many other aspects of text. We are beginning to think more systematically now about the role that these big shapes play in learning written language, and *The Reading Book*, soon to be published by CLPE, will have more to say about their importance in learning to read. Given the importance of genre as an idea, it is disappointing that it is not being developed and used more positively and interestingly by the genre linguists. Like many others in language education, their first response to finding out something important about the way that language works has been to codify their findings, develop rules of use, and advocate the teaching of these rules. If, however, we can broaden out the 'genre debate' and look at genre in a more exploratory and constructive way, we shall be able to consider how genre fits into children's learning of written language, how children's use of written genres develops, what the influences on this development are, and what this developing use of genres reveals about the relationship between language and learning.

References

Acts of Meaning, Jerome Bruner, *Harvard University Press, 1990*.
English for ages 5 to 11 (The Cox Report), *DES, 1988*.
Awakening to literacy, Goelman, Hillel, Oberg, A Antoinette and F Smith, *NH: Heinemann Educational, 1984*.
Learning how to mean, M A K Halliday, *E Arnold, 1975*.

Learning to write, Gunther Kress, *Routledge & Kegan Paul, 1982.*

Genre in a social theory of language, Gunther Kress, in **The Place of genre in learning** Ed. Reid, *Denkin University Press, 1987.*

Social processes in education, J R Martin, F Christie and J Rothery, *in* **The Place of genre in learning** Ed. Reid, *Deakin University Press, 1987.*

More than stories: the range of children's writing, Thomas Newkirk, *NH: Heinemann Educational, 1989.*

The development of genres – primary to junior secondary school, *in* **Language studies: Children's writing: Study guide**, Joan Rothery, *Deakin University Press, 1984.*

Thought and language, Lev Vygotsky, *MIT Press, 1962.*

The Meaning Makers, Gordon Wells, *Holder & Stoughton, 1987.*

Children's argumentative writing, Janet White, *Deakin University, 1989.*

58

GENRE AND LITERACY

Modeling context in educational linguistics

James R. Martin

Source: *Annual Review of Applied Linguistics* (1993) 13: 141–172.

Introduction

Christie (1992), in the previous year's volume of the *Annual Review of Applied Linguistics*, reviewed literacy initiatives in Australia which drew on systemic functional linguistics, focusing on three themes: differences between speech and writing, written genres, and the study of spoken language. This paper is designed to complement her review, highlighting ongoing research within the same general theoretical framework, and focusing on the general question of modeling context in educational linguistics.

By way of general orientation, the research in question attempts to read culture as broadly as possible in linguistic terms in order to give as rich a contextualization of literacy issues as possible. The intention of this broad reading has been to promote educational linguistics in Australia as a **transdiscipline**, characterized by intruding linguistic expertise, rather than as an interdiscipline, featuring complementary expertise. This has in turn enabled negotiation (you try my bit and I'll try yours) alongside cooperation (you do your bit and I'll do mine). A few of the results of this ongoing dialogism are briefly reviewed below under five headings: 1) modeling context as genre, 2) modeling context as register, 3) reconciling integration and diversity, 4) critical literacy, and 5) pedagogy.

Modeling context as genre—a functionally integrated perspective

Following Halliday (1978), systemic functional linguistics treats language as a social semiotic which plays an instrumental role in construing the social contexts in which we live[1]. Turning this around, language is, at the same time, construed by social context. Ecologically speaking, the

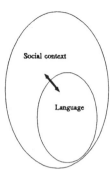

Figure 1 Language as the realization of social context.

relationship is symbiotic—one of mutual engendering. Linguistically speaking, the relationship is **realization**, as modeled in Figure 1.

On one reading, Figure 1 models a realization relationship between a social system (social context) and a semiotic system (language).[2] In Australian educational linguistics however, the preferred 'intrusive' reading has involved reconstruing social context in linguistic terms, as a semiotic system contextualizing language (as a connotative semiotic, following Hjelmslev). One critical component in this reconstrual has been the concept of genre, which in the early 1980s was a major point of departure for interventions in literacy debates.

Martin, *et al.* (n.d.) characterize genres as staged goal-oriented social processes. In systemic functional linguistics, this amounts to characterizing social context as a system of genres. A few of these processes (or genres) received special attention in light of their relevance to the educational contexts in which this approach was applied, e.g., report, recount, procedure, exposition, discussion, explanation, exploration, serial, anecdote, exemplum, observation, and news story (as introduced in Martin 1984/1991; 1985/1989; 1992a). As it turned out, the perspective was remarkably similar to that proposed by Bakhtin:

> All the diverse areas of human activity involve the use of language. Quite understandably, the nature of forms of this use are just as diverse as are the areas of human activity.... Language is realized in the form of individual concrete texts (oral and written) by participants in the various areas of human activity. The texts reflect the specific conditions and goals of each such area not only through their content (thematic) and linguistic style, that is the selection of the lexical, phraseological, and grammatical resources of the language, but above all through their compositional structure. All three of these aspects—thematic content, style, and com-

positional structure—are inseparably linked to the *whole* of the text and are equally determined by the specific nature of the particular sphere of communication. Each separate text is individual, of course, but each sphere in which language is used develops its own *relatively stable types* of these texts. These we may call *speech genres*

(1986: 60, writing in 1952–1953). [The term *text* has been substituted for *utterance* throughout.]

By way of illustration, consider texts 1 and 2 below, from Veel's (1992, in press) work on the language of school science.[3] Text 1 is a procedure; for Veel, the staging for this genre appears to involve a Title, optionally conflated with (i.e., acting as) or followed by its Aim, optionally followed by a specification of Materials needed, followed by the Steps in the experiment. In text 1, the Title is conflated with the Aim, and the Materials needed stage is omitted.

1 *Procedure* {Title, Aim, (Materials needed), Steps}
Title/Aim: Seed experiment

Steps:

- Collect 2 petri dishes.
- Place a thin layer of soil in one dish and some cotton wool in the other dish.
- Label the dish with soil "soil" and the other dish "no soil."
- Next, place about 20 seeds in each petri dish.
- Spray each dish with water until it is damp to touch.
- Finally, put the dishes in a warm sunny spot in the classroom.

Text 2, on the other hand, is a procedural recount (i.e., a telling of the instantiation of a procedure). For Veel, the staging for this genre involves a Title, followed by Aim, followed by a Record of Events, followed by Conclusion.[4] All four stages are represented in text 2.

2 *Procedural recount* {Title, Aim, Record of events, Conclusion}
Title: Seed experiment

Aim: On the 23rd of September Stuart and Sean did an experiment to see if seeds needed soil to germinate.

Record of events:

    We collected 2 petri dishes and 40 seeds. We placed a thin layer of soil on one petri dish and some cotton wool on the other. We put an equal number of seeds in each petri dish and lightly sprayed them with water. We labelled them 'Soil' and 'No soil'.

The next day we took the lid off both petri dishes. No seeds had germinated in the 'Soil' dish, but I seed had germinated in the 'No soil' dish.

The following day 16 seeds in the 'Soil' dish had germinated. In the other dish 13 seeds had germinated.

Findings:

In conclusion, we found that seeds do not need soil to germinate.

From the point of view of school science, these familiar genres complement each other as far as experimentation is concerned. The procedure enables an experiment while the procedural recount provides a record of its enactment. Concomitantly, the language of the two genres construes them as complementary social processes. They share, for example, a large part of their experiential grammar—especially with respect to the actions undertaken (TRANSITIVITY[5]) and the things acted upon (nominal group structure). They differ, on the other hand, in MOOD (imperative vs. declarative), THEME (initial processes vs. initial actors or circumstances of location in time), and TENSE (tenseless vs. past or past in past tense). The language of the two texts makes the distinct meanings that construe the scientific activities involved; alternatively, the two scientific contexts can be read as telling language what to do. The language redounds with the genre.

The holistic perspective on context afforded by this kind of theory of genre proved invaluable in initial educational interventions which were, in the first instance, directed at literacy in primary schools. By focusing on overall staging (sequences in the structuring of genres) and global construals of meaning across a text, as exemplified above, this analysis drew educators' attention to the very narrow range of writing undertaken in process writing classrooms. Generally, writing tasks consisted of one or another type of 'story' genre, and there was a tendency for large numbers of students to get stuck on a single genre throughout their first seven years of school (often observation or recount). Generic structure proved relatively easy to bring to teacher's consciousness and quite straightforward for their students to learn—including the technical terminology for different genres and their staging. This social perspective reinforced the connections between genres and school learning, and between genres and social processes in the communities served by schools (see also Christie 1992).

Before turning to the question of register, it is important to emphasize that the genre theory underlying this research was developed as a theory of social processes within the general transdisciplinary framework of social semiotics. Related work on scripts, schemas, and frames, on the other hand, has tended to be pursued within the very different interdisciplinary framework of cognitive science. The politics and pedagogical implications of these divergent intellectual orientations will be touched on in passing below.

Modeling context as register—a functionally diversified view

The holistic perspective on social context outlined above evolved out of 'traditional' approaches to modeling context in systemic functional linguistics as exemplified in the work of Halliday (e.g., 1985b). This traditional view presents a more diversified perspective, based on the intrinsic functional organization of language itself (for discussion, see Martin 1991a). Following Halliday (e.g., 1974; 1978), language systems and structures are organized by metafunctions—interpersonal, ideational, and textual. The different orders of 'reality' construed by these metafunctions are outlined in Table 1, following Matthiessen (1991) and Halliday (1974).

This intrinsic functionality is modeled[6] as interacting with the organization of social context (with field, tenor, and mode respectively), as outlined in Figure 2. The realization relationship between language and social context is thus construed as a 'natural' one.

Halliday's 1985a characterizations of **extrinsic** functionality are as follows:

Field: **the social action**: '*what is actually taking place.*'
[This] refers to what is happening, to the nature of the social action that is taking place: what [activity/topic] is it that the participants are engaged in, in which the language figures as some essential component (1985a/1989: 12).

Tenor: **the role structure**: '*who is taking part.*'
[This] refers to who is taking part, to the nature of the participants, their statuses and roles: what kinds of

Table 1 Metafunctions and orders of reality construed.

METAFUNCTION	'reality' construed	work done
IDEATIONAL	'natural' reality	(observer)
INTERPERSONAL	intersubjective reality	(intruder)
TEXTUAL	semiotic reality	(relevance)

301

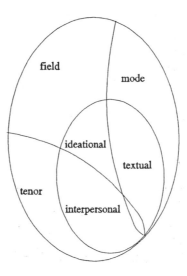

Figure 2 A metafunctionally diversified view of language and social context.

role relationship obtain among the participants, including permanent and temporary relationships of one kind or another, both the types of speech role that they are taking on in the dialogue and the whole cluster of socially significant relationships in which they are involved (1985a/1989: 12). [This notion includes what Halliday 1978: 33 refers to as the "degree of emotional charge" in the relationship.]

Mode   **the symbolic organization**: '*what role language is playing.*'

[This] refers to what part language is playing, what is it that the participants are expecting the language to do for them in the situation: the symbolic organization of the text, the status that it has, and its function in the context, including the channel (is it spoken or written or some combination of the two?)[7] (1985a/1989: 12).

The second phase of the literacy interventions in Australia based on systemic functional linguistics drew heavily on this model of language and social context. The problems which were faced included 1) developing literacy within a genre once the basic staging was in place; and 2) developing literacy in secondary school and workplace contexts in which discipline-specific discourses are dealt with in greater detail.

The potential power of this model for pedagogy is examined in greater detail below. Specifically, the roles played by the extrinsic functions of social context (field, mode, and tenor) are explored in terms of their realizations as different patterns of language forms and genre structures.

1 Field—language and 'natural' reality

With respect to the discourses of science and technology, the main challenge is to develop the register variable *field* (e.g., Wignell, *et al.* 1990, Martin 1990; 1992a). This has been pursued from the complementary perspectives of 'things' and 'processes.' As far as scientific 'things' are concerned, this work concentrated on the development of **uncommon-sense technical taxonomies** (including partonomies). In particular, there is a concern with the role played by 'definitions' in translating common sense or less specialized knowledge into technical terms as well as the ways in which science discourse establishes relationships (i.e., *valeur*) among these technical terms. Text 3 exemplifies the genre that does the bulk of the meaning construal in this area; the taxonomy it construes is outlined in Figure 3.

3 Taxonomizing report; *field of science*

(a) As far as the ability to carry electricity is concerned, (b) we can place most substances into one of two groups. (c) The first group contains materials with many electrons that are free to move. (d) These materials are called **conductors** (e) because they readily carry or conduct electric currents. (f) Conductors are

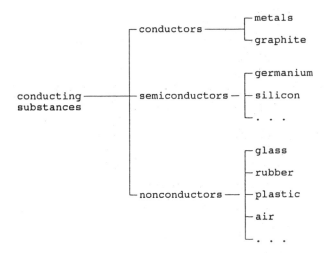

Figure 3 Classification of conducting substances in text 3.

mostly metals (g) but also include graphite. (h) The second group contains materials with very few electrons that are free to move. (i) These materials are called **nonconductors** (j) and are very poor conductors of electricity. (k) Nonconductors can be used to prevent charge from going where it is not wanted. (l) Hence they are also called **insulators**. (m) Some common insulators are glass, rubber, plastic and air. (n) There are a few materials, such as germanium and silicon, called **semiconductors**. (o) Their ability to conduct electricity is intermediate between conductors and insulators. (p) Semiconductors have played an important role in modern electronics (Heffernan and Learmonth 1983: 212).

Complementing taxonomizing reports of this kind are scientific explanations which establish **uncommon-sense accounts of processes**. This family of genres breaks phenomena down into steps, with one step logically implying another (**implication sequences**); explanations also generate technical terms, generally as distillations of several links in implication chains—for example, *vibrating, compression, rarefaction*, and *sound* in text 4 below.

4 Explanation; *field of science*

(a) If we look at how a tuning fork produces sound (b) we can learn just what sound is. (c) By looking closely at one of the prongs (d) you can see that it is moving to and fro (**vibrating**). (e) As the prong moves outwards (f) it squashes, or compresses, the surrounding air. (g) The particles of air are pushed outwards (h) crowding against and bashing into their neighbors (i) before they bounce back. (j) The neighboring air particles are then pushed out (k) to hit the next air particles and so on. (l) This region of slightly 'squashed' together air moving out from the prong is called a **compression**. (m) When the prong of the tuning fork moves back again (n) the rebounding air particles move back into the space that is left. (o) This region where the air goes 'thinner' is called a **rarefaction** (p) and also moves outwards. (q) The particles of air move to and fro in the same direction in which the wave moves. (r) Thus **sound** is a compression wave that can be heard.

(Heffernan and Learmonth 1982: 127).

The genres concerned with doing science, such as procedure and procedural recount, have already been reviewed above. In science, macro-genres such as textbook chapters combine the genres illustrated in texts 1 through 4 (procedure, procedural recount, report, and explanation); the chapters as a whole are structured as macro-reports with procedures, procedural recounts, and explanations dependent on reporting co-text (Derewianka 1992). Images of various kinds (figures, tables, photographs, etc.) also play a critical role in these macro-genres, and an account of these draws heavily on Kress and van Leeuven (1990; forthcoming). Recently, deconstructions of this kind have been extended to technological discourse in workplace contexts, as reported in Rose, *et al.* (1992). In this research, a large number of procedural genres have been distinguished, reflecting the enabling function of specialized and technical discourse in science-based industries.

Modeling *field* in terms of taxonomies and implication sequences along these lines provides tools for deconstructing discipline-specific literacy. This enables an analysis beyond the global staging of a genre which deals directly with the uncommon-sense knowledge that the various genres are mobilized, stage by stage, to construct. This in turn provides frameworks for sensitively situating genres within a discipline. Thus, a set of genres operate in a field and are essential to the construction of registers of scientific language. These frameworks have proved critical for literacy interventions in secondary school, which have to be undertaken within key learning areas (e.g., Veel 1992, Rothery 1992).

2 Mode—language and semiotic reality

Research into differences between spoken and written language were reviewed by Christie (1992) and so will be touched on only briefly here. The theoretical foundation in this area derives from work by Halliday on grammatical metaphor (1985a; 1985b) and the evolution of scientific English (1988; 1990, Halliday and Martin in press). Halliday's account is particularly relevant to deconstructions of uncommon-sense (field-specific academic) discourse in the humanities which, unlike the discourse of science and technology, do not foreground technicality but are at the same time equally, if not more, abstract. To illustrate this point, consider text 5 below from a senior secondary history textbook focusing on the Chinese revolution.

5 Historical recount; *degrees of abstraction (Buggy 1988: 224–225)*

The Breakout: 16 October to 25 November
This most successful phase of the Long March owes a great deal to the diplomatic skills of Zhou Enlai and to the bravery of the rear-guard.

Knowing that the south-west sector of the encircling army was manned by troops from Guangdong province, Zhou began negoti-ations with the Guangdong warlord, Chen Jitang. Chen was concerned that a Guomindang victory over the Communists would enable Chiang Kaishek to threaten his own independence. Chen agreed to help the Communists with communications equipment and medical supplies and to allow the Red Army to pass through his lines.

Between 21 October and 13 November the Long Marchers slipped quietly through the first, second and third lines of the encircling enemy. Meanwhile the effective resistance of the tiny rearguard lulled the Guomindang army into thinking that they had trapped the entire Communist army. By the time the Guomindang leaders realized what was happening, the Red Army had three weeks' start on them. The marching columns, which often stretched over 80 kilometers, were made up of young peasant boys from south-eastern China. Fifty-four per cent were under the age of 24. Zhu De had left a vivid description of these young soldiers:

> They were lean and hungry men, many of them in their middle and late teens . . . most were illiterate. Each man wore a long sausage like pouch . . . filled with enough rice to last two or three days.
>
> (A. Smedley, *The Great Road*, Calder, New York, 1958, pp. 311–312)

By mid-November life became more difficult for the Long Marchers. One veteran recalls:

> When hard pressed by enemy forces we marched in the daytime and at such times the bombers pounded us. We would scatter and lie down; get up and march then scatter and lie down again, hour after hour. Our dead and wounded were many and our medical workers had a very hard time. The peasants always helped us and offered to take our sick, our wounded and exhausted. Each man left behind was given some money, ammunition and his rifle and told to organize and lead the peasants in partisan warfare when he recovered.
>
> (Han Suyin, *The Crippled Tree*, London: Jonathon Cape, 1970, pp. 311–312) . . .

The first sentence in this text is, in Halliday's terms, one of its most metaphorical. The key phrases construing this abstraction are underlined below:

This <u>most successful phase</u> of the <u>Long March owes a great deal</u> to the <u>diplomatic skills</u> of Zhou Enlai and to the <u>bravery</u> of the rearguard.

On Halliday's interpretation, written discourse of this kind is read against a 'spoken' alternative of the following kind:

> Zhou Enlai was able to negotiate skillfully with Chen Jitang and the soldiers who were left to guard the rear were very brave, so the Red Army successfully escaped.

Step by step, the correlations between the spoken and written readings can be unpacked as follows:

concrete spoken	**abstract written**
{transferred reading}	{literal reading}
process + manner + time	quality + thing
[successfully escaped in Oct./Nov.]	[This most successful phase]
process + duration	quality + thing
[marched for 12 months]	[the Long March]
process + manner	quality + thing
[negotiated skillfully]	[the diplomatic skills]
process + attribute	thing
[were brave]	[bravery]
logical connection	process + thing
[so]	[owes a great deal]

Halliday's suggestion is that grammatical metaphor can thus be interpreted as introducing tension between grammar (a text's wording) and semantics (a text's meaning) so that the language has to be read on at least two levels—one level directly reflecting the grammar and, beyond that, another symbolically related level reflecting the semantics. In abstract written discourse, the overwhelming drift of this skewing between meanings and wordings is in the direction of the noun. This is clearly reflected in text 5's first sentence which grammaticalizes participants (e.g., *Zhou Enlai*), processes (e.g., *the Long March*), qualities (e.g., *bravery*), all in nominal form. Even the sentence's logical connection, *owes a great deal to*, distributes its realization across nominal (*a great deal*) and verbal (*owes*) forms. The nominalizing drift of this inter-stratal tension (between forms and meanings) is summarized in Figure 4.

Overall, text 5 is textured as successive waves of generalization followed by specification, and these waves correlate with a shift from more written to more spoken grammaticalization. The second of the eye-witness citations, as a recount of events, reveals this shift.

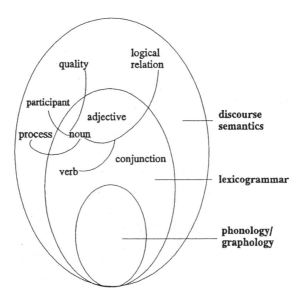

Figure 4 Nominalization as stratal tension.

> When hard pressed by enemy forces we marched in the daytime and at such times the bombers pounded us. We would scatter and lie down; get up and march then scatter and lie down again, hour after hour. Our dead and wounded were many and our medical workers had a very hard time. The peasants always helped us and offered to take our sick, our wounded and exhausted. Each man left behind was given some money, ammunition and his rifle and told to organize and lead the peasants in partisan warfare when he recovered.

Here, participants come out as participants (nouns: e.g., *we, bombers, peasants*), processes come out as processes (verbs: e.g., *marched, scatter, offered*) and logical relations come out as logical relations (conjunctions: e.g., *when, and, then*). For the most part grammar and semantics harmonize; there is no tension between the two. The text only has to be read on one level to get its meaning across[8]. In passages of this kind, then, a natural relationship is established between strata. The language sounds simple, authentic, convincing—a first hand account of what went on.

The basic insight deriving from this work has to do with the way in which humanities discourse textures itself as waves of more and less metaphorical text, with the more metaphorical passages enabling (or demanding) interpretation[9] (as with the first sentence of text 5 above). As a larger generalization, it appears that the institutional boundary between primary and secondary school symbolizes the ontogenesis of grammatical metaphor in students' language development; and discipline-specific secondary school discourses depend on abstract metaphorical text to construe their specialized knowledge. Such a transition makes apprenticeship into written abstraction a fundamental rite of passage in secondary school. Devising ways of facilitating this apprenticeship across subjects has thus become a priority as far as secondary school literacy interventions are concerned (e.g., Derewianka 1992, Rose, *et al.* 1992, Rothery in press, Veel in press).

3   Tenor—language and intersubjective reality

Halliday's (1982; 1985b) work on grammatical metaphor also provides tools for dealing with interpersonal dimensions of secondary school and community discourse, particularly with respect to appraisal—the range of systems deployed to express degrees of attitude, and to assess probability, usuality, obligation, inclination, and ability (for a review, see Martin 1992b). Appraisal resources are particularly important in the secondary English curriculum, in which writing and responding to story genres is central. Elsewhere in the humanities, social sciences, and sciences, the evaluations that these resources afford tend to be marginalized because so much of the meaning potential of the clause[10] is dedicated to constructing uncommon sense. For this reason, too much appraisal is treated as an intrusion, as in text 6 below (from Martin and Rothery 1991).

6   Observation; *personal reaction*

Explain the climate of Sydney (Year 8 geography)

Sydney is a beautiful place to visit it has one thing that I don't really like that is the weather. It's climate is always different one day it could be rainning and the next day it would be so hot that you would have to have a cold shower. I like Sydney's weather when i is nice and Sunny I like Summer that is my favorite season of the year, because it is mostly Sunny. Although this year in Sydney I't wasn't as sunny as I thought it would be. Because half of Summer it was either rainning or was very windy and very cold.

[Teacher's comment: "You need to write a geography paragraph on temperature and rainfall ... not an English essay."]

A number of observations can be made about a reactive discourse of this kind. For one thing it makes use of attitudinal description to express the writer's feelings—a *beautiful* place, *nice* and Sunny, my *favorite* season. In addition, along various parameters, meanings are graded by degree—intensified (*really* like, *always* different, *mostly* Sunny, *very* windy, *very* cold, *half of* Summer) and compared (*so hot* you would have to have a cold *shower, as sunny as I thought it would be*). The discourse also includes a number of assessments of modality (probability, usuality, and obligation) coded through modal verbs—*could be raining, would be, would have to have*. Further, the writer subjectively expresses thoughts and feelings—*I don't really like, I like, I like, I thought.* In short, this discourse is designed to engage interpersonally in solidarity contexts, typical with family and friends who are interested in negotiating how you feel.

However, public appraisal, such as the evaluation prized in the secondary English curriculum, and deployed across a range of community genres, is very different in kind. By way of illustration consider the following letter, published on the front page of the *Sydney Morning Herald* in 1991. The author's father, Australia's leading heart specialist, had recently been murdered; the then state premier, Mr. Greiner, had won a number of key seats for the Liberals in the previous election by campaigning against Labor's recently imposed gun control policies. Labor's controls were lifted once Greiner's Liberals had won office.

7 Hortatory exposition; *public evaluation*

Dear Mr Greiner,
WHY HAVEN'T GUN LAWS BEEN CHANGED?
THE SHOCKING AND SENSELESS KILLING OF MY OWN FATHER, VICTOR CHANG, FORCES ME TO WRITE THIS LETTER. I CANNOT BELIEVE THAT HIS DEATH AND THE MURDER OF SO MANY OTHERS IN THE LAST TERRIBLE WEEKS HAS NOT PROMPTED AN IMMEDIATE RESPONSE FROM THE GOVERNMENT!

After the needless killing of over a dozen people in the last two months I must emphasise the desperate need to review and reform existing policies on the possession of arms in this state. Policies which, at present, are NOT stringent enough to prevent the slaughter of innocents.

How many more tragedies will have to occur? How many families will have to live with the anguish of not only the death of their loved one, but the thought that it could have been prevented?

I appeal to you, Mr. Greiner, to realise past mistakes and help rectify the existing situation now, before more lives are sacrificed. I know that criminals cannot be stopped but surely we can limit or STOP their easy access to lethal weapons!

It would be irresponsible to ignore Australia's plea to reform antiquated gun law policies!
Sincerely,
VANESSA CHANG [*Sydney Morning Herald*, Thursday, August 29, 1991: 1]

In texts of this kind, grammatical metaphor is mobilized for interpersonal considerations. For example, one of Chang's achievements in her letter is to construe her father as a Christ-like figure whose life has been unnecessarily sacrificed. To accomplish this, she draws on nominal group resources for constructing attitude—and this involves extensive nominalization. The key passages are as follows, with the evaluation highlighted in bold face and their attendant nominalizations underlined.

> The **shocking and senseless killing** of my own father, Victor Chang
> the **needless** killing of over a dozen people
> the **slaughter** of **innocents**
> How many more *tragedies*
> the **anguish** of not only the death of their **loved** one
> more lives are **sacrificed**.

Grammatical metaphor is also mobilized to manipulate modal responsibility. Chang is in a strong position to speak out and be heard, and she explicitly projects her opinions from this position until near the end of her appeal:[11]

I CANNOT BELIEVE ...   [high certainty; explicit subjective]
{cf. surely ...}

I must EMPHASISE the desperate   [high obligation; explicit subjective]
   need ... {cf. you must ...}

I appeal to you Mr Greiner ...   [high obligation; explicit subjective]
{cf. you must ...}

I know that ...   [high certainty; explicit subjective]
{cf. admittedly ...}

Late in the letter Chang shifts her ground, preferring the involving *surely we* as she prepares for her final appeal:

but SURELY we can ...   [high certainty; implicit objective]

Finally, she draws again on grammatical metaphor, but this time to objectify her position explicitly instead of explicitly subjectifying it as in the four examples considered above:

It would be irresponsible ...   [high obligation; explicit objective]

The effect is to subjugate Mr. Greiner to his ministerial responsibilities, having just consolidated his responsibility with hers (*surely we*), and having previously driven home her right to speak (*I cannot believe, I must emphasize, I appeal, I know*).

311

Overall the dialectic of evaluation construes Greiner as Pontius Pilate. The interpersonal message is clear: "Pay for your sins." It's a powerful message; and it's a message that only public evaluation, as mobilized by grammatical metaphor, can effectively construe.

In secondary school, public evaluation of this kind is typically learned (or not) in English in the context of writing and responding to narrative. Traditionally, these resources are passed on very selectively according to students' ethnicity, class, and gender. Bringing the relevant interpersonal metaphors to teachers' consciousness in order to overcome this gatekeeping role is currently one of the major challenges faced by Australian educational linguistics.

Reconciling integration and diversity—stratifying register and genre

Recent research in systemic functional linguistics has attempted to reconcile holistic and functionally diversified perspectives by stratifying a model of social context, treating field, mode, and tenor as the 'expression form' of genre. One projection of a model of this kind is outlined in Figure 5 (a reconciliation of Figures 1 and 2). The theoretical and descriptive advantages of this stratified model are argued for in Martin (1991a; 1992a). More relevant here are the practical pay-offs which will be briefly reviewed.

The value of the holistic perspective in bringing text structure to teachers' and their students' consciousness is noted in section 1 (raising teacher and student awareness of the variety of genre structures and their differing purposes). Once the different staging of genres is brought to consciousness, it is possible to move forward, to draw educators' attention to families of genres—the different types of stories, reports, procedures, or explanations which adapt form and meaning more delicately to the range of social tasks at hand. In short, genre is a way in; it works to raise awareness, and it works in a way which register analysis alone had not been able to work before.

At the same time, by stratifying context, this analysis was able to improve on[12] the relations between register categories (field, mode, tenor) and metafunctions outlined above. Strong language/context linkage of this kind proves invaluable when bringing grammar to consciousness in educational contexts since it naturally foregrounds the connections between linguistic choices and relevant educational issues; these include the difference between common sense and technical understandings (field), the complementarity of spoken and written explanations (mode), or the advantages of an authoritative as opposed to an authoritarian pedagogy (tenor). The grammar of a language is more deeply buried than any other aspect of its organization, and without the strong functional motivation register-solidarity provides, it is often difficult to convince educators to rethink

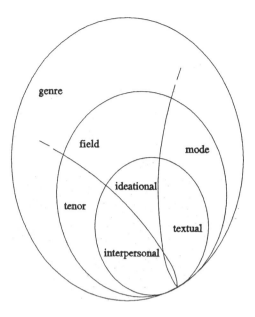

Figure 5 Modeling tenor, field, and mode as the realization of genre.

literacy instruction. Promoting the study of grammar, for register's sake, has proven to be a most challenging task.

This interest in genre has also opened up an extremely valuable dialogue with contemporary critical theory which had been more directly influenced by Bakhtin (e.g., Cranny-Francis 1990; 1992a, Cranny-Francis, *et al.* 1991, Kress and Threadgold 1988, Thibault 1989; 1991, Threadgold 1988; 1989; 1991). In Sydney, members of the Literacy and Education Research Network (LERN) and the Newtown Semiotic Circle have explored ways in which genre studies could be positioned in a model of context which attends explicitly to ideological issues (as taken up below). These discussions have also made important contributions to the evolution of a transdisciplinary social semiotics in Australia (as reflected in the new journal *Social Semiotics*, edited by Cranny-Francis, Matthiessen, Threadgold, and van Leeuven).[13] Christie, *et al.* (1991) synthesized this dialogue as the basis for their recommendations on the pre-service training of teachers for teaching English literacy.

Critical literacy—further diversification

From the beginning, this genre-based research was conducted within the general framework of critical discourse analysis, as reviewed by Kress (1991). Bernstein's (e.g., 1990) deconstructions of traditional and progressive pedagogy, class, and coding orientation provides important tools for understanding the ongoing frustration that systemic functional researchers and teacher trainers have with progressive literacy teaching (with 'process writing,' and then 'whole language' classrooms). In Australia during the 1980's, as far as literacy teaching was concerned, 'benevolent inertia' ruled the day—reacting to this position, many educational linguists felt strongly that, without guidance, non-mainstream students were being stranded in common-sense discourses, cut off from most of the publicly empowering discourses of the culture. In order to address these issues from the perspective of a functional model of language, genre-based researchers further contextualized the social-semiotic model with a layer of ideology, as in Figure 6 below.

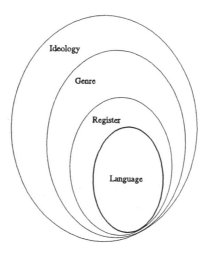

Figure 6 Language in relation to its connotative semiotics—ideology, genre, and register.

At the level of ideology, two descriptive styles of this approach have evolved. One is more dynamically oriented and attempts to deal with the textual ramifications of ideology in crisis. This issue-oriented perspective is introduced in Martin 1986 (see also Martin 1985/1989, Cranny-Francis and Martin 1991), and it is the perspective used to deal pragmatically with the volleys of discursive resistance to the ongoing critique of progressive literacy pedagogy (see Christie, *et al.* 1989; cf. the commentary by McCormack in Cranny-Francis, *et al.* 1991, Martin, *et al.* n.d.).

A complementary approach is more synoptic, and focuses on mapping out the major dimensions along which literacy is distributed in our culture. Its basic cartography is presented in Figure 7 below. Note that the model is built up around the notion of naturalized mainstream discourses in tension with resistant construals of meaning.[14]

314

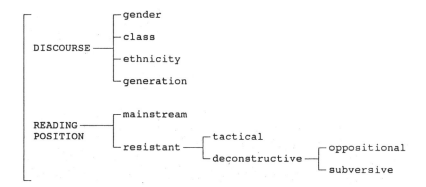

Figure 7 Dimensions of discourse and reading position.

This approach to the social construal of discourse contrasts sharply with perspectives deriving from cognitive paradigms. In Australia, however, the more significant contestation has been with the romantic liberalism underpinning process writing and whole language literacy pedagogy. This came to a head in 1988 at the Language in Learning Symposium held at Mount Gravatt College of Advanced Education in Brisbane; the relevant quotation from proponents of the whole language perspective runs as follows, and suggests that frameworks such as that developed above actually get in the way of literacy learning.

> We sometimes think that socio-economic status, restricted and elaborated codes, class, role, genre, well-formedness, I.Q., developmental stages, and other constructs are simply blocking variables hallucinated by neo-behaviourists in linguistics, psychology, and sociology so that they would have something to run their statistical data against. They should have no a priori reality in a new theory of literacy. We all play many roles even in the same context. It depends on the mind of the beholder. Social class is a state of mind. Social class is more an attitude than a fixed state of being. Even yuppiehood can be outgrown (Harste and Short 1988).

Gee (1990; 1992) pointedly deconstructs intellectual ostrichism of this kind while still maintaining reservations about the extent to which social subjects from non-mainstream discursive positionings can fully 'acquire' mainstream discourse (1992: 118–119 on 'mushfake discourse'). To his credit, Gee does not allow these misgivings to distract him from a commitment to redistributing some measure of control over mainstream discourses. But there remain those with reservations about teaching mainstream discourses to non-mainstream students on the grounds that this will in some sense de-value, or perhaps even destroy, their working class, or their Aboriginal, or their non-patriarchal, or their child-like subjectivity.

Consider then the following two texts. The first was written by a young female Aboriginal student in an inner-city junior secondary school (Year 8, age 13/14); it was produced in her English classroom, and it is representative of the kind of writing produced by students from this background in progressive literacy classrooms up until the point at which they leave school (usually Year 10 or earlier). The text is a good example of tactical resistance; it makes space for the student in her school, but in no sense deconstructs or challenges the mainstream discourses that have her struggling for space in the first place.

8   Personal recount

Fucken Hell man, who the hell told you I liked doing this kind of shit. On Saturday I saw Brian and Brendon and his Girlfriend at Waterloo, I was waiting to catch the bloody bus, anyway they started talking to me so that killed alot of time. Anyway I had to go to the Laundromat Yesterday and I saw my ex-boyfriend man he looks fucken ugly god knows what I went out with him, he looks like a fucken dickhead

ANY WAYS HE WAS

so ugly only a blind woman would go out with him. I ran into this elderly man that lived down one of my old streets and because I had a bag of clothes the stupid cunt said to us are you running away from home which is bull-shit because the sooner that I got home the happier I would have been. Then my ex-boyfried comes up which makes it even worse and he starts calling this old cunt a cradle snatching little ass-hole. I mean as if its any of his business, and like this is totally humiliating cause I mean everybody and I mean everybody tried to see who the hell was making all the fucken noise and yes there I was trying to hide my face as soon as possible . . .

The second is from a composite Year 5/6 class (students aged 10/12) in a primary school with a very high density migrant population. The text is representative of writing in one of the genres into which the students were being explicitly apprenticed at the school.

9 Exposition

I strongly agree with the building of the Wiley park ampitheatre for the following reasons, its free, the residents dont get mad because there is no rock concerts, alot of people will come to Lakemba, It will put Lakemba on the musical map also its suitable for all ages.

My first issue is that its all free so people get entertained for nothing also people who can't afford it can have a nice day out and at the same time their not paying for it.

My next matter is the residents don't get mad because there is not any rock concerts so the residents dont wake up in the middle of the night and go and complain.

Another issue is more people will come to Lakemba and it will put Lakemba on the musical map, and at the same time Lakemba will be becoming a highly populated area.

Finally the ampitheatre is suitable for all ages for instance classical for the old and music bands for the young.

I hope after reading this that you will reconsider your issue on the Wiley Park ampitheatre.

In Australia the genre-based approach has strongly advocated the interventionist pedagogy reflected in the exposition (text 9) rather than the benevolent inertia leading to the recount (text 8). These sympathies in other words lie with Gee, rather than Harste—but without Gee's misgivings. It is the view of genre-based researchers and teacher trainers that subjectivity changes by evolution, not revolution, and that teaching powerful discourses expands a student's meaning potential; language learning is simply not a question of new discourses coming in to replace the old. Beyond this, powerful discourses are not regarded as so ineffable that they cannot be taught; and in Australia there is plenty of evidence that mainstream discourses can be commandeered—and used by women, by Aboriginal people, or by Irish Catholics to change their world. Indeed, the post-progressive literacy initiatives presented here are by and large driven by 'dislocated' subjectivities of this kind. Is their discourse actually powerful 'mushfake' (cf. Gee 1992)? How so? Which are the 'mushfake' discourses among the Australian references presented throughout this paper? Which are the 'genuine' article, having been 'naturally' acquired by their middle class subjects? Who's 'faking' it? And who is recognizable as the real thing?

Pedagogy

As noted above, Bernstein's deconstructions of progressive pedagogy were used heavily when formulating curriculum genres to effect a more negotiated pedagogy. The development of such a pedagogy is in response to the perceived weaknesses of whole-language approaches. Following Bernstein, Australia's process writing and whole language classrooms are classrooms with the following characteristics:

1   The control of the teacher over the child is implicit rather than explicit.
2   Ideally, the teacher arranges the context which the child is expected to rearrange and explore.
3   Within this arranged context, the child apparently has wide powers over what he selects, over how he structures tasks, and over the time-scale of his activities.
4   The child apparently regulates his own movements and social relationships.
5   There is a reduced emphasis upon the transmission and acquisition of specific skills.
6   The criteria for evaluating the pedagogy are multiple and diffuse and so not easily measured.

(Bernstein 1975: 116)

Underlying this practice lie theories of learning and language acquisition of the following kind (deriving largely from the work of Piaget and Chomsky):

1   The theories in general will be seeking universals and thus are likely to be developmental and concerned with sequence. A particular context of learning is only of interest inasmuch as it throws light on a sequence. Such theories are likely to have a strong biological basis.
2   Learning is a tacit, invisible act; its progression is not facilitated by explicit public control.
3   The theories will tend to abstract the child's personal biography and local context from his cultural biography and institutional context.
4   In a sense, the theories see socializers as potentially, if not actually, dangerous, as they embody an adult-focused, therefore reified, concept of the socialized. Exemplary models are relatively unimportant and so the various theories in different ways point towards *implicit* rather than explicit hierarchical social relationships. Indeed, the imposing exemplar is transformed into a *facilitator*.
5   Thus the theories can be seen as interrupters of cultural reproduction and therefore have been considered by some as progressive or even revolutionary. Notions of child's time replace notions of adult's time, notions of child's space replace notions of adult's space; facilitation replaces imposition and accommodation replaces domination.

(Bernstein 1975: 122–123)

These theories, and the practices they entail, involve what Bernstein refers to as an invisible pedagogy, which he contrasts with a visible pedagogy as follows:

'An **invisible** pedagogy is created by:

1   implicit hierarchy;
2   implicit sequencing rules;
3   implicit criteria.

The underlying rule is: '**Things must be put together**'.

(Bernstein 1975: 119–120)

'A **visible** pedagogy is created by:

1   explicit hierarchy;
2   explicit sequencing rules;
3   explicit and specific criteria.

The underlying rule is: '**Things must be kept apart**.'

For political reasons, advocates of a genre-based curriculum feel compelled to reject the invisible literacy pedagogy deriving from progressivism. Its distribution of discursive resources appears to be even more reactionary than the already skewed distribution of the traditional visible pedagogy it had overthrown; and unlike traditional pedagogy, where failure could be blamed on the school, progressive pedagogy places blame for failure directly on the individual who, for some reason (intelligence?, family background?, motivation?), is unable to learn to write by osmosis in the purportedly rich literacy environments provided. Against this trend, genre-based researchers and teacher trainers have worked towards a visible pedagogy, such as that outlined by Bourdieu:

> ... a rational and really universal pedagogy, which would take nothing for granted initially, and would not count as acquired what some and only some of the pupils had inherited, would do all things for all and would be organised with the explicit aim of providing all with the means of acquiring that which, although apparently a natural gift, is only given to the children of the educated classes.
>
> (Bourdieu 1974: 133, quoted in Freebody 1991: 108)

This endeavor is aided considerably by the Vygotskyan and Hallidayan learning theories out of which the genre-based pedagogy has evolved. Gray (1985; 1986; 1987; 1990) has drawn heavily on Vygotskyan learning theory (via Bruner); and Rothery (e.g., 1986; 1989) has taken her inspiration from systemic studies of early language development in the home

Intra-individual

invisible pedagogy	visible pedagogy
Progressive pedagogy (e.g. Rousseau, Piaget, Chomsky, Goodman)	Behaviourist pedagogy (e.g. Skinner, phonics, basal readers)

Acquisition _____ liberal | conservative _____ Transmission
[competence]   radical | subversive   [performance]

| Critical pedagogic theories (e.g. Friere, Giroux) | Social/psychological pedagogic theories (e.g. Vygotsky, Bruner, halliday, |

Inter-group

Figure 8 Theories of instruction (after Bernstein 1990: 72 and 213).

(e.g., Halliday 1975, Painter 1984). By blending together learning discourses of this kind, genre-based curricula has come to occupy the bottom right-hand quadrant in the chart of pedagogies presented as Figure 8 (adapted from Bernstein 1990: 72 and 213). Bernstein unpacks this territory as follows:[15]

> The vertical dimension would indicate whether the theory of instruction privileged relations internal to the individual, where the focus would be *intra-individual*, or whether the theory of instruction privileged not relations within the individual but relations *between* social groups (inter-group). In the first case, intra-individual, the theory would be concerned to explain the conditions for changes within the individual, whereas in the second the theory would be concerned to explain the conditions for changes in the relation between social groups. The horizontal dimension would indicate whether the theory articulated a pedagogic practice emphasizing a logic of acquisition or one emphasizing a logic of transmission. In the case of a logic of acquisition the focus is upon the development of shared competences in which the acquirer is active in regulating an *implicit* facilitating practice. In the case of a logic of transmission the emphasis is upon *explicit* effective ordering of the discourse to be acquired by the transmitter.
>
> (Bernstein 1990: 213–214)

The instructional practices for the visible pedagogy which has evolved draws upon Bernstein (1975; 1990); one example of this is the ongoing

320

work in the Sydney Metropolitan East Region Disadvantaged Schools Program (see Rothery in press, Veel in press for details).[16] Instruction in a **curriculum genre**, which takes up a number of lessons, consists of four main stages: Negotiating the Field, Deconstruction of Relevant Genres, Joint Construction of Text, and Independent Construction of Text. This pedagogy employs, in Bernstein's terms, both the weak classification and framing of an invisible pedagogy and the strong classification and framing of a visible pedagogy, deployed in successive waves through the implementation of the curriculum genre. Unfortunately, space does not allow for a detailed presentation of the approach. In closing, it should be noted that the model of social context presented in this chapter directly supports the development of these teaching practices and provides the framework by which students can be apprenticed into publicly empowering discourse.

Notes

1 This is not to argue that language is the only semiotic system involved (cf. Kress and van Leeuwen 1990 on images, van Leeuwen 1988 on music); nor is it claimed that the social context construed by language is identical to that construed by other semiotic systems.

2 Unidirectional notions of cause and effect, as often deployed in the interpretation of physical and biological systems, are quite inappropriate.

3 Examples are taken from Veel's pre-publication manuscript.

4 The labeling of stages is designed to reflect relationships among genres, i.e., connections between procedures and procedural recounts; connections between science procedures and other enabling texts (e.g., instructions or recipes); and connections between procedural recounts and recounts of other kinds (e.g., personal recounts of holidays, historical recounts of settlement patterns). The motivation for Veel's labeling is thus too large an issue to explore here.

5 Throughout the paper, lexicogrammatical analyses are based on Halliday 1985b, discourse semantics analyses on Martin 1992a.

6 Historically in systemic functional linguistics, the accounts of extrinsic functionality (field, tenor, and mode) and intrinsic functionality (ideational, interpersonal, and textual) evolved independently and were subsequently correlated by Halliday in the late 1960s.

7 Halliday continues: "... and also the rhetorical mode, what is being achieved by the text in terms of such categories as persuasive, expository, didactic, and the like." 1985a: 12. This aspect of mode is treated under genre in the model being developed here.

8 The realization of qualities as Heads of nominal groups in this text works against this pattern: *our dead and wounded, our sick, our wounded and exhausted*. These could, of course, be viewed as fossils, borrowed directly from poetic discourse.

9 Metaphorical grammar also enables the construal of technical uncommon sense in science discourse; cf. the nominalized criteria for taxonomizing in text 3 (*the ability to conduct electricity*) and the nominalized distillation in text 4 (*compression, rarefaction, and sound*); see Martin 1991b, Halliday and Martin in press.

10 The impersonality of these discourses results from the pressures of field and mode on clause grammar; impersonality was not in itself a driving force in their evolution (cf. Halliday 1988, Halliday and Martin in press).

11 The analysis of modality used here draws on Halliday (1985b).

12 Moving such categories as persuasive, expository, didactic, and the like out of register to the more abstract level of genre in fact clarifies the predictive relations suggested by Halliday between field and ideational meaning, tenor and interpersonal meaning, and mode and textual meaning.

13 Available through the Department of English, University of Sydney, Sydney, NSW 2006, Australia.

14 For work on discourse and gender see especially Cranny-Francis 1990; 1992b, Gilbert 1989, Gilbert and Taylor 1991, Poynton 1985/1989; discourse and ethnicity is explored in Walton 1990, Walton and Eggington 1990; discourse and class is discussed in Cranny-Francis and Martin 1991, Giblett and O'Carroll 1990; childism in relation to literacy teaching is considered by Martin 1985/1989; strategies of resistance are explored in Cranny-Francis 1990; 1992b, Cranny-Francis and Martin 1992. For a general introduction to the role of ideology in the overall model of context see Martin 1991a; 1992a.

15 Bernstein comments further as follows: "It is a matter of interest that this top right-hand quadrant is regarded as conservative but has often produced very innovative and radical acquirers. The bottom right-hand quadrant shows a radical realization of an apparently conservative pedagogic practice ... each theory will carry its own conditions of contestation, 'resistance', subversion" (Bernstein 1990: 73).

16 For reasons of space, addresses for practical resourses and instructional material could not be included. The author welcomes all enquiries for further information. [Dept. of Linguistics, University of Sydney, Sydney N. S. W. 2006, Australia].

Unannotated bibliography

Bakhtin, M. M. 1986. The problem of speech genres. In *Speech genres and other late essays*. [Trans. V. McGee.] Austin, TX: University of Texas Press. 60–102.

Bernstein, B. 1975. *Class, codes and control. Volume 3: Towards a theory of educational transmissions*. London: Routledge and Kegan Paul.

—— 1990. *Class, codes and control 4: The structuring of pedagogic discourse*. London: Routledge.

Bourdieu, P. 1974. The school as a conservative force. In J. Eggleton (ed.) *Contemporary research in the sociology of education*. London: Methuen.

Buggy, T. 1988. *The long revolution: A history of modern China*. Sydney: Shakespeare Head Press.

Christie, F. 1992. Literacy in Australia. In W. Grabe, *et al.* (eds.) *Annual Review of Applied Linguistics, 12. Literacy*. New York: Cambridge University Press. 142–155.

—— (ed.) 1989. *Literacy for a changing world: A fresh look at the basics*. Hawthorn, Victoria: The Australian Council for Educational Research. [Theme Monograph Series. Radford House, Frederick Street, Hawthorn, Vic. 3122, Australia.]

—— (ed.) 1991. *Literacy in social processes: Papers from the inaugural Australian Systemic Linguistics Conference, held at Deakin University, January 1990*.

Darwin: Centre for Studies of Language in Education, Northern Territory University. [Casuarina, NT 0810, Australia.]

——, J. R. Martin and J. Rothery. 1989. Genres make meaning: Another reply to Sawyer and Watson. *English in Australia*. 90.43–59.

——, *et al*. 1991. *Teaching English literacy: A project of national significance on the preservice preparation of teachers for teaching English literacy*. 3 Volumes. Canberra: Department of Employment, Education and Training and Darwin: Centre for Studies of Language in Education, Northern Territory University.

——, *et al*. 1992. *Exploring explanations*. Sydney: Harcourt Brace Jovanovich. [Levels 1–4 and Teacher's Book.]

Cranny-Francis, A. 1990. *Feminist fiction: Feminist uses of generic fiction*. Cambridge: Polity.

—— 1992a. The value of 'genre' in English literature teaching. *English in Australia*. 99.27–48. [Theme issue on Contested Orthodoxies.]

—— 1992b. *Engendered fictions: Analysing gender in the production and reception of texts*. New South Wales: University Press.

——, A. Lee, J. R. Martin and R. McCormack. 1991. Danger – shark: Assessment and evaluation of a student text. In F. Christie (ed.) *Literacy in social processes: Papers from the inaugural Australian Systemic Linguistics Conference, held at Deakin University, January 1990*. Darwin: Centre for Studies of Language in Education, Northern Territory University, 245–285.

—— and J. R. Martin. 1991. Contratextuality: The poetics of subversion. In F. Christie (ed.) *Literacy in social processes: Papers from the inaugural Australian Systemic Linguistics Conference, held at Deakin University, January 1990*. Darwin: Centre for Studies of Language in Education, Northern Territory University. 286–344.

Derewianka, B. 1991. *Exploring How Texts Work*. Sydney: Primary English Teaching Association.

—— 1992. Reading secondary science textbooks. In J. Scott (ed.) *Science and language links: Classroom implications*. Melbourne: Australian Reading Association. 67–80.

Freebody, P. 1991. Inventing cultural-capitalist distinctions in the assessment of HSC papers: Coping with inflation in an era of 'literacy crisis.' In F. Christie (ed.) *Literacy in social processes: Papers from the inaugural Australian Systemic Linguistics Conference, held at Deakin University, January 1990*. Darwin: Centre for Studies of Language in Education, Northern Territory University, 96–108.

Gee, J. P. 1990. *Social linguistics and literacies: Ideology in discourses*. London: Falmer.

—— 1992. *The social mind: Language, ideology, and social practice*. New York: Bergin and Garvey.

Giblett, R. and J. O'Carroll (eds.) 1990. *Discipline – dialogue – difference: Proceedings of the Language in Education Conference. Murdoch University, December 1989*. Perth: 4D Duration Publications, School of Humanities, Murdoch University. [Murdoch, WA 6150, Australia]

Gilbert, P. with K. Rowe. 1989. *Gender, literacy and the classroom*. Melbourne: Australian Reading Association.

—— and S. Taylor. 1991. *Fashioning the feminine: Girls, popular culture and schooling*. Sydney: Allen and Unwin.

Gray, B. 1985. Helping children to become language learners in the classroom. In F. Christie (ed.) *Aboriginal perspectives on experience and learning: The role of language in Aboriginal education*. Geelong, Victoria: Deakin University Press. 87–104.

Gray, B. 1986. Aboriginal education: Some implications of genre for literacy development. In C. Painter, and J. R. Martin (eds.) *Writing to mean: Teaching genres across the curriculum*. Applied Linguistics Association of Australia. 188–208. [Occasional Papers 9.]

—— 1987. How natural is 'natural' language teaching: Employing holistic methodology in the classroom. *Australian Journal of Early Childhood*. 12.4.3–19.

—— 1990. Natural language learning in Aboriginal classrooms: Reflections on teaching and learning. In C. Walton and W. Eggington (eds.) *Language: Maintenance, power and education in Australian Aboriginal contexts*. Darwin, NT: Northern Territory University Press. 105–139.

Halliday, M. A. K. 1974. Interview with M. A. K. Halliday. In H. Parret (ed.) *Discussing language*. The Hague: Mouton. 81–120. [Janua Linguarum Series Maior 93.]

—— 1975. *Learning how to mean: Explorations in the development of language*. London: Edward Arnold.

—— 1978. *Language as a social semiotic: The social interpretation of language and meaning*. London: Edward Arnold.

—— 1982. The de-automatization of grammar: From Priestley's 'An Inspector Calls'. In J. M. Anderson (ed.) *Language form and linguistic variation: Papers dedicated to Angus MacIntosh*. Amsterdam: Benjamins. 129–159.

—— 1985a. *Spoken and written language*. Geelong, Victoria: Deakin University Press. [Republished by Oxford University Press 1989.]

—— 1985b. *An Introduction to Functional Grammar*. London: Edward Arnold.

—— 1985c. Context of situation. In M. A. K. Halliday and R. Hasan. *Language, context and text*. Geelong, Victoria: Deakin University Press. 3–14. [Republished by Oxford University Press 1989.]

—— 1988. On the language of physical science. In M. Ghadessy (ed.) *Registers of written English: Situational factors and linguistic features*. London: Pinter. 162–178.

—— 1990. Some grammatical problems in scientific English. *Australian Review of Applied Linguistics*. 6.13–37. [Series S.]

—— 1991. Linguistic perspectives on literacy—A systemic-functional approach. In F. Christie (ed.) *Literacy in social processes: Papers from the inaugural Australian Systemic Linguistics Conference, held at Deakin University, January 1990*. Darwin: Centre for Studies of Language in Education, Northern Territory University. 2–22.

—— and J. R. Martin. In press. *Writing science: Literacy and discursive power*. London: Falmer.

Harste, J. C. and K. G. Short. 1988. What educational difference does your theory of language make? Paper presented at the Language in Learning Symposium. Mount Gravatt, Queensland, Australia, 1988.

Hasan, R. and J. R. Martin (eds.) 1989. *Language Development: Learning language, learning culture. Meaning and choice in language: Studies for Michael Halliday*. Norwood, NJ: Ablex. [Advances in Discourse Processes 27.]

Heffernan, D. A. and M. S. Learmonth. 1982. *The world of science—Book 3*. Melbourne: Longman Cheshire.

—— 1983. *The world of science—Book 4*. Melbourne: Longman Cheshire.

Kress, G. 1991. Critical discourse analysis. In W. Grabe, *et al.* (eds.) *Annual Review of Applied Linguistics, 11. Discourse analysis*. New York: Cambridge University Press, 84–99.

—— and T. Threadgold. 1988. Towards a social theory of genre. *Southern Review*, 21.215–243.

—— and T. van Leeuven. 1990. *Reading images*. Geelong, Victoria: Deakin University Press.

—— Forthcoming. *A grammar of diagrammes, maps and charts*.

Lemke, J. L. 1990. *Talking science: Language, learning and values*. Norwood, NJ: Ablex.

Martin, J. R. 1984. Types of writing in infants and primary school. In L. Unsworth (ed.) *Reading, writing, spelling: Proceedings of the fifth Macarthur Reading/Language Symposium*. Sydney: Macarthur Institute of Higher Education. 34–55. [Republished in *Working with genre (Papers from the 1989 LERN Conference, University of Technology, Sydney, 25–26 November 1989)*. Sydney: Common Ground. 33–44, 1991.]

—— 1985. *Factual writing: Exploring and challenging social reality*. Geelong, Victoria: Deakin University Press. [Republished by Oxford University Press 1989.]

—— 1986. Grammaticalising ecology: The politics of baby seals and kangaroos. In T. Threadgold, E. A. Grosz, G. Kress and M. A. K. Halliday (eds.) *Language, semiotics, ideology*. Sydney: Sydney Association for Studies in Society and Culture. 225–268. [Sydney Studies in Society and Culture 3.]

—— 1990. Literacy in science: Learning to handle text as technology. In F. Christie (ed.) *Fresh look at the basics: Literacy for a changing world*. Melbourne: Australian Council for Educational Research. 79–117.

—— 1991a. Intrinsic functionality: Implications for contextual theory. *Social Semiotics* 1.1.99–162.

—— 1991b. Nominalisation in science and humanities: Distilling knowledge and scaffolding text. In E. Ventola (ed.) *Recent systemic and other functional views on language*. Berlin: de Gruyter.

—— 1992a. *English text: System and structure*. Amsterdam: Benjamins.

—— 1992b. Macroproposals: Meaning by degree. In W. A. Mann and S. A. Thompson (eds.) *Discourse description: Diverse analyses of a fund raising text*. Amsterdam: Benjamins. 359–395.

Martin, J. R., F. Christie and J. Rothery, n.d. Social processes in education: A reply to Sawyer and Watson (and others). In I. Reid (ed.) *The place of genre in learning: Current debates*. Geelong, Victoria: Centre for Studies in Literary Education 46–57. [Typereader Publications 1.] [More fully published in *The Teaching of English: Journal of the English Teachers' Association of New South Wales*. 53.]

—— and J. Rothery. 1991. *Literacy for a lifetime – teachers' notes*. Sydney: Film Australia.

Matthiessen, C. M. 1991. Language on language: The grammar of semiosis. *Social Semiotics*. 1.2.69–111.

Painter, C. 1984. *Into the mother tongue: A case study of early language development*. London: Pinter.

—— and J. R. Martin (eds.) 1986. *Writing to mean: Teaching genres across the curriculum*. Applied Linguistics Association of Australia [Occasional Papers 9.] [Available from Department of Modern Languages, University of Wollongong, P.O. Box 1144, Wollongong, NSW 2500, Australia.]

Poynton, C. 1985. *Language and gender: Making the difference*. Geelong, Victoria: Deakin University Press. [Republished by Oxford University Press, 1989.]

Rose, D., D. McInnes and H. Korner. 1992. *Scientific literacy (Literacy in industry research project – Stage 1)*. Sydney: Metropolitan East Disadvantaged Schools Program.

Rothery, J. 1986. Teaching genre in the primary school: A genre based approach to the development of writing abilities. *Writing project – report 1986. Working Papers in Linguistics*, 3–62. [Department of Linguistics, University of Sydney.]

—— 1989. Learning about language. In R. Hasan and J. R. Martin (eds.) *Language development: Learning language, learning culture. Meaning and choice in language: Studies for Michael Halliday*. Norwood, NJ: Ablex. 199–256. [Advances in Discourse Processes 27.]

—— In press. *Literacy in school English*. Sydney: Metropolitan East Disadvantaged Schools Program.

Thibault, P. 1989. Genres, social action and pedagogy: Towards a critical social semiotic account. *Southern Review*. 22.338–362.

—— 1991. *Social semiotics as praxis: Text, social meaning making and Nabakov's "Ada"*. Minneapolis: University of Minnesota Press. [Theory and History of Literature 74.]

Threadgold, T. 1988. The genre debate. *Southern Review*, 21.315–330.

—— 1989. Talking about genre: Ideologies and incompatible discourses. *Cultural Studies*, 3.1.101–127.

—— 1991. Postmodernism, systemic-functional linguistics as metalanguage and the practice of cultural critique. In F. Christie (ed.) *Literacy in social processes: Papers from the inaugural Australian Systemic Linguistics Conference, held at Deakin University, January 1990*. Darwin: Centre for Studies of Language in Education, Northern Territory University, 60–82.

van Leeuven, T. 1988. Music and ideology: Notes towards a sociosemiotics of mass media music. In T. Threadgold (ed.) *Sydney Association for Studies in Society and Culture working papers*, 2.1/2.19–44. Sydney: Sydney Association for Studies in Society and Culture.

Veel, R. 1992. Engaging with scientific language: A functional approach to the language of school science. *Australian Science Teachers Journal*, 38.

—— In press. *Literacy in school science*. Sydney: Metropolitan East Disadvantaged Schools Program.

Walton, C. 1990. The process vs genre debate: An Aboriginal education perspective. *Australian Review of Applied Linguistics*, 13.1.100–122.

—— and W. Eggington (eds.) 1990. *Language: Maintenance, power and education in Australian Aboriginal contexts*. Darwin, NT: Northern Territory University Press. [Casuarina, NT 0810, Australia.]

Wignell, P., J. R. Martin and S. Eggins. 1990. The discourse of geography: Ordering and explaining the experiential world. *Linguistics and Education*, 1.359–392.

59

THE EMERGENCE OF GENRES

Some findings from an examination of first-grade writing

Marilyn L. Chapman

Source: *Written Communication* (1994) 11(3): 348–380

From an emergent literacy perspective, writing is considered part of a continuum beginning at birth. Much of the research in emergent literacy has viewed learning to write as part of a more general symbolic development. As such, children's writing is seen as interrelated with other forms of communication, especially oral language and drawing (Dyson, 1986; Gardner 1986). One aspect of children's literacy development entails differentiating the unique aspects of written language (Dyson, 1984; Sulzby, 1986). Although earlier research sought identifiable patterns or stages of development in writing (e.g., DeFord, 1980), the concept of emergent literacy is not one of "ages and stages" in the Piagetian sense. Rather than being an invariant series of successive approximations toward conventional ways of reading and writing (e.g., Holdaway, 1984), research findings indicate individual differences among children (Sulzby, 1985), diversity in different contexts of situation (Harste, Woodward, & Burke, 1984), and sociocultural variations (Heath, 1983).

Literacy is, above all, a set of "socially constructed and embedded practices based on cultural symbol systems and organized around beliefs about how reading and writing might be or should be used to serve particular social and personal ends" (Hull, 1993, p. 34). Emergent literacy can be thought of as a cultural process, accomplished through active construction, in which the child internalizes social action as well as independently explores written language (Teale, 1987). Thus, writing is "cultivated" rather than imposed (Vygotsky, 1978). Children are socialized into literacy through participation in a kind of social dialogue: The words of others "are processed dialogically into one's own/others' words with the help of different 'others' words' (heard previously) and then in one's own words" (Bakhtin, 1979/1986, p. 163). Taking the role of apprentices who appropriate their culture's ways of using written language, children learn literacy via those who are more adept or advanced (Resnick, 1990; Rogoff, 1990).

Rich, descriptive studies of young children's writing from a perspective of emergent literacy have been conducted in the context of the home (Bissex, 1980; Taylor, 1983), the preschool (Ferreiro, 1978; Schickedanz, 1987), and the kindergarten (Dyson, 1985, 1989; Sulzby, 1986). Considerably less research conducted from this perspective has focused on writing in first grade, perhaps because the emphasis in first-grade instruction has traditionally been the teaching of "basic skills." For first-grade writers, spelling is a major concern (Graves, 1982), yet because spelling growth is so obvious, it is easy to overlook other aspects of growth (Calkins, 1986). Many studies of children's writing have ignored the level of discourse (Scinto, 1986). Shuy (1981) urges researchers to focus on whole written discourses in order to develop a holistic theory of writing development integrating all the components of written language. "Writing is a process of making, and what the writer makes is not a word or a sentence but a text, or a whole discourse. Children, if given the chance, compose whole discourses from the beginning of their development as writers" (Gundlach, 1981, p. 138). Gundlach maintained inquiry at the discourse level "will turn up both interesting common lines of development and important information about differences among children and their growth as writers" (p. 140).

One aspect of learning to write entails mastering the structural and organizational patterns of written language (Martin & Rothery, 1986; Perera, 1984) and "the acquisition of a repertoire of discourse forms" (Hudson, 1986). In much of the research on writing, discourse forms are divided into two broad categories, narrative (time-related) and nonnarrative (non-time-related) (Harris, 1986). Because narrative writing is considered by many to be easier for children than nonnarrative writing (Burgess, 1973; Wilkinson, Barnsley, Hanna, & Swan, 1980), it is apparently more highly valued than nonnarrative in the primary grades (Christie, 1986; Collerson, 1986). However, for most young children, learning to write true narratives is usually difficult, and many early attempts are but "frame stories," which often include little more than formulaic openings and closings and content that is a setting without elaboration (Sutton-Smith, 1979). In *The Child's Concept of Story*, Applebee (1978) traced the development of children's oral narratives, describing how two basic processes, centering and chaining, produce increasingly mature narrative forms, from "heaps" to narratives. More recently, Applebee's sequence has been revisited by Moninghan-Nourot, Henry, & Jones (1988). These researchers, who used the dictated stories of 4- and 5-year-old children, revised Applebee's developmental schema, finding that chaining and centering can occur at the same developmental level.

Few developmental classifications of nonnarrative forms exist. In

Factual Writing, Martin (1985) categorizes factual writing along two dimensions: "particular/general" and "event/thing focus." These produce four general types of children's writing into: recounts (what happened), procedures (how things are done), descriptions (what some particular thing is like), and reports (what an entire class of things is like). Newkirk (1987), applying a modified Langer-Meyers coherence analysis (Langer, 1985), used relationships between clausal units to develop structural categories. In his schema, the label (one word or one sentence identification of a picture) and list (a series of names, dates, facts, etc., usually not in sentence form) are the basic structural forms. As topic statements are elaborated, more complex forms develop.

In proposing a schema to account for development of both narrative and nonnarrative forms, Martin and Rothery (1986) classified children's writing into three basic genres: "observation/comment," a direct reference to the child's own experience, with more or less random strings of observations; "recount," a series of events from the child's own experience, sequenced chronologically; and "report," a set of facts describing an object, usually from the child's own experience. They hypothesized a sequence, with observation/comment as the basic genre from which, with the addition of the elements of time and topic, more sophisticated genres develop.

Defining genre

Implicit in much of the research into the structure of children's written discourse are assumptions that genres are fixed text types that children need to gain mastery of or to learn to perform in conventional ways. However, traditional notions of genre are currently being challenged, due to a surge of interest in the work of Bakhtin (1979/1986). New questions are being posed: How should we define genre? Are genres properly understood as fixed text forms or types? Or are they better thought of as typical forms, models or templates, ways of organizing our discourse to suit the specific conditions and goals in different areas of human activity (Bakhtin, 1979/1986, p. 78)? According to Bakhtin, genres are compositional structures that are embedded in and develop out of the various spheres of human activity. "Each sphere of activity contains an entire repertoire of speech genres [oral and written] that differentiate and grow as the particular sphere develops and becomes more complex" (p. 60). These socially constructed genres provide a set of signals that enable a speaker/writer and listener/reader to interpret the particulars of a specific communicative interaction.

Central to any exploration of genre is some sort of working definition about how a genre can be characterized and what counts as a description of a genre (Fahnestock, 1993). According to Freedman (1993a, 1993b), genres are actions, events, and/or responses to recurring situations or contexts that involve complex interrelationships among substance, form, context, and motive or intention. The recurring nature of specific contexts leads to ritualized social actions (Miller, 1984), thus genres can be thought of as "typified rhetorical actions based on recurrent situations" (Miller, 1984, p. 159). However, although "genres are only definable by regularities" (Fahnestock, 1993, p. 270), such as typical openings, topics, and discourse arrangements, they are not fixed algorithms. Indeed, textual regularities are secondary to and a consequence of actions, events, and responses (Freedman, 1993a). A working definition of genre in the context of this study, then, is: A typified form of discourse or way of organizing or structuring discourse, shaped by and in response to recurring situational contexts (in this instance, Writing Workshop in a first-grade classroom). Although a genre is characterized by a regular discourse pattern, it is open and flexible rather than fixed or immutable and reflects an interplay of substance, form, context, and intention.

The present study, part of a large examination of first-grade children's writing, focuses on the genres embedded in and growing out of their daily Writing Workshop period. Using a case study method, it treats all texts produced by six children of varying abilities during Writing Workshop in their first-grade school year. The study addresses the general question: Do genres emerge in first-grade children's writing in ways analogous to other aspects of writing development? Specific research questions include:

1   What are the written genres produced by a particular group of first-grade children in the context of Writing Workshop? How are their drawing and writing products structured or organized?
2   How does the children's writing evolve and change throughout first grade when examined from the perspective of genre?
3   What similarities and differences are evident in the children's writing when examined from the perspective of genre?

The issue is seen as complex, one that cannot be resolved by determining a strict linear developmental sequence. Because different contexts and different kinds of writing make differing demands on the writer, there is often a wide range of structural patterns and complexity both among the compositions produced by children of the same age and among the compositions produced by the same child within what would be considered the same moment of development. Because young children weave talk, pictures, and text to create meaning (Dyson, 1985; Newkirk, 1982), any examination of young children's writing cannot consider written texts in isolation. Thus, in this study, analyses of discourse structure and the resulting genre classification system consider children's pictures and texts as interrelated wholes. It must also be noted that in this investigation, genres are viewed as typical models or ways the children organize their written discourse to suit the context of the writing Workshop in their first-grade classroom. Thus, although genre is thought of as a form of discourse that is "relatively stable" (Bakhtin, 1979/1986, p. 60), it is not considered to be a fixed text type.

Method

The study was conducted in a first-grade classroom in an urban center in British Columbia, Canada, in which the teacher based her program on a sociopsycholinguistic view of language and language learning (Goodman, Smith, Meredith, & Goodman, 1987). From the very beginning of the school year, the teacher viewed the children as meaning makers and authors and encouraged them to write for themselves without concern for adult standards of correctness. Handwriting, spelling, punctuation, and other orthographic features of written language were modeled, explained, practiced, and learned in context throughout the school day. The teacher did not use a hierarchically arranged sequence for teaching writing or phonics skills, basal readers, workbooks or worksheets. Rather, she based the language arts program on two central notions: Reading and writing are similar processes and should be taught together from the beginning; and oral and written language develop best through personal and functional use (Gunderson & Shapiro, 1987).

Each day of the school year started with a routine that quickly became familiar to the children. First, the children gathered together at the group meeting area, which was demarcated by a large rug and a portable chalkboard. After greetings were shared and the children settled, the teacher led "Morning News," in which the children told the group about current events in their lives. The teacher recorded their ideas on the chalkboard, "thinking aloud" as she wrote and asking the children to provide "assistance" in the spelling of words, suggestions for wording, sequencing, and so on. After the Morning News was recorded, the teacher and children read it together. Morning News was followed by shared reading of "big books" and chart stories. Immediately after these collaborative writing and reading activities, the children participated in Writing Workshop, a time in which they communicated their ideas about things that interested them through writing and drawing. During this time the teacher circulated among the children, had conferences with them about their writing, and provided assistance and instruction (in the context of the child's writing) where needed. At the end of the period, the children stamped their work with the date stamp and filed it in their writing folders. In Writing Workshop children were invited, but never forced to write. The only assigned writing was on "Project Day," which occurred once a week. On Project Day the children were requested to write about their projects, describing

331

them and explaining how they worked. The teacher described such writing as "scientific writing" because it related to environmental studies (social studies and science). In addition to the formal writing times, the teacher reported that all of the children integrated writing (for example, labels, signs, letters and plans) into their play activities.

Focal children

Six focal children, three boys and three girls, were selected, in consultation with the classroom teacher, to encompass a range of abilities or developmental levels (from "advanced" to "delayed") to ascertain whether or not changes that occur in writing throughout first grade might be limited to one developmental group or another or occur across developmental levels. As well, an attempt was made to eliminate confounding factors such as mental and physical conditions considered to be beyond a "normal" range and possible interference of languages other than English. Table 1 shows the developmental levels and genders of the focal children in this study. In subsequent tables, these focal children are referred to by the numbers shown in Table 1.

Data collection and analysis

Information related to the children's classroom and home literacy experiences was obtained through classroom observations (approximately one day per month), interviews and conversations with the teacher, and questionnaires completed by the children's parents. All of the focal children's writing and drawing products created in Writing Workshop throughout the school year provided the raw data for the study, revealing the children's growth over time. All of the children's products were filed immediately after the Writing Workshop by the children and accumulated in monthly files. To analyze differences across the school year, the corpus of

Table 1 Gender, developmental levels, and ages* of subjects

Subject	Developmental level		
	Advanced	Average	Delayed
Boys	1. Matthew (6.6)	2. Alan (6.4)	3. Brandon (6.0)
Girls	4. Caitlin (6.7)	5. Janet (5.10)	6. Lindsey (6.0)

Note
* Ages at the beginning of first grade.

writing was divided into three time segments: Beginning (September-November), Middle (December-February), and End of Year (March-June).

In the context of this study, discourse structure refers to the organization of a piece in terms of the relationships among the meaning units within the text (including relationships between the writing and drawings); structural complexity considers the type and quality of the relationships, for example, coherence and elaboration. Genre refers to a typical model or form of written (and in this instance, drawn) discourse or way of organization that is considered to be "changeable, flexible, and plastic" rather than fixed (Bakhtin, 1979/1986, p. 80). Because discourse structure, structural complexity, and genre are interrelated, analyses were conducted in an interactive, recursive process. Initially, the drawing/writing products were sorted into two general categories, chronological and nonchronological, using verb forms and temporal adverbials as guides. Chronological texts were classified loosely as narratives, and nonchronological texts as nonnarrative. Next, individual clauses and connectives were identified. The clause was selected as the unit for analysis rather than the T-unit because clausal analysis can show relationships within T-units and can more finely identify the kind of coherence links the subject has used (Newkirk, 1987). This method provided a tentative assignment of genre to each text. Structural complexity was determined by examining the number of clauses in each piece and the type of linkages between clauses. Determining structural complexity led to a reexamination of the genre codings and a refinement of the genre analysis.

Analytical categories for genre were developed both from previous studies and from the data of this study. As stated, each writing/drawing product was classified first as chronological/narrative or non-chronological/nonnarrative, using the following criteria as guides (Perera, 1984):

Chronological:
— action verbs
— usually past or future tense, rarely present tense
— temporal connectives (e.g., then, next)
— temporal adverbials (e.g., yesterday, after school, in two days, at Christmas).
Nonchronological:
— verbs of attribution (e.g., are, have, got) or of attitude (e.g., like, want)
— usually generalized present tense.

Both chronological and nonchronological texts were analyzed using a Langer-Meyers coherence analysis (Langer, 1985) modified by Newkirk (1987). Clause units were identified, then each piece of writing was diagrammed to show the relationship of individual clauses to preceding and following clauses, and the hierarchical structure of the text. The diagram represented the hierarchical structure which showed the ways in which focal children related each clause unit to the topic and subtopics, thus providing an "x-ray" of each text (Newkirk, 1987). Linkages between clauses were classified as (a) random, (b) relational, or (c) chronological. Random clauses were those that could be rearranged without changing the meaning of the text. Relational links were those that could show any nonchronological relationship such as statement-attribute, statement-example, question-answer, or assertion-reason (Newkirk, 1987). In the event that a text coded as nonchronological had chronological linkages, it was rejected from the nonchronological category, recoded as chronological, and assigned the appropriate chronological genre. Random, relational, and chronological linkages are similar to Applebee's (1978) "heaped," "centered," and "chained" structures, respectively.

A few of the nonchronological texts could not be analyzed using the coherence analysis alone, which led to reexamination of the data in an attempt to account for all of the drawing/writing products. As a result, four new genres were identified: Word Play, Note/Letter, Written Dialogue, and Picture Dialogue/Sound Effects. Word Play included repetition and rhyme; Note/Letter and Written Dialogue were interactive in nature, having a high incidence of the pronoun "you," implying a known audience; Picture Dialogue/Sound Effects were embedded within children's artwork.

Independent ratings, by the three raters trained in the classification system, produced an interrater reliability of 90%. As with Newkirk's (1987) study, disagreements involved categories that were similar, for example: Recount/Narrative, Attribute Series/Hierarchical Attribute Series, Expanded Record/Recount, and Label/Basic Record. Once the categories of analysis were established, each piece was coded for genre. Only one genre was assigned to each piece of writing. Each category was then tabulated for each subject per term (beginning, middle, and end), and for the entire school year.

Results

From an examination of the entire corpus of writing/drawing products, 15 genres were identified. The genre categories, which were arrived at inductively, are described in Table 2, which also provides examples of the genres from the writing of the children in this study.

Two of the genres, Label and Picture Dialogue/Sound Effects, were defined in terms of the relationship between the text and the picture. Five of the children embedded text within their pictures by representing the talk of characters in their pictures and sound effects related to action, such as POW and BANG! During the first term, 99% of the texts were

Table 2 Genre categories, descriptors and examples

Genre	Descriptors	Examples
Chronological	time-related; action verbs; usually past tense ("replays") or future tense ("pre-plays"), occasionally present tense; may have temporal adverblals, e.g., yesterday; may have temporal connectives, e.g., then; may be true or invented.	
1. Basic Record	single clause statement of action/event;	At night time I was kicking footballs up in the air.
2. Expanded Record	two or more related clauses, such as: one action/event and information, or two or more related events;	Yesterday my mom had a piano recital. It was a pretty good recital. We got treats at it.
3. Basic Record Series	a series of two or more unrelated action/event statements consisting of single clause units;	In fourteen days it is my birthday. I went to The Fox and The Hound. For a week it has rained. Two days ago it was Easter.
4. Expanded Record Series	a series of two or more unrelated actions/events consisting of two or more related clauses;	Gary came to our house. He left today. My tooth is wiggly. It will fall out. My Dad is going. He is going to Vancouver.
5. Recount	three or more related actions sequenced chronologically, usually has temporal connectives, no real crisis or complication;	When I was at the beach I caught my pointer finger. It started to bleed. But I didn't cry.
6. Narrative	three or more related actions, sequenced chronologically, with basic schematic structure: orientation, complication, resolution, coda; usually past tense;	Far, far away in another galaxy a rocket has been lost. No one has ever found it. The rocket crashed in Bloodland. Everything is blood. The people are blood. The astronauts were running out of the fire. They went out of the rocket. They got chased by the blood people. They got blood on their feet.
Nonchronological	nontime-related; verbs of attribution (e.g., are, have, got); verbs of attitude (e.g., like, want); generalized present tense.	

Table 2 continued

Genre	Descriptors	Examples
7. Label	exophoric reference, nonverbal context (i.e., picture) provides much of the message, identifies picture or parts of picture, may be a word, phrase, or sentence, may be a series of labels;	This is a soccer game. Once upon a time there was a sky with no clouds in it.
8. List	series of items, not usually in sentence form;	team I an
9. Attribute Series	series of one clause units to comment on a topic, may state attributes (e.g., details of a picture) or attitudes toward the topic, random order rather than logical;	This is an army ant base. I like it. There is a trap door.
10. Couplet	two related clause units, e.g., identification and information, question and answer, statement and reason, statement and example, statement and comment;	This is Slimer. Slimer has a sandwich.
11. Hierarchical Attribute Series	series of units with more than one related clause, i.e., clusters of information;	I am sick today. And my tummy is sore. I am going to throw up. I have a back ache. I called my Mom and she wasn't home. I have an ear ache. I feel my cat sit in my hand. I hear my cat purr. Both of my legs are broken. Both of my arms are broken. I have a broken neck. I have a broken nose. I have a broken ear. I called my Dad and so we went to the doctor. I am very sick. I am history.
12. Word Play	rhymes and repetitive phrases;	Fuzzy Wuzzy was a bear. Fuzzy Wuzzy had no hair. Fuzzy Wuzzy was a wuzzy A bear wuzzy.

13. Note/Letter	implied reader through use of pronoun YOU, salutations and/or closing, use of TO and FROM;	To Mom and Dad, love Caitlin
14. Written Dialogue	one or a series of statements or questions written by one writer and answer(s) or response(s) written by another;	CAITLIN: Do you want to play with me today? LINDSEY: Yes. CAITLIN: Do you really want to play with me? LINDSEY: No! CAITLIN: Do you like me? LINDSEY: Yes! CAITLIN: Did you go to the tea party? LINDSEY: No!
15. Picture Dialogue and Sound Effects	embedded in and part of a picture, represents speech of characters in picture or sound effects related to action;	"Good night!" POW!
Mixed	two or more unrelated segments incorporating both chronological and nonchronological forms.	It is Valentine's day today. This is a weirdo. He is flying.

Table 3 Pictures associated with text

Subject	Percentage (frequency)			
	September–November	December–February	March–June	Year
1. Matthew	98	76	16	45
2. Alan	98	84	36	77
3. Brandon	100	94	100	98
4. Caitlin	100	95	79	93
5. Janet	100	74	84	87
6. Lindsey	100	100	98	99
$\bar{X}$	99	77	67	82

accompanied by pictures. Throughout the year there was a downwards trend in writing accompanied by drawing, as children were able to convey more of their meanings lexically, although one student, Lindsey, continued to combine drawing and writing almost exclusively through the year. Table 3 summarizes the results of the analysis of picture-text associations across the school year.

As the children wrote, they often made explicit references to their drawings. These references were made in one of two ways, either lexically or by the use of arrows linking text and picture (see Figure 1). In some instances, a child would embed dialogue in the picture and make a direct reference to this dialogue in the body of the text (see Figure 2).

Individual differences were noted in the frequency with which children produced the various genres. For Matthew, the most frequent genre was the Expanded Record. Comprising 34% of his writing, this genre was found almost twice as frequently in his writing as the second most frequent genre. On the other hand, Brandon produced two genres with similar frequency, Basic Record (25%) and Label (26%). The three girls each had a single genre that stood out as most frequent. Caitlin and Lindsey wrote Labels most frequently (32% and 35%, respectively), although Janet's most frequent genre was the Expanded Record (21%).

Changes were observed in the distribution of the genres between the beginning, middle, and end time segments in both number of genres observed and the frequency with which they were produced. Eight of the 15 genres were observed during the first term, 6 new genres were identified during the second term, and an additional genre arose during the final term. Thus, as one would expect, the children were increasing their repertoires of written genres. Changes were also noted in the frequency of the various genres throughout the year. During the first term, the Label accounted for almost half of the writing (49%), with the Basic Record the next most frequent at 18%. During the second term the Label decreased

Figure 1 Kate's t-shirts (April)

Transcription: We got T-shirts at school today. I like them. They are nice. *Names connected to arrows*: Dad, Mom, Kate, Jim, Eve, Ali, J-P.

in frequency (to 10%), as the children wrote in a wider variety of forms, with the Basic Record and Attribute Series gaining prominence at 20% and 21%, respectively. During the final term, the Attribute Series became even more frequently used (24%), but was surpassed in frequency by the Expanded Record (31%). Table 4 summarizes the changes in genres throughout the year.

When one examines the changes in genres during the school year, a strong pattern emerges. From the perspective of genre, all children increased in range and complexity. For all of the children, single clause genres were dominant during the first term. For Janet, this was the Basic Record, for the other five children, it was the Label. During the last term, however, all of the children produced more complex forms than single clause forms. Brandon and Lindsey produced Attribute Series the most often, whereas the other four children produced Expanded Records most frequently. Differences in timing were noted between the various ability levels. Children identified by the teacher as "advanced" or "average" in ability produced expanded records by the middle term, whereas those children who were identified as "delayed" produced this form only in the last

339

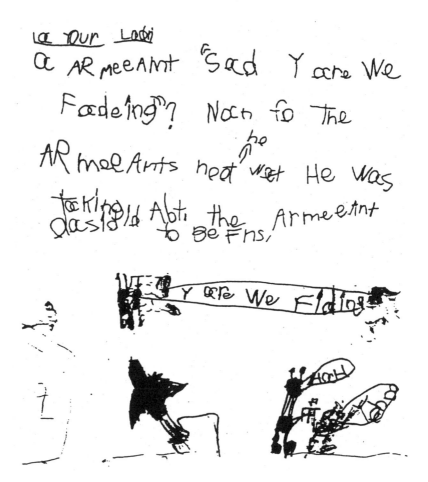

Figure 2 Brandon's army ants (May)

Transcription: **At Your Leader** An army ant said "Why are we fighting?" None of the army ants knew what he was talking about. The army ants decided to be friends. *Words in the picture*: Why are we fighting? Hah. Yahoo.

term (Brandon) or not at all in their first-grade year (Lindsey). Likewise, though advanced and average children produced Recounts or Narratives by the middle term, the delayed children did not produce the Recount until the last term, and produced no true Narratives during their first-grade year.

The genres identified may be classified into two groups, chronological and nonchronological. Within each of these categories, the genres are hierarchically ordered to some extent, by order of increasing complexity. In the chronological category, the simplest form is the Basic Record,

Table 4 Frequency distribution of genres, beginning, middle, and end of year

Genre	Percentage (frequency)			
	September–November	December–February	March–June	Year
Chronological				
1. Basic Record	18	20	1	14
2. Expanded Record	6	18	31	17
3. Basic Record Series	0	5	3	2
4. Expanded Record Series	0	4	9	4
5. Recount	0	4	13	5
6. Narrative	0	<1	1	<1
Nonchronological				
7. Label	49	10	1	22
8. List	2	<1	0	1
9. Attribute Series	<1	21	24	14
10. Couplet	3	7	3	5
11. Hierarchical Attribute Series	0	<1	1	<1
12. Word Play	0	1	1	<1
13. Note/Letter	5	<1	0	2
14. Written Dialogue	0	0	1	<1
15. Picture Dialogue and Sound Effects	4	2	6	3
Mixed	0	3	3	2
Insufficient Decodable Text	15	4	<1	6
Total number of texts (raw scores)	273	229	226	728

which consists of a single statement related to an action or event. These statements usually consist of single clause units; occasionally, they are phrases or sentence fragments. Expanded Records consist of two or more clause units that are related to the same event. When chronological sequencing is added, a Recount evolves. Then, with the addition of a crisis of complication, Narrative develops. Two of the genres, Basic Record Series and Expanded Record Series, are lists of separate or unrelated events, with the Basic Record Series consisting entirely of single clause units.

Within the nonchronological category, there are two sets of genres, one of which has a hierarchical or possibly developmental nature. This set of genres includes the List, which usually consists of single words; Label, single clause units; Couplets, two related clause units; Attribute Series, consisting of lists of single clause units related to a central topic; and the Hierarchical Attribute Series, an extension of the former, with the addition of subtopics with associated clusters of information. The other four

341

Text Structure	Diagram	Genres
Single Clause (may be a series of single unrelated clauses)		Label Basic Record Basic Record Series
Coupled	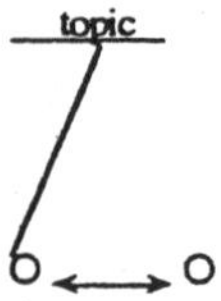	Couplet Expanded Record Exp. Record Series
Centered	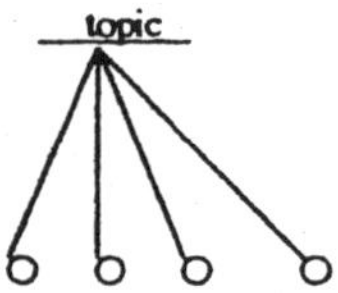	Attribute Series
Chained		Expanded Record Recount Narrative
Centered + Chained (centering may occur at any point in a chain)	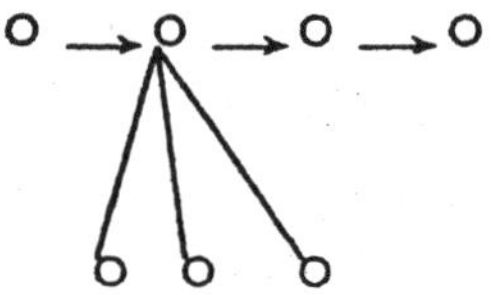	Recount Narrative

Figure 3 Text structures

nonchronological genres have unique characteristics and are not hierarchically ordered. Figure 3 provides a visual representation of the structure of the hierarchically ordered genres.

Centering and chaining

According to Applebee (1978), clauses are linked by one of two processes, centering and chaining. In chaining, there is a shared idea between two clauses; one idea expands on the previous idea, thus producing pairwise connections. These connections are often, but not necessarily, chronological. In the chaining process, a shared word may provide the link, or a pronoun in the following clause may refer to a noun phrase in the previous clause. Examples of pairwise connections, two-clause chains, include identification + information, statement + reason, or statement + example. Examples of longer chains include relating a sequence of events or giving directions. In the centering process, clauses are related to a central nucleus, producing an associative clustering rather than a logical or sequential pattern. Centering often involves attributes or attitudes. Examples of such connections include descriptions about characters or settings. In this study, many examples of centering and chaining were found in the children's texts. Sometimes, but not often, texts were found to have both types of links.

Examples:

1. Chaining

   - Two days ago I couldn't play soccer because they said it was too wet.
   - I found a dead cat in my back yard. Its name is Tuffy. It was under a tree.
   - The chick went to the moon. He landed on the moon. He decided to live on the moon.

2. Centering

   - This is a picture of Hawaii, me watching the sea, and the sun shining in the picture.
   - This is a castle. The castle is Craigdarroch Castle. The castle is huge. I like the castle.
   - Once upon a time there was a girl. The girl was not an ordinary girl. The girl was a princess. The girl's name was Sarah.

3. Centering + Chaining

   - Long, long ago there was a ghost. It was inside my house. It was a nice ghost. But it was hungry, so I fed it. And then I got hungry, and it fed me. We made friends. We went to the park.
   - My Dad got a new bike. It is red and yellow. I like it. It is nice. He loves it too. We had a bike ride. We went up hills and down hills. It was nice. We went to see Stewart at his new house. When we got home I went to bed. I'm sorry to say, but I have to go.

The genres identified in this study may be organized across the chronological/nonchronological boundary according to the types of links. Labels and Basic Records are single-unit texts; Couplets are pairwise chains;

Attribute Series are centered. Expanded Records, Recounts and Narratives are primarily chained, although they often incorporate small clusters or pairwise connections. More elaborate narratives often contain fairly large clusters. Expanded Record Series may be classified as pairwise or chained, depending on the structure of the particular text.

Changes in discourse structure throughout first grade

As the children in this study gained experience with writing, the structures of their texts became more complex, as demonstrated in Table 4. To see more readily the changes throughout the year, the data were organized to show the changes in structure from the beginning to the end of the year. Table 4 shows the most frequent discourse structures during the first three terms: single unit, coupled (pair-wise), centered, chained, and centered + chained within one text. This chart does not include all forms, for example Lists, which usually do not have clause units, and Record Series, in which the clause units are not linked, or fragments or texts that were not sufficiently decodable.

Table 5 reveals that single clause units were the most frequent discourse structure during the first term, comprising 69% of the texts, and decreased in frequency to 1% in the last term. Pairwise connections increased during the second term, but then decreased. This indicates that the children's

Table 5 Most frequent structural types

Percentage (frequency)		Subjects						
		1	*2*	*3*	*4*	*5*	*6*	*X̄*
Single clause	B	64	68	82	86	44	69	69
	M	21	22	34	22	19	28	24
	E	0	0	4	0	0	3	1
Coupled	B	16	11	2	9	12	2	9
	M	45	31	20	16	9	22	24
	E	16	28	15	6	11	6	14
Centered	B	0	0	0	2	0	0	<1
	M	10	13	29	49	21	26	25
	E	18	21	46	30	34	77	38
Chained	B	0	0	0	0	4	0	1
	M	21	6	0	3	21	6	10
	E	51	29	27	49	47	10	36
Centered +	B	0	0	0	0	0	0	0
chained	M	0	3	0	8	7	0	3
	E	6	7	8	12	3	3	7

Note
B = beginning of year; M = middle of year, E = end of year.

344

texts were becoming increasingly complex in comparison to the first term, but that pairwise connections diminished as the children began to write longer texts. Centering and chaining gradually increased throughout the year, with centering becoming apparent in greater frequency than chaining, yet by year's end, centering and chaining were similar in frequency (38% and 36%) and accounted for the vast majority of the texts. Finally, centering + chaining within a text increased from 0% to 7% at year's end.

In addition to producing texts with more complex structures as the school year progressed, the children's texts increased in length. This can be demonstrated two ways, first by examining mean clause length per text, and secondly, by showing examples of the same genre early and late in the school year. During the first term, most of the children's texts were one clause in length. By the end of the year, all of the children wrote texts averaging more than three clauses long, ranging from an average of 3.15 to 5.52 clauses per text. Examples of increasing length and complexity are demonstrated with the following examples from Matthew's writing, all references to soccer:

- At Windsor Park I played soccer with my brother. (September)
- Yesterday after school Alex came to my house and we played soccer. (December)
- Every day I go to soccer. Every day after school I play soccer. Sometimes my Dad plays with me. (January)
- My soccer games are almost over. At Easter weekend my soccer coach is having a tournament. I am going to the tournament. At the tournament we are going to have three games. I am going to get a shirt. (February)
- Last Saturday and Sunday my brother went to soccer tournaments. There was two tournaments a day. His team was in third place. At the end every team got a trophy even though the team might not have won. And everyone got a popsicle. Last Saturday and Sunday I was sick. (March)

Sometimes the children reworked a particular theme over a period of several days or weeks, each time adding something new. Examples of such "variations on a theme" are selected from Brandon's files:

- Long, long ago in the woods there was a Wolfman. He destroys anybody who comes near him. His friend is Frankenstein. (January 9)
- This is Wolfman. He destroys anybody who comes near him. His friend is Frankenstein. He lives on the rocks. (January 23)
- This is Wolfman. He destroys anybody who comes. His friend is Frankenstein. He lives on the rocks. His name is the Mummy. (February 1)

As well as thematic reworking, the children would sometimes experiment with a particular textual pattern over a period of time. For example, Caitlin went through a phase of ending her writing with a question and later on, a question and answer:

- This is a birthday party. It is fun. Where are you?
- The Ghost Busters are happy now that the ghost is gone. Where is he?
  I know. Maybe the Ghost Busters save Slimer. The end.

Reworking a theme through different genres of formulating their own discourse patterns, then, was part and parcel of the process of writing development for these children.

Structural differences among children

All of the children began the year writing predominantly single-clause texts. By the middle term, single-clause texts were still the dominant form for the two children rated by the teacher as delayed in development, Brandon and Lindsey. During this term, two-unit texts were most frequently observed in Matthew's and Alan's writing (45% and 31%, respectively), whereas Caitlin wrote mostly centered texts (49%), and Janet wrote either centered or chained texts (21% and 21%, respectively). By the end of the year, however, the advanced and average children wrote mostly chained texts, whereas the delayed children wrote more centered texts. As the year progressed, as one would expect, all of the children's texts increased in length.

The sequence in which the structure of text changed varied with the individual child. Apart from the fact that the single unit structure developed first, development of text structure varied among the children. The sequences for each child were as follows:

Matthew: (1) single unit (2) coupled (3) centered/chained
Alan: (1) single unit (2) coupled/centered (3) chained
Brandon: (1) single unit (2) coupled/centered (3) chained
Caitlin: (1) single unit (2) coupled (3) centered (4) chained
Janet: (1) single unit (2) coupled/chained (3) centered
Lindsey: (1) single unit (2) coupled (3) centered (4) chained

Drawing, talking, reading and writing

The children differed greatly in the way in which they related drawing and writing. Almost all of the writing was accompanied by drawings in the first term. For Matthew, drawing became increasingly less associated with

346

writing, so that by year's end, only 16% of his writing was accompanied by drawing. Four of the children, including all three girls, on the other hand, continued for the most part to weave drawing and writing to express their ideas throughout the school year.

Aspects of oral language and literate language are also evident in the children's writing. One of the most obvious demonstrations of the link to oral language is the presence of dialogue represented through "speech balloons" and sound effects within the children's pictures and in the body of a text. In organizing their written discourse, the children drew on their knowledge of centering (ideas related to a topic) and chaining (elaborating an idea or relating a sequence of events). As well, the children used aspects of literate language through phrases such as "Far, far away, in another land" and "Once upon a time," and through depictions of signs in pictures (BEWARE! KEEP OUT!). In addition, the children occasionally emulated the work of authors the teacher read to them, as did Alan, for example, in response to *Memorable Prose* by Michael Rosen:

> I am sick today. And my tummy is sore. I am going to throw up. I have a back ache. I called my Mom and she wasn't home. I have an ear ache. I feel my cat sit on my hand. I hear my cat purr-rr. Both of my legs are broken. Both of my arms are broken. I have a broken neck. I have a broken nose. I have a broken ear. I call my Dad and so I went to the doctor. I am very sick. I am history.

Discussion

Four assumptions about literacy are central to a discussion of genre as an emergent dimension in young children's writing: (a) Growth in literacy is a continuum that begins at birth and involves both quantitative and qualitative changes; (b) writing is related to other symbol systems and processes, in particular, oral language and drawing; (c) written discourse is embedded in and shaped by specific contexts; each sphere of activity contains a repertoire of genres that differentiate and grow as the particular sphere develops; (d) becoming literate involves participation in socially embedded and constructed practices; children do not invent literacy anew, rather, they are socialized into literacy through interactions with their literate communities. Interpreting the results from this study in relation to these four assumptions, I will argue that for this particular group of children, genres emerged in the context of Writing Workshop.

Emergence of genre: qualitative and quantitative changes

During the children's first-grade year, genres emerged both in terms of quantity, that is, increasing repertoires, and quality. Quantitatively, the range of genres identified in the Writing Workshop products almost doubled, from 8 in the beginning term to 15 at year's end. As their written language evolved, the children began to extend and elaborate their ideas in writing. From single-clause texts, more complex structures developed. This development did not occur in an invariant sequence, however. For example, pairwise connections did not always precede centering and chaining. And, as Moninghan-Nourot et al. (1988) found in their investigation, the processes of centering and chaining sometimes occurred at the same level of development, rather than centering preceding chaining as Applebee (1978) suggested. Rather than an invariant sequence, different children's writing developed complexity in different ways. Apart from beginning with single-clause units, these first-grade children wrote their way to a combination of centering and chaining through different routes, yet they all reached this destination by the end of the school year.

Although the developments suggested by Lindfors (1985)—from non-verbal to verbal, from shorter to longer, from "building blocks" to "ivy," and from simple to complex—are verified by the children's writing in this study, growth was irregular and uneven. Children would sometimes seem to reach a plateau, reworking the same theme or pattern repeatedly. At other times, a child who seemed to be progressing rather slowly would suddenly produce a much more complex text. Sometimes growth involved the production of longer pieces; at other times it was evidenced through texts of similar length but a greater degree of complexity. When one takes a step back and looks first at the children's early writing and then at their later efforts, it is evident that along the dimension of genre, the children's writing evolved both quantitatively and qualitatively. Unfortunately, because the study is limited to the writing produced in one school year, it is not possible to determine the continuity of the children's genre development or acquisition with either previous or subsequent years. Neither is it possible to estimate the true extent of the children's repertoires of written genres because the data were limited to Writing Workshop and did not include the writing related to their projects or to their play. Nevertheless, the data do suggest that within the context of Writing Workshop, this group of children's written genres did emerge both quantitatively and qualitatively during their first-grade year. The big question remains, however, would the children's writing over a longer period, from preschool through the elementary years, still exhibit the trend noted throughout first grade?

Tapestries: drawing, talking, reading and writing

In the present study, various written genres emerged not in isolation but in relation to other ways of communicating as the children wove together their drawings, talking and writing to compose meaning (Dyson, 1985). In the early stages, drawing often preceded the writing, with writing gradually taking on a larger role. At the end of the school year, most of the children's writing could stand alone in conveying their meanings, although in most cases the children chose to draw as part of their writing processes. Because of this interrelationship between drawing and writing, many of the children's written genres were picture related. In fact, the earliest genre to appear was the "Label," usually written after the picture was drawn. Later, children integrated writing with their pictures, creating, for example, single-word labels (usually accompanied by arrows), sound effects (e.g., POW), dialogue (YAHOO), and written signs (WATCH OUT!). Toward the end of the year, thes representations of oral language and signs were conveyed both within the picture and in the body of the text (Figure 2).

The genres "Written Dialogue," "Picture Dialogue" and "Sound Effects," and "Note/Letter" also demonstrate the connections children made between talking and writing. Less obvious are the chronological genres, from "Basic Record" to "Narrative." Clearly, children are able to structure their oral discourse in a variety of chronological genres, and this repertoire provides a storehouse of knowledge which they can draw on in their writing. "Labels" and "Attribute Series" are reminiscent of children's talk and oral commentary about their pictures (e.g., "This is a haunted castle. I like it. It's neat.") Thus, in the same way that children's written vocabulary resembles their speech (e.g., overgeneralizations of verbs, such as "hurted" and "brang") the children's written genres reflect their oral discourse structures. Similarly, literary language (from reading or being read to) has an impact on their written discourse, as for example, when Janet wrote "Once upon a time there was a girl who lived in the woods" (a label for a picture) and in her penchant for songs and rhymes. Literary genres also appear to have influenced Caitlin's production of the following "Recount" (What *was* she reading? Who's been reading to her?):

Another place, another time

If there was an answer, he'd find it there. He kept on going and he got to a castle. He knew he'd find something. And he did.

In this first-grade classroom, drawing and talking were valued by the teacher and considered by her to be facilitative of children's writing processes. However, in many classrooms, while drawing may be allowed in the early stages, it is often assumed that children grow out of (or should grow out of) the need to draw. (It should also be noted that some children sometimes get frustrated with drawing and don't want to draw.) What happens to children when they are denied opportunities to use drawing as a way of generating or expressing their ideas? Likewise, what happens to children when they are discouraged from talking? When writing time means quiet time? Are their written genres constrained, and if so, how?

In a similar vein, as in other areas of literacy development, it is likely that being read to has an impact on the children's repertories of genres. It is interesting to note, however, that one of the children in the study, Brandon, was not read to by his parents before he started school and, in fact, his older siblings did not have much success in reading and writing at school. At the beginning of the year, Brandon had very little knowledge of the alphabet and his writing consisted of letter and letter-like strings. Yet 10 of the 15 genres identified in this study (all except Basic Record Series, Narrative, List, Word Play and Note/Letter) were apparent in his writing. Figure 2 shows the richness with which Brandon wove together drawing, writing, written dialogue, and picture dialogue. Would this tapestry have occurred if Brandon had not participated in collaborative literacy events mediated by the teacher and had many opportunities to explore interconnections among drawing, talking, and writing?

Genres in a first-grade writing workshop

From the data, 15 genres are identified from the writing produced in the daily Writing Workshop periods. Earlier genres were simple in structure, and these were replaced by more complex ones. Some of the genres are hierarchically ordered to some extent: chronologies (Basic Record through Narrative), which are organized primarily through a chaining process, and centered texts (Labels, Couplets, Attribute Series, Hierarchical Attribute Series). (The Label can be seen as a centered text in that it is topically connected to the picture and is usually stated in the generic present tense.) When one looks at the genres with the hierarchically ordered and dialogic forms in groups, the children's repertoires of genres in Writing Workshop include:

- chronologies or chained texts (Basic Record through Narrative);
- centered texts (Labels, Couplets, Attribute Series and Hierarchical Attribute Series);
- dialogues (Written Dialogue, Picture Dialogue, Note/Letter);
- Lists; and
- Word Play.

From this clustering of similar genres, the range seems fairly limited. Or is it perhaps that, because the writing was drawn from a particular recurring context in the school day, the extent of the repertoire is to be expected? It is interesting to consider that although the children wrote "scientific writing" every Wednesday (Project Day), they did not do this kind of writing in Writing Workshop. Did the children perceive that scientific writing is not an appropriate genre in the context of Writing Workshop?

Freedman (1993a) suggested that genres themselves form part of the discursive context. What influenced the children to shape their writing in these particular ways? Where did these genres come from? Part of the answer lies perhaps in the activities that preceded Writing Workshop each day: Morning News and Shared Reading. As described earlier, in Morning News the children talked about the events in their lives and the teacher recorded their ideas on the chalkboard. In shared reading, they read many stories and poems together. Did the genres embedded and constructed in Morning News and Shared Reading serve as models for the chronological genres and for Word Play? In this classroom, the children wrote most frequently about their personal experiences. Is this a result of their "egocentrism" as suggested by Piaget (1983)? Or is it perhaps an indicator that participating in collaborative writing during Morning News and *watching their teacher write* had a more powerful effect on them as writers than the authors, unknown to them, of the stories and poems they read together?

Because the children were encouraged to draw and talk as well as write, many of their products were integrated, thus Labels, Couplets, Attribute Series, Written Dialogue, Note/Letter, and Picture Dialogue/Sound Effects were outgrowths of their multimedia activities. Indeed, these children continued to be "symbol weavers" (Dyson, 1985) throughout first grade. Although the genres have been divided into large categories of chronological and nonchronological discourse types, in reality, the two are not distinctly separate in the children's writing. Rather than leaping directly into narrative by shaping their discourse like the stories they read together, the children often created imaginary worlds through integrated drawing, talking, and writing. Earlier in the year these creations were constructed as nonchronological genres, contradicting a commonly held belief that narrative is more suitable or perhaps easier for primary children than nonnarrative (see Newkirk, 1987). As the school year progressed, however, a text that started out as a Label sometimes evolved into a Narrative, for example, this text Caitlin wrote in June:

> This is a duckling. Its name is Fuzzy. One day Fuzzy thought that
> the moon fell in the lake. He called the farmer.
> The farmer said, "What is it?"
> "The moon fell in the lake."
> The farmer said, "There is no moon in the lake. It is the reflection
> show. Now go to bed."
> "O.K."

It is also interesting to note that although the children's classroom context was shared, and that there were similarities in their written genres, the classroom events and actions seem to have had differential effects on their writing. Individual children had preferences for some genres over others. For example, Matthew's writing seems to have been greatly influenced by Morning News. During the first two months of school, most of his writing consisted of labels integrated with his imaginative drawings. Yet starting in November, with few exceptions, his genres were chained texts. From February on, his writing was rarely accompanied by drawing. On the other hand, Alan's, Caitlin's and Janet's genres were more equally distributed across the chronological and nonchronological genres. Lindsey chose to label and comment on her drawings for the most part, and Janet produced most of the notes or letters.

Although the genres were identifiable because of their regularities, differences in the children's writing styles were apparent within genres. For example, Matthew was the only child who incorporated either past and present events or future and present events within a chronological text. In attribute series, Caitlin liked to use questions and imperatives whereas Brandon often used lexical repetition. Both Brandon and Caitlin liked to weave action and dialogue into their texts, both chronological and nonchronological genres. Rather than emerging as either fixed forms or generalized verbal actions, various genres appear to have been adapted by the children as verbal written practices, reflecting their individuality, their voices (Bakhtin, 1979/1986).

Literate socialization: a first-grade literacy community

The teacher of the classroom under study has strong beliefs about literacy and learning and created the classroom environment to socialize the children into literacy quite deliberately. She believes that children will acquire considerable knowledge of literacy through "immersion," that demonstrations of literacy are important, that children will develop skills (e.g., spelling) when they have opportunities to read and write without an overemphasis on mechanics, that explanations and instruction in the context of meaningful literacy activities are more beneficial than decontextualized instruction, and that drawing and talking facilitate literacy development. Although the teacher stated her intention to address variety in terms of personal, realistic, imaginative, and "scientific" forms of writing, genre was not a conscious focus in the language arts program. Yet although specific genres were not explicit instructional objectives, the structure of the children's writing reflects the conditions and goals of the context in which it occurred. Genres resulted from participating in the social dialogue, the literate socialization processes, at play in the classroom.

Conclusions and recommendations for future research

Although the insights provided by this study may be specific to these children, they do suggest that there are trends in the way first-grade writing changes when examined from a perspective of genre. Although the study is not large in scale or scope, it can contribute to our understanding of how children's writing continues to emerge after they enter school and contribute to a developmental theory of writing (Shuy, 1981). Although many studies conducted from an emergent literacy perspective have described the emergence of various aspects of orthography in children's writing, this study highlights how first-grade writers develop the discourse structure of their writing and construct a repertoire of genres.

The children in the focal classroom had many opportunities to explore writing collaboratively and independently; however, many first-grade classrooms are dominated by worksheets, skill exercises, fill-in-the blanks "writing activities," and a concern for correctness in spelling and punctuation. What and how do written genres develop in this type of classroom? What happens to children's written discourse in the intermediate grades with increasing pressure for "academic writing?" Because school literacy programs and environments vary according to our values and beliefs about how literacy is learned and should be used, children are socialized into literacy in different ways. Thus, there is a need to look at the development of genres in more breadth and depth: in a variety of contexts within classrooms (for example, in response to literature, in science and mathematics, in learning centers, and in play), in the interrelationships between children's written genres and reading programs (for example, in basal classrooms and in literature-based classrooms), in different classrooms across grade levels, and in case studies conducted over several years.

For the most part, a discourse structure approach has dominated empirical analyses of children's writing. Indeed, a structural analysis was used in the present study. However, in order to better understand the development of written genres in different contexts, Bakhtin's (1979/1986) work suggests that we must address the issue of function. Because genres reflect an interplay of substance, form, context, and intention, what we need to explore from a methodological standpoint are various ways of integrating functional and formal analyses for examining children's written discourse. Hopefully, the renewed interest in and reconceptualizing of genre precipitated by Bakhtin will lead to the development of such tools.

References

Applebee, A. N. (1978). *The child's concept of story: Ages two to seventeen.* Chicago, IL: University of Chicago Press.

Bakhtin, M. M. (1986). *Speech genres and other late essays* (C. Emerson & M. Holquist, Eds.; V. W. McGee, Trans.). Austin: University of Texas Press. (Original work published 1979.)

Bissex, G. L. (1980). *Gnys at wrk: A child learns to write and read.* Cambridge, MA: Harvard University Press.

Burgess, C. (1973). *Understanding children writing*. Harmondsworth, England: Penguin.

Calkins, L. (1986). *The art of teaching writing*. Portsmouth, NH: Heinemann.

Christie, F. (1986). Writing in schools: Generic structures as ways of meaning. In B. Couture (Ed.), *Functional approaches to writing: Research perspectives* (pp. 221–240). London: Frances Pinter.

Collerson, J. (1986). *Genres and process*. Unpublished manuscript, Milperra, NSW, Australia.

DeFord, D. (1980). Young children and their writing. *Theory Into Practice, 29*, 157–162.

Dyson, A. H. (1984). Reading, writing, and language: Young children solving the written language puzzle. In J. M. Jensen (Ed.), *Composing and comprehending* (pp. 166–171). Urbana, IL: ERIC Clearinghouse on Reading and Communication Skills.

Dyson, A. H. (1985). Individual differences in emerging writing. In M. Farr (Ed.), *Advances in writing research: Vol. 1. Children's early writing development* (pp. 59–125). Norwood, NJ: Ablex.

Dyson, A. H. (1986). Transitions and tensions: Interrelationships between the drawing, talking, and dictating of young children. *Research in the Teaching of English, 20*, 379–409.

Dyson, A. H. (1989). *Multiple worlds of child writers: Friends learning to write*. New York: Teachers College Press.

Fahnestock, J. (1993). Genre and rhetorical craft. *Research in the Teaching of English, 27*, 265–271.

Ferreiro, E. (1978). What is written in a written sentence? A developmental answer. *Journal of Education, 160*, 25–39.

Freedman, A. (1993a). Show and tell? The role of explicit teaching in the learning of new genres. *Research in the Teaching of English, 27*, 222–251.

Freedman, A. (1993b). Situating genre: A rejoinder. *Research in the Teaching of English, 27*, 272–281.

Gardner, H. (1986). The development of symbolic literacy. In M. E. Wrolstad & D. Fisher (Eds.), *Toward a new understanding of literacy* (pp. 39–56). New York: Praeger.

Goodman, K. S., Smith, E. B., Meredith, R., & Goodman, Y. (1987). *Language and thinking in school: A whole-language curriculum* (3rd ed.). New York: Richard C. Owen.

Graves, D. (1982). Research update: How do writers develop? *Language Arts, 59*, 173–179.

Gunderson, L., & Shapiro, J. (1987). Some findings on whole language instruction. *Reading-Canada-Lecture, 5*, 22–30.

Gundlach, R. (1981). On the nature and development of children's writing. In C. H. Frederiksen & J. F. Dominic (Eds.), *Writing: The nature, development, and teaching of written communication: Vol. 2. Writing: Process, development and communication* (pp. 133–151). Hillsdale, NJ: Lawrence Erlbaum.

Harris, J. (1986). Children as writers. In A. Cashdan (Ed.), *Literacy: Teaching and learning language skills* (pp. 88–110). Oxford: Basil Blackwell.

Harste, J., Woodward, V., & Burke, C. (1984). Examining our assumptions: A transactional view of literacy and learning. *Research in the Teaching of English, 18*, 84–108.

Heath, S. B. (1983). *Ways with words: Ethnography of communication, communities, and classrooms*. Cambridge: Cambridge University Press.

Holdaway, D. (1984). *Stability and change in literacy learning*. Exeter, NH: Heinemann; and London, Ontario: University of Western Ontario.

Hudson, S. (1986). Context and children's writing. *Research in the Teaching of English, 20*, 294–316.

Hull, G. (1993). Hearing other voices: A critical assessment of popular views on literacy and work. *Harvard Educational Review, 63*, 21–49.

Langer, J. (1985). The child's sense of genre. *Written Communication, 2*, 157–188.

Lindfors, J. (1985). Understanding the development of language structure. In A. Jaggar & M. T. Smith-Burke (Eds.), *Observing the language learner* (pp. 41–56). Newark, DE: International Reading Association; and Urbana, IL: National Council of Teachers of English.

Martin, J. R. (1985). *Factual writing: Exploring and challenging social reality*. Victoria, Australia: Deakin University Press.

Martin, J. R., & Rothery, J. (1986). What a functional approach to the writing task can show teachers about "good writing." In B. Couture (Ed.), *Functional approaches to writing: Research perspectives* (pp. 241–265). London: Frances Pinter.

Miller, C. (1984). Genre as social action. *Quarterly Journal of Speech, 70*, 151–167.

Moninghan-Nourot, P., Henry, J., & Jones, J. (1988, April). *The baby and the platypus: Expanding notions of children's narrative forms*. Paper presented at the American Educational Researcher's Association Conference, New Orleans, LA.

Newkirk, T. (1982). Young writers as critical readers. *Language Arts, 59*, 451–457.

Newkirk, T. (1987). The non-narrative writing of young children. *Research in the Teaching of English, 21*, 121–144.

Perera, K. (1984). *Children's writing and reading*. London: Basil Blackwell & Andre Deutsch.

Piaget, J. (1983). Piaget's theory. In P. H. Mussen (Ed.), *Handbook of child psychology: Vol. 1. History, theory and methods*. New York: Wiley.

Resnick, L. (1990). Literacy in school and out. *Daedalus, 119*, 169–185.

Rogoff, B. (1990). *Apprenticeship in thinking*. New York: Oxford University Press.

Schickedanz, J. (1987, May). *How children show us what they know: Insights from classroom episodes*. Paper presented at the 32nd annual convention of the International Reading Association, Anaheim, CA.

Scinto, L. (1986). *Written language and psychological development*. New York: Academic Press.

Shuy, R. (1981). Toward a developmental theory of writing. In C. H. Frederiksen & J. F. Dominic (Eds.), *Writing: The nature, development, and teaching of written communication: Vol. 2. Writing: Process, development and communication* (pp. 119–132). Hillsdale, NJ: Lawrence Erlbaum.

Sulzby, E. (1985). Kindergarteners as writers and readers. In M. Farr (Ed.), *Advances in writing research: Vol. 1. Children's early writing development*. Norwood, NJ: Ablex.

Sulzby, E. (1986). Writing and reading. Signs of oral and written language organization in the young child. In W. H. Teale & E. Sulzby (Eds.), *Emergent literacy: Writing and reading* (pp. 50–89). Norwood, NJ: Ablex.

Sutton-Smith, B. (1979). Presentation and representation in fictional narrative. In

355

E. Winner & H. Gardner (Eds.), *Fact, fiction, and fantasy in childhood*. San Francisco, CA: Jossey-Bass.

Taylor, D. (1983). *Family literacy*. Exeter, NH: Heinemann Educational Books.

Teale, W. H. (1987). Emergent literacy: Reading and writing development in early childhood. In J. Readence & R. S. Baldwin (Eds.), *Research in literacy: Merging perspectives* (36th yearbook of the National Reading Conference, pp. 45–74). Rochester, NY: National Reading Conference.

Vygotsky, L. S. (1978). *Mind in society* (M. Cole, V. John-Steiner, S. Scribner, & E. Souberman, Eds.). Cambridge, MA: Harvard University Press.

Wilkinson, A., Barnsley, G., Hanna, P., & Swan, M. (1980). *Assessing language development*. New York: Oxford University Press.

60

GENRE IN A SOCIAL THEORY OF LANGUAGE

Gunther Kress and Peter Knapp

Source: *English in Education* (1994) 26(2): 4–15

Access to forms of language, kinds of texts, and levels of literacy more generally, are not distributed evenly in societies such as those of Britain or Australia. If you do not have the kind of position in a bureaucracy that requires
you to read and write texts of a certain kind – reports, memos, surveys,
precis, minutes – it is unlikely that you will develop a knowledge and working
command of those forms. If your job, or your position in your community,
does not call on you to speak frequently in public and formal situations, then
it becomes very difficult for you to develop either the knowledge of those
forms of language, or the skills of putting that knowledge into use.

It is here where teaching about language becomes important in the curriculum. On the one hand, this kind of knowledge, unlike some human
practices, does not come naturally – even though that has been a long-held
and implicit assumption in much thinking about language. On the other
hand, this kind of knowledge, and the skills of its application and use, can
be taught, even though there has been and continues to be a quite strong
tradition which treats language as simply "expressive", as something that
comes spontaneously from within, as something which escapes formalisa-
tion and therefore the possibility of teaching.

In this paper we make a small contribution towards the possibility of
teaching some aspects of knowledge about language. We are particularly
concerned with knowledge of the forms of larger stretches of language, of
texts, and of the social and cultural reasons for the existence of particular
kinds of texts, of genres. Our assumption is that it is possible to make
schoolchildren aware of the manner in which differing social situations
lead to different kinds of texts, and that by making children sensitive to
the relations between social factors and forms of language in texts they
will gain a knowledge both about language and about society from which
they will be able to generalise, and which they will be able to use productively in making texts of their own.

357

Our approach lies squarely within what has become known as the genre-approach in Australia and, increasingly, in Britain. One fundamental factor in our approach is that we see texts as produced in a response to, and out of, particular social situations and their specific structures. As a result our approach to genre puts most stress on the social and cultural factors, rather than on merely linguistic factors. For us texts are always social objects, and the making of texts is always a social process.

We concur with other writers in the "genre school" in two crucial matters. One: in any society there are types of texts of particular form: because there are recurring types of social encounters, situations, events, which have very similar structures. As these are repeated over and over and over, certain types of texts appear over and over and over. They become recognisable and recognised in a society by its members, and once recognised they become conventionalised. When they have become conventionalised, they appear to have an existence "of their own", with recognisable rules. Knowledge of those forms and of their social meanings can and should be taught.

Two: a knowledge of how language works, in other words a knowledge of grammar, is an essential component of a thoroughly productive relation to one's own language, or to the language one needs to use. We don't see this as an end in itself, in the sense that learning Latin and latinate grammar used to be thought a good thing in itself – as a kind of mental discipline, encouraging rigour, providing intellectual training or whatever, an intellectual equivalent perhaps of a good caning. Rather we see this knowledge of grammar as a means of gaining a full understanding of the range of things which it is possible to mean, to say, to write in a particular culture, and to do with its language. Beyond that we see knowledge of language at the level of grammar as one means of a detailed and critical understanding of the forms and meanings of a culture.

So while we want to respond to a 'need' articulated by a variety of groups in many varied ways, our aims are not simply pragmatic, but rather are educational in an old-fashioned and yet entirely contemporary sense. We would like to make available to anyone who needs or wants to know the kinds of knowledge which will make access to knowledge about language and literacy more possible for members of all social and cultural groups in our kind of society.

In the following pages we sketch out a view of language and literacy which supports the kinds of issues which we have just outlined.

A social theory of language

Broadly speaking, there are three approaches to thinking about language. One takes language as simply being there, and sees its task as that of providing a formal account of its rules, that is, providing a grammar. This approach can be traced back to Greek and then Roman grammars, which became the basis of the English (and generally the European) tradition of grammar teaching. It is the tradition some of us can still remember as pretty formal and sterile. It has left a legacy of ill-will and suspicion towards the teaching of grammar. It is also the tradition which has left us with the largest number of and the best-known grammatical terms: noun, verb, subject, object, etc.

A second approach sees language as a fundamentally psychological phenomenon. Here the assumption is that language is a uniquely human phenomenon, and is to be most plausibly explained on the basis of the structure of the human brain. In other words, language is as it is because of the kinds of brains which have produced langauge and still use and (re)produce it. This has been – and continues to be – the most influential view, and one which promises much for an application in educational contexts. Education in this approach is, after all, about the training of developing human brains – "minds". A psychological approach might tell us much about mental development. Grammars within this theory tend to emphasise structure, regularity, generality, and, in some cases universality ("all human languages are essentially the same"). The structure, regularity, and universality are assumed to be effects of the structure of the brain. This tradition has been particularly influential in second and other language teaching programmes.

The third approach, the one we adopt, emphasises the cultural and social dimensions which enter into the formation and constitution of language. This approach does not deny the importance of psychological factors in language, but rather assumes that whatever is psychological is common to all human beings, and therefore to all cultures. In one sense, then, what is common is seen as less important and less interesting than those factors which make languages different, and specific to particular cultures. In educational terms our approach offers the possibility of understanding language-in-culture and langauge-in-society to allow us to focus on those matters which reveal cultural and social significance, difference, and relevance. Grammars in this approach are much more oriented towards *meaning* and *function*: what does this bit of language *mean* because of what is *does*?

Because of our interest in meaning and function, our emphasis is therefore not on parts of speech – nouns, adjectives, adverbs, verbs, prepositions – and the rules of their combination, nor on an account of formal aspects of structure. Both are important, and we draw on this tradition and its terminology where necessary. But neither is as important, in our view, as an understanding of what language is *doing* and *being made to do* by people in specific situations in order to make particular meanings. The latter tells us about the social needs and the cultural values and meanings of its users. It connects with all the hurly-burly and messiness of life in the midst of social processes and cultural values and demands. Ultimately it connects equally with the pragmatic goals of politicians, business people, bureaucrats, as well as the perhaps less pragmatic goals of those interested in an increasingly equitable, a morally better society.

Thinking about language as a social phenomenon requires some considerable reorientation in relation to well-established and commonsense notions of what language is. First and foremost we need to rethink what the main focus of a theory of language is. Commonsense, folsky, notions of language are that it is "made up" of sounds, words, and sentences. And indeed linguistic theorising through most of this century has reinforced this view: grammar has either been about descriptions of parts of speech and the rules governing their form and combination, or, more recently, grammar has attempted to describe the structure of sentences.

In a social theory of language, however, the most important unit is the *text*, that is *a socially and contextually complete unit of language*. For instance: in English speaking cultures, when two people meet briefly and casually, they will exchange greetings, will probably make a brief enquiry about each other's well-being, and perhaps that of near friends and relatives, and will then exchange some concluding and farewelling remarks. Something like this (to be spoken with a full-on Australian accent):

Mike: Oh, g'day John! How's things?

John: Hi, Mike, not too bad, not too bad. How's things with you? How's work?

Mike: Can't complain, can't complain, be going on holidays soon. By the way, how's Mary and the kids?

John: Good, real good actually.

Mike: Well look, got to dash, good seeing you – catch up with you later.

John: Yeah, look, let's have a coffee soon.

Mike: OK, great; see you then.

John: Yeah, see you.

This exchange constitutes a text. Its origin is entirely social, as is its function. Its characteristics are specific to a particular cultural group, though in an abstract form it is common to very many cultures. It is entirely conventional and recognisable; that is, it is a text with a recognisable and oft repeated structure, with a particular way of expressing (coding) social relationships – whether of familiarity and solidarity as here, or of formality, distance, and power differences as in other instances of this kind of text. The conventionalised aspect of this interaction is what we recognise as being *generic*, as making of this text a particular *genre*.

Notice that while the conventions have become entirely automatic and "natural" to a member of the social or cultural group which uses them, there is in fact nothing natural about them. This becomes quickly apparent when we meet a member of a different culture and see him or her struggling with an unknown convention – or when we find ourselves out of our culture, not knowing "how to behave", not knowing what the right thing to do might be.

We want to bring some of these conventions into focus, show what kinds of social situations produce them and what the meanings of those social situations are. In the example above the meanings would be something like: a wish to accord recognition to a familiar person, to indicate friendliness, to affirm existing solidarity and intimacy, and to provide for the continuation of this relationship in these terms. *And* we want to provide a sufficient understanding of *grammar as a dynamic resource for making meaning* to enable teachers to understand the texts of their students as well as the texts which they would wish their students to be able to produce.

Several theoretical categories are therefore particularly important in our account. We have already touched on the three most significant: text, genre and grammar. We will give a more thorough account of these in a moment, but here we will briefly mention some other issues which are essential to a social account of language, and give just a thumbnail sketch of them. These are as follows:

1   In thinking about topics which we speak or write about, we need to consider *how* we talk or write about a topic. For instance, a scientific 'discovery' will be written about in very different ways in a popularising account, in a primary school text, or in a scientific journal, or in an upper level secondary school text. This question we deal with under the heading of *discourse*.

2   The second point we want to raise concerns the differences between speech and writing. In thinking about language we need to be quite precise about the distinction between the structures, forms and meanings of *speech*, and the structures, forms, and meanings of *writing*.

3   Following from 2, it will be clear, we hope, that writing is much more, and something quite other than the mere transcription of speech. That is, literacy is never simply a matter of transliteration from one medium (sound) to another (visual marks). So we will have some discussion of the broader question of *literacy*, of what literacy is and what it makes possible: a discussion of literacy as a cultural technology.

Text as the social unit of language

Consider this text. It is the front page of a local council election pamphlet distributed through letter boxes in a northern English town:

FOCUS (SOCIAL & LIBERAL DEMOCRATS)

AXE THE POLL TAX

Household budgets continue to be squeezed by the excessive demands of the Poll Tax. Shirley Templeforth shares the widespread feelings of anger against this unjust tax and wants to see it replaced by a Local Income Tax, which would be fairer and cheaper:

FAIRER because it is related to ability to pay,

CHEAPÉR because it costs less to collect.

But until it is scrapped, what can be done to bring the Poll Tax down?

Luneceaster City Council must play its part by cutting out waste and promoting greater efficiency, but it is responsible for only 10% of the bill, and so cannot have much impact on the total.

But the Government could help by restoring the £16 million it chopped from this year's grant.

The County Council could contribute by holding down the massive salary rises it gives to its chief officers and the generous perks that go to county councillors (meals subsidised by over £200,000 last year).

In Luneceaster, we need to look at all job vacancies, try to slim down the administration and take advantage of new technology. Do we really need to employ 37 people to count the cash from the city's car parks? Could this not be automated? Shirley Templeforth believes that greater efficiency could produce savings and keep the Poll Tax down.

CONSULTING PEOPLE FIRST

First and foremost our point is that any explanation of language has to start with text as the relevant unit of analysis: not the *word* and not the *sentence*, but the *text*. Beyond that, the point we wish to make is that everything significant about this text can be explained by asking *who produced it?, for whom was it produced?, in what context and under what constraints was it produced?* In other words, our argument is that all aspects of this text have a social origin, and can be explained in terms of the social context in which it was made. We don't have anything particularly startling to say about this text, other than our main point: any interesting explanation of a text must draw on social categories to give that explanation: without them, nothing of great relevance can be said about any text.

We'll start our brief discussion with a very simple point. The piece of paper which came through the letter box was an A4 sheet in size. It had been folded in half to produce a four 'page' leaflet. The decision to use an

A4 sheet may well have been due to the amount of money the candidate could afford to spend (this was a leaflet put out by a minority party in a council by-election). However, the decision to fold the piece of paper, rather than leaving it unfolded, was not made for *financial* but for *generic* reasons. To leave it unfolded would have made it into a typical local 'newsletter', Folding it made it into something with four pages, more like a local 'newspaper' than a 'newsletter'.

Once this step had been taken, some of the generic conventions of (the front-page of) a newspaper take over, as it were. There has to be a name for the paper, a 'masthead' and a 'logo'; there has to be a front-page story; there have to be aspects of typical newspaper language, and so on. Last but not least, in this case, the front-page story can't go beyond the front page, so that the size of the piece of paper also determines just how *big* this text will be.

Newspaper stories are written by reporters, or that at least is the fiction, and so we have here a 'reporter' reporting the candidate's views, her anger, her solutions. This generic convention allows Shirley Templeforth (who, after all, may have written this herself) to appear as the subject of a report. Had the publication been a 'newsletter' she would have had to speak to her readers herself, as the writer of a letter "I think ... I feel ... I am angry ...". The objectivity of the report makes possible a certain distance, and lends a different credence to the candidate's opinions. The generic conventions (in this case of the 'tabloid' paper) also introduce a certain kind of language: words and phrases such as "squeezed", "excessive demands", "scrapped", "chopped from the grant", "massive rises".

We don't wish to do any detailed description of this text here. Our point is, as we mentioned above, that it is the *text* in its full social and cultural context which provides the relevant starting point for any useful speculation about the forms, uses and functions of language. A lot more could be said about this text from that point of view (for instance, why is there the sudden appearance of the personal "we" in the last paragraph?).

What we do want to suggest is that every text, and every aspect of a text, needs to be thought about in these terms. The texts produced by school children in the course of their passage through the education system, at *any* point at all, are no exception. This approach can provide a teacher with a new way of thinking about the writing produced by children, no matter at what stage, or in what subject. It can also provide an interesting way of thinking about a teacher's demands and expectations of children.

Kinds of texts: genre

In one way the most interesting point about the 'Focus' text is its lack of conformity to the generic conventions of a front-page newspaper report.

The explanation for that can be found in the social context of the production of the two kinds of text. A newspaper reporter operates, from the point of view of the writing of a text, in a stable, well-known, well-understood environment. There is the notion of 'news'; which it is the reporter's task to report; readers buy the newspaper because they think that they want to be informed. The reporter promises to inform the readers, without distortion or bias, fairly. The reporter is, or should be, detached from the event. All of this leads to a relative stability in the kind of text that is produced. We can recognise immediately that we are reading a front-page report from paper X, even if we see only a small part of it – provided of course that we know paper X.

The 'Focus' piece by contrast has no such stability. For one thing it has no existing readership; it has to create it. Given the heterogeneity of any electorate, that is a difficult task. Despite the overt appearance of a wish merely to report and inform, Shirley Templeforth wants to persuade: hence the two little slogans: "Fairer ... cheaper ..."; to cajole: "what can be done ...?"; to bring readers on side: "*we* need to ...", "Do *we* really need to ...?" In other words, the relation with the audience is quite unstable; it is all over the place. This makes for the oddness of the text overall. But this also makes, by contrast, the point about generically strong texts: because they are written in a situation of a stable social relation of writers and readers, they can have the appearance of being 'all of a piece'. The stability, the repeatability of that social situation leads to texts with a similar stability, a marked conventionality, which makes the text seem simply natural and makes its constructedness unnoticeable.

This is the crux of the argument about the teaching of conventions of textual structures, the teaching of genres. In any society there are regularly recurring situations in which a number of people interact to perform or carry out certain tasks. Where these are accompanied by language, of whatever kind, the regularity of the situation will give rise to regularities in the texts which are produced in that situation – whether as here, as a political pamphlet masquerading mildly as a little newspaper; or whether in a science classroom, the writing up for the teacher of the report of an experiment; or whether in a primary classroom in the writing down of some recollection; or whether in any of the myriad generic forms which make up the inventory of a literate society. In our approach we would like to focus on making available at least the following knowledge about genres:

- an understanding by teachers and students that texts are produced in order to do some specific social thing;
- an understanding by teachers and by children that nearly all our speaking or writing is guided to a greater or a lesser extent by conventions of generic form;
- an understanding by teachers and students that generic form is always

the product of particular social relations between the people involved in the production of a text;

- an understanding that while generic conventions provide certain dimensions of constraint, generic form is never totally fixed, but is rather always in the process of change (a job interview in 1991 is very different from a job interview in 1931);
- an understanding of the ways in which degrees and kinds of power and power-difference enter into the production and maintenance of generic form;
- an understanding, in the context of what we have said above, of the possibilities for change, innovation and creativity;
- an understanding by all teachers of the role which the functions, forms and structures (the grammar) of language play in the production of texts and their meanings;
- and an understanding by students of the social role which the functions, forms and structures of language play in their own production of texts – an understanding sufficient for the task at hand.

Grammar

We suggested above that the teaching of grammar has fallen into some disrepute over the last two decades or more. Now there is a clamour on the part of sections of the community for a re-introduction of grammar teaching. There were good reasons for the decline of grammar teaching; and there are good reasons for its re-introduction. The good reasons for the decline had to do with the fact that a certain kind of grammar (latinate, formal) was being taught for reasons which had long since ceased to exist: At a time when formal education had as one of its aims to produce young adults who were trained to accept forms of knowledge, forms of rules, as a necessary means for 'fitting' to a segment of adult society, classical, latinate grammar functioned very well as one means of achieving this (along with liberal use of the cane, reciting of tables, much rote learning of various kinds). As the social and cultural goals of formal education (were) shifted, in the sixties and seventies, to produce young adults who were to question, to understand processes rather than forms, to become adaptable in a social environment that was seen as more rapidly changing than it had been hitherto, the teaching of classical latinate grammar lost its raison d'être. It became to a large extent a pointless exercise.

It is at this point that we must be wise in our response to the call for the re-introduction of grammar teaching. It has two significant aspects. On the one hand, it may amount to nothing much more than a nostalgic yearning for the days when there was a particular kind of order, of discipline, of standards, an unquestioning deference to authority. On the other hand, calls for grammar teaching are now linked far too closely to pragmatic economic goals (mainly in English-speaking societies, which are experiencing severe economic difficulties). If only all school leavers could parse and spell, so the argument goes, our economy would be fine again, billions could be saved – a micro-economic reform of seemingly unlimited potential.

If we take the calls for the reintroduction of grammar teaching seriously – and there is every reason to do so – our response needs to be considered; the reasons have to be better than the two we've reproduced just now. The reasons for bringing back grammar need to be better than those for bringing back the cane. The most cogent reasons that we can advance have to do with issues of equity, and with the facts of social, economic, industrial life as they will be in the late twentieth/early twenty-first century. Issues of equity demand that all members of society have the fullest understanding of the principles underlying the production of meaning through language. That makes grammar essential knowledge. Issues of competence of participation in societies whose economic foundations have shifted to information, in all its forms, again demand that all children growing into that kind of society have the fullest understanding and competence in the production and use of information in language. This too requires knowledge of grammar.

The question that needs to be answered is 'what kind of grammar?' In our view the answer is plain: it has to be a kind of grammar which is able to reveal what langauge does and what it can be made to do. Old-fashioned grammar had partial answers to questions about what language consists of, what it is. The demands of contemporary society are demands for an understanding of how language functions in social and cultural life. If I have certain social, political, cultural, economic aims, how can I use language to achieve these? And, as importantly, how can I use knowledge about language to let me understand what others (my neighbours, partner, boss, the media, the tax office, the gas company) are trying to achieve with their use of language towards me'.

Old-fashioned grammar cannot do this. The contemporary social demands made by us on language need a different grammar, a functional grammar. There is a problem in this: however much we didn't like the old grammar, nevertheless its terms, its insights, its implicit theory have become part of popular consciousness. The man or woman in the street, if pressed to give an answer about language or about grammar, will give an answer which depends on the terms of old-fashioned grammar.

Consequently, any attempt to introduce a new grammar will "go against the grain", will evoke a strong resistance, couched in terms of a resistance to "yet more jargon". Nevertheless, we advocate an attempt to introduce such a grammar, avoiding 'jargon' where we can, explaining it where we introduce it, convinced of the need to start making this attempt.

As the briefest possible sample of what this kind of grammar will do, consider the first sentence of the 'Focus' text. What questions will the "new grammar" ask about this? What will it tell us? "Household budgets continue to be squeezed by the excessive demands of the Poll Tax." Every journalist is told that good journalistic writing avoids passives, as ungainly, as lacking in punch; and is told to use active forms wherever possible. Why is this rule honoured only in the breach? The new grammar tells us that this writer wishes to make "household budgets" the starting point of the argument, to give it the prominence which the writer assumes it has for all readers. Hence "Household budgets" is made into the *theme* of this sentence. That is the *function* of this form. Old-fashioned grammar would have spoken about "Household budgets" as the *subject* of the sentence, a description which is not as illuminating. The new grammar gives us a reason for a writer's use of passive constructions, and give us a reason for their frequency in journalistic writing: journalists are more often interested to tell us about what happened to someone or to something, than to inform us about who was responsible for that action, never mind the constraints imposed by the laws of libel.

The new grammar will pose yet further questions about this sentence: not only "what sort of a noun (phrase) is *the excessive demands of the poll tax*", but "what does it tell us about this writer's language and this writer's general cultural and cognitive make-up, to use such a complex and abstract noun-thing as the *agent*, the doer of the action "squeezed"? What are we actually saying or thinking when we say "The (excessive demands of the) Poll Tax squeezes household budgets"? Are we using "squeezed" here in the same way as we are when we talk about squeezing lemons or someone's hand? And if not, what are we doing? Is this level of abstraction unusual? Should we teach it to children? Must we teach it to children to give them necessary literacy skills? When do we start teaching forms of this kind?

None of these questions could arise in old-fashioned grammar. All of them are crucial to a full command of literacy skills, and to participation in social and cultural life.

Discourse: or, habitual ways of talking

It may be that our point about abstractness will strike you as fussy, pedantic, too erudite, or just plain silly. Perhaps we haven't even got our point across. Language tends to habituate us to such an extent, that even the oddest things seem natural. Try to visualise the excessive demands of the poll tax squeezing the household budget. Cartoonists do this all the time of course, by personalising abstract notions like *war, famine, liberty, democracy*, etc. And it is quite likely that we do exactly that when we read a sentence such as that one, though we do it so habitually that we are no longer aware of what we do. It is most unlikely that Shirley Templeforth would see anything at all unusual in this form: she, along with most of us, lives in a world where you talk like that, where this has become a kind of new reality, a second nature.

All institutions develop ways of talking which reflect the characteristics of that institution's practices. To anyone who has become institutionalised, that is the way you talk, and that is the way things are. Consider two kinds of examples. The first example illustrates how science (in this case Biology) talks about its practices, its world. (Both examples are taken from Greg Myers' *Writing Biology*.) In the first of these two brief extracts scientists are talking to each other, in the highly prestigious journal *Evolution*. This is the opening paragraph of an article about sexual selection in a dungfly:

> The present series of papers is aimed towards constructing a comprehensive model of sexual selection and its influence on reproductive strategy in the dungfly, *Scatophaga stercoraris*. The technique used links ecological and behavioural data obtained in the field with laboratory data on sperm competition, for which a model has already been developed.
>
> (Parker, 1970s, from *Evolution*)

In the second extract scientists are talking to the intelligent layperson, in the popularising science magazine *New Scientist*:

> Why do peacocks sport outrageously resplendent plumage compared with their more conservative mates? Why do majestic red deer stags engage in ferocious combat with each other for possession of harems, risking severe injury from their spear-point antlers?
>
> (From *New Scientist*)

In the first extract the world of science is one in which "series of papers" have aims, and the aims are "towards constructing a comprehensive *model*", and it is "this model", according to the syntax, which has an influence on the "reproductive strategy *in* the dungfly". Mating, it seems, is definitely not a straightforward matter for the dungfly. All those strategic discussions! And it is the "technique" (*not* the investigator) which links "ecological data" with "laboratory data". In other words, the language which biologists use in talking to each other about their discipline is one which suggests a strange world: not one in which humans or other living things act, but one in which abstractions act on other abstractions. Nor is this discipline concerned with an account of what nature is like; rather this language tells us what biologists are most concerned about: producing papers, constructing models, techniques, laboratory data, and so on.

368

The popularising account, by contrast, is very much concerned with nature: living things engaged in real actions. The language, it has to be said, strives a bit for sensationalism – which presumably reflects the writer's view that even the intelligent man or woman in the street needs this kind of lurid description to become interested.

While the terminology used in the first example is specific to biology, the grammar is not. It is quite common to all the 'scientific' disciplines, from physical sciences to the social sciences.

Literacy

The fabric of western technologically advanced societies rests on the techno-logy of literacy. This may seem a perverse and paradoxical statement to make in an age which is all bedazzled by the wonders and speed of elec-tronic technologies. However, the whole edifice of that technology rests on the achievements of literacy, and is secured by its continued dominance.

Literacy practices vary, of course, both through history and between classes and other cultural groups. We need to be specific therefore when we speak of literacy, to be aware that we are indulging in a sweeping generalisa-tion. But consider literacy in the form in which we meet it in the paragraph from the scientific journal, for instance, and contrast that with an oral tradi-tion as it might be represented by the brief spoken text above. Consider the enormously complex syntax of noun-forms such as "a comprehensive model of sexual selection", or "ecological data obtained in the field". How would we translate either of these into informal speech, the kind of speech which our neighbour wouldn't judge as "stuck up" or "affected"?

This little, perhaps trivial, exercise gives an indication of the gulf that separates the cultural and cognitive worlds of speech and writing. You would, literally, have to turn these noun complexes on their head, go right back to some quite different beginning: "Well, you know, I'm interested in how dungflies select each other when they want to mate, and when I've found that out I'd like to make a model, a little theory, you know what I mean, which includes all the various ways in which they do that . . ."

The grammar of speech belongs to a world and a culture in which ideas are developed bit by bit, one thing is added to another, bits are repeated, building *over time* a picture of the complex whole. The grammar of writing belongs to a world and a culture in which things are stacked inside other things, on top of things, or dangling off the side of a bit of the structure, building *all at once* a complex, encapsulated, integrated structure. The former has advantages: it attends to the understanding of the hearer, devel-oping arguments at the hearer's pace and leisure. The latter has advantages, developing complex constructs which redefine the world, compacting and abbreviating it. It is the language which likes the control of hierarchy and space; the former is the language which likes control of time and sequence.

369

These are, we believe, foundational facts about the cultures which make up our kind of society. It is knowledge which must form part of every child's education for the multi-cultural, information-based society of the next decades. If English is to retain its culturally and politically salient place in the curriculum these are some central questions – there *are* others – in any thinking about the future of the subject.

Bibliography

Andrews, R. (ed) (1989) *Narrative and Argument*, Milton Keynes: Open University Press.

Christie, F. (ed) (1990) *Literacy for a Changing World*, Hawthorn, Victoria, Australia: The Australian Council for Educational Research.

Gilbert, P. (1990) "Authorising disadvantage: authorship and creativity in the language classroom" in Christie, F. (ed).

Halliday, M. A. K. (1985) *Introduction to Functional Grammar*, London: Edward Arnold.

Knapp, P. (1989) *The Discussion Genre*, Erskineville, NSW: Disadvantaged Schools Project.

Knapp, P. & G. R. Kress (1992) *Genre & Grammar*, Melbourne: Thomas Nelson.

Kress, G. R. (1988) "Texture as Meaning" in Andrews, R. (ed).

Kress, G. R. (1989) *Linguistic Processes in Socio-cultural Practice*, London: Oxford University Press.

Kress, G. R. (1992) *Learning to Write* (revised edition), London: Routledge.

Martin, J. (1989) *Factual Writing*, London: Oxford University Press.

Martin, J. (1990) "Literacy in Science" in Christie, F. (ed).

Myers, G. (1990) *Writing Biology*, Madison: University of Wisconsin Press.

Reid, I. (ed) (1987) *The Place of Genre in Learning: Current Debates*, Centre for Studies in Literary Education, Deakin University.

White, J. (1990) "On Literacy and Gender" in Christie, F. (ed).

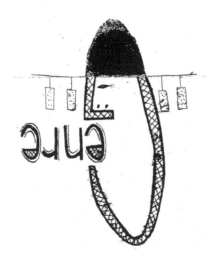

61

THE NATIONAL CURRICULUM IN ENGLISH

Does genre theory have anything to offer?

Leslie Stratta and John Dixon

Source: *English in Education* (1994) 26(2): 16–27

New insights in writing

Over the last ten to fifteen years there have been fascinating new advances in writing in school, and in the teaching of it. For the moment, we will highlight four of these.

a   During the later 1970s, teachers interested in Communication 'opened up the fourth wall of the classroom'[1]: thus they pioneered a new range of writing that was actually designed for people outside the classroom – writing to inform, advise, guide, warn them, and so on[2].

b   In place of the deficit model of the past, teachers have been learning both to look positively at what students have written, and to respond with constructive suggestions for development and improvement. Drafting has become a valuable practice. What's more, in several varieties of writing, it has become possible to start mapping 'signs of progress'[3].

c   Stemming from earlier work on 'sense of audience', there have been further fundamental changes in the role of the teacher. As the London Writing Research team put it in 1975: "There will be many children whose relations with their teacher have to be established and maintained principally by what *each writes for the other*"[4] [our emphasis]. In line with this revolutionary idea, we now have dialogic journals, in which groups learning together (with the teacher) can share, comment on, advise, encourage and develop what they have each been thinking, through writing extended responses in each others' journals.

d   Finally for the moment, there has been a valuable impetus from the work in socio- and psycho-linguistics (including Vygotsky, Labov,

Hymes, Volosinov, Halliday, and Bakhtin): we have been learning to look at writing as part of social interaction, shot through with ideological and cultural assumptions. The institutional formation of written varieties is not an 'innocent' or 'natural' matter. In fact, as we ourselves have shown, institutions like traditional exam boards set questions that betray a whole range of suspect theories, presuppositions, and associated practices[5].

How then does the National Curriculum measure up to these changes? Let's start with the way the Cox Report laid out the guidelines.

Cox on writing – and reading

In a government report representing the best work in English, we'd expect these ideas to be prominent. Has this happened? In some form or other they all appear in *English for ages 5 to 16* (1989) – but, as often happens with committee reports, they are not held together by a consistent theoretical perspective, we would argue.

Let's start with a clear indicator – a case where the language used channels our thinking. For oral English, the key concept is "Speaking and listening"; the two are seen as inextricably related. But when it comes to the written mode, "Writing" and "Reading" are given separate chapters and separate treatment in the programmes of study and attainment targets.

The committee undoubtedly wanted a variety of "audiences" to read what students had written; they explicitly called for writing "in different forms for different purposes and audiences", for writing in a style "appropriate to the purpose, audience and subject matter" (section 17.15). And they spelt this out in greater detail at various points.

When it comes to reading, the treatment is less confident, though. They started off on the right foot, calling for "the development of the ability to read, understand and *respond* to all types of writing" (16.1, our emphasis). And so far as written "response" to literature is concerned, they spoke with obvious confidence: "We particularly urge that children should be encouraged to write fiction, poetry, plays, diaries, book reviews and so on, in response to the literature they have enjoyed and shared and discussed ..." (16.14). So a dialogic relation between reading and writing is strongly encouraged here. However, so far as we can see, a dialogic written response to other forms of reading is missing – despite the fact that they listed a catholic range (16.6–8).

This is all the more significant when there's such a clear emphasis on dialogic response under "Speaking and listening". Here we note:

a   students should not only "assimilate" but "act appropriately on information, explanation and instructions";

b   students should give "weight to ... the opinions of others"; perceive "the relevance of contributions"; time their "contributions, adjusting and adapting to views" already expressed;

c   students should grasp the idea of "turn-taking" and, among other things, "voice disagreement courteously with an opposing point of view."

(15.26)

Of course, in everyday life it is much easier to recognise that speaking and listening involve interplay. It has taken all of us – NATE included – a long struggle to realise that an active response to what we read is equally normal, though much less obvious – especially in silent reading. For years, the tradition of decontextualised "comprehension" and "precis" exercises has channelled our perceptions[6].

So we shouldn't really be surprised, perhaps, that an authoritative report still bears the marks of those formative experiences, especially if, as we believe, a new dialogic theory of "writing and reading" has yet to be developed.

Unfortunately, looking round the International Federation (IFTE), we see little or no chance of help from the major English-speaking country, the USA, where Reading is characteristically a monolithic enterprise, organised by Reading specialists, and Writing – through to College Composition – may actually be taught by different people. However, as attentive NATE members will have noted, there is a newly fledged theory of writing from Australia, which is now finding its way into UK publications[7]. So our next question is: how does this theory match up to emerging achievements in the teaching of English? Has it anything to offer us?

The Australian theory of genre

Over the past ten years, four university teachers – Frances Christie, Gunther Kress, Jim Martin and Joan Rothery – have been collaborating to produce a theory of writing in school, and beyond. Their thinking derives, they claim, from the work of the distinguished linguist, Michael Halliday, especially his systemic theory of language. As Christie and Rothery recently put it:

> Our is a systemic linguistic theory which holds that language is a resource people use for the construction and negotiation of meaning. The theory holds further that because language is used to build meaning, the people in any given culture develop characteristically patterned ways of using language in order to serve the complex set of functions humans have. Such characteristic patterns, then, are social constructs, fashioned out of the constant

373

and ongoing need of people to organise, control and hence make sense of their world[8].

This is a sophisticated claim, which affects both writing and reading. However, as we intend to show, the emphasis in their published work so far – including recent curriculum material from New South Wales – is very much on "characteristic patterns" of language, rather than the dialogic "construction and negotiation of meaning".

Whatever the case, their recent work in Australia has amounted to something like a crusade, especially among primary teachers. Here, they have serious criticisms, as they see it, of current classroom practices:

> The whole movement toward child-centred education has foundered on the idea that children can understand and undertake history, geography and other subject areas 'in their own words'. That this is a necessary starting point, none would deny, especially not those interested in genre-based approaches to writing development. But that children should be stranded there, writing stories for example as their only genre in infant and primary school, is impossible to accept[9].

In our opinion, this is an extremely confused – and confusing – argument. Child-centred teachers as a group do not insist that children can "undertake" history or any other subject merely in their own words. Surely, none of the school texts children read are in *their* words, for a start? Nor do child-centred teachers insist on written stories as the only genre. In fact, we find it difficult to imagine any school where children between the ages of five and eleven are writing and reading nothing but stories. This kind of stereotyping of progressive movements in teaching is familiar enough in the popular press; we are amazed to find it being used by academic colleagues.

However, though we have serious reservations about the negative side of their case, we do have sympathy with their concern that students be helped to achieve social empowerment through writing, for as they say:

> Without the capacity to handle the written genres in which information is processed and understood in the contemporary world, people will be truly left out, unable to participate in a world of increasingly sophisticated information, construction and exchange[10].

So we now propose to examine the theory in more detail.

Is there a consistent genre theory?

Our first problem is that we find it difficult to discern a consistent model. In fact, right from the start in 1982, Gunther Kress conceded, 'I have used the term "genre" in a quite non-technical and non-specific way: *mode of writing* might have been a better term'[11]. And in a relatively recent (1989) article he had this to say:

> *Genre theory in education is not, at this stage, a highly unified body of theory.* The contributors to this debate represent a significant range of distinctive positions ... The debate ranges from a position which treats genres as fully determined in all essential characteristics and therefore as outside the scope of effective individual action, to positions which treat genres as relatively fluid structures, subject to the actions of socially located individual agents[12] [our emphasis].

This reveals a fundamental, disagreement. Those who take the first position must surely be teaching pre-existing, fully determined, forms within which there can be no variation, given the social context. Those who take the second, will have to acknowledge that students, as they write, are dealing with relatively fluid structures and thus should construct their meaning according to their sense of the social situation.

It follows that there will be two further key issues about which genre theorists are not agreed.

1   Is there a fixed number of genres? Here, Kress has rejected his earlier position. In 1982 he confidently asserted that 'there exists a small and fixed number of genres in any written tradition'[13]. By 1987 he believed that 'genres change historically; hence new genres emerge over time, and hence, too, what appears as 'the same' generic form at one level has recognizably distinct forms in differing social groups'[14].

    Christie and Rothery, on the other hand, asserted in 1989 that "most members of a given culture would participate in some dozens of these [genres]"[15]. In principle, it seems as if they could count them, then. Yet in 1987 Kress had pointed to a student producing "what is in effect a new generic type ... The text shows *a generic mix, or blend; something not at all unusual* in other kinds of text produced by competent writers or speakers"[16] [our emphasis].

    Again this disagreement has fundamental consequences. On the one hand, there are said to be some dozens of self-sufficient genres, which presumably must be taught. On the other, there are hundreds, even thousands, of blends, which could well outrun any linguistic classification, not to mention any attempt to teach them.

2   How and when do new genres appear? If they change historically, how quickly does this happen – can new ones pop up in any classroom, as Kress seems to imply? Furthermore, if one and the same genre has "recognizably distinct forms in differing social groups", are we to assume that each social group (and there must be dozens of them) will structure any given genre differently? If so, we begin to wonder how it can be defined, formally?

Disagreement on such questions is serious enough. But they lead to the $64,000 question: is there any agreement among the group about what constitutes a 'genre'? Has this new theoretical use of the term any stable sense?

What is a genre?

As we see it, the new definition of 'genre' has been emerging piecemeal over the last ten years; but let us put it together here in the most coherent way we can.

The definition begins, then, with language in context, in society. So that's common ground. Thus, the basis for genres lies in the fact that 'given the relative stability of social structures, social situations recur, and the purposes and goals of participants in these situations have a certain regularity, even predictability . . .'[17].

We welcome the idea that a theory of writing and reading will have to account for the 'purposes and goals of participants' – the readers as well as the writers – and 'a certain regularity, even predictability' in what goes on. But let us note straight away that the wording 'a certain regularity' already allows for less regular and less predictable things to arise.

However, there may well be a conflict here with an earlier view that is certainly still operational. According to the 1984 Deakin University study guide, 'genre':

> refers to any staged, purposeful cultural activity, and it thus includes oral language genres, as well as written language genres. A genre is characterised by having a *schematic structure* – a distinctive beginning, middle, and end[18].

Here we leave common ground: for, if each individual genre is characterised by its schematic structure, this implies that every example of a given species is structurally identical. That seems to fly in the face of the facts – and would certainly have to be demonstrated by a massive analysis for all the 'dozens' of genres that are currently proposed.

Besides, the idea of a distinctive 'beginning, middle and end' seems an extremely vague way of characterising 'structures' – unless it suggests a further step towards the formulaic.

These efforts at a new definition take us so far, then, but they leave a number of gaps and ambiguities, as we have indicated. Such ambiguities are further compounded when the group actually offer instances of specific 'genres'. Thus, in 1987, examples include 'jokes, letters to the editor, job applications, lab reports, sermons, medical examinations, appointment making, service encounters, anecdotes, weather reports, interviews and so on'[19]. Each of these apparently has a characteristic structure. We would certainly like to see that demonstrated – on a random sample! Martin himself disagrees about letters, arguing elsewhere that 'the term *letter* refers to a mode not to a genre ... [Thus,] as a channel letters can be used to transmit all kinds of different genres'[20].

However, Martin's own claims turn out to be – if anything – even wilder. His 1989 list of 'staged, purposeful cultural activities' offers some pretty incredible candidates: 'religious ceremonies, participation in polit-ical processes, marriage ... political marches and rallies, sit-ins, pamphlets, graffiti, sabotage, kidnapping and hijacking...'[21].

Lists like these are all the more bewildering when the group consis-tently claims that 'ours is a systemic linguistic theory'[22]. We can see nothing systemic about either of the previous lists. According to Halliday, 'Systemic theory is a theory of meaning as choice, by which a language, or any other semiotic system, is interpreted as networks of interlocking options'[23]. So at some point we expect to be told what these options are, at what social, cognitive, affective and linguistic levels they operate, and what typical contrasts in meaning result from a given set of semiotic choices. We're still waiting.

Nevertheless, despite its internal problems, this theory is actually being implemented in practice. Let us turn to the latest work we have seen, *A Genre-Based Approach to Teaching Writing in Years 3–6*[24].

From theory to practice

In the material we currently have access to, only two genres have been dealt with in detail. We propose to analyse the genre called 'Report', which is discussed at length in 'Book 2: Factual Writing'.

Let us start from our common ground with this theoretical model. The "social situation" they are dealing with is a class of primary pupils working with their teacher on a scientific enquiry. Within that situation, the pupils are being required to write. Every member of the class will be required to write a piece in the same genre, 'Report'.

So there are two issues. The first is, how to introduce and foster a particular type of scientific enquiry, bearing in mind that pupils of this age range will be at very different stages of cognitive development? The second, how to set up an occasion for 'Reports' to be written – and then responded to by an appropriate readership?

We can already see a tension here, in terms of social relationship and power. Scientific enquiry, at its best, calls for observation, raising questions, speculating, formulating hypotheses, setting up experiments, collecting and organising data, selecting, tabulating and so on ... and, at various stages, presenting one's findings and submitting them to discussion. (One of us has actually seen excellent videotapes of this going on, in a primary classroom in Victoria, Australia.) All of this requires active learners, who are given opportunities – with appropriate guidance – to take the initiative and formulate ideas in their own terms. In direct conflict with this, producing a 'Report' such as the genre group envisage places the main emphasis, as we shall show, on following a formulaic cognitive and linguistic structure.

The actual product required – as a 'model' – is a written 'Report' on dolphins. In other words, the subject is one where real-life observation and experiment is pretty well ruled out. Instead, the basis of the enquiry is a text – a reference book and some labelled diagrams and pictures (pp 16–19). So, in terms of social power, the pupils are made dependent on second order information. This is a severe constraint on any kind of scientific thinking.

After introductory talk about 'scientific reports', teachers are given a definition: 'Reports give information about things in the world' (p18). This is followed by a series of examples. As a definition this seems surprisingly vague. However, when the 'schematic structure' and 'text organisation' are outlined and discussed, the focus suddenly becomes extremely narrow. In fact, a 'Report' is effectively redefined as a *General classification*, followed by a *Description of appearance* and a *Description of habits*, sometimes with a 'finishing off' statement (pp24–9). And a "Model" on these lines is actually given to the class to discuss:

Stages	**DOLPHINS**
General Classification	Dolphins are sea mammals. They have to breathe air or they will die. They are members of the Delphinidae family.
Description of appearance (parts and their uses)	Dolphins have smooth skin. Only baby dolphins are born with a few bristly hairs on their snouts. These hairs soon fall out. They have a long tail and the fin on the top of their backs keeps the dolphin from rolling over. The female dolphins have a thick layer of fat under their skin to keep them warm when they dive very deep. The dolphin's front fins are called flippers. They use them to turn left and right. Dolphins grow from 2 to 3 metres long and weigh up to 75 kilograms.

Description of habits (everyday)	Dolphins hunt together in a group. A group of dolphins is called a pod. They eat fish, shrimps and small squid. They live in salt water oceans. Dolphins can hold their breath for six minutes.
Description of habits (unusual)	When dolphins hear or see a ship close by they go near it and follow it many kilometers. Dolphins can leap out of the water and do somersaults. Sometimes they invent their own tricks and stunts after watching other dolphins perform.
	Dolphins are very friendly to people and have never harmed anyone. They are very playful animals.

How do these procedures affect the 'purposes and goals of participants'? On the teaching side, the goal seems to be reduced to teaching the approved formula; on the students' side, to reproducing it for all reports they subsequently write.

In effect, the Genre group have selected a highly specific sub-species of writing: a type of junior encyclopedia article, or school textbook outline, perhaps. Even then, they have over-defined it. Many examples of this kind of writing will still not fit inside the boundaries they set up, for the *language features* that they insist on limit still further what can, or cannot, be written – excluding narrative events from the description of behaviour, for instance. (We discuss this more fully in a previous article.[25])

'The Message'
a.) Report

We don't wish to deny that learning to classify, and learning to think about systems of classification, is a valuable goal, given the right context. And when Book 2 proposes that the teacher should work with the class in 'joint negotiation of text' to build up 'taxonomies', while introducing the use of tree diagrams and matrices, possibilities for a new kind of social relation certainly emerge (p55, p47). This flexible interest in diagrams, as well as continuous prose, might well have been taken further, we would say; why, for example, should they be excluded from 'Reports'?

Of course, the decision whether and where to include diagrams depends on readers' needs and interests. Yet, despite the fact that several 'model texts' of reports on dolphins are given in Phase One, their potential readers are never discussed. Nor are readers with scientific interests ever expected to write or speak in response to these examplars, apparently.

The thrust in this Phase is to get the model right. After that, in Phase Three – Independent Construction of Text – the students will be allowed to break free, 'to pursue their own interests within a particular field' (p62), so long as they continue to follow the formula when writing their reports, no matter what they have discovered. (No blends are allowed for!)

Finally, in the section on Assessment (pp69–86), teachers are given five examplars of increasingly sophisticated 'achievements'. Is the focus on making scientific meaning, or on linguistic features, you may wonder. It is clear that scientific enquiry takes second place – if it gets a mention.

Instead, the teacher's attention is directed towards: co-ordinated or complex sentences, use of conjunctions, use of technical language, consistency of generic reference, 'reasoning expressed as nouns and verbs, as well as conjunctions' ... There is no discussion of the quality of the scientific thinking. Nor is there any reference to the criteria students need to use

'The Message'
b) Information

for selecting and organising what they have found out – whether about appearance or behaviour. (If 'audience' had been taken into account, questions like these would have naturally arisen – not least when potential readers were asked what they expected, or whether they had got what they needed.)

The focus is not on a scientific project, but on a restricted linguistic model. At a time when one-hour pen and paper tests are being advocated for National Assessment, the dangers are obvious.

What does the genre model still need to include?

Martin, Kress, and Rothery are all named as consultants in the above project, and we must assume that it has their imprimatur. If so, what can we say constructively in response?

1   In the world outside school, most writing is going to be part of a dialogue or a social transaction. Within many schools we're not so sure this is currently the case. So the first thing we need is for teachers and students to ask themselves habitually: What am I trying to interest my readers in? – What am I hoping to get from them, in response? – What am I hoping they will think or do, as a result of reading my work? – Can they help me by offering questions and suggestions? What kind of response am I inviting?

We acknowledge that this is not an easy transition to make. For one thing, it requires a fundamental change in the teacher's roles – both as reader and as fellow-writer. For another it requires imagination to set

'The Message'
c/ Gossip

up situations (real or simulated) where questions like these naturally arise.

2   If we want to guide teachers about writing in science, we need to study the most interesting and exciting classrooms, where rigorous, adventurous scientific thinking and learning go hand in hand. The same would apply in history or any similar subject. In other words, we need to understand the nature of enquiries in that subject.

Thus, for example, one of the fundamental processes we would expect to observe in science would be the development and refining of questions. Another would be the decision where to be tentative, where to be confident, given the evidence. Students have to learn to examine the validity of their ideas and to become self-critically aware. These are just three of the many signs that might count as progress in scientific thinking.

3   Once we are clearer what might count as scientific progress, we'll be in a better position to look for linguistic indices – among other things. We've no doubt that such indices would help to alert teachers about what to be on the lookout for. But diagrams, statistical tables and the design of experiments will also offer powerful evidence, too. They need further consideration.

4   Rather than invent new definitions of scientific reports (and other 'factual' genres), it seems more sensible to accept Kress's case for 'blends'. It's then possible to talk about classifying, describing appearance, describing behaviour, and so on as *structural elements* in certain blends, rather than argue that a discrete 'genre', with a restricted defi-

'The Message'
d./ Scandal

nition, is a prerequisite for genuine scientific enquiry. And we might add that the way such elements are threaded together to make a text seems to be better considered as a 'strategy'. Strategies vary according to the participants' goals on a specific occasion – rather than follow a predetermined 'structure'[26].

5   Finally, we suggest that generic choices must be related, in some way, to speech acts. After all, many of the everyday terms for genres or species of writing derive from verbs like reporting, persuading, arguing, describing, instructing, or explaining (as the Cox committee recognised, when they used these verbal forms in preference to the derivative nouns, in 17.46).

It's well known, too, that there are some thousands of these verbs in English, and – as one of us has pointed out – they can be divided in a preliminary way into three (overlapping) families:

a   external speech acts (instruct, explain . . .)
b   inner speech acts (ruminate, reflect . . .)
c   dialogic acts (assent and dissent, negotiate . . .)[27]

Surely this is something we should all be following up? In doing so, we will also have to take account of the stubborn fact that different listeners, or different readers, may well construe the 'same' situation and linguistic signs in different ways. In other words, no writing theory worth serious consideration can go on ignoring the problems of readers' constructions – something the genre theorists have so far failed to acknowledge.

Notes

We would like to acknowedge the help we've had from Ken Watson and from the articles he has written in collaboration with Wayne Sawyer (see Reid 1987 and *English in Australia* 1989/90).

1 The phrase arose from the work of Paul Clark at Kingsway College, London, in the mid-1970s.

2 See J. Dixon, J. Brown & D. Barnes's report on the English 16–19 Project: *Education 16–19: the Role of English and Communication* (1979), Macmillan and more recently, J. Brown, S. Clarke, P. Medway, A. Stibbs & R. Andrews (1990) *Developing English for TVEI*, University of Leeds.

3 See A. Wilkinson, G. Barnsley, P. Hanna & M. Swan (1980) *Assessing Language Development*, Oxford University Press; Bretton Language Development Unit (1981) *A Policy for Writers*; and J. Dixon & L. Stratta (1986) *Writing Narrative – and Beyond* (available through NATE).

4 J. Britton, T. Burgess, N. Martin, A. Mcleod, H. Rosen (1975) *The Development of Writing Abilities 11–18*, Macmillan.

5 J. Dixon & L. Stratta (1985) *Character Studies – Changing the Question*, and *Examining Poetry – the Need for Change* (both available through NATE).

6 See J. Dixon & L. Stratta (1987) *Reading and Responding with Understanding* SREB (available through NATE).

7 See, for example, *Knowledge about Language and the Curriculum: the LINC Reader* ed. Ronald Carter (1990) Hodder & Stoughton.

8 F. Christie & J. Rothery (1989) *Genres and Writing: a response to Michael Rosen*, pp3–4 in *English in Australia* 90, AATE.

9 J. R. Martin, F. Christie & J. Rothery (1987) *Social Processes in Education* in I. Reid ed. *The Place of Genre in Learning*, Centre for Studies in Literary Education, Deakin University, (available in UK from John Dixon).

10 F. Christie & J. Rothery (1989) ibid, p9.

11 G. Kress (1982) *Learning to Write*, Routledge.

12 G. Kress (1989) *Texture and Meaning* in R. Andrews ed. *Narrative and Argument*, Open University Press.

13 G. Kress (1982) ibid, p125.

14 G. Kress (1987) *Genre in a Social Theory of Language* in I. Reid ed., see above (9).

15 F. Christie & J. Rothery (1989) ibid.

16 G. Kress (1987) ibid.

17 M. Macken et al. (1990?) *A Genre-based Approach to Teaching Writing in Years 3–6: Book 1*, NSW Department of Education, p7.

18 F. Christie et al. (1984) *Language Studies: Children Writing Study Guide*, Deakin University.

19 J. Martin, F. Christie & J. Rothery (1987) ibid.

20 J. Martin (1985/9) *Factual Writing: exploring and challenging social reality*, Oxford University Press.

21 J. R. Martin (1985/9) ibid.

22 F. Christie & J. Rothery (1989) ibid.

23 M. Halliday (1985) *An Introduction to Functional Grammar*, Arnold.

24 M. Macken et al. (1990?) ibid.

25 J. Dixon & L. Stratta (1991) *New Demands on the Model for Writing in Education – What does Genre Theory Offer?* to be published in the proceedings of the Fourth International Convention: Language and Literacy, University of East Anglia.

26 J. Dixon (1987) *The Question of Genres* in I. Reid ed., see above (3).

27 J. Dixon & A. Freedman (1988) *Levels of Abstracting: Invitation to a Dialogue*, Carleton University, Ottawa (available in UK from J. Dixon).

62

THE EFFECTS OF WHOLE LANGUAGE ON CHILDREN'S WRITING

A review of the literature

Steve Graham and Karen Harris

Source: *Educational Psychologist* (1994) 29(4): 187–192

The whole-language movement and its underlying principles have engendered considerable and often acrimonious debate (Edelsky, 1990), most often centering on learning to read. Much less attention has focused on the effects of whole language on learning to write. Many of the beliefs about learning underlying the whole-language movement, however, have considerable potential for improving writing instruction.

One potential value of the whole-language approach is that students will spend more time writing. In conventional classrooms, students appear to do very little writing. Christenson, Thurlow, Ysseldyke, and McVicar (1989), for instance, observed that the elementary schools in their study allocated only 20 min of the entire school day to composing. Bridge and Hiebert (1985) also reported that young students spend very little time composing (most of which involved transcription), seldom compose text longer than a sentence, and rarely write for a real audience. In contrast, whole-language advocates place considerable emphasis on the role of learning to write in literacy development (Goodman, 1992). Fisher and Hiebert (1990), for example, found that students in whole-language classes spent six times as much time writing as students in skills-oriented classes.

Other potential benefits of whole language for writing development include the emphasis placed on choice, ownership, authenticity, and self-evaluation. These principles are aimed at creating environmental conditions that are believed to encourage self-regulation and self-confidence (Corno, 1992). Both of these are important ingredients in becoming a skilled writer (Graham & Harris, 1994). Whole-language teachers also strive to create classroom conditions that are supportive, pleasant, and

385

nonthreatening. A supportive classroom environment may have a positive impact on both interest and writing development. Soltis and Walberg (1989), for example, found that students who shared their compositions with their peers were better writers and more interested in writing than those who did not. Finally, whole-language teachers believe that learning is integrative and encourage students to use their experiences with other forms of langaµge to support their growth and development as writers. There are numerous examples in the literature that provide support for this view, including acquiring rhetorical knowledge by reading (Bereiter & Scardamalia, 1984) and using vocabulary knowledge to spell a word (e.g., use a related word to spell a reduced vowel: *combine, combination*).

Although there are many reasons why whole language should be an effective approach for helping students learn to write, some educators worry that children in whole-language classrooms do not learn all they need to know (cf. Spiegel, 1992). Because whole language primarily relies on indirect versus direct methods of instruction, critics have questioned whether children adequately acquire the knowledge, skills, and strategies underlying skilled writing. In this article, we examine the impact of whole language on learning to write. This includes a review of studies where whole-language students' writing, thinking about writing, or learning patterns during writing instruction were assessed.

Effects of whole language on writing

Through a computer search of the Educational Resources Information Center (ERIC; using the descriptor *whole language*) and an examination of references of obtained articles, including prominent reviews and discussion papers (cf. Edelsky, 1990; Stahl & Miller, 1989), we located 33 studies examining the effects of whole language on students' knowledge, performance, and/or behavior.[1] Only 14 (42%) of the studies examined the impact of whole language on students' writing; 27 (82%) looked at the effects of whole language on reading. Thus, despite the emphasis that whole-language proponents place on the role of writing in literacy development, researchers have focused more of their attention on learning to read. Of the 14 studies examining writing, 6 were quasi-experimental studies comparing whole-language to skills-based instruction, 6 were qualitative analyses of whole-language classes, 1 was a study on the effects of strategy instruction in whole-language classes using a single-subject design, and 1 was a descriptive investigation of the writing produced by students in whole-language classrooms.

Writing performance

Most of the investigations focused on the effects of whole language on students' written products. Gunderson and Shapiro (1988), for example, described the writing progress of first-grade children in two whole-language classrooms. Papers written by one child were used to illustrate the authors' claims that children in these classes "produced a huge volume of writing" and "made tremendous growth in writing ability" (pp. 433–434). They also noted, but provided no supportive evidence, that students in whole-language classrooms were "dramatically" better writers by second grade than students without a whole-language background.

In a separate report, Shapiro and Gunderson (1988) examined these same first-grade students' papers to determine the types of words they used when writing. They found that the high-frequency words used by the students corresponded quite well to the high-frequency words used in a popular basal series. They further reported that the lower frequency words used by the students were not common to the basal series and were more "current." The basis for this latter claim is unclear, however. The basal series was already 10 years old at the time of the study. Furthermore, Shapiro and Gunderson made an implicit assumption that students using a basal reading series learn only the words presented in that series. This is an unnecessarily restrictive view of students' learning.

Westby and Costlow (1991) also described the writing progress of children in a whole-language program. The participants in their study were 5- to 9-year-olds with language and learning disabilities. Students' growth from writing figures and lines to writing letters and extended narratives was illustrated with several examples drawn from the children's writing over the course of several years. Although the authors indicated that many of the children participating in the program learned to write as well or better than their normally achieving counterparts, evidence to support this claim was not presented.

Whereas the Gunderson and Shapiro (1988) and Westby and Costlow (1991) investigations illustrate how children can grow as writers in a whole-language classroom, it is important to note that their observations quality more as reportage than research. They provided glowing descriptions and uncritical evaluations of the classrooms observed. Negative evidence was not presented nor did the researchers raise questions about whether the evidence really supported their hypothesis or conclusions.

In contrast, Allen (1988) provided a more critical analysis of seven kindergarten classrooms using whole language. Examination of students' writing over the course of the school year showed that 84% of the students progressed as writers. However, 8.5% of the students appeared to make no progress and another 5% regressed. An additional 2.5% of the students who were among the best writers in the class throughout the year also made little or no progress. Participation in whole language, therefore, does not ensure that *all* children will grow and progress as writers. No single method of instruction is suitable for all children; whereas this may appear to be an obvious point, it is worth making all the same. As Reyes (1991) observed, teachers may fail to provide needed instructional mediation during writing because they expect their instructional approach to work exactly like it is supposed to and want to remain faithful to their ideal.

Allen (1988) also found that the entry reading behaviors of the kindergarten children participating in her study did not predict their writing growth during the year; most children progressed regardless of their initial levels. In contrast, other researchers have found that children beginning school with few literacy skills are likely to have difficulty learning to write. Dahl and Freppon (1991) reported that many of the kindergarten children in their study of whole-language classrooms who did poorly on literacy measures at the beginning of the school year made only minimal gains in writing by the end of the year. Similarly, Klesius, Griffith, and Zielonka (1991) indicated that students who began first grade low on either phonemic awareness skills, reading, or writing were not as capable writers at the end of the year as students who began high in these skills. Neither a skills-oriented nor whole-language program was able to close the gap between children who were high and low in incoming ability. Thus, although a school's program may change the outcome for some students as in the study by Allen (1988), no conclusions about the effects of whole language as the catalyst for change can be drawn from the existing literature at the present time.

Finally, three quasi-experimental studies comparing the writing performance of students in whole-language classrooms with students from more traditional classrooms were located. Varble (1990) collected writing samples at the end of the school year from second- and sixth-grade students taught by teachers using either a whole-language or skills approach. There were no differences between the writing of the sixth-grade students. The papers written by second-grade students in the whole-language classes, however, were of higher quality on a holistic rating of content than those written by students in skills-oriented classes. No differences were found for holistic ratings on the mechanics of writing for the two groups of second graders. In contrast, Hagerty, Hiebert, and Owens (1988) reported that there were no differences in the writing of second-, fourth-, and sixth-grade students participating in either whole-language or skills programs. Likewise, Klesius et al. (1991) found no differences in either the writing or spelling performance of first-grade children in either whole-language or skills-oriented classrooms. Both groups of students made similar levels of improvement in writing from the beginning to the end of the year.

Although these three studies failed to find reliable differences between whole-language and skills-oriented instruction, such differences may in fact exist. A variety of methodological problems were evident in each study, clouding interpretation of the available data. In all three studies, reliability of the written language measures were either absent or low. Students were also required to write about an imposed topic during a single session in each study. Because whole-language proponents advocate student choice in topic selection and writing for extended periods, this may have biased the evaluation toward students in skills-oriented classes in which writing for shorter periods of time about assigned topics is more common. The Hagerty et al. (1988) and Varble (1990) studies contained an additional methodological confound; students' prior instructional experiences were not taken into account. Prior to participating in a whole-language class, students may have received one or more years of skills-oriented instruction.

Knowledge of writing

In addition to examining students' writing samples, investigators have further examined the effects of whole language on students' thinking about writing. In a quasi-experimental study by Hagerty et al. (1988), second-, fourth-, and sixth-grade students participating in either a whole-language or skills program were asked to define writing and to describe what they did when they had trouble writing. Answers were scored as either a skills-based (emphasizing the skills of writing) or meaning-based response (emphasizing communication). No information on the reliability of scores was provided. Students in the whole-language classrooms moved from a view of literacy as skill-based at the beginning of the year to a view of literacy as meaning-based by the end of the year. Students in the skills-oriented classes maintained a skill-based view throughout the school year.

Differences between whole-language and skills-oriented instruction were also reported by Gambrell and Palmer (1992). At the end of the school year, they asked students participating in either whole-language or skills-oriented classes a series of questions about writing. First-grade students in whole-language classes were more likely than students in the skills-oriented classes to identify independent strategies for spelling words, provide an elaborate description for their best writing during the year, and describe good writers as thinking about meaning when they write. For students with an additional year of experience in the two programs, differences were even more pronounced. Second graders in whole-language classes were more likely to classify themselves as good writers, identify pleasure as a purpose for writing, identify a broader range of reasons why writing might be difficult, and describe good writers as thinking about meaning when they write.

Similarly, in a study by Rasinski and DeFord (1985), first-grade students participating in a class emphasizing either whole language, a basal reading series, or mastery learning of words and letter-sound combinations were asked to define writing and describe how they wrote. Responses were scored on a 7-point scale ranging from *skills-based* (1) to *meaning-based* (7; no information on the reliability of scores was provided). Students in the whole-language class were more likely to describe writing using meaning-based referents than students in the basal reading or mastery learning classes.

The three studies reviewed in this section focused on the effects of a total program on students' thinking about writing. A qualitative study by Boljonis and Hinchman (1988), however, suggests it may be more profitable to focus on specific instructional processes. They asked first graders why people, including grown-ups, need to know how to write. Students were either in a class emphasizing whole language, a basal reading series, or a basal reading series supplemented by shared writing and reading activities. Each student was able to articulate functional adult-type uses for writing. Children in the traditional basal classroom focused on parental literacy (helping kids learn to write), whereas students in the whole-language class and the basal series class, supplemented with shared reading and writing activities, concentrated on connections between writing and reading: "If they write something and didn't know how to write, the people wouldn't be able to read it" (p. 112). In these two classes, writing was done on a regular basis and the connections between reading and writing were emphasized; this was not the case in the traditional basal classroom. Thus, differences in students' thinking about writing mirrored specific instructional processes that occurred in either a whole-language or skills-oriented program.

Finally, Stewart (1992) asked kindergarten children in a whole-language and a skills-oriented classroom how they were learning to read. Although the participating students were able to explicitly describe how they were learning to read, writing as a vehicle for learning to read was rarely mentioned by children in either group. This finding was unexpected, because students in the whole-language class composed and read with the teacher a language experience chart nearly every day.

Patterns of learning

The whole-language movement has generated considerable controversy among educators working with children who are most likely to experience difficulty learning to write and read (cf. Spiegel, 1992). Skeptics are concerned that the instructional methods used by whole-language teachers are not powerful enough to help these children learn to write and read adequately (cf. Mather, 1992). Students who have problems learning may require more extensive, structured, and explicit instruction to learn skills and processes that other children learn more easily (cf. Brown & Campione, 1990; Harris & Graham, 1992). To illustrate, Reyes (1991) found that students in a bilingual class did not adopt models of conventional form in their writing even though their teacher used common whole-language instructional practices such as capitalizing on teachable moments to model the desired skills.

390

Nevertheless, several qualitative studies have shown that whole-language teachers are sensitive to individual patterns of learning and adjust their instructional interactions accordingly. In a study by Dahl and Freppon (1991), 12 children in whole-language classes were observed during their kindergarten year. The children were all from urban schools, comprised mostly of students from low-income families. Three different patterns of behaviors were identified by the investigators. One pattern of behavior involved students who were confident, self-directed, intensely engaged, and willing to experiment. These students all began kindergarten with some degree of knowledge about writing and were able to make considerable progress without extensive individual help from the teacher. A second pattern of behavior included students who actively participated in writing activities, but were often dependent on the teacher or peers for learning new concepts and were reluctant to experiment with unfamiliar writing. These students' knowledge of writing at the beginning of the school year was quite varied, ranging from students with few literacy skills to those with some degree of knowledge about writing. Teachers provided these students with a lot of scaffolding and extended guidance aimed at helping them extend their writings skills. The final pattern of behavior involved students who had a cautious or negative attitude toward writing, were unwilling to take risks, and were highly dependent upon the teacher for direction and structure. These students had few writing skills upon entering kindergarten and made only limited progress over the course of the year, despite teachers' efforts to provide more direction and structure.

Allen, Michalove, Shockley, and West (1991) also reported that the whole-language teachers participating in their study found that creating a "literate environment" was not enough for all children. Students in their classrooms who were most likely to have difficulties learning to write and read needed and received active, intentional support designed to increase their success.

In the studies by Allen et al. (1991) and Dahl and Freppon (1991), the types of assistance provided to children that teachers were worried about ranged from on the spot help to directly teaching sound-letter combinations. Whereas the role of explicit and more direct instruction is often viewed as undesirable by whole-language advocates (cf. Edelsky, 1990; Goodman, 1992), many whole-language teachers use both direct and indirect teaching methods in their classrooms (Slaughter, 1988). An interesting twist on this issue is the recommendation that students in whole-language and other process-oriented writing classrooms be explicitly taught strategies for planning and revising as well as managing the writing process (Routman, 1991). We have conducted several studies that have examined the impact of embedding strategy instruction within classes based on whole-language principles.

In the first study (MacArthur, Schwartz, & Graham, 1991), a reciprocal peer revising strategy was taught to fourth through sixth-grade children participating in Writers' Workshop, a process approach to teaching writing. All of the children in the study were receiving special services for learning disabilities in self-contained classrooms. The strategy was taught through a series of extended mini-lessons and was designed to guide students in both the cognitive and social aspects of providing and receiving recommendations for revising. Students who were taught the strategy made more revisions and produced papers of higher quality when revising with peer support than students in a process approach control group. Learning the strategy also affected students' thinking about writing. Following instruction, they demonstrated a greater awareness of substantive criteria for evaluating their writing.

In a second study using a single-subject experimental design (Danoff, Harris, & Graham, 1993), students in three whole-language classes were taught a strategy to help them generate ideas for writing stories. The skills of students in each of these classes were quite varied, and each class included one student who had been identified as having a learning disability by the participating school. The strategy was taught through an extended series of mini-lessons, and the writing progress of two students from each class (one average writer and the child with a learning disability) was monitored. In previous investigations (Graham & Harris, 1989; Sawyer, Graham, & Harris, 1992), we found that learning the strategy had a positive effect on the writing of children with learning disabilities. The effects of the strategy on children without learning difficulties had not been investigated.

Integrating strategy instruction into the participating whole-language classes had a positive impact on the writing performance of the six students monitored. The schematic structure and the quality of their stories improved substantially following instruction. A qualitative case study of one of the classes (Harris & Graham, 1993) further revealed that instruction in the strategy had positive benefits for most of the students in the class. This and the previous study by MacArthur et al. (1991) suggest that students, particularly children who experience difficulty with writing, benefit from more extensive, structured, and explicit instruction in the cognitive processes underlying skilled writing than they receive in whole-language classrooms. Including strategy instruction as part of the classroom routine may make important cognitive processes more visible and concrete for these young writers.

Conclusions

The effects of whole language on learning to write is an important educational issue that has yet to be adequately addressed. Although the status of writing in the whole-language movement is commensurate with that of reading, only a handful of studies have examined the impact of whole language on writing development. Drawing conclusions from this small and fragmented data base is further complicated by the fact that many of the available studies are methodologically flawed. With these caveats in mind, we offer the following conclusions.

The most notable effect of whole language was on students' thinking about writing. Students in whole-language classes commonly held a meaning-based view of writing and writing processes, whereas their counterparts in conventional classes had a skills-based view of writing. Because the beliefs that students hold about writing can affect how frequently and how well they write (cf. Daly & Shamo, 1978), such differences may well have an important impact on students' future development as writers. Additional research is needed, however, to verify that this relationship does in fact develop over time and to more specifically identify the instructional processes responsible for the observed differences.

The impact of whole language on students' writing was not as pronounced as the effects on students' thinking about writing. In general, the writing of students in whole-language classes in kindergarten through second grade improved over the course of the school year. Reliable differences between the writing of students in whole-language and more conventional classes, however, were not found, possibly because of bias in the methods used to collect writing samples. In addition, it was not possible to draw any meaningful conclusions regarding the effects of whole language on the writing of students beyond second grade. The writing of older students was the subject of only two investigations. In one of these studies (Varble, 1990), writing was only assessed at the end of sixth grade and no differences were found between whole-language and conventional classes. In the other investigation (Hagerty et al., 1988), differences between whole-language and conventional instruction were also not found, and writing improved in only one of the four whole-language fourth- and sixth-grade classes over the course of the year.

It is noteworthy that even in kindergarten, where the effects of whole language may be most pronounced (Stahl & Miller, 1989), some children did not make much progress in writing and required considerable teacher assistance. For these children and older students who are likely to have difficulty with writing, integrating more extensive, structured, and explicit teaching procedures such as strategy instruction into the whole-language class may prove to be beneficial. Likewise, it may be possible to improve students' writing and thinking about writing by integrating activities common to the whole-language movement into skills-oriented classes.

Finally, we encourage researchers to extend the length of their studies as well as to expand the scope of their evaluations to include measures of students' affect and indices of how they plan, revise, and regulate the writing process. Whole language should have a positive impact on motivation to write and attitudes toward writing, because choice, ownership, authenticity, cooperation, and acceptance are emphasized. Although the study by Gambrell and Palmer (1992) provided some tentative support for this thesis, additional research is needed to verify and extend their findings. Similarly, we know little about the processes and strategies that students in whole-language classrooms employ as they learn to write. As Hagerty et al. (1988) noted, the full impact of whole language on writing will only be known when "an extensive research literature has been amassed that includes attention to a variety of measures and to long-term patterns" (p. 459).

Note

1 A list of the studies are available from Steve Graham and Karen Harris.

References

Allen, J. (1988). *Literacy development in whole language kindergartens* (Tech. Rep. No. 436). Urbana: University of Illinois at Urbana-Champaign, Center for the Study of Reading. (ERIC Document Reproduction Service No. ED 300 780)

Allen, J., Michalove, B., Shockley, B., & West, M. (1991). "I'm really worried about Joseph": Reducing the risks of literacy learning. *The Reading Teacher, 44*, 458–472.

Bereiter, C., & Scardamalia, M. (1984). Learning about writing from reading. *Written Communication, 1*, 163–188.

Boljonis, A., & Hinchman, K. (1988). First graders' perceptions of reading and writing. In J. E. Readence & R. S. Baldwin (Eds.), *Dialogues in literacy research* (pp. 107–114). Chicago, IL: National Reading Conference.

Bridge, C., & Hiebert, E. (1985). A comparison of classroom writing practices, teachers' perceptions of their writing instruction, and textbook recommendations on writing practices. *Elementary School Journal, 86*, 155–172.

Brown, A., & Campione, J. (1990). Interactive learning environments and the teaching of science and mathematics. In M. Gardner, J. Green, F. Reif, A. Schoenfield, A. di Sessa, & E. Stage (Eds.), *Toward a scientific practice of science education* (pp. 112–139). Hillsdale, NJ: Lawrence Erlbaum Associates, Inc.

Christenson, S., Thurlow, M., Ysseldyke, J., & McVicar, R. (1989). Written language instruction for students with mild handicaps: Is there enough quantity to ensure quality? *Learning Disability Quarterly, 12*, 219–229.

Corno, L. (1992). Encouraging students to take responsibility for learning and performance. *Elementary School Journal, 93*, 69–83.

Dahl, K., & Freppon, P. (1991). Literacy learning in whole-language classrooms: An analysis of low socioeconomic urban children learning to read and write in kindergarten. In J. Zutell & S. McCormick (Eds.), *Learner factors/teacher factors: Issues in literacy research and instruction* (pp. 149–158). Chicago, IL: National Reading Conference.

Daly, J., & Shamo, W. (1978). Academic decisions as a function of writing apprehension. *Research in the Teaching of English, 12*, 55–56.

Danoff, B., Harris, K., & Graham, S. (1993). Incorporating strategy instruction within the writing process in the regular classroom: Effects on normally achieving and learning disabled students' writing. *Journal of Reading Behavior, 25*, 295–322.

Edelsky, C. (1990). Whose research agenda is this anyway? A response to McKenna, Robinson, and Miller. *Educational Researcher, 19*(8), 8–11.

Fisher, C., & Hiebert, E. (1990). Characteristics of tasks in two approaches to literacy instruction. *Elementary School Journal, 91*, 3–18.

Gambrell, L. B., & Palmer, B. M. (1992). Children's metacognitive knowledge about reading and writing in literature-based and conventional classrooms. In C. K. Kinzer & D. J. Leu (Eds.), *Literacy research, theory, and practice: Views from many perspectives* (pp. 215–223). Chicago, IL: National Reading Conference.

Goodman, K. (1992). I didn't found whole language. *The Reading Teacher, 46*, 188–199.

Graham, S., & Harris, K. R. (1994). The role and development of self-regulation in the writing process. In D. H. Schunk & B. J. Zimmerman (Eds.), *Self-regulation of learning and performance: Issues and educational applications* (pp. 203–228). Hillsdale, NJ: Lawrence Erlbaum Associates, Inc.

Graham, S., & Harris, K. R. (1994). A components analysis of cognitive strategy instruction: Effects on learning disabled students' compositions and self-efficacy. *Journal of Educational Psychology, 81*, 353–361.

Gunderson, L., & Shapiro, J. (1988). Whole language instruction: Writing in first grade. *The Reading Teacher, 42*, 430–437.

Hagerty, P. J., Hiebert, E. H., & Owens, M. K. (1988). Students' comprehension, writing and perceptions in two approaches to literacy instruction. In S. McCormick & J. Zutell (Eds.), *Cognitive and social perspectives for literacy research and instruction* (pp. 453–459). Chicago, IL: National Reading Conference.

Harris, K., & Graham, S. (1992). Self-regulated strategy development: A part of the writing process. In M. Pressley, K. Harris, & J. Guthrie (Eds.), *Promoting academic competence and literacy in school* (pp. 277–309). San Diego: Academic.

Harris, K., & Graham, S. (1993). Cognitive strategy instruction and whole language: A case study. *Remedial and Special Education, 14*, 30–34.

Klesius, J. P., Griffith, P. L., & Zielonka, P. (1991). A whole language and traditional instruction comparison: Overall effectiveness and development of the alphabetic principle. *Reading Research and Instruction, 30*, 47–61.

MacArthur, C., Schwartz, S., & Graham, S. (1991). Effects of a reciprocal peer revision strategy in special education classrooms. *Learning Disabilities Research and Practice, 6*, 201–210.

Mather, N. (1992). Whole language reading instruction for students with learning disabilities: Caught in the cross fire. *Learning Disabilities Research and Practice, 7*, 87–95.

Rasinski, T., & DeFord, D. (1985). *Learning within a classroom context: First graders' conceptions of literacy*. (ERIC Document Reproduction Service No. ED 262 393)

Reyes, M. (1991). A process approach to literacy using dialogue journals and literature logs with second language learners. *Research in the Teaching of English, 25*, 291–313.

Routman, R. (1991). *Invitations*. Portsmouth, NH: Heineman.

Sawyer, R., Graham, S., & Harris, K. R. (1992). Direct teaching, strategy instruction, and strategy instruction with explicit self-regulation: Effects on learning disabled students' compositions and self-efficacy. *Journal of Educational Psychology, 84*, 340–352.

Shapiro, J., & Gunderson, L. (1988). A comparison of vocabulary generated by grade 1 students in whole language classrooms and basal reader vocabulary. *Reading Research and Instruction, 27*, 40–46.

Slaughter, H. (1988). Indirect and direct teaching in a whole language program. *The Reading Teacher, 42*, 30–34.

Soltis, J., & Walberg, H. (1989). Thirteen-year-olds' writing achievements: A secondary analysis of the Fourth National Assessment of Writing. *Journal of Educational Research, 83*, 22–29.

Spiegel, D. (1992). Blending whole language and systematic direct instruction. *The Reading Teacher, 46*, 38–44.

Stahl, S. A., & Miller, P. D. (1989). Whole language and language experience approaches for beginning reading: A quantitative research synthesis. *Review of Educational Research, 59*, 87–116.

Stewart, J. (1992). Kindergarten students' awareness of reading at home and in school. *Journal of Educational Research, 86*, 95–104.

Varble, M. E. (1990). Analysis of writing samples of students taught by teachers using whole language and traditional approaches. *Journal of Educational Research, 83*, 245–251.

Westby, C., & Costlow, L. (1991). Implementing a whole language program in a special education class. *Topics in Language Disorders, 11*, 69–84.

63

CONTEXTS FOR WRITING

The social construction of classroom writing

Jane Medwell

Source: Wray, D. and Medwell, J. (eds) *Teaching Primary English: The State of the Art* (1994)
London: Routledge, 112–121.

The importance of context

Current theories and practices of teaching writing place a great deal of emphasis upon the importance of providing an appropriate and enabling context for children's writing. Teachers are urged to become literate models for their pupils, and to create a print rich classroom environment which replicates as closely as possible the literate environment of the real world. The National Writing Project has encouraged many teachers to develop an interest in the processes of writing and a key factor in this has been the provision of authentic purposes and audiences for children's work. The Project has also given teachers a set of stimulus points from which to consider the ways in which they might teach writing and the class-room conditions they might try to create. The National Curriculum has set out a range of skills which children should use and specified that these should be used in a range of contexts.

One of the implications of recent work in the general field of literacy is that for teachers concerned with developing the literacy of their pupils the major task is to provide appropriate contexts for that development. The features of these contexts have been expressed in terms of a set of 'conditions for learning' (Cambourne, 1988), prominent among which are plentiful demonstrations of accomplished literate behaviour, the opportunity to learn through progressive approximations to this behaviour, all set into a responsive, 'scaffolded' environment. Applying these ideas to writing, it has begun to seem that the teaching of writing is largely about getting the context right. It is tempting to assume that if the optimum classroom context could be established, this would in itself lead to an improved product and process in children's writing.

However worthy this assumption, it still leaves the problem of determining just what the best context for writing is and the role that the context plays in the child's learning. Unfortunately, our theory of which factors in context are important is as yet an ad hoc one. It has tended to be assumed that such context-producing teaching strategies as conferencing, drafting, collaboration and revising have a beneficial effect upon the process and product of writing. We have yet to formalise a theory to explain why this should be true and just how, and indeed if, these factors help.

What constitutes context?

The first step towards developing any such theory must be to decide what constitutes the context of children's writing, and only when this has been done can the ideas involved be investigated. The common-sense approach to this might be to list all the factors which seem to impinge upon the child writer as he/she works on a piece of writing in school. This listing might include such factors as:

- school and county policies on teaching writing,
- recent in-service work in the school, or undertaken by a particular teacher,
- the teacher's views about writing and the learning of writing,
- the setting in which writing takes place, including the social and physical organisation of the classroom,
- the range of writing that a child has experienced in the past,
- the nature and range of the audiences for which the child has written,
- the teacher's intended outcome for a specific piece of writing,
- the intended outcome of the child for that piece of writing,
- any intervention by the teacher in the form of task description and subsequent response to the outcome,
- the subject, genre, purpose and audience of each particular piece.

These factors can be classified into two distinct groups:

a   global factors operating over a range of pieces of writing and a period of time, that is, fairly permanent influences,
b   local contextual factors which might have influence upon the creation of a particular piece of writing. By their nature these would be more temporary in effect.

This provides a complex web of contextual factors which are interrelated and may be differentially perceived by the participants in the process, namely teachers and children.

The operation of contextual factors

In order to investigate the operation of this web of factors, a number of case studies were undertaken into the contexts provided for children's writing in primary classrooms. Each case study focused upon the work over a period of one term (approximately twelve weeks) of one lower junior classroom in South Wales. The schools were selected from a range of schools which had recently undertaken a school based in-service programme on writing. The classes were run by teachers selected as successful in the teaching of writing by the head teacher of those schools. Each case involved study at several levels:

- the teachers were interviewed to ascertain their general approaches to writing in the class, and to establish their aims and intentions for the particular writing tasks which they set or encouraged.
- two children in each class were selected and interviewed to establish both their general views about writing and their perceptions about particular writing tasks.
- copies of the writing of these two children, at various stages of development, were collected over the case study period.
- a range of writing sessions were observed (by tape recording and extensive field notes) and discussed with the children.
- parents were visited and interviewed about their children's experiences of writing, and the children asked to keep writing diaries to include home-based activities over a two week period.

Each case study yielded vast amounts of data, including pieces of writing, transcripts of interviews and observation notes, and much of this remains to be analysed in detail. There is space here only to report some of the broad implications which have begun to emerge from the studies. This chapter will attempt to contrast some of the data from two of the classes in order to sketch some of the similarities and differences of context and the implications of these findings for the teaching of writing.

These two classes were studied during the second term of the children's 4th primary year. The schools were of a similar size (350 children) on large housing estates. Both schools had completed a term long in service education course about children's writing, led by a local advisory teacher. The schools had been recommended as successful in the teaching of writing and the teachers volunteered to take part in the research. The teachers involved were seen as successful, in that the children in these classes achieved high standards. However, the classes were very different. Class A (whose teacher I shall refer to as Mr Jones) can be termed a 'traditional' writing class, whilst class B (whose teacher I shall refer to as Mrs Evans) is an example of a 'process writing' class. The classroom organisation in these two classes can be contrasted from the brief summary below:

The traditional class

The traditional class was described by its teacher as a secure environment for work, in which children knew what was expected and received praise for effort. The teacher was most concerned to match the work to the child's level of attainment and felt the writing tasks were ideal as 'they can be tackled at any level'. Mr Jones recognised that the children did some writing in a number of subjects, but said that it was essential to practise writing for itself, particularly if new skills such as drafting were to be mastered. He felt under pressure to introduce a drafting approach, but said that on the whole he already encouraged the children to check their spellings before submitting work for marking. He felt that the ability to reshape the content of the story was probably beyond the abilities of children of this age.

The school day consisted of assembly, mathematics before play and English after play. Other subjects were tackled at various times in the afternoons. There were clear rules for classroom activity. The main teacher-needs were for a smooth running, orderly day without obvious noise, and the provision of activities within the capabilities of all the children so that as little disruption as possible occurred. With the exception of maths all tasks were tackled by the whole class at the same time. Co-operation between pupils was not encouraged, but quiet talk not interrupted.

English tasks consisted mainly of short answer or cloze-based scheme work with a creative writing session each week. The teacher would assign a title from a list of ideas which had been successfully used before. The children also retold a bible story each week, wrote a report of a science lesson and did short answer work for history and geography. The main allocations of time were as follows:

1   Work time – children had to complete work as neatly as possible, work quietly, and if in difficulties go to the teacher's desk,
2   Talking time – characterised by the teacher talking to the class, introducing a topic, and asking questions of the children,
3   Transition time – children moved between activities, to and from their classroom. At this time books were collected in or given out.

There was a low hum of activity and children talked, mainly about work-centred issues. If the noise level rose the teacher would call out a name and the class would instantly become quiet. Work was collected by a named individual at the end of each session. The work was marked, mainly for transcription details and returned, sometimes with a verbal or written comment.

The 26 children in the class were cooperative and responsible workers who were keen to participate in the teacher-led discussions and attempted

to complete the work they were given. The teacher was at pains to anticipate the needs of the children before lessons and planned carefully to
avoid confusion. This allowed little scope for child-initiated decisions.
Most conversational exchanges before work started were to clarify directions for completing a task. The children in this class has an exceptionally
positive, warm and humorous relationship with their teacher.

The process writing class

Mrs Evans described her class as 'a context for learning about the writing
process, a garden of opportunities'. This teacher stated that she wanted
her children to become independent learners and support each other in
learning the craft of writing. She was very enthusiastic about the writing
process and committed to giving the children every possible support in
learning to revise and edit their work. She gave a high profile to literacy
activities and had provided a comfortable, well stocked reading area and
plenty of teacher-made posters on the wall emphasising various aspects of
literacy and children's individual achievements.

The school day started with assembly followed by a news time when
individuals were given the opportunity to share important news. Almost
all tasks for the week were given out to the groups on the Monday by the
teacher, with a record sheet for each group which the children filled in as
they completed the tasks. Typical tasks involved worksheets and scheme
work or writing up experiences, stories or letters. The children worked as
groups of six, and although most work was individual they were encouraged to cooperate and help each other. The groups were responsible for
deciding the order in which they tackled the week's tasks, but in practice
everyone knew that maths work was done until play, then tasks involving
writing until lunch. Occasionally the teacher would set aside a time for the
whole class to have a session together where she would introduce a task to
everyone. Writing tasks were usually related to topic work or literature
and most writing was done into rough books to be recopied later into the
appropriate exercise book or onto paper. Most, but not all drafted work
reached a finished stage. The teacher allocated the tasks, although not all
children did the same tasks. Children were keen to have their work chosen
for 'publication' in class books and displays. The children in this class
generally worked round their home table, but did not have fixed places
and sat with friends. Privacy was available in areas, and the cloakroom, for
those who preferred it.

During sessions the teacher would either work with a group, perhaps on
their group reading task which was done as a whole group, or help individual children to complete tasks. This sort of intervention was often child-
initiated and characterised by teacher instruction and questioning.

The main allocations of time were as follows:

1   Work time – children completed tasks, helped each other or sought advice,
2   Sharing time – children shared news or, when asked by the teacher, read out work completed or in progress.
3   Reading time – all the children read their own, school, or class published books,
4   Story time – the teacher read daily to the class,
5   Transition time – children moved activities, changed for games, put work away or onto the teacher's desk for marking.

There was a moderate level of noise in the class and generally one or more children moving around. If the teacher thought the noise too loud she would stand up wherever she was and say 'Excuse me'.

Contrasts and similarities

During the course of the case studies it was already clear that there were striking differences between the contexts in both classes, and also unexpected similarities. The differences which were observed existed not only between classes, as might have been expected, but also on a number of other levels. There were, of course, examples from children in both classes of excellent writing, very appropriate to its purpose and audience, and others which were obviously not so well thought out, but it was difficult to link this variation infallibly to particular elements of the context of either class.

Although both teachers had recently participated in prolonged in-service work about writing, with the same advisory teacher, they had each reached very different conclusions about the teaching of writing. They differed in the ways in which they talked about writing. For example, Mr Jones talked about writing as a skill learnt through practice and felt that the weekly 'creative writing' session was essential practice for becoming a mature writer. He expressed the belief that other types of writing should be taught, for example, letter writing, but that this could be satisfactorily dealt with through exercises. Mrs Evans also stressed that children need to practice writing but she emphasised that her children needed to practice a range of writing skills which could only be done through experience of a range of types of writing. The manner and degree to which these expressed beliefs were realised as classroom practice differed in each class. For example, on a number of occasions Mrs Evans expressed concern with audience and purpose, and specifically structured writing tasks to focus upon these aspects. However, her notions of audience and purpose were not shared by the children, who still seemed to feel that they were writing for the teacher but that the rules had changed slightly. This was clearly seen on one occasion when the children were asked to write thank-you letters to the local vicar who had shown them around his church. She gave a full introduction to the whole class, discussing the purpose of the letter and the content and language which might be used. Talking to the children during their writing of these letters, however, it became clear that they were more concerned with 'what Miss told us to write' and whether they would meet her criteria and criteria agreed amongst themselves about length and spelling than with the needs of the vicar as a audience. In fact a number did not remember that the letters were intended for the vicar. Some were not sure whether they would actually be sent at all. It is doubtful, therefore, whether in cases such as this the intended audience and purpose were actually part of the context for writing as perceived by the children.

The ways the children discussed the writing process also differed, but not directly according to their situation or the teacher's instruction. Mr Jones placed a strong emphasis upon neatness and accuracy and would mention these qualities in every introduction to a writing task. Both the studied children in this class, however, seemed, on occasion, to go beyond the emphases of their teacher and talked about the writing process in terms of content, revision and audience as well as neatness and accuracy. In one instance a girl in class A attributed to her teacher critical facilities about writing with which he actually showed no evidence of being concerned. She suggested that in writing, 'You have to have the right ideas and they have got to be interesting. You can put stuff in to make it longer but that isn't really ideas and Sir'll know.' Mr Jones was flattered, but agreed that the child was going 'beyond her teaching' in the sense that he had never discussed these aspects.

The similarities between the two classes were also notable. In discussing the features of writing products the children in the traditional class usually prioritised neatness and accuracy. However in the process writing class the children were also very concerned about the length of writing and neatness of work, although these were aspects that the teacher was keen to play down. Mrs Evan's continual stress on rough work, and disregard for correct spelling in preliminary drafts seemed to have had little effect. Not surprisingly, this was a source of some frustration to the teacher who felt that her children were bound to be used to traditional school demands and it would take some time before her new demands resulted in a change of perceptions.

Looking at a number of discussions with members of both classes, it seems that there were clear rules for writing which were recognised by the children. These show a surprisingly high degree of similarity from class to class. What is clear, from even a cursory examination of the evidence provided by these two case studies, is the immense complexity of the relationship between contextual factors and writing processes and products.

Context as individual

These observations seem to call for a re-evaluation of the notion of context and a shift in a theoretical conceptualisation of contexts for writing. It may be that the whole idea of context as a set of identifiable factors acting upon the individual is inadequate and it may be more helpful, in fact, to consider context as mental, that is as not having an external existence identifiable to an observer. The context of writing might be considered as a construct which has no existence outside of the feelings and perceptions of the participants in it. This is similar to the conclusion arrived at by Edwards & Mercer (1987) who studied the ways in which shared understandings were created through classroom discourse. Context is, according to Mercer (1990), 'everything that the participants know and understand (over and above that which is explicit in what they say) which they use to make sense of what is said and done' (p. 31). This is further elaborated by Mercer: 'What counts for context for learners, as for analytic linguists, is whatever they consider relevant.' (Mercer, 1992, p.31). If this is the case then the contextual factors described earlier do not exist in an objective sense. They are only given meaning to the extent to which they are perceived as important by the participants. It is clear that these perceptions of the participants are not simply derived from any current experiences, but are a product of these experiences and previous experiences, the effects of which continue to reverberate for a considerable time. Edwards & Mercer (1987) talk about 'continuity' as 'a characteristic of context, being context as it develops through time in the process of joint talk and action' (p. 161).

Context as culture

Whilst the differences in context perceived by individuals may lead us to consider context as mental it is also worth noting the high level of similarity between the understandings of children in the same class, and in some cases between all the children. The tape transcripts, field notes and photographs reveal that each classroom had a unique culture – complete with values, norms, beliefs and organisational structures. This appears as a set of shared understandings to which none of the participants explicitly shows adherence, yet in the light of which each acts. An interesting example of this occurred in one case study when the teacher, after an initial stimulus and discussion about pirates (which, incidentally, was exciting and bloodthirsty and thoroughly enjoyed by the children) asked the class for 'a really exciting story about pirates'. While the children were writing, he wrote requested spellings on the blackboard and, when the stories were completed, he marked them, concentrating on spelling accuracy and making no response whatsoever to content. When asked what they thought the teacher wanted from this piece of writing, the children replied with variations on 'two pages with no spelling mistakes!' Excitement, although requested, was not a priority, and this knowledge guided the actual actions of everyone involved.

The children seemed able to incorporate new rules into this system. In the process writing class the teacher produced a range of notices on the walls of the classroom about the various stages of writing. Then children were given the opportunity to discuss which processes would be suitable for a particular task. The teacher was at pains to talk to the children about the stages. This was not, however, reflected in the children's discussions. They referred to the stages they had discussed as a rule system which applied to the writing they did in this class (but not in other classes and not at home). They did not consider that the writing task they engaged in should influence the stages they would use although the teacher had explicitly told them that it might. It seemed as if one rule system had been substituted for another without any apparent increase in the children's levels of awareness about writing processes.

As mentioned above, Mrs Evans was most concerned to provide authentic audiences and purposes for her children so that they could be involved in 'real' writing. Their discussions, however, seemed to indicate that they continued to view these as school tasks, primarily done for the teacher. The question of ownership further supported this impression, as the children in the process class did not feel that the work was theirs, whilst on some occasions a child in the traditional class expressed strong ownership of stories she had written.

Another revealing aspect to emerge in these case studies was a difference in the way writing was approached at school and at home. One child said she disliked writing. Her parents confirmed this and said she never wrote at home. However, in the course of the home visit it became clear that her home writing, although not regarded as such by her parents, actually showed signs of more mature writing processes than her work at school. For example, she had produced written 'rules' for a club she was running which had been carefully and obviously revised, yet revision was something to which she was very resistant at school.

Thus in both these classes there was a strong culture in the sense of a set of social norms, rituals, conduct rules and meaning systems, which was clearly a school culture. Within these classes the rules and meaning systems about writing were school rules and meanings about the activity of writing in school – a process seen as different from writing at home, and as Neisser (1976) suggests, it is not unusual for children to 'leave their life situations at the door' in approaching school tasks. Moreover, the rules in both classes showed a very high degree of similarity, despite the very different conceptions of writing held by the teachers. The process writing teacher was keen to talk about this. She felt that she had done all the right things to change the way children wrote, but realised that they had not gained the insights into the writing processes she had expected.

Implications

In a general sense it is obvious that the context of all writing is socially shaped. All writers write for socially significant audiences and purposes and the genres they use reflect relationships between individuals and socially agreed conventions of style. School writing, therefore, has particular features shaped by its social setting. The context of any piece of writing can be considered as whatever the individual perceives to be relevant to the task of producing it. In the classroom the major part of these perceptions stem from the rules, norms and accepted practices of writing which form part of the prevailing culture in that class. What is striking is the fact that in this study it seemed that children's perceptions of these features were broadly similar across classes, even where one teacher had deliberately tried to change the children's understandings about writing.

It seems that this teacher's attempted introduction of real purposes and audiences for the children in her class had not really changed her children's perceptions of the audiences for whom they were writing. Given this, therefore, it might be thought reasonable to expect that the children would apply the understandings of writing and the writing processes with which they were familiar. The rules about writing might have changed as the teacher tried to introduce a process writing model, but as the classroom culture was essentially unchanged, then new understandings about writing did not need to be generated.

The key to the problem raised here may be to do with the concept of authenticity in classroom writing. Authentic audiences and purposes are not necessarily those provided by the teacher, however real the teacher may consider them to be. Authenticity of task needs to be recognised by an individual within the classroom culture. In assigning 'real' tasks to the children, teachers may unwittingly transform them into teacher-set tasks which are no more authentic than traditional imaginative writing exercises. In the classrooms examined in this study the audiences and purposes for writing were largely teacher dominated because they originated in a teacher controlled curriculum. An authentic task is, by definition, one whose purpose is defined by the author.

In trying to teach children about writing it may therefore be necessary to negotiate new perceptions about writing through renegotiation of the classroom culture. This cannot be done by simply changing one element of the rules. Perhaps what needs to be renegotiated, in order to offer authentic purposes and audiences, is not the rule system, but control of the writing curriculum itself. It may be that only in a situation where young writers are able to negotiate tasks for purposes which they can recognise and have some say in, can the classroom culture, and the perceptions and context of the individuals within it, significantly increase young children's understandings about writing. Authorship is, after all, about exercising control over a particular medium to meet specific social demands. The purposes of writing will be dictated by the culture that gives rise to them and the processes for writing will be those agreed as appropriate within that culture. In classrooms there will always be a social context for writing which is formed by, and gives rise to individual contexts for specific writing experiences. Change in the writing demands in a class must be created and recognised by all concerned. It is not something which can be imposed.

References

Cambourne, B. (1998) *The Whole Story*. Auckland, NZ: Ashton Scholastic

Edwards, D. & Mercer, N. (1987) *Common Knowledge*. London: Methuen

Mercer, N. (1990) 'Context, continuity and communication in learning', in Potter, F. (ed.) *Reading, Learning and Media Education*. Oxford: Basil Blackwell

Mercer, N. (1992) 'Culture, context and the construction of knowledge in the classroom', in Light, P. & Butterworth, G. (eds) *Context and Cognition*. Hemel Hempstead: Harvester Wheatsheaf

Neisser, U. (1976) 'General, academic and artificial intelligence', in Resnick, L. (ed.) *The Nature of Intelligence*. London: Chambers/Murray

64

ERRORS IN THE RESEARCH INTO THE EFFECTIVENESS OF GRAMMAR TEACHING

David Tomlinson

Source: *English in Education* (1994) 28(1): 20–26

In November 1992, I received a telephone call in Japan, relayed from the secretary of the National Curriculum Committee in London. It asked me to send as soon as possible information the committee had learned I had about research into the effectiveness of teaching grammar. For many years now, opponents of grammar in the classroom have been able to shut down debate by saying that scientifically rigorous studies have repeatedly shown grammar teaching to have absolutely no effect on developing writing skills. They are mistaken. I am one of the few who actually search out and read the studies, as opposed to simply taking on board the conclusions, and so far I have not seen one that stands up to critical examination. This article is a shortened version of the paper I prepared on the subject for the NCC, though for space reasons without the section on the theoretical case studies for teaching sentential analysis.

The studies are not as many as one is led to believe. Many references turn out to be simply polemic. Those that are genuine research follow a pattern. There is an introductory piece of polemic, followed by a summary of past research in which the author, without scrutinising the research itself, accepts all the conclusions that show grammar teaching to be ineffective; and then comes the author's own research. The method is usually to attempt to quantify pupils' knowledge of grammar, or an aspect of it; secondly, to quantify similarly their standard of written English; and then to show that no valid statistical correlation obtains between the two. Assuming this to be a viable procedure (and this is not the place to discuss whether it is possible to assign precise numerical values to such complexities) we can see straightaway that such studies need to be designed with extreme care. Clearly there are likely to be several ways of arriving at a negative statistical correlation other than the one you are hoping to demonstrate. So far I have not seen a study that is not so flawed in design as to make its conclusions worthless. Researchers and supervisors alike, they are usually so convinced in their own minds that grammar teaching is pointless that, as long as the research findings are consonant with their opinions, they do not look closely at how those findings are obtained.

I propose to demonstrate this by examining two well-known studies. Because the 1989 Cox Report believed such studies were mainly done between the 1920s (actually 1903) and the 1950s, with the implication that they are too antiquated to be relevant, I have picked two of the later ones, from 1959 and 1962 respectively. I also wanted to take two which, although unpublished (as is usually the case), are readily available to the general public. You do not have to believe what I write: you can go and check for yourself.

My first choice is Nora Robinson, 'The relation between knowledge of English Grammar and ability in English composition' (M.Ed. thesis, University of Manchester, 1959, and held there in the John Rylands Library). It was first brought to wider attention in four well-known and highly misleading pages in Andrew Wilkinson, *The Foundations of Language*, Oxford University Press, 1971, pp. 32–35. Despite his approval, Wilkinson seems not to have read it: his reference is to the 700-word abstract in the *British Journal of Educational Psychology*, XXX, 1960, pp. 184–6, not to the thesis itself.

Robinson conducted her research in 1958 in four maintained grammar schools in the Manchester area. She picked grammar schools because it used to be said grammar teaching benefited only the most intelligent: if it had any beneficial effect it would show up in the work of grammar school pupils (p. 30). She administered tests of grammatical knowledge to all second and fourth year pupils and asked them to write three 30-minute 'free compositions', with the intention of comparing the two. She did not study all of the work produced. She picked five pupils at random from each of the 29 classes involved, and this gave her a random sample of 145 pupils. So far, excellent. Robinson is to be commended also for deciding to test simply the actual knowledge of the pupils. She did this in order to avoid tangling with what is actually meant by the phrase 'formal grammar teaching', a problem we shall ourselves have to contend with later. She did not wish to concern herself with what sort of grammar was taught or how, only with what the pupils had picked up about basic sentence structure and whether their achievement in written work correlated with this knowledge. Her study is in many ways a model of procedure, and I wonder what the result would have been if it had been more carefully supervised.

The first problem comes with the assessment of the compositions. Robinson had these 'impression-marked' by three experienced examiners, whose marking was compared and found statistically reliable. They were not allowed to analyse their marks. Though Robinson nowhere says why, she insisted on this in her instructions to them: 'No analytical method should be used' (Appendix, p. xxii). But if you are assessing the effect of grammatical knowledge on written work, there is no point in insisting on impression-marking. Why not? The impression mark depends to an unexpected extent on variables unrelated to grammatical knowledge, e.g. vocabulary choice and spelling, and indeed to further aspects difficult to relate to English teaching at all, e.g. the amount of content and its originality, or the ability to summon relevant facts and marshal them into a composition. Comparison with an analytical marking scheme makes this clear. I have picked one of roughly the same date as Robinson's thesis: that devised in 1965 by John Sheard, King's College, London, for marking the free composition in the West African Exams Council O level exams. Sheard's total mark was 40, and compositions of under 400 words had their marks proportionally reduced. He divided his 40 marks into four categories as follows, instructing his examiners to consider each aspect separately:

CONTENT:
10 marks
Quantity and quality of material;
relevance to the topic selected.

EXPRESSION:
15 marks
Sentence construction; variety of
structures and cohesion; clarity;
width of vocabulary and aptness,
etc.

ORGANISATION:
5 marks
Logical arrangement of ideas;
paragraphing; good opening
and conclusion.

MECHANICAL ACCURACY:
10 marks
1/4 mark deducted for each error of
spelling, capitalisation and
punctuation in the first 400 words,
and the remaining mark to be the
MA score. Blemishes to be counted
under expression.

His actual instructions cover six pages, those for Mechanical Accuracy being especially detailed. But even from this brief description, it will be clear that only about half the 40 marks could be related to grammatical knowledge. Three compositions could all score, say, 22, and be so scored for different reasons. One might be moderately competent all round but with many spelling errors. Another might have plenty of content and few MA errors but be ineptly written, with chains of simple sentences joined by 'and' and 'but'. A third might score high on expression but be marked down for content and organisation and have a reduced MA mark. Because impression marking balances out in this way so many disparate variables, the final score is unrelatable to any single aspect of English teaching, no matter what you take. Do I make this clear? Robinson's statistical analysis is in itself impressive, carefully worked through and difficult to fault. Yet when she took scores for grammatical knowledge tests and calculated the statistical correlation with the impression mark of free compositions, the negative correlations she obtained prove nothing, because the two scores were never relatable in the first place.

The assumption that a grammar test score could correlate with an essay mark assessing a whole bundle of variables seems to have been widespread. I have seen it in three earlier studies; it appears in the later study examined below (not however as an invalidating flaw); and though I have not personally examined the very early studies of the 1900s, if the descriptions of them are accurate (e.g. Robinson's of the American Hoyt study of 1906), they too have it. Was the same procedural error reproduced over a period of 50 years, from study to study?

So far nothing has been said about Robinson's measure of the subjects' grammatical knowledge. She set eight 10-minute tests on aspects of traditional grammar: adjectives, pronouns, subject-verb-object, etc. Considered simply as tests, they were excellently constructed. The first half of each consisted of half a dozen easy questions on the lines of 'Pick out the adjective/noun/preposition in each sentence'. The second half had more difficult questions on the lines of 'Which verb is in the subjunctive/passive/imperative?' Constructed in this way, there was a good chance the test would differentiate between those who know a little, those who know a fair amount and those who are knowledgeable. The problem comes with the topics of the tests. The first seven cover: I. nouns; II. verbs; III. adjectives; IV. pronouns; V. adverbs; VI. prepositions; VII. conjunctions. In the eighth and last, the first half has questions on subject-verb-object, and the second half a few sketchy questions on identifying clauses as either noun, adjectival or adverbial. Seven-eighths of Robinson's grammar test consists of parts of speech. She admits (p. 38) that there was 'little attempt to assess the relative importance of different grammatical concepts'. She also admits that the second year subjects, who comprised half her sample, had 'only some acquaintance with the techniques of sentence analysis'.

There undoubtedly were those in the profession who believed that teaching parts of speech improved writing ability, but could any intelligent professional take this seriously? No one believes that teaching the names of letters of the alphabet improves spelling – although spelling cannot be learned without it. Similarly with parts of speech: 'Common' versus 'Proper' nouns teaches basic capitalisation but, for the rest, these labels are only the prerequisite information for discussing errors and for teaching grammar. Robinson was testing little that could carry over into pupils' written work. Her study stopped at the point really where it should have started.

It is clear then that nothing at all can be concluded from Robinson's research, except perhaps how easy it is to bamboozle with a barrage of statistics. I may be thought over-censorious. It was only an M.Ed. thesis; not intended for publication, and certainly not intended to stand up to the sort of public drubbing it is getting here. Yet there is reason for exposing its flaws. As I have already mentioned, it was the most recent of the

411

studies cited by Wilkinson in his influential text *The Foundations of Language*, to support his claim that research into the teaching of grammar has repeatedly shown it to be without any practical value:

> *The ... claims for [grammar teaching] are nearly all completely without foundation, as has been demonstrated by massive research over seventy years. The researches are carried out with traditional grammar, but there is no reason to think their findings would be any different with other systems.*

(p. 32)

> *They depend on the differences between an analytical categorising activity and a synthesizing specific activity rather than on the merits of any particular system.*

(p. 35)

Contrary to Wilkinson, my experience is that the conclusions of the research do not stand up to scrutiny, and his last sentence is damaging nonsense. There is no such separation as he alleges between synthesizing and analytical activities. Skill at synthesizing, creative activities – I amend Wilkinson's descriptions slightly – is enhanced by information derived from the analytical, categorising, diagnostic activities, and this applies as much to language learning as to scores of other activities. Yet this assertion by Wilkinson became the starting point for a booklet of advice for ILEA teachers by three ILEA inspectors: Welch, Thornton and Ashton, *London English Papers 1: Helping Pupils to Write Better*, ILEA, 1979, p. 3. From flawed research to fallacious language pedagogy to misguided advice for teachers in the classroom. . . .

Those pages in Wilkinson were the first of two authorities the ILEA inspectors used to stop their teachers from teaching London pupils the grammar of standard English. The other was an article by R. J. Harris, one-time Deputy Head of Woodberry Down School, North London, which appeared in the journal *The Use of English*, in 1965. (The ILEA inspectors' reference to its having appeared in Quirk's *Use of English*, 1968, is wrong.) As Harris' article was based on his Ph.D. thesis, the second study I shall analyse is therefore: R. J. Harris, 'An experimental enquiry into the functions of and value of formal grammar in the teaching of English. With special reference to the teaching of correct written English to children aged twelve to fourteen', unpublished Ph.D. thesis, London, 1962, and readily available at the Institute of Education library, London University.

Harris' is a Ph.D. thesis, and at 300 pages long, is not as easy to summarise as Robinson's concise, focused study. But it follows the usual pattern, first recapitulating the findings of earlier research, with some good knockabout fun at the expense of the gullible traditionalists, before

412

turning (p. 110) to his own experiment. Three times Harris makes a special point of the lack of correlation between clause analysis marks and essay, comprehension and precis marks in the London GCE exam for 1956 (pp. 24, 111, and 206) assuming, as Robinson did, that it was a valid statistic. It is not, however, integral to his own study and we can therefore ignore it.

His experiment was carried out over a period of two years with a pair of classes in five London schools: two grammar, two comprehensive, one girls' secondary modern. All were first years who were followed into their second year. Pupils in one class had one period of instruction in formal grammar, whilst pupils in the other used the time saved to write a long story. The aim was to test whose English improved the more: in Harris' words, the 'grammar class' that had the grammar lesson or the 'non-grammar' class that had the writing practice instead. It was ostensibly a test of the effectiveness of the grammar lesson, with a control class that did not have it. By carrying out his experiment over a period of two years, Harris was trying to test for long-term transfer. Each class would write a composition at the beginning of the two-year period and another on the same subject at the end of it, and these would be scored for errors. Pupils would also take two parallel tests of grammatical knowledge. The experiment was not, however, well set up, and compares badly with the care taken by Robinson. For example, Harris was unable to match the classes in intelligence, background or attainment (p. 113). And where the same teacher took both classes, which was usually the case, there was no way of ascertaining whether the teacher was impartial in attitude or equally adept at both methods of teaching (p. 115). Nevertheless, I agree with Harris that 'weaknesses in design [were] not decisive' (p. 205). Only the use of the same teacher for both classes was a possible prejudicing factor.

Space does not permit a summary of the parameters Harris used in evaluating writing skill, and how the pairs of classes fared on each. However, when the results of his experiment were statistically analysed, Harris found that it was the pupils in the 'non-grammar' class who most often improved their English, whilst the 'grammar' classes rarely showed it. But this was not uniform across the participating schools, and Harris was cautious about making large claims for his findings. Further, where schools on their own initiative set an additional essay after nine months, and scores from these were considered, it was seen that advantages gained after nine months had sometimes vanished or been reversed by the final essay (p. 207). Harris was therefore inclined to give the credit for any improvement only to the fact 'that an extra writing period in place of grammar [had] in fact probably doubled the time given each week to actual written work in class'. However, the study of English grammatical terminology, it was clear from this experiment, had had only a negligible effect.

All this is fair enough until you discover that Harris' 'non-grammar' classes, the supposed control group, those who spent their weekly lesson on a writing task, were in fact, also being taught grammar. At this point we must confront the problematic meaning of 'formal grammar teaching' that Robinson skirted. The phrase is ambiguous, covering as it does two altern-ative noun phrase structures: 'formal teaching of grammar' and 'teaching of formal grammar' – and indeed also the two conflated. Space prevents me from going through all the possible interpretations; but in Harris' thesis, the meaning of 'formal grammar teaching' is the teaching of formal grammar, and by 'formal grammar', he means traditional formal grammar. This is what his 'grammar' classes were taught: a rigid heavily taxonomic, traditional grammar which, for example, went into four classes of adjec-tive. It was also taught in a formal way, from a standard textbook: Humphreys and Roberts, *Active English Course*, ULP, 1939, Books 1 and 2 – ten lessons of grammar alternating with ten composition lessons sup-posedly based on it. (The course content is set out on pp. 138–9.) But when Harris labelled his control groups the 'non-grammar' classes, he did not mean that they were not taught grammar, only that they were not taught *'formal'* grammar.

Harris' 'non-grammar' classes wrote their stories but then had informal instruction, as far as possible without using grammatical terms, on what was wrong with their sentences. Pupils 'were given help in re-phrasing a sen-tence' and had discussions about, for example, their tendency to use London dialect. They also seem to have been coached in avoidance of the common errors Harris looked for when scoring their final essays. 'Teachers did natu-rally keep in mind the elimination of particular errors listed in the "common errors" in appendix 1' (p. 131). Most good teachers coach for exams, but it is doubtful whether this should have been allowed in a research experiment. Since in four of the schools the same teacher took both classes, it is incon-ceivable to me that the teacher did not use concepts of formal grammar taught to the 'grammar' class, translated into simple English, to help the 'non-grammar' pupils with their sentence structure. Indeed, Harris gives a lengthy example (pp. 131–2) of such a teacher explaining what was wrong with 'Jim and me was going into the cave' without using the terms subject and object pronoun. Now this is an excellent way to teach syntax to 12- and 13-year-olds. However, it is highly misleading to label such classes the 'non-grammar' classes. When contrary to his expectations the 'non-grammar' classes slightly increased their score on the grammatical knowledge test (p. 118), Harris did not see this as a sign that something was wrong with his experiment. He says they were probably getting their grammatical know-ledge from their modern language lessons. Perhaps they were. They were also getting it from their English teacher.

There are then two flaws in Harris' research. He set out to measure over a period of two years the effect of teaching formal, traditional grammar to one class and of not teaching it to a parallel control class. And if you read the perfunctory summaries of this research in the literature, this is what happened. Thus Walmsley, 'The uselessness of formal grammar' *British Association of Applied Linguistics Newsletter* No. 23, 1986, p. 11; 'The control group followed a basic course in English, with no grammar'. In fact, it was a comparison between two ways of teaching grammar: a formal, rigidly structured way and an informal, practical way. Since the pupils were at the beginning of their secondary school career, not at the other end approaching their GCE, the result was a foregone conclusion. The pupils who showed most improvement were those who had benefited from two years' informal grammatical discussion of their written work – not to mention their coaching in error avoidance. Whether this method, limited as it is to the level of what pupils are currently able to produce, is enough to generate a high standard of written work by the time of the fifth year school-leaving examination is, however, another matter.

The second flaw was the type of grammar taught to Harris' 'grammar' classes: detailed taxonomic grammar of the most arid kind, that is, parts of speech. It was, once again, not grammatical knowledge of a kind that could carry over into the written work of 12- and 13-year-olds. As with the Robinson study, the teaching of formal grammar stopped at the point where work on the more generally useful sentential analysis began. My strictures on Robinson thus apply here also. Harris' thesis is not worthless in the way that Robinson's is, but flaws in design meant that it did not cover the areas of grammar teaching that needed investigation. To conclude on the basis of teaching parts of speech to 12- and 13-year-olds that grammar teaching, even the teaching of traditional grammar, had no value in the secondary school, is, if not specious nonsense, certainly a *non sequitur*. It was, however, what many in the education establishment wanted to hear. Indeed, approving references to these studies are still common today, which is why I have analysed these two at length. It is my hope that we shall now hear less of them.

... Some writers have a fondness for the dash and employ it in places where the comma or semi-colon would do equally well. Sterne in the last century and Mr. Besant in our own make free use of the dash.

65

TEACHING FACTUAL WRITING

Purpose and structure

David Wray and Maureen Lewis

Source: *The Australian Journal of Language and Literacy* (1997) 20(2): 43–52

Introduction

As members of a postmodern literate society, we need to read and write a wide range of texts, including factual texts. However, much of the research in the United Kingdom into the development of children's writing has concentrated on personal and fictional texts while factual literacy has been relatively neglected. Our work with teachers in the Exeter Extending Literacy (EXEL) project (see, for example, Lewis, Wray, & Rospigliosi, 1994) demonstrated that although many classroom practitioners recognised the need to widen the range and quality of children's non-fiction writing they were unsure as to how to do this. This article sets out to describe the theoretical background to our project and some of its practical outcomes.

Genre theory: new insights, new approaches

There has been an increasing interest in encouraging students to write for a particular purpose, for a known audience, and in an appropriate form. However, what constitutes an appropriate form is often presented in general lists of different text types; for example, "notes, letters, instructions, stories, and poems, in order to plan, inform, explain, entertain and express attitudes or emotions" (Department of Education and Science, 1990).

Such lists imply that teachers and students know what differentiates one text type from another. At one level this may be true—we all know that a story or narrative usually has a beginning, a series of events, and an ending. We have a general sense that this differs from a recipe. And many teachers discuss these differences with their students. However, it is still relatively rare, in the UK anyway, for teachers of elementary school students to discuss non-fiction texts by drawing on knowledge of the usual structure of a particular text type in order to improve students' writing.

It has been argued (e.g., Martin, 1985) that our implicit knowledge of text types and their forms is quite extensive, and one of the teacher's roles is to make this implicit knowledge explicit. Theorists in this area have been referred to as "genre theorists," and they base their work on a functional approach to language (Halliday, 1985). They see all texts, written and spoken, as being "produced in a response to, and out of, particular social situations and their specific structures" (Kress & Knapp, 1992, p. 5) and, as a result, put stress on the social and cultural factors that form a text as well as on its linguistic features. They view a text as a social object and the making of a text as a social process. They argue that in any society there are certain types of text—both written and spoken—of a particular form, because there are similar social encounters and events which recur constantly within that society. As these events are repeated over and over again certain types of text are created over and over again. These texts become recognised by the members of a society and, once recognised, they become conventionalised, i.e. become distinct genres.

These distinct genres, however, need to be learned by our children. And we need to help to make explicit the purpose and features of such genres for them.

Written genres in the classroom

Several ways of categorising the written genres used in classrooms have been proposed over the years. Collerson (1988) categorises written genres into early genres (labels, observational comment, recount, and narratives) and factual genres (procedural, reports, explanations, and arguments or exposition), while Wing Jan's (1991) categories are factual genres (reports, explanations, procedures, persuasive writing, interviews, surveys, descriptions, biographies, recounts, and narrative information) and fictional genres (traditional fiction and contemporary modern fiction).

In our project, we took as our model the categories of non-fiction genres identified by linguists Martin and Rothery (1980, 1981, 1986). The six non-fiction genres they identified were recount, report, procedure, explanation, argument, and discussion. Of these, recount was overwhelmingly the most used in student writing.

Martin and Rothery argue that being competent in the use of non-fiction written genres in our society offers the language user access to power. Persuasion, explanation, report, explanation, and discussion are powerful forms of language that we use to get things done and, thus, have been labelled the "language of power." It can be argued that students who leave our classrooms unable to operate successfully within these powerful genres are denied access to becoming fully functioning members of society. This suggests we can no longer accept the overwhelming dominance of recount in our students' non-fiction writing. Our challenge as teachers is to provide students with the language of power.

The problems of writing non-fiction

For the inexperienced writer this overuse of "written down talk" or written recount can indicate a lack of knowledge about the differences between speech and written language.

Bereiter and Scardamalia (1987) highlight the supportive, prompting nature of conversation where somebody speaks, which prompts someone else to say something and so on. This reciprocal prompting or turn taking is missing from the interaction between a writer and a blank sheet of paper. Bereiter and Scardamalia's research has shown that a teacher's oral promptings during writing can extend a student's written work, with no drop in quality. The prompts act as an "external trigger of discourse production" (p. 97). The teacher-student and peer conferences have become part of writing classrooms, it would seem, to support this process. Bereiter and Scardamalia further suggest that students need to "acquire a functional substitute for . . . an encouraging listener."

Other problems students experience when reading and writing non-fiction text are caused by the complexity of the cohesive ties used, the use of more formal registers, and the use of technical vocabulary (Anderson & Armbruster, 1981; Halliday & Hasan, 1976; Perera, 1984).

An approach to helping students

Our challenge was to find ways of supporting students in their learning to write non-fiction. Vygotsky proposed that children first experience a particular cognitive activity in collaboration with expert practitioners. The child is firstly a spectator as the majority of the cognitive work is done by the expert (usually a parent or a teacher), then a novice as he or she starts to take over while under the close supervision of the expert. As the child grows in experience and capability of performing the task, the expert passes over greater and greater responsibility but still acts as a guide, assisting the child at problematic points. Eventually, the child assumes full responsibility for the task with the expert still present in the role of a supportive audience. This model fits what is known theoretically about teaching and learning. It is also a model which is familiar to teachers who have adopted such teaching strategies as paired reading and an apprenticeship approach. An adaptation of this model to the teaching of writing can be seen in Figure 1.

In busy, over-populated classrooms, however, it can be difficult to use this model, constructed around an ideal of a child and an expert working

| Demonstration (Teacher modelling) |
| Joint Activity (Collaborative writing) |
| Independent Activity (Independent writing) |

Figure 1 An apprenticeship model of teaching writing

together on a one-to-one basis, as a guide to practical teaching action. In particular, it seems that students are too often expected to move into the independent writing phase before they are ready. Often the pressure to do so is based on the practical problem of teachers being unable to find the time to spend with them in individual support. What is clearly needed is something to span the Joint Activity and Independent Activity phases.

We proposed a scaffolded phase, where we offer our students strategies to aid writing but strategies that they can use without an adult necessarily being alongside them (see Figure 2).

One such strategy we have been exploring is that of *writing frames*. A writing frame consists of a skeleton outline to scaffold students' non-fiction writing. The skeleton framework consists of different key words or phrases, according to the particular genre. The template of starters, connectives, and sentence modifiers which constitute a writing frame gives

| Demonstration (Teacher modelling) |
| Joint Activity (Collaborative writing) |
| Scaffolded Activity (Supported writing) |
| Independent Activity (Independent writing) |

Figure 2 A revised apprenticeship model of teaching writing

419

students a structure within which they can concentrate on communicating what they want to say while scaffolding them in the use of a particular genre. And, in the process of using the genre, students become increasingly familiar with it. The frame should be developed with the students drawing on how the various non-fiction genres are structured in what they read.

How writing frames can help

The work of Cairney (1990) on story frames and Cudd and Roberts (1989) on "expository paragraph frames" first suggested to us that children's early attempts at written structures might profitably be scaffolded. Cairney describes story frames as "a form of probed text recall" and a "story level cloze," whilst Cudd and Roberts claim that expository frames "provide a bridge which helps ease the transition from narrative to content area reading and writing." Using these as a model to develop frames that would introduce students to a wider range of genres, we have evolved and developed, in collaboration with teachers, a range of writing frames for use in the classroom. These frames have been widely used with children throughout the elementary and middle school years and across the full range of abilities, including students with special needs. On the strength of this extensive trialling, we are confident in saying that not only do writing frames help students become familiar with unfamiliar genres but that they also help overcome many of the other problems often associated with non-fiction writing.

There are many possible frames for each genre and we have space here for only two examples (see Lewis & Wray, 1995; and Lewis and Wray, 1996, for much more extensive discussion).

Recount genre

Using the recount frame given in Figure 3, nine-year-old Rachel wrote about her trip to Plymouth Museum (Figure 4). The frame helped structure her writing and allowed her to make her own sense of what she had seen. It encouraged her to reflect upon her learning.

Although I already knew that..
I have learnt some new facts. I learnt that ....
I also learnt that ....
Another fact I learnt was ....
However the most interesting thing I learnt was ....

Figure 3 A recount frame

A trip to Plymouth Museum

Although I already knew that they buried their dead in mummy cases I was surprised that the paint stayed on for all these years. I have learnt some new facts. I learnt that the River Nile had a god called Hopi. He was in charge of the River Nile and he brought the floods. I also learnt that sometimes people carried a little charm so you tell a lie and you rubbed the charm's tummy and it would be OK. Another fact I learnt was that they put pretend scarab beetles on their hair for decoration. However the most interesting thing I learnt was they mummified cats and sometimes mice as well.

Figure 4 Rachel's framed recount

Discussion genre

Using the discussion frame in Figure 5 helped eleven-year-old Kerry write a thoughtful discussion about boxing (Figure 6). The frame encouraged her to structure the discussion to look at both sides of the argument.

How the frames might be used

The use of a frame should always begin with discussion and teacher modelling before moving on to joint construction (teacher and students together) and then to the student undertaking writing supported by the frame. This oral, teacher-modelling, joint construction pattern of teaching is vital, for it not only models the generic form and teaches the words that signal connections and transitions but it also provides opportunities for

---

There is a lot of discussion about whether..

The people who agree with this idea, such as ....

claim that..

They also argue that ....

A further point they make is ....

However there are also strong arguments against this point of view.

....believe that..

Another counter argument is...

Furthermore ....

After looking at the different points of view and the evidence for them I think..............

....because ....

Figure 5 A discussion frame

There is a lot of discussion about whether boxing should be banned. The people who agree with this idea, such as Sarah, claim that if they do carry on boxing they should wear something to protect their heads. They also argue that people who do boxing could have brain damage and get seriously hurt. A further point they make is that most of the people that have died did have families.

However, there are also strong arguments against this point of view. Another group of people believe that boxing should not be banned. They say that why did they invent it if it is a dangerous sport. They say that boxing is a good sport, people enjoy it. A furthermore reason is if this a good sport, people enjoy it. A furthermore reason is if they ban boxing it will ruin people's careers.

After looking at the different points of view and the evidence for them I think boxing should be banned.

Figure 6 Kerry's framed discussion

developing students' oral language and their thinking. Some students, especially those with learning difficulties, may need many oral sessions and sessions in which their teacher acts as a scribe before they are ready to attempt their own framed writing.

It would be useful for teachers to make "big" versions of the frames for use in these teacher-modelling and joint-construction phases. These large frames can be used for shared writing. It is important that the child and the teacher understand that the frame is a supportive draft and that words may be crossed out or substituted, extra sentences may be added, or surplus starters crossed out.

We are convinced that writing in a range of genres is most effective if it is located in meaningful experiences. The concept of "situated learning" (Lave & Wenger, 1991) suggests that learning is always context-dependent. Thus, we have always used the frames within class topic or theme work rather than in isolated study skills lessons (Lewis & Wray, 1995).

We do not advocate using the frames for the direct teaching of generic structures in skills-centred lessons. The frame itself is never a purpose for writing. Our use of a writing frame has always arisen from students having a purpose for undertaking some writing, and the appropriate frame was then introduced if they needed extra help.

We have found the frames helpful to students of all ages and all abilities (and, indeed, their wide applicability is one of their most positive features). Teachers have commented on the improved quality (and quantity) of writing that has resulted from using the frames with their students.

It would, of course, be unnecessary to use a frame with writers already confident and fluent in a particular genre, but they can be used to introduce such writers to new genres. Teachers have noted an initial dip in the quality of the writing when comparing the framed new genre writing with the fluent recount writing of an able child. What they have later discovered, however, is that, after only one or two uses of a frame, fluent language users add the genre and its language features into their repertoires and, without using a frame, produce fluent writing of high quality in that genre.

The aim with all students is for them to reach this stage of assimilating the generic structures and language features into their writing repertoires. Use of writing frames should be focussed on particular children or small group of students as and when they need them.

Conclusion

We need to give greater attention to teaching students to write effective and well-structured non-fiction texts. The concept of genre gives a useful framework, while writing frames are a strategy that helps us help students to reach our goals.

References

Anderson, T., & Armbruster, B. (1981). *Content area textbooks* (Reading Education Report No. 24). Champaign-Urbana, IL: University of Illinois, Center for the Study of Reading.

Bereiter, C., & Scardamalia, M. (1987). *The psychology of written composition.* Hillsdale, NJ: Erlbaum.

Cairney, T. (1990). *Teaching reading comprehension.* Milton Keynes, UK: Open University Press.

Collerson, J. (1988). *Writing for life.* Newtown, NSW: Primary English Teaching Association.

Cudd, E., & Roberts, L. (1989). Using writing to enhance content area learning in the primary grades. *The Reading Teacher, 42*(6), 392–404.

Department of Education and Science. (1990). *English in the national curriculum.* London: HMSO.

Halliday, M. (1985). *An introduction to functional grammar.* London: Arnold.

Halliday, M., & Hasan, R. (1976). *Cohesion in English.* London: Longman.

Kress, G., & Knapp, P. (1992). Genre in a social theory of language. *English in Education, 26*(2).

Lave, J., & Wenger, E. (1991). *Situated learning.* Cambridge, UK: Cambridge University Press.

Lewis, M., & Wray, D. (1995). *Developing children's non-fiction writing.* Leamington Spa, UK: Scholastic.

Lewis, M., & Wray, D. (1996). *Writing frames.* Reading, UK: Reading and Language Information Centre, University of Reading.

Lewis, M., Wray, D., & Rospigliosi, P. (1994). "... And I want it in your own words." *The Reading Teacher, 47*(7), 528–536.

Martin, J. (1985). *Factual writing: Exploring and challenging social reality.* Oxford, UK: Oxford University Press.

Martin, J., & Rothery, J. (1980). *Writing Project Report No. 1*. Sydney, NSW: Department of Linguistics, University of Sydney.

Martin, J., & Rothery, J. (1981). *Writing Project Report No. 2*. Sydney, NSW: Department of Linguistics, University of Sydney.

Martin, J. & Rothery, J. (1986). *Writing Project Report No. 4*. Sydney, NSW: Department of Linguistics, University of Sydney.

Perera, K. (1984). *Children's reading and writing*. Oxford, UK: Blackwell.

Wing Jan, L. (1991). *Write ways: Modelling writing forms*. Melbourne, Victoria: Oxford University Press.